COMMUNICATION THEORIES

Origins • Methods • Uses

A TAXONOMY OF CONCEPTS IN COMMUNICATION
by Reed H. Blake and Edwin O. Haroldsen

COMMUNICATIONS AND MEDIA
Constructing a Cross Discipline
by George N. Gordon

ETHICS AND THE PRESS
Readings in Mass Media Morality
Edited by John C. Merrill and Ralph D. Barney

DRAMA IN LIFE
The Uses of Communication in Society
Edited by James E. Combs and Michael W. Mansfield

INTERNATIONAL AND INTERCULTURAL COMMUNICATION
Edited by Heinz-Dietrich Fischer and John C. Merrill

EXISTENTIAL JOURNALISM
by John C. Merrill

THE COMMUNICATIONS REVOLUTION
A History of Mass Media in the United States
by George N. Gordon

COMMUNICATION ARTS IN THE ANCIENT WORLD
Edited by Eric A. Havelock and Jackson P. Hershbell

EDITORIAL AND PERSUASIVE WRITING
by Harry W. Stonecipher

ENTERTAINMENT
A Cross-Cultural Examination
Edited by Heinz-Dietrich Fischer and Stefan R. Melnik

COMMUNICATION THEORIES
Origins • Methods • Uses
by Werner J. Severin and James W. Tankard, Jr.

Humanistic Studies in the Communication Arts

Communication Theories

ORIGINS • METHODS • USES

by

WERNER J. SEVERIN
The University of Texas at Austin

and

JAMES W. TANKARD, JR.
The University of Texas at Austin

COMMUNICATION ARTS BOOKS

HASTINGS HOUSE, PUBLISHERS
New York 10016

Library of Congress Cataloging in Publication Data

Severin, Werner Joseph.
  Communication Theories.

  (Humanistic studies in the communication arts) (Communication arts books)
  Includes bibliographies and index.
  1. Communication. I. Tankard, James W., joint author. II. Title.
P90.S4414   001.5   79-16468
ISBN 0-8038-1274-4
ISBN 0-8038-1275-2 pbk.

Published simultaneously in Canada by
Copp Clark Ltd., Toronto

Designed by Al Lichtenberg
Printed in the United States of America

Contents

Preface   *viii*

Foreword by George N. Gordon   *ix*

1 **INTRODUCTION**
Mass communication; theory; some questions about the media; definition
of mass communication.   *1*

2 **SCIENTIFIC METHOD**
What is the scientific method?; inductive and deductive logic; generalizations; hypotheses; theories, laws; models; survey research; content
analysis; experimental design; case studies; statistics; validity and reliability.   *11*

3 **MODELS IN SCIENCE AND COMMUNICATION RESEARCH**
What are models?; functions of a model; evaluation of a model; communication models: Lasswell, Shannon and Weaver, Osgood, Schramm, Newcomb, Westley-MacLean, Gerbner.   *28*

4 **INFORMATION THEORY**
The concept; sources; destinations; messages; transmitters; receivers; signals; channels; encoding and decoding; channel capacity; feedback; entropy; redundancy; noise. Information theory applied: systems; gatekeepers; functional systems; coupling, communication networks; application
to measuring readability.   *43*

5   **GENERAL SEMANTICS—A LOOK AT ENCODING**
Encoding; founding of general semantics, Korzybski, Johnson, Hayakawa; characteristics of language; misuse of language; kinds of statements; studies of objectivity; implications for encoding.   *51*

6   **THE MEASUREMENT OF READABILITY**
Need for; history of readability measurement; Flesch; Gunning; using
a formula; applications of readability formulas: textbook evaluation, mass
communication, new literates, government documents, insurance policies;
Taylor's Cloze Procedure.   *67*

7   **MEASURING CONNOTATIVE MEANING: THE SEMANTIC DIF-
FERENTIAL**
Need for; connotative and denotative meanings; theory and development
of the semantic differential; semantic space; factor analysis; use of differential for comparisons; generality of findings; application to newspapers,
broadcasting, opinion measurement, advertising, marketing, politics and
political campaigns, image evaluation, identification of opinion leaders;
misunderstandings and misuse.   *89*

8   **PROPAGANDA**
The roots of later research; definitions and history of; propaganda devices
and their effectiveness; "bullet theory" of media effects.   *113*

9   **PERCEPTION AND COMMUNICATION**
Selective perception; decoding; assumptions and perception; cultural expectations and perception; attitude and perception; perception and mass
communication; selective exposure (attention) and selective retention;
subliminal perception.   *128*

10   **GROUPS AND COMMUNICATION**
Primary, reference and casual groups; group norms and pressures; changing food habits; groups and political attitudes; groups as instruments
of change; groups and mass communication.   *143*

11   **COGNITIVE CONSISTENCY AND MASS COMMUNICATION**
The notion of consistency and examples; Heider's Balance Theory; Newcomb's Symmetry Theory; Osgood and Tannenbaum's Congruity Theory
and media examples; attacking source credibility; selective attention,
perception, denial or incredulity, selective retention; Festinger's Theory
of Cognitive Dissonance; decision making; forced compliance.   *154*

12 **BEGINNINGS OF ATTITUDE CHANGE RESEARCH**
Persuasion; Carl Hovland and military research; concept of attitude; one-sided and two-sided messages; Yale communication research program; source credibility; fear appeals; resistance to counterpropaganda.
165

13 **FURTHER DEVELOPMENTS IN ATTITUDE CHANGE**
Katz's functional approach; McGuire's Inoculation Theory; attitudes and behavior; Lerbinger's five designs; stimulus-response, motivational, cognitive, social, personality.
182

14 **INTERPERSONAL COMMUNICATION AND THE MEDIA**
Concern with all-powerful media; voting studies; opinion leaders and two-step flow; adoption of a new drug; findings about opinion leadership; criticisms of the two-step flow; the diffusion of innovation, homophily, heterophily, innovation process over time, individual mental processes, attributes of an innovation, advantages of various channels, combination of channels, media forums.
200

15 **MASS MEDIA IN MODERN SOCIETY**
Functions and dysfunctions of the media; Lippmann and our mental pictures; conditions of media effectiveness; social control in the newsroom and mass communication and sociocultural integration with examples from the media.
212

16 **NEWSPAPER CHAINS AND MEDIA CONGLOMERATES**
Newspaper chains; broadcasting concentration; media conglomerates; abuses, real and potential; media cross ownership and effects of; calls for change; an employee-owned prizewinning major daily; arguments against increasing concentration; suggested remedies.
231

17 **THE EFFECTS OF MASS COMMUNICATION**
The bullet theory; limited effects model; moderate effects model; information seeking paradigm; uses and gratification approach; agenda setting function; cultural norms theory; powerful effects model; effects of media on political behavior; effects of television violence.
246

18 **THE OVERALL PICTURE**
The theory and findings fit into the Westley-MacLean Model; research for audience studies, message content and design, effect studies, communicator analysis; related fields.
267

Index *273*

Preface

This book was written to introduce communication theory to undergraduate students who intend to pursue careers in the mass media. It was designed to be suitable for students majoring in a variety of fields, including journalism, radio-television-film, advertising and public relations.

The authors, who have both taught communication theory for a number of years, have not been able to find any one book that accomplishes this purpose. A recent survey by the Association for Education in Journalism suggests that other "theory" instructors have also had this difficulty: Of 79 titles mentioned, no one book was used by more than eight schools.

We have attempted to avoid the pitfall of some other books that have dealt with mass communication theory in highly abstract terms. We have tried to give concrete examples of theoretical concepts at work and to be explicit about how ideas and techniques can be applied. Many theory books seem to be written for scholarly colleagues or for graduate students. Ours is specifically addressed to undergraduate students. Much of the material has withstood the test of fire—the examples and methods of presentation come from 19 semesters of teaching an undergraduate theory course by one of the authors and 12 semesters by the other.

While the book is not addressed primarily to fellow scholars, we have attempted to make it as up-to-date as possible. Thus, we have included sections on major recent topics in communication research and theory—the effects of television violence, the agenda-setting function, the uses and gratifications approach and the "powerful effects" model.

We have included extensive references for readers who want to pursue a topic further and for instructors who might want additional material for lectures.

Foreword

What is communication theory?

Outsiders in the "real world" frequently ask me this, and my reluctance to answer in precise terms (because I cannot) is embarrassing, particularly on occasions when I am playing the role of a paid "communications consultant." After twenty-seven years in the world of communications education at various colleges and universities, I should be able to come up with an answer, even if it is, "There ain't no such thing." Unfortunately, I cannot.

The question is ill phrased—as nebulous, I suppose, as "What is Oriental philosophy?," the answer to which is, "It ain't," (in the Western sense), but it *may* become many things, possibly as many as one wants or needs.

Should we ask, "What *are* communications theory," we compensate for our grammatical damage by posing a question that *can* indeed be answered in proper English and makes some sense. The response begins with the reply that most people who are in a position to hold responsible opinions on the matter agree that *one* cogent communications theory indeed exists! Many of them can spell it out quite precisely and sensibly. What occurs, however, is that different people from different intellectual backgrounds happily label entirely different sorts of theoretical statements "communications theory." And most of them have impressive reason for doing so. It all depends upon whether they are psychologists, sociologists, electronic specialists, photographers, semanticists, advertising executives, therapists, clerics or recreation directors at summer resorts.

I am not certain that any *single* unifying statement about communications has ever been articulated—or may even be contrived—that is not also a discouraging and banal platitude wearing the mask of wisdom. "Who says what to whom and how and with what effects?" is not a theoretical statement.

But it sounds like one and creates a noise redolent of the chimes of wisdom. I can think of half a dozen other platitudes (some employing numbers instead of words) that make the same sort of noise and are dignified by loose associations with such respectable intellectual figures as Bertrand Russell, I. A. Richards, Suzanne Langer, Bernard Berelson, George Herbert Mead, Charles Cooley, J. R. Pierce, and Martin Buber. I suppose also that after careful cryptology one may even discover a theory of communications somewhere in the collected works of H. Marshall McLuhan, although I have never met anyone who has!

Personal preference leads me also to be cryptic whenever I think seriously of so ubiquitous and curious a phenomenon as communication in theoretical terms. The only omnibus attempt to capture a satisfactory but powerful structural theory of communications, that I can both identify and feel, I find in the collected paintings of Salvador Dali. But I cannot explain my reasons in less than one hundred thousand words. I also remember the punch-line to a long and tedious joke, wherein a cat says, "What the hell is the good of talking, if nobody is going to listen to you?" The statement has neat theoretical coloration, but it too is a platitude. And speaking of cats, I believe that George Herriman's classic and magnificent comic strip, *Krazy Kat,* exhibited certain assumptions about society that, over the years, took on many attributes of well-tested theory, unfortunately too complex and allegorical for most scholarly stomachs.

Negative theoretical statements about communication, however, grow as thick as weeds in an untended garden. Some of them are interesting, mostly because they bespeak the kind of courageous unilateralism one finds in various "laws" attached to names like "Murphey." Samuel S. Vaughn, for instance, the president of the Doubleday Publishing Division (and who should know), once said, "The only medium of communication that fails to transmit information is the interoffice memo." Vaughn's wisdom is, however, non-fertile because of its negativism. Those of us who live in a world replete with interoffice memos know that the theory is unhappily entirely true beyond contest, but there is nothing that we can do about it. This applies also to communication consultant Bert Cowlan's old claim that the only words that cannot be communicated in *any* language are "No starch!"— a worthy notion, true enough before the invention of wash-and-wear shirts that do not shrivel up like prunes.

All of which leads to the prefatory observation that some of us involved in the *Humanistic Studies in the Communication Arts* feel strongly that it is about time that this remarkably fecund series face squarely the issue of communication theories as they are expounded and used and abused by the media at the present time. This does *not* mean that theory has not had its place in many of the volumes in this series listed a few pages back. But no single book has been devoted to the relationship of communication theories to the sum total of those activities that attempt to link up human communication, mediated or non-mediated, with empirical or normative regularities that may be called, in any of its many senses, "scientific."

Theory building requires no logical defense for anybody who had experience conducting the kind of research that transcends mere jot gathering for journalistic purposes or to feed a computer. The British behavioral psychologist, H. J. Eysenck, has recently stated that "a good theory is often more reliable than empirical determinations," quoting T. H. Huxley's famous axiom, "Those who do not go beyond the fact, seldom get as far as the fact," adding that "all facts *must be* embedded in a theoretical framework . . ."

Tankard and Severin's *Communication Theories* makes me both happy and nostalgically sad. I am happy because I believe, as the authors have noted in their *Preface,* that this book will find its widest use in college classrooms, where far too often the value of communication theories is derided or dismissed or (and this is unfortunate) is beyond the comprehension of instructors. I am sad, because I am reminded how arduously all of us involved in the study and teaching of humanistic communications will eventually have to work to clean up or clear up much quasi-theory, pseudo-theory and non-theory that is fractured and useless but nevertheless represents our best knowledge at present. A surge of nostalgia rises in me, for instance, when I note those shaky categories once articulated (probably in their time as propaganda devices) by the now dead Institute for Propaganda Research which supposedly describe a handful of "propaganda techniques." Can it be that these chestnuts are now more than *forty* years old? Where have the years gone?

In fact, I think we are all fortunate that Tankard and Severin have written a book that is both old and new, concrete and abstract, as well as rich in its exposition of our current state of knowledge—and ignorance—concerning the theoretical domains of communication studies. I cannot stress too strongly its value for students and other neophytes who are now entering this particular academic territory in ever increasing numbers. They *need* an education in theory just as much as they *want* more comfortable training in facts and skills, if their study of the Communication Arts is designed to be both productive for themselves and for society as well.

GEORGE N. GORDON
Muhlenberg College
Cedar Crest College

Chapter 1

Introduction

M ASS COMMUNICATION is part skill, part art, and part science.[1] It is a skill in the sense that it involves certain fundamental learnable techniques such as focusing a television camera, operating a tape recorder or taking notes during an interview. It is an art in the sense that it involves creative challenges such as writing a script for a television program, developing an aesthetic layout for a magazine ad or coming up with a catchy lead for a news story. It is a science in the sense that there are certain principles involved in how communication works that can be verified and used to make things work better.

Many people want to pigeonhole mass communication as one or two of these aspects to the exclusion of the others, and this has caused some problems. It is our position that all three aspects are valid and valuable, and that taking one approach does not mean that the others must be excluded.

This book focuses on the aspects of communication that can be approached scientifically, but it attempts to view them from the perspective of the communication practitioner, whether this person is a newspaper reporter, a television director, an advertising copy writer, or a public relations specialist. Many important questions about mass communication that can't be dealt with any other way can be dealt with scientifically.

Since we are taking a scientific approach, when we use the word *theory* in this book, we will be referring to scientific theory. Theory can be thought of as our understanding of the way things work (MacLean, 1972). Taken

---

[1] We are expanding here on Mitchell Charnley's observation that reporting is a craft and an art (see Charnley, 1975).

in this sense, we always have *some* theory about anything we are doing. In the field of mass communication, much of our theory in the past has been *implicit*. People have relied on folklore, traditional wisdom, and "common sense" to guide much of the practice of mass communication. Sometimes these assumptions are never even stated or written down anywhere. Other times they take the forms of oversimplified *aphorisms* or *maxims*. The statement sometimes heard around newsrooms that people are interested in "women, wampum and wrongdoing" is one example. Extensive research from readership studies and studies of news values suggests that this is an oversimplified and vague definition of news.

The communication scientist argues that since we have some theory operating all the time anyway, why not try to make it the best theory that we can? The scientist believes that the greatest faith should be placed in those statements about the way things work that have been tested and verified and that have some generality and predictive power. These are the kinds of statements that make up scientific theory. And these statements are *useful;* as social psychologist Kurt Lewin has said in an often quoted remark, "There is nothing so practical as a good theory" (Marrow, 1969, p. viii).

The science of communication is a young science. Two of the oldest works we will discuss—Walter Lippmann's *Public Opinion* and Alfred Korzybski's *Science and Sanity*—come from the 1920s and 1930s. Much of the research based on careful applications of scientific method—Carl Hovland's work on attitude change, Kurt Lewin's work on groups, Harold Lasswell's thinking about the role of communication in society, and Claude Shannon's development of information theory—came from the 1940s. Charles Osgood's work on the measurement of meaning and Leon Festinger's work on dissonance theory came in the 1950s. Much of the important work in this field is not yet thirty years old.

Some Questions about Mass Communication

What are some of the important questions about mass communication that can't be dealt with any other way except scientifically? Some examples will help to bring out the variety of such questions.

A question of some concern, particularly during the Nixon Presidency, was whether or not television news is biased. Vice President Spiro Agnew charged in his famous Des Moines speech in November of 1969 that television news coverage of the Nixon administration had been unfair, that television newscasters had been "hostile critics" and that one commentator had engaged in "slander" of Nixon. Agnew's speech also carried the threat of governmental action; he said the power of television was so great that it shouldn't be measured by "the traditional democratic standards." A few years later, President Nixon himself stated during a press conference that television coverage of his administration had been "outrageous, vicious [and] distorted." Some citizens apparently agreed with Nixon and felt that national television news had a liberal or left wing bias.

How could such a question be answered? Is it possible to get an objective answer, separate from the opinions of people who have strong feelings one way or the other? The answer is yes, if a scientific procedure known as content analysis is used. There are a number of steps that would have to be done carefully and properly, but it could be done. (See Chapter 2 for more detail on research methods.) Without these scientific procedures, statements about the amount of bias in television news are largely personal opinion. Even some attempts at a systematic study of bias, such as Edith Efron's *The News Twisters* (1971), have been badly flawed in their procedures. Efron apparently did not measure *coder reliability*—whether different persons could agree on what was biased and what was not. Other weaknesses in her procedures have been pointed out by a group of communication researchers who replicated her study (Stevenson, Eisinger, Feinberg and Kotok, 1973).

Another question of recent interest has been whether or not television has harmful effects on young people. This is really a set of questions, including these: Are television commercials teaching young people unhealthy eating habits? Are commercials for nonprescription drugs and other self-medications making young people more inclined to experiment with illicit drugs? Does watching television violence lead to aggressive behavior in young people? The public has shown growing concern about these questions, as indicated by the formation of the group Action for Children's Television and the fact that the National PTA and the American Medical Association have taken stands opposing television violence. All three of these questions about television are essentially questions of cause and effect. The best way to answer a question of cause and effect is through a *controlled experiment* in which one group of persons is exposed to one situation (or condition) and an equivalent group of persons is exposed to another situation (or condition).

Many experiments of this type have been done on the question of television violence. Some of the most carefully done were conducted as part of an inquiry by the Surgeon General of the United States. The Surgeon General's committee issued a report in 1972 presenting its somewhat tentative finding of a causal relationship between watching television violence and aggressive behavior.

Communication research of this type is coming to be used more and more in communication policy making. The television networks origination of the "family viewing time" can be traced back fairly directly to the report of the Surgeon General's committee. So can the refusal of a growing number of advertisers to sponsor programs with violent content.

Another example of communication research being used in communication policy making deals with the question of whether advertisements for drugs on television might have a harmful effect on young people, such as influencing them to try illicit drugs. In a case in 1976, the attorney general of the state of Massachusetts asked the Federal Communication Commission to ban over-the-counter drug advertising prior to 9 P.M. to protect children (Comstock, 1976). The government convened a hearing to review the scientific evidence on the effects of drug advertising on the use and abuse of drugs. The principal study reviewed, which was based on a three-and-a-half year investigation of 13- to 15-year-old boys, indicated that exposure to drug advertising was unrelated to later illicit drug use, although it was modestly related to over-the-counter drug use. The attorney general's petition was rejected for lack of supporting evidence, but we can see the importance that research had in the decision. If the research results had given more support to the attorney general's claim, it appears that drug advertising would have been banned.

A third general question that can be approached scientifically is one that has probably been of concern throughout history—what are the most effective methods of persuading people? Persuasion—trying to influence other people to our point of view or to take some action—is not only basic to much of mass communication, but it seems to be a big part of our interpersonal communication with friends, family and strangers alike. Persuasion is theoretically a neutral tool—it can be used for good or evil purposes. Thus it can be used in advertising or public relations in which the purpose is primarily to serve the source by selling goods or a favorable image of a company. But it can also be used in ways that might benefit the receiver more. A political campaign, which is a basic component of democracy, would be inconceivable without persuasion. And persuasion can be used in messages promoting health—campaigns to encourage people to stop smoking, to get more exercise, or to handle disagreements with other people in ways conducive to mental health. Particularly as the field of medicine begins to stress prevention rather than cures, as it seems to be doing, we might see much greater use of persuasion by means of mass communication aimed at improving people's mental and physical health.

Communication researchers, along with social psychologists, have done an enormous amount of research on the most effective methods of persuasion. Communication researcher Nathan Maccoby (1963) has called this work "the new 'scientific' rhetoric," because it is similar in purpose to the old rhetoric developed by Aristotle and others. Much of this new work falls in the area known as attitude change research.

The question of what methods of persuasion are most effective is another question of cause and effect, and the experiment is again the most effective method of investigating it. If we wanted to know whether a large amount of fear in a message or a small amount of fear was most effective in getting people to wear seat belts, we could devise an experiment to find out. Such an experiment would begin to provide conclusive evidence about the effectiveness of the two different types of messages. When the same kind of research is repeated in other experiments with many other variables, and not just the level of fear in a message, then we have the beginnings of the "new scientific rhetoric" that Maccoby was talking about.

A fourth example of the way a scientific approach can be useful to mass communicators is in providing *feedback*. One of the main differences between mass communication and interpersonal communication is that feedback is much weaker in mass communication. In face to face communication, we get information immediately about how our messages are being received. This is not true in mass communication. In the case of broadcast media— radio and television—even the simplest kind of feedback indicating how many people are receiving the message is difficult to obtain. The rating services— A. C. Nielsen, Trendex, Arbitron, and others—have come into existence just to fulfill this vital need. And of course these rating services rely on scientific procedures to allow them to generalize from the small sample they study to the audience as a whole.

Another type of feedback comes from evaluation research aimed at determining the effectiveness of communication programs or messages. This might involve a commercial effort such as measuring the effectiveness of a new advertising campaign designed to change the image of Budweiser beer. Or it could involve a project in the health area aimed at getting people to reduce the risk of heart attack by cutting down on smoking, getting more exercise and changing their diets. One such project, the Stanford Heart Disease Prevention program (Maccoby and Farquhar, 1975), had an evaluation component built in from the very beginning. People in government and in business are becoming less willing to spend millions of dollars on communication campaigns (as well as other projects) without obtaining some evidence that the campaigns are having the desired effect. This may mean that in the future we will see less and less of the old "fly by the seat of your pants" approach to mass communication campaigns and more of the scientific approach.

Definitions of Communication

Before we go too much further in discussing communication theory, we ought to give some attention to what we mean by communication. The question of "What is communication?" is not one that has led scholars to a single satisfactory answer. In fact, there has been a plethora of articles with titles like "On Defining Communication: Another Stab" (Miller, 1966) and "On Defining Communication: Still Another View" (Gerbner, 1966). Professor F. E. X. Dance (1970) of the University of Wisconsin at Milwaukee once compiled a list of 98 different definitions of communication that had been proposed by scholars. Without going into that many different definitions, it may be worthwhile to point out some of the basic differences in the way communication has been viewed.

1. *Definitions that stress sharing.* One way to begin to consider the meaning of any word is to look at the etymology of the word, or the words in

other languages from which it was derived. The word communication comes from the Latin word *communicare,* which means "to make common." A number of definitions stress this notion of making common, or sharing. One example is Alexander Gode's definition (quoted in "What Is Communication?" 1959): "It [communication] is a process that makes common to two or several what was the monopoly of one or some" (p. 5). A similar definition that is more specific is this one by communication theorist Wilbur Schramm (1971): "Today we might define communication simply by saying that it is the sharing of an orientation toward a set of informational signs" (p. 13). Notice that it is not enough that the signs themselves be shared. The same sign may have different meanings to two people, or may have some meaning for one person and no meaning for another person. It is the *meaning* that must be shared, not the signs, and Schramm's definition brings this out. This advantage of these "sharing" definitions is that they seem closely related to the root meaning of the word and also to the way we often think of communication. One disadvantage of this kind of definition is that it is hard to go from it to a measurement of whether or not communication is taking place. It may not be as *operational* as some other kinds of definitions. How do you measure whether there is a sharing of meaning? There are some ways to do this (see Chapter 7 on the semantic differential), but they may not be easy in specific communication situations.

2. *Definitions that stress intentional influence.* Some scholars have defined all communication as being essentially persuasion. One example is this definition by psychologists Carl Hovland, Irving Janis and Harold Kelley (1953): "the process by which an individual (the communicator) transmits stimuli (usually verbal) to modify the behavior of other individuals (the audience)" (p. 12). Another example comes from communication theorist David Berlo (1960), who wrote: "All communication behavior has as its purpose the eliciting of a specific response from a specific person (or group of persons)" (p. 16). These definitions have the advantage of being operational. They give you a basis for determining whether or not communication has taken place: you find a way to observe or measure the change in behavior or the response that the communication was aimed at producing. These are useful definitions from the point of view of the communication source. They can also be helpful for the communication consultant—if you can get your client to say that he wants to increase sales by 5 per cent or get more votes at the ballot box than his opponent, then you have a specific goal to design your communication program around and a criterion for measuring your communication success. The disadvantage of this kind of definition is that it really doesn't seem to fit all kinds of communication. Two friends or lovers telling each other about their day do not have to have an intent to modify the behavior of the other person—the telling can be an end in itself. Or a television sports announcer doesn't really have an intent to modify the audience's behavior when he or she gives them some baseball scores. The announcer is simply fulfilling a communication role, which is to give people information.

This kind of definition also excludes certain types of incidental learning from communication. A young girl might learn something about courtship behavior from watching soap operas, when the intent of the program producers was to provide dramatic entertainment and attract an audience for the commercials.

Finally, the view of communication as always involving persuasion seems rather a Machiavellian way of looking at communication. It certainly leaves out the kind of communication that philosopher Martin Buber (1958) has referred to as an *I-Thou* relationship.

3. *Definitions that include any kind of influence or response (with or without intent).* Definitions in this category are the very broadest definitions of communication. They include Warren Weaver's (1949, p. 3) "all of the procedures by which one mind may affect another" and S. S. Stevens' "the discriminatory response of an organism to a stimulus" (quoted in Cherry, 1966, p. 7). These are broad enough to include someone learning about courtship behavior by watching soap operas as a type of communication. Weaver (1949, p. 3) has argued that sometimes it may even be necessary to go beyond the breadth of these definitions to include "the procedures by which one mechanism . . . affects another mechanism." The disadvantage of these definitions—particularly the last two—is that they seem to be *too* all-inclusive. The discriminatory response of an organism to a stimulus could refer to a rat pushing a bar to get a food pellet or a plant turning toward the sun to receive its rays. If we define communication that broadly, how do we distinguish between the field of communication and the fields of psychology and biology?

The search for *one* single definition of communication seems to be a futile quest. Some of the definitions that have been discussed work well for some purposes, but work less well for other purposes. For instance, the second type of definition, stressing persuasion, can be a useful way of looking at communication from the source's point of view. It can make the source think through the desired outcome of the message or communication that will be presented. But the third kind of definition, including any kind of influence or response, whether intended by the source or not, can be a useful way of looking at communication from the receiver's or audience's point of view. The receiver might find interesting and useful things in a message that were never intended by the source.

It is helpful to remember that the process we call communication can serve a number of different functions, and that the process can operate somewhat differently depending on the function. Schramm (1971) has pointed out that communication can serve the functions of persuasion, informing, teaching, and entertaining. In each of these cases, there is a different set of assumptions about what is going on. And often the source and the receiver share these assumptions. For instance, a person performing the informing role is expected to stick to the truth, while a person involved in the persuading role is often expected to hedge the truth slightly (one term for it in advertising is "puffery"). Usually these expectations are understood by parties on both sides. We don't have to be "on our guard" when we are listening to the television weather announcer in quite the same way that we might when we are listening to a paid advertisement for a political candidate. Entertainment can involve still a different mental set on the part of the audience; often there must be a "suspension of disbelief" for entertainment to be effective. Greeting television commercials with the same kind of "suspension of disbelief" could leave a person an easy target for advertisers.

Mass Communication

The term *mass communication* can, in a sense, be defined more easily than the term *communication*. Or at least we can point out the characteristics that distinguish mass communication from interpersonal communication.

Mass communication is distinguished by three characteristics:

1. *The audience is large.* Some mass communication audiences are enormous—528 million people all over the world watched the live television broadcast of the Apollo 11 moon landing in 1969. But a country newspaper that reaches a few thousand people is also engaged in mass communication.
2. *The source is an institution or organization.* There have been a few one-person communication efforts that have reached fairly large audiences, such as *I. F. Stone's Weekly,* but in general mass communication is put out by a group of people working together, often a corporation.
3. *Some kind of mechanism is used to reproduce messages.* The mechanism can be a printing press, a radio transmitting tower and the receivers built to receive its signals, a motion picture projector, a cable TV system, etc. But something, as Schramm (1973) points out, "multiplies" the message.

While we are talking about terminology, we should point out that *mass media* is a plural term referring to several different (or sometimes *all* the different) means of communication—newspapers, television, radio, magazines, and so forth. It is grammatically incorrect to use the phrase with a singular verb. Furthermore, using it with a singular verb also implies that the mass media are monolithic and in agreement, which is rarely the case.

CONCLUSIONS

The science of communication is a young science. Much of the important work is barely thirty years old. The value of the scientific approach to communication is that it can answer questions that can't be answered in any other way. Examples of these kinds of questions are: Is television news biased? What are the effects of television violence on viewer behavior? What are the most effective methods of persuasion? Is a given program of communication achieving its intended effect? Answers to these questions can help practitioners in the mass communication field to do their jobs better.

A knowledge of communication theory can also benefit the consumer of mass communication—and that includes all of us. Knowing something about mass communication, the methods of persuasion it uses, and the effects it might be having on us can serve as a kind of "inoculation." It can help to give the consumer of mass communication what Ernest Hemingway called a "built-in, shockproof crap detector."

REFERENCES

Berlo, D. (1960). *The Process of Communication: An Introduction to Theory and Practice.* San Francisco: Rinehart Press.

Buber, M. (1958). *I and Thou.* 2nd ed. New York: Charles Scribner's Sons.

Charnley, M. V. (1975). *Reporting.* 3rd ed. New York: Holt, Rinehart and Winston.

Cherry, C. (1966). *On Human Communication: A Review, a Survey, and a Criticism.* 2nd ed. Cambridge, Mass.: The M.I.T. Press.

Comstock, G. (1976). The Role of Social and Behavioral Science in Policymaking for Television. *Journal of Social Issues* 32, no. 4:157–178.

Dance, F. E. X. (1970). Some Definitions of Communication(s). Unpublished manuscript, February, 1970.

Efron, E. (1971). *The News Twisters.* Los Angeles: Nash Publishing.

Gerbner, G. (1966). On Defining Communication: Still Another View. *Journal of Communication* 16:99–103.

Hovland, C., I. L. Janis and H. H. Kelley. (1953). *Communication and Persuasion: Psychological Studies of Opinion Change.* New Haven: Yale University Press.

Maccoby, N. (1963). The New "Scientific" Rhetoric. In W. Schramm (ed.) *The Science of Human Communication,* pp. 41–53. New York: Basic Books, Inc.

Maccoby, N., and J. W. Farquhar. (1975). Communication for Health: Unselling Heart Disease. *Journal of Communication* 25:114–126.

MacLean, M. (1972). Journalism Education: Whence and Where To. Paper presented at a conference honoring Professor Henry Ladd Smith on his retirement, University of Washington, Seattle, Washington.

Marrow, J. (1977). *The Practical Theorist: The Life and Work of Kurt Lewin.* New York: Teachers College Press.

Miller, G. A. (1966). On Defining Communication: Another Stab. *Journal of Communication* 16:88–98.

Schramm, W. (1971). The Nature of Communication Between Humans. In W. Schramm and D. Roberts (eds.) *The Process and Effects of Mass Communication,* rev. ed., pp. 3–53. Urbana: University of Illinois Press.

Schramm, W. (1973). *Men, Messages, and Media: A Look at Human Communication.* New York: Harper & Row.

Stevenson, R., R. A. Eisinger, M. Feinberg and A. B. Kotok. (1973). Untwisting *The News Twisters:* A replication of Efron's Study. *Journalism Quarterly* 50:211–219.

Weaver, W. (1949). Recent Contributions to the Mathematical Theory of Communication. In C. E. Shannon and W. Weaver, *The Mathematical Theory of Communication.* Urbana: University of Illinois Press.

"What is Communication?" (1959). *Journal of Communication* 9, no. 1:5.

Chapter 2

Scientific Method

S CIENCE serves as a guard against untested assumptions about the world
we live in. The scientific method differs from other methods of obtaining
knowledge in that it is based upon observation and the testing of our assumptions (hypotheses) against the evidence of the "real" world (empiricism).

To a great extent this book will deal with the findings of research from
a number of different disciplines or fields. Nearly all of the findings are
derived, however, from the application of scientific method, in this case in
what have come to be known as the social or behavioral sciences.

Thomas H. Huxley, a great nineteenth century scientist, once defined
science as "trained and organized common sense," and added that theory
building is something you engage in "every day and every hour of your
lives."

The father of the relativity theory, Albert Einstein, said, "the whole
of science is nothing more than a refinement of everyday thinking."

This is not to imply that first rate science does not require large quantities
of imagination—in identifying significant areas of inquiry, in the ability to
perceive unrecognized relationships and causes, in the ability to translate
abstract hypotheses into real world variables (operational definitions) which
can be measured, in the ability to devise measuring instruments to "get a
handle" on elusive data, and in many other aspects of science.

Certainly it took imagination for Nicolaus Copernicus to visualize the
sun at the center of our solar system and to break with the astronomy of
Ptolemy, which, for fifteen centuries, had held that the sun revolved around
the earth. It also took imagination for Galileo to see the possibilities of apply-

11

ing a new instrument, the spyglass, to the heavens, and to demonstrate that Copernicus' guess, or hypothesis was right. In doing so, Galileo created the modern scientific method: he built the apparatus, did the experiment and published the result.

There were, of course, many who felt their authority threatened by Galileo's findings, as is so often the case, and they did everything within their power to suppress the new notions of the universe. (Bronowski [1973] has an excellent brief account.)

Every scientist assumes an approach or a particular orientation when dealing with a subject or issue. This approach determines the concepts, questions, perspectives and procedures the scientist applies. It also shapes the hypotheses which are tested and eventually the theory which is generated. The approach, then, is the framework within which a theory is tested.

As has often been observed, the business of science is theory. Put another way, theory is what science is all about; it is the product of scientific research. The scientist seeks to make generalizations about the nature of reality. In our field we wish to be able to make generalizations about the way people communicate. Verified theory then enables us to make predictions about the outcome of certain events. In this case the goal is to make predictions concerning the process and effects of communication.

Science, as all scholarship, is also *cumulative,* that is, it builds on the work which has preceded it. Sir Isaac Newton summed this up three centuries ago when, in one of the most important aphorisms in the history of science, he said, "If I have seen further, it is by standing on the shoulders of giants."

Robert K. Merton, a pioneer in the sociology of science, has pointed out that Newton's aphorism "does not only apply to science. In its figurative meaning it explains the growth of knowledge and culture in virtually every area of learning you can mention." Merton adds, "Newton's aphorism means that no investigator starts out with a tabula rasa, or clean slate. It denies the great man notion." (Whitman, 1976)

This cumulative nature of scholarship, and science, is made possible by its transmissibility, its ability to overcome barriers of geography, language, and social, economic and political systems. Transmissibility is possible, in part, because science and all knowledge deals with abstractions about reality. The special language of any discipline is composed of these abstractions.

In order for cumulation to take place, scholars must share an approach or orientation, or at least a system of scholarly values. If scholarship is to be transmissible across various social classes and political systems it must, to a great extent, be, in the words of one author "detached, objective, unemotional and nonethical." (Westley, 1958, pp. 240–1)

The history of science is filled with attempts to impose philosophical and political positions on scientific findings and make scientific findings conform with untested pre-conceived notions.

Well known and already mentioned was the reaction of established authority to Galileo's verification of Copernicus' hypothesis which placed the sun and not the earth at the center of our solar system. In our own century Soviet agriculture and genetics had Marxist dogma imposed upon it by Trofim Lysenko. He rejected conventional theories of heredity and asserted that the basic nature of plants and even animals could be radically affected by changes in environment. Discussion and experimentation related to opposing views was forbidden and it is claimed that Soviet agriculture was set back by 25 years (Salisbury, 1976).

The scientist seeks to make generalizations about the nature of reality. He or she accomplishes this by repeatedly testing (replication) generalizations (hypotheses) about reality until sufficient confirmations are obtained to warrant calling these generalizations tentative laws. In science the tests of generalizations are accomplished through controlled observations. The scientist must be able to demonstrate that any variables which could provide an alternative explanation for the findings of an experiment have been controlled. This must be accomplished in such a way that it can be repeated by another investigator. It is the replicability and verifiability of science which serve as its guard against fraud and bias.

As has been pointed out, the end product of science is theory to enable the making of predictions. A hypothesis (or scientific proposition) is usually framed in what is known as a conditional form ("if. . . . then. . . ."). When the scientist establishes a conditional relationship he or she is dealing with cause and effect. It is these causal relations that science ultimately seeks.

The scientist assumes that the subject matter he or she deals with is natural phenomena or a part of nature, ordered in a natural way and not a result of supernatural ordering. This implies that the objects of investigations are determined, and causal connections can be found to account for them.

As a scientific discipline develops it works toward the explanations which are the most *parsimonious*. As one writer so aptly puts it, "The parsimonious explanation is the one that accounts for the most variance with the fewest propositions." (Westley, p. 249). In other words, science tries to explain as much as possible with the fewest generalizations. A twin goal of science, along with parsimony, is a striving for *closure*. If the scientist works with lawful, ordered or natural data, then it is assumed that eventually the universe is knowable and the sciences work toward understanding those areas which are unknown—the goal of closure.

While every scientist assumes an approach or orientation when dealing with an issue, science concerns itself with what is, what exists, or what happens when, not with questions of what is right or what should be. This is not to say that social sciences do not deal with ideologies, attitudes and value systems, but that the social scientist, in selecting or framing his methods of inquiry, must take into account the observer's or investigator's biases in these areas. Questions of values, or what should be, are dealt with by the fields of religion, ethics and philosophy rather than science.

The safeguard of science against bias or fraud lies in the publications of findings and *replication* of results, as has been noted. Can colleagues in a discipline agree that the hypotheses have been put to a valid test? Are the conclusions drawn from the data reasonable? Are the generalizations made from the data within the bounds of the phenomena examined or do the conclusions go beyond the data? Can the findings be replicated? As two famous authors in the area of logic and scientific method have said, "By not claiming more certainty than the evidence warrants, scientific method succeeds in obtaining more logical certainty than any other method yet devised." (Cohen and Nagel, 1934, p. 396)

Scientific inquiry employs both the methods of induction and deduction. *Induction* uses particular or specific instances as observed by the scientist to arrive at general conclusions or axioms. This is the use of data or evidence to arrive at generalities, often called empiricism. The mathematical expression of induction is found in statistical inference where the scientist examines many cases and arrives at a conclusion. *Deduction,* on the other hand, begins with what is general and applies it to particular cases, often called logic or rationalism. Deduction is employed by the scientist in making the leap from an hypothesis (a generalization) to an operational definition so that the hypothesis can be tested with specific "real world" phenomena or cases.

Some Definitions

At this point it is necessary to deal with several definitions. Two authors of a well-known text in comparative politics provide these reasoned and, for our purposes, highly useful definitions (Bill and Hardgrave, 1973, p. 24):

> *Generalization:* A statement of uniformities in the relations between two or more variables of well-defined classes.
> *Hypothesis:* A generalization presented in tentative and conjectural terms.
> *Theory:* A set of systematically related generalizations suggesting new observations for empirical testing.
> *Law:* A hypothesis of universal form that has withstood intensive experimentation.
> *Model:* A theoretical and simplified representation of the real world.

It is important to remember that a model is neither a generalizing nor an explanatory device.

> A model is a theoretical and simplified representation of the real world. It is an isomorphic construction of reality or anticipated reality. A model, by itself, is not an explanatory device, but it does play an important and directly suggestive role in the formulation of theory. By its very nature it suggests relationships. . .The jump from a model to a theory is often made so quickly that the model is in fact believed to be a theory. A model is disguised as a theory more often than any other concept . . ." (Bill and Hardgrave, 1973, p. 28)

The following chapter will deal with models and more specifically, communication models, in greater detail.

In communication research several methods are frequently employed to acquire empirical data in a systematic fashion. The most common are: survey research; content analysis; experimental design; and case studies.

Surveys

The sample survey is used to answer questions about how a large group of subjects feel, behave, or are, especially for those variables which change over time.

Survey research is the study of a portion, or a sample of a "population" the researcher is interested in (e.g., magazine subscribers, newspaper readers, television viewers, the population of a community or state, etc.). If done according to statistical principles, generalizations can then be made from the sample to the "population" with a given degree of assurance or confidence. A sample is less costly than a census, which is an enumeration of all the members of a population. However, the sample forces the researcher to make generalizations about the population within a given degree or range of probability (called the "confidence interval") which can be calculated statistically for any given sample.

Sample surveys can also compare relationships between variables by correlation (moving toward answers to questions of cause and effect). Often variables of interest to the researcher cannot be manipulated in an experiment (e.g., age, race, occupation) and the survey allows for comparisons between people who differ on a given characteristic with differences in their behaviors (e.g., how individuals of various ages, occupations, or educational levels, differ in their perceived credibility of the media or in their media use patterns).

An example of the survey technique applied through the use of *mail questionnaires* is its use to check on news accuracy. Tankard and Ryan (1974) clipped articles dealing with science news over a three month period from a random sample of 20 newspapers taken from the 167 newspapers in the 26 states east of the Mississippi which have a circulation exceeding 50,000. Cover letters, questionnaires, clippings and return envelopes were mailed to 242 scientists involved in the news articles. The scientists were asked to indicate possible types of errors in the articles on a checklist of 42 kinds of errors, to express their attitudes toward science news coverage in general and to provide information regarding his or her recent activities with representatives of the press.

The survey resulted in 193 usable returns (only two refused to cooperate and 13 were returned for lack of a complete address out of the original mailings).

The investigators were able to specify the types of errors the scientists perceived as most often made, the scientist's agreement or disagreement with nine short statements regarding science writing in general and the relationship between nine "predictor" variables and perceived error rate (e.g., such things as content category (medicine, biology, social sciences, etc.), origin of report (staff, wire service, etc.), circulation size of newspaper, whether or not a story was bylined, etc.).

Tankard and Ryan reported that the mean number of kinds of errors was 3.50 when the scientist read the story before publication and 6.69 when the scientist did not read the story before publication. The attitude items indicated strong criticism by the scientists of the accuracy of science news reporting in general. Large majorities of the sample indicated that headlines on science stories are misleading and that information crucial to the under-standing of research results often is omitted from news stories. (Tankard and Ryan, p. 334)

An example of the sample survey using *personal interviews* in communica-tion research is a study done by Westley and Severin (1964b) concerning perceived media credibility. A sample of 1200 households was drawn from the population of an entire state and one randomly selected adult in each household was interviewed by a professional interviewer. The sample resulted in 1,087 usable completed interviews.

In the course of the interviews the interviewees were asked to indicate which medium (television, radio or newspaper) they would be most likely to place their trust in should they receive conflicting reports concerning several types of news and also to indicate the time they spent on a typical day with each of the media. Questions were also asked concerning the interviewees behavior in several other areas (voting, group memberships, offices held, visit-ing patterns, etc.) as well as data on "demographic" variables (age, sex, educational level, occupation, income, place of residence, etc.).

It was then possible to "cross tabulate" responses to identify the types of persons who claim to place the greatest trust in one of the media and the types of persons who report the greatest and least amount of time spent with each of the media.

The investigators concluded, among other things, that the "ideal type" of media user who was especially likely to assign relatively high credibility to the newspaper is a man who had at least some college, resided in an urban area, and had a high-status occupation. He regarded himself as middle class and his father also had a high social status. He was most likely to be an independent in politics and if he acknowledged any party to have had only a weak party identification. He belonged to a moderate number of organ-ized groups and tended to hold office in them but was not especially gregarious. (Westley and Severin, 1963b, p. 334)

In another analysis of data from the same survey the investigators profiled the daily newspaper non-reader. They found the non-reader to be most often a rural or small town resident with few memberships in formal organizations, including churches, and to be infrequent in attending church and in visiting with friends and relatives. The non-reader tended to have no political identifi-cation or even political leaning and to be a non-voter. (Westley and Severin, 1964a, p. 51)

Ten years later the survey was replicated in another state by another group of researchers. They concluded that by and large the newspaper non-reader was approximately the same type of person found earlier. A discouraging factor these researchers found was that significantly larger numbers of people had decided not to read the newspaper, especially the poorer and the less educated. (Penrose, Weaver, Cole and Shaw, 1974)

Because these samples were drawn according to sampling theory and an error term for these specific samples was calculated, the researchers were able to make generalizations about the media use and assigned credibility patterns for the population of a state as a whole within stated parameters with a high degree of assurance. In the Westley and Severin (1964b) study survey research allowed making generalizations to a population of more than four million from a sample of little more than one-thousand.

Content Analysis

Content analysis is a method of analyzing message content in a systematic way. It is a tool for observing and analyzing the messages of certain communicators. Instead of interviewing people or asking them to respond to questionnaires as in survey research, or observing behavior as in the human experiment, the investigator using content analysis examines the communications that have been produced at times and places of his or her own choosing. Bernard Berelson described it as the "objective, systematic and quantitative description" of communication content (Berelson, cited in Budd, et al., 1967, p. 3).

A sophisticated use of content analysis couples it with additional information about source, channel, receiver, feedback or other conditions of the communication situation, such as attitude, personality or demographic characteristics. This enables predictions to be made about the communication process. In such cases content analysis is a tool used with other methods of inquiry to link message content with other parts of the communication setting. It allows the investigator to deal with larger questions of the process and effect of communication.

After selecting a question to be investigated or an hypothesis to be tested, the content analyst must define the "population" he or she will work with (i.e., the publication(s), newscast(s), the time span, etc). If the population is large, a sample is drawn, as in survey research. Categories must then be defined for classifying message content (a crucial step) and the content of the sample is coded according to objective rules. The coded content may be scaled or differentiated in some way so as to arrive at scores. If the content is to be related to other variables these scores can then be compared with them. As with all quantitative research, these scores must then be analyzed (usually using the data reduction techniques of statistical analysis) and the findings interpreted according to the concepts or theories which have been tested.

An early application of content analysis to stereotyping in the mass media is a study by Berelson and Salter (1946) to examine treatment of majority and minority groups in mass magazine fiction. The investigators were interested in what kinds of people, in terms of racial, religious and national backgrounds, appear in typical magazine short stories and how they were treated.

A sample of 198 short stories published in eight mass circulation magazines in 1937 and 1943 were examined to investigate the effect of World War II on magazine fiction. The war was not found to increase the number of minorities portrayed or otherwise modify their treatment.

From their analysis the investigators concluded that American minorities appeared much less frequently in magazine fiction than in the population. Also, the heroes and heroines were rarely minorities and were usually depicted as of lower social and economic status than the "pure" Americans. Furthermore, the investigators pointed out that the fiction saw little need to justify or explain the "pure" American's claim on society's rewards. They said, "Their acceptance at the top, without elaboration, subtly suggested that they belonged there." However, when minorities were depicted at the top, their positions had to be explained, because they did not belong there.

Only one per cent of the "pure" Americans were depicted in illegal or "suspect" occupations, while 15 per cent of "the Others" were. Whenever on-the-job social interaction occurred, members of minority and foreign groups were usually in subordinate roles. They worked for, and served, "the Americans." As the researchers put it, "In these stories, the world belonged to them (The Americans), and they ran it."

It appears, say the investigators, that the closer to the norm of "The Americans" the character is (i.e., white, Protestant, English-speaking, Anglo-Saxon) the better treatment he receives. Even within "The Others," some came off better than others. Minorities from European and Oriental countries, deprived as they were, still received preferential treatment in these stories over two other American minorities, Negroes and Jews, who never appeared as heroes or heroines or as members of the armed forces. They had the lowest occupational ratings and were the only groups with more disapproved than approved traits.

The investigators conclude that magazine fiction perpetuates the myth of the "100 per cent American" in its subtle and consistent differentiation between "The Americans" and representatives of minority groups. They say that readers of popular magazine short stories are constantly exposed, implicitly, to the prejudices and stereotypes attached to minority problems in the United States, but they are almost never exposed to the problems themselves. In the researchers' words, "Minority representatives are consistently deprived within an atmosphere which acknowledges no basis for such deprivation."

From their content analysis of popular magazine fiction the researchers then went on to speculate about the presumed intent and effects of this trend. Having established to their satisfaction the existence of certain patterns they set the stage for additional research.

A more recent content analysis deals with the portrayal of women and blacks on prime-time television. Lemon (1977) investigated inter-sex and inter-race dominance patterns by focusing on two-person interactions between men and women and blacks and whites to see if there is equal interaction or if one person dominates.

In this study the race and sex of each participant was noted and he or she was classified as the dominator, the dominated or an equal. These factors were also related to a number of program and character variables. A sampling was then made of situation comedies and crime dramas broadcast in prime-time during the latter half of March 1975.

Lemon found that only 28 per cent of the major character interactants were female, about the same in both crime dramas and situation comedies. Blacks had stronger portrayals than whites in situation comedies, but were more often unfavorably portrayed in crime dramas. From the data the researcher estimated that about 36 percent of the interactants in situation comedies were black, and seven per cent of those in crime dramas were black. Situation comedies were found to offer more favorable portrayals of both women and blacks than did crime dramas.

In inter-sex interactions women were dominated less frequently in situation comedies than in crime dramas, but men still outdominated women in both genres. Also, the situation comedies less frequently portrayed blacks as dominated than did the crime dramas. The most egalitarian patterns of interactions between men and women were found in the family context.

Both investigations are good examples of how content analysis can be applied to media content to measure objectively how groups in our society are portrayed. The effect of these portrayals on the socialization of children and on the society as a whole is, of course, a matter for additional investigation. Content analysis is also often used to measure alleged bias in the media in politics, in media positions taken on various other issues, and changes in media positions, often in correlation with events (e.g., editorial positions toward the Arab world before and after the oil embargo of 1973).

Experimental Design

Experimental designs are the classic method of dealing with questions of *causality.* An experiment involves the control or manipulation of a variable by the experimenter and an observation or measurement of the result in an objective and systematic way. When it is possible to use the experimental method it is the research method most apt to provide answers of cause and effect. The classical experiment will answer questions of whether and to what degree a variable (the experimental or *independent variable)* affects another variable (the *dependent variable).*

In the most simple form of the classic experiment two matched groups are randomly selected from a population (which has been defined by and is of interest to the experimenter), and one is given the experimental variable (in communication research it may be a news story, documentary film, piece of propaganda, etc.). After the experimental group has been exposed to the variable in question both groups are observed or measured and the differences between them is the effect of the experimental treatment.

Many experiments modify the classic design for reasons of practical difficulties, costs, etc. Often experiments are far more complex to provide answers to additional questions (e.g., how long the effects of a message will last, the effects of various types or combinations of messages, the effect of a number of different independent variables which may interact, etc.).

A classic experiment in communication research was conducted by Hovland and Weiss (1951) which dealt with the effects of communicator credibility on acceptance of the content of a message. Identical messages were presented to two groups, one from a source of high credibility, and the other from a source of low credibility. Opinions were measured before and after the messages were presented and also one month later. Four different topics were used (each in affirmative and negative versions) and presented to some subjects by trusted sources and to other subjects by sources held in much lower trust.

Each subject received one article on each of the four topics with the source given at the end of each article. Before reading the articles the subjects indicated their trust in each of a long list of sources including those used in the experiment. The four high credibility sources used in the experiment were judged so by 81 to 95 per cent of the subjects, with the low credibility sources the percentages were only 1 to 21 per cent.

The initial attitudes held toward the sources clearly affected how the subjects evaluated the presentations. Those from low credibility sources were judged "less fair" and conclusions "less justified" than those by high credibility sources, even though the articles were identical. The researchers concluded that "judgments of content characteristics, such as how well the facts in a given communication justify the conclusion, are significantly affected by variations in the source." (Hovland, Janis, Kelley, 1953, p. 29).

The researchers found greater opinion change in the direction advocated by the message when the source was of high credibility than when it was one of low credibility.

However, when opinion data were obtained four weeks later, the differential effectiveness of the sources had disappeared. There was less acceptance of the viewpoints of high credibility sources and greater acceptance of the positions advocated by low credibility sources. At that time measures were also obtained of the subject's memory of the sources for each communication.

After ruling out alternate explanations, the researchers concluded that there exists a "sleeper effect" for subjects who showed increased belief in messages attributed to sources of low credibility or, in the investigator's words, "there is decreased tendency over time to reject the material presented by an untrustworthy source" (Hovland, Janis, Kelley, 1953, p. 256).

The main advantages of the experimental method are the control it allows the investigator and the inherent logical rigor it offers. However, many experiments are "artificial" or oversimplified in their settings and the findings must be translated to the "real" world. Because of this and a number of other reasons, often seemingly conflicting results are obtained from experimental designs and survey research. Carl Hovland, a pioneer in communication research, addressed this problem as it applies to studies of attitude change and suggested methods for its resolution. He concluded by noting the virtues of each method and the need for both methods in communication research (Hovland, 1959).

Often "natural" experiments can be set up outside the laboratory. An example of a planned natural experiment in communication is the "split run" technique where two versions of an advertisement or other message are run and the relative effectiveness of each is assessed. This may be done through follow-up questions asked over the telephone or in personal interviews, or through tabulation of responses from coupons coded to identify which version has resulted in the response, or through other means.

Sometimes the experimenter may be interested in a theoretical question or in testing a hypothesis and can design a study and wait for an appropriate natural event. The experimenter is then prepared to "follow up" the event immediately with field work. Such can be the case with "diffusion studies" where the experimenter waits for an appropriate news event and then attempts to chart the flow of information about the event within a specified population (residents of a community, members of a profession, etc.)

An early example of a diffusion study which was partly experimental in nature was an investigation by Danielson (1956) of the news impact of President Eisenhower's announcement that he would seek a second term. Because everybody knew approximately when such an announcement of whether or not Eisenhower would seek re-election would be made, the investigator was able to plan to study the event.

A sample of 198 residents of Palo Alto, California, was interviewed two weeks before the news event (Eisenhower's announcement of his decision to seek a second term). On the weekend following the announcement interviewers were able to reach 129 of those originally interviewed. (Technically this is known as a "panel" study.)

Three hypotheses were tested involving the effects of Eisenhower's announcement to seek a second term. There were:

1) that respondents would see a greater chance for a Republican victory in November;
2) that Republicans would be more apt to be more optimistic concerning peace and prosperity than Democrats;
3) that there would be an increase in expressed intent to vote for Eisenhower.

Danielson then presented his reasoning for each hypothesis.

In the same study the investigator also obtained data on the dissemination of the news among the interviewees. Data were also gathered and reported on the medium from which the respondent first got the news, sources of additional information, and on images the respondents held of the candidates.

The hypothesis was supported that respondents saw an improvement in Republican chances if Eisenhower ran again, as was the hypothesis concerning peace and prosperity. The third hypothesis was not supported by the data. The news reached more than half the respondents within four hours and 96 per cent within twelve hours. Radio was the fastest source and reached the most people. The candidate image study indicated Democratic respondents saw Eisenhower as kind, good and fair, but also slow and ill, while Nixon was perceived as cruel, unfair and bad, but also fast and healthy. The same patterns held for Republicans, but with smaller differences. (Danielson, 1956, p. 441).

Case Studies

The case study is used to examine many characteristics of one subject (e.g., a communicator, a newsroom, a newspaper, news syndicate, television station, ad agency, etc.) as compared with a survey which examines fewer characteristics of many subjects or units. The case study usually tries to learn "all" about the area the investigator is interested in for the specific case over a period of time.

"Gate-keeper" studies are classic media case studies. With the cooperation of the wire editor of a morning newspaper with a 30,000 circulation in a mid-western city of 100,000 White (1950) was able to compare wire copy used with that actually received during one week from three major wire services.

The wire editor saved all unpublished wire copy, about nine times as much as that which was published and at the end of each day spent from one and one-half to two hours noting his reasons for rejecting each item not used.

With the data available, the investigator was able to compare the amount of wire copy actually received for each of a number of categories, both in column inches and in percentages of the total received, as compared to that used. He was also able to tabulate the number of times stories were rejected for various reasons.

The "gatekeeper" was then asked to consider at length four broad questions about the basis upon which he selected news, his own prejudices, his concept of the audience he was making selections for and any specific tests of subject matter or style which may enter into selection of stories.

The researcher carefully qualified his conclusions with the parenthetical remark, "if Mr. Gates is a fair representative of his class," recognizing that a case study deals with one example and is not a sample which can be logically or scientifically generalized. The study has, of course, provided considerable insight and information which serves as the basis for further investigation.

Another example of the case study applied to the media is a study of a Supreme Court reporter at work for an afternoon daily by Grey (1966). Permission was obtained to observe and later, discuss, the reporting of Dana Bullen of the Washington Evening Star on a "typical" day of reporting the court. A week earlier a practice run-through was held.

Grey maintained a minute-by-minute diary of Bullen's activity. He then followed this with commentary about Bullen's news judgment patterns, observed that the study provides "insight" into how reporters monitor their competition, provides reinforcement of studies on the importance of peer groups, and discussed this reporter's basic approach and his relationship with the national desk of his newspaper.

He concluded by discussing the implications of his case study for further research and more carefully controlled situations. He suggested questions raised in his study to be later turned into hypotheses. As he said, "The general objective would be a more thorough and theoretically advanced understanding of how the newsman works . . . and, thus, the end news product communicated."

Most histories of media institutions can also be classified as case studies. While they provide long-term, in depth examination of a specific newspaper, magazine, broadcasting station, ad agency, public relations department, news agency, etc., and may provide much valuable insight, they cannot, in the scientific sense, be generalized to other, like institutions. Additional information is nearly always needed before generalizations can be made.

An exception in communication research is an investigation of three centuries of the British press and its regulation by Siebert (1952). In this non-quantitative study hypotheses are formulated and tested and conclusions drawn, giving it some of the properties of the scientific approach. A more recent example is a test of one of Siebert's propositions in North Carolina by Shaw and Brauer (1959), using the historical method in focusing on one editor and the Newcomb A-B-X Model of symmetry (Chapters 3 and 11) from the field of social psychology to make predictions.

Case studies usually are not designed to prove anything because the results are based on a single example and rarely are hypotheses formulated and tested making it difficult if not impossible to generalize to other similar situations. The method does provide a great many observations, ideas and insights which can then be followed up with other types of investigations which will yield results that can be generalized.

Statistics

Scientific investigators rely on statistics to aid them in making inferences from the object of their studies to the populations they seek to generalize about. Statistics is a tool which is used in the process of reasoning about the data gathered.

Statistics can be used in a number of ways. One of the most common uses is data reduction, that is, in bringing large quantities of data to manageable form by providing summaries. These are known as descriptive statistics which provide information such as the mean, median, variance, percentiles, etc., for a body of data.

Perhaps even more important for our purposes is the use of sampling or probability statistics to enable the scientist to make estimates of population characteristics. It is this use of statistics which enables the scientist to draw inferences from data at given levels of confidence. A scientist using the sample survey method can make inferences from the sample data to the population from which the sample was drawn. This is done within parameters which can be calculated after the confidence level or "odds" which the scientist is willing to accept of being in error have been specified. For example, the range of the mean daily television viewing of a population can be predicted from a random sample from that population once the chances we are in error are stated (e.g., the 5 per cent level or 1 chance in 20) . As the scientist increases the degree of confidence he or she expects in the prediction, the interval within which he or she can make the prediction (confidence interval) also increases.

The investigator who employs the experimental method randomly assigns subjects to various groups. The random assignment assures that there will be no systematic bias in subject assignment. After the experimental group or groups have been exposed to the variable in question, observations and measurements are made about the effects of the variable. The resulting data are analyzed with statistical methods to determine if any differences between groups in the effects of the experimental variable could have been by chance, and at what level of probability. For example, what is the probability that the group which received a specific message and scored higher on an attitude measure following the message did so only by chance? If the probability is very low, and if other basic requirements of the experimental method were observed, the scientist can then infer that the difference between the groups is due to the different treatment (in this case the message).

Validity and Reliability

When evaluating scientific findings and the generalizations made from them the scientist asks questions regarding validity and reliability. The question is raised, did the experiment, or survey, or content analysis measure what the investigator claims to measure? More specifically, *external validity* deals with the question of whether the phenomena observed and measured by the investigator are representative of the "real world" phenomena the scientist wishes to generalize to. The act of translating abstract hypotheses to real world phenomena is called "operationally defining" the hypotheses. For example, an hypothesis that, "If an individual is a social isolate, then that individual is less apt to use the mass media than one who is socially integrated into his community," needs to be defined in terms which can be measured. The investigator can define "social isolate" and "socially integrated" in terms of frequency of visits with neighbors, relatives, co-workers and others, and media use in terms of reported time spent with the mass media. A comparison can then be made between those individuals who report little social interaction with others and those who report considerable social interaction with others and how each sub-group reports their time spent with various mass media. The question of validity then becomes whether the measures of social integration actually measure what we mean by that term.

Internal validity is required in experimental research if conclusions are to be drawn from the data. It raises the question of whether differences obtained resulted from the experimental treatment or whether they can be explained by other factors. Internal validity deals with extraneous or alternate variables which must be controlled in the research design to rule out their being a cause of any effects which may be observed. Put another way, the experimenter wishes to rule out any explanation for the results or findings other than the experimental or independent variable. (cf. Campbell and Stanley, pp. 5–6).

Reliability deals with the consistency of measurement. *External* reliability is the ability of a measure to provide the same results time after time, within acceptable margins of error, if applied to the phenomena under the same conditions. *Internal* reliability refers to the question of whether various sub-parts of a test provide comparable data.

CONCLUSIONS

As the scientist in any field of investigation develops and tests hypotheses about the nature of the world in his or her area of interest, the process of observation, testing, replication, cumulation and closure, as described earlier, continues. All of this, of course, is toward the building of theory which will provide explanations and allow for predictability.

In communication research there has been a gradual and long-term shift from applied research to basic research (sometimes, with unfortunate connotations, called "pure" science). The point here is that the field of communication research, like so many other fields, is moving from answers to specific questions dealing with immediate problems toward theory building to provide the general explanations of how humans communicate.

REFERENCES

Backstrom, C. and G. Hursh (1963). *Survey Research.* Evanston, Ill.: Northwestern University Press. A good introduction to survey research.

Berelson, B. and P. Salter (1946). Majority and Minority Americans: An Analysis of Magazine Fiction. *Public Opinion Quarterly* 10:168–97. Reprinted in B. Rosenberg and D. M. White (1957, 1964) *Mass Culture.* New York: The Free Press, pp. 235–50.

Berelson, B. and G. A. Steiner (1964). *Human Behavior: An Inventory of Scientific Findings.* New York: Harcourt, Brace and World. Especially Chapter 2, "Methods of Inquiry."

Bill, J. A. and R. L. Hardgrave, Jr. (1973). *Comparative Politics: The Quest for Theory.* Columbus, Ohio: Charles E. Merrill Publishing Co. Especially pp. 21–40 dealing with the scientific method.

Bronowski, J. (1973). *The Ascent of Man.* Boston: Little, Brown and Co. Especially Chapter 6, "The Starry Messenger" dealing with Copernicus, Galileo and the birth of the scientific method.

Budd, R., R. Thorp and L. Donohew (1967). *Content Analysis of Communications.* New York: The Macmillan Company. Remains a good introduction to content analysis.

Campbell, D. T. and J. C. Stanley (1966). *Experimental and Quasi-Experimental Designs for Research.* Chicago: Rand McNally & Co. Reprinted from N. L. Gage (Editor) *Handbook of Research on Teaching* (1963). American Educational Research Association Chicago: Rand McNally & Co. A concise introduction to experimental design.

Cohen, M. R. and E. Nagel (1934). *An Introduction to Logic and the Scientific Method.* New York: Harcourt Brace and World.

Danielson, W. A. (1956) Eisenhower's February Decision: A Study of News Impact. *Journalism Quarterly* 33:433–41.

Grey, D. L. (1966). Decision-Making by a Reporter Under Deadline Pressure. *Journalism Quarterly* 43:419–28.

Hovland, C. (1959). Reconciling Conflicting Results Derived from Experimental and Survey Studies of Attitude Change. *The American Psychologist* 14:8–17. Reprinted in Schramm, W. and D. Roberts (Editors) *The Process and Effects of Mass Communication,* Revised Edition (1971). Urbana: University of Illinois Press, pp. 495–515.

Hovland, C., I. L. Janis and H. H. Kelley (1953). *Communication and Persuasion.* New Haven: Yale University Press.

Hovland, C. and W. Weiss (1951), The Influence of Source Credibility on Communication Effectiveness. *Public Opinion Quarterly* 15:635–50.

Kerlinger, F. (1973). *Foundations of Behavioral Research.* New York: Holt, Rinehart and Winston, Inc.

Lemon, J. (1977). Women and Blacks on Prime-Time Television. *Journal of Communication* 27:70–9.

Penrose, J., D. Weaver, R. Cole and D. Shaw (1974). The Newspaper Nonreader 10 Years Later: A Partial Replication of Westley-Severin. *Journalism Quarterly* 51:631–8.

Salisbury, H. (November 24, 1976). Trofim L. Lysenko Is Dead at 78; Was Science Overlord Under Stalin. *New York Times,* p. 36.

Siebert, F. S. (1952). *Freedom of the Press in England 1476–1776.* Urbana: University of Illinois Press.

Shaw, D. and S. Brauer (1969). Press Freedom and War Constraints: Case Testing Siebert's Proposition II. *Journalism Quarterly* 46:243–54.

Tankard, J. and M. Ryan (1974). News Source Perceptions of Accuracy of Science Coverage. *Journalism Quarterly* 51:219–25.

Westley, B. (1958). Journalism Research and Scientific Method. *Journalism Quarterly* 35:161–9; 307–16. Reprinted in R. O. Nafziger and D. M. White (1963) *Introduction to Mass Communications Research* as "Scientific Method and Communication Research" (Chapter 9) Baton Rouge: Louisiana State University Press.

Westley, B. and W. Severin (1964a). A Profile of the Daily Newspaper Non-Reader. *Journalism Quarterly* 41:45–51.

Westley, B. and W. Severin (1964b). Some Correlates of Media Credibility. *Journalism Quarterly* 41:325–35.

White, D. (1950). The "Gate Keeper": A Case Study In the Selection of News. *Journalism Quarterly* 27:383–90.

Whitman, A. (February 6, 1976). Newton's Other Law Is Hailed on Its Tercentenary. *New York Times,* p. 21.

Williams, F. (1968). *Reasoning With Statistics: Simplified Examples in Communications Research.* New York: Holt, Rinehart and Winston, Inc.

Chapter 3

Models in Science and Communication Research

W HETHER we realize it or not, we are using models every time we try to systematically think about, visualize or discuss any structure or process, be it past, present or future. The effectiveness of such activity will depend in large measure on how well our model fits the thing we supposedly are modeling.

In the previous chapter we discussed the nature of the scientific method, the role of theory and the advantage of being able to make predictions. We gave a definition of a model and quoted two authors who observe that models are often confused with theories.

If a model is not a theory and if theories are "the business of science," what then are models, why use them, how does one evaluate them and what are some of the more important models in communication research? The answers to these questions are the topic of this chapter.

The structures and processes we are interested in modeling have to do with how humans communicate, especially with the mass media. This can be the way one individual deals with reality within his own mind, how a newspaper, television network, advertising agency or information office is structured and functions, how information flows in a society, or how innovations are adopted or rejected in a social system.

In Chapter 2 we cited Bill and Hardgrave's definition of a model as "a theoretical and simplified representation of the real world." They explain that a model is not an explanatory device by itself, but that it helps to directly formulate theory. It suggests relationships, and it is often confused with theory because the relationship between a model and a theory is so close and made so quickly.

Another author, Deutsch (1952, p. 357) points out that a model is a structure of symbols and operating rules which is supposed to match a set of relevant points in an existing structure or process. They are indispensable for understanding the more complex processes. This is a form of selection and abstraction, which, as we shall see (Chapters 5, 9, 11 and elsewhere) is used far more often than most of us realize. Because we select the points we include in a model, a model implies judgments of relevance and this, in turn, implies a theory about the thing modeled. Of course, abstraction carries with it the danger of oversimplification.

A model provides a frame within which we can consider a problem, even if in its early versions it does not lead to successful prediction. It may also point out important gaps in our knowledge which are not apparent and suggest needed areas of research (the goal of "closure"). Failure of a model when it is tested may lead to an improved model.

The use of theoretical models unites the natural and social sciences, as does the scientific method itself. In nearly all areas of scientific endeavor symbols are used to describe the essential aspects of reality the particular scientist wishes to focus upon.

Functions of a Model

Deutsch (1952, pp. 360–1) has discussed the uses of communication models in the social sciences. He cites four distinct functions of models: organizing, heuristic, predictive and measuring.

The *organizing* function of a model is seen in its ability to order and relate data and to show similarities and connections between data which had previously not been perceived. If a new model explains that which has not been understood then it almost always implies *predictions* which can be made. If it is operational a model implies predictions which can be verified by physical tests.

Predictions, even if they cannot be verified at the time for lack of measuring techniques, can be *heuristic* devices which may lead to new unknown facts and methods. Models also allow a range of predictions from the simple yes-or-no type to completely quantitative predictions which deal with when or how much.

When a model allows us to make completely quantitative predictions with a degree of precision about when or how much it becomes related to *measurement* of the phenomena we are interested in. If the processes which link the model to the thing modeled are clearly understood, the data obtained with the help of a model are a measure, whether those measures are only rank orderings or full ratio scales.

Evaluation of a Model

Each of these functions, in turn, form a basis for evaluating models.

1. How *general* is a model, or how much material does it organize, and how effectively?
2. How *fruitful* or *heuristic* is the model? How helpful is it in discovering new relationships, facts or methods?
3. How *important* to the field of inquiry are the predictions which can be made from it? How *strategic* are they at the stage of development a field is in?
4. How *accurate* are the *measurements* which can be developed with the model?

Deutsch (1952, pp. 362–3) also adds the following criteria for the evaluation of models:

1. How *original* is the model? Or put another way, how *improbable* is it? How much new insight does it provide? This is the opposite of the obvious, probable or trite.
2. What is the model's *simplicity,* or economy of means, or *parsimony?* This is linked to the model's efficiency or its attainment of an intended goal with the greatest economy. (An unsurpassed example is Einstein's theory that energy and matter are interchangeable, expressed as $E=mc^2$)
3. The *realism* of a model or the degree to which we may rely on a model as a representation of physical reality.

Some Communication Models

An early verbal model in communication is that of Lasswell (1948):

Who
Says What
In Which Channel
To Whom
With What Effect?

Lasswell's model allows for many general applications in mass communication. He implies that more than one channel can carry a message. The "who" raises the question of the control of the messages (as for example the "gatekeeper" study cited in Chapter 2). The "says what" is the subject of content analysis (e.g., the studies of the portrayal of minorities in the media). Communication channels are studies in media analysis.

"To whom" deals with the receiver and audience analysis (e.g., the newspaper non-readers in Chapter 2). The diffusion study and the communicator credibility studies cited in Chapter 2 can be viewed as effect studies.

Lasswell's model has been criticized because it seems to imply the presence of a communicator and a purposive message. It has also been called oversimplified, but, as with any good model, it focused attention on important aspects of communication.

Norbert Wiener published *Cybernetics* in the same year (1948), which emphasized two important concepts, the statistical foundation of communication and *feedback,* one of the most frequently borrowed concepts in communication.

The Mathematical Theory of Communication

Claude Shannon's *The Mathematical Theory of Communication,* (1949), has been the most important and influential stimulus for the development of other models and theories in communication. The Shannon model is based upon the statistical concept of communication which was first emphasized by Wiener. In the second part of *The Mathematical Theory of Communication,* Warren Weaver presented a schematic diagram of communication which resulted in many other models of the communication process.

Figure 1

A schematic diagram of Shannon's general communication system.

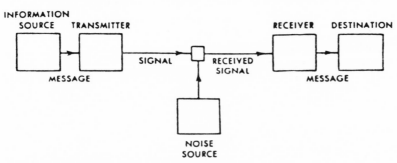

From Shannon and Weaver (1949). *The Mathematical Theory of Communication.* Urbana: University of Illinois Press. Copyright 1949 by the Board of Trustees of the University of Illinois. Reprinted by permission.

In this model the information source produces a message to be communicated out of a set of possible messages. The message may consist of spoken or written words, or music, pictures, etc. The transmitter converts the message to a signal suitable for the channel to be used. The channel is the medium which transmits the signal from transmitter to receiver. In conversation the information source is the brain, the transmitter is the voice mechanism producing the signal (spoken words) transmitted through the air (the channel).

The receiver performs the inverse operation of the transmitter by reconstructing the message from the signal. The destination is the person or thing for whom the message is intended.

Other major contributions are Shannon and Weaver's concepts of a message composed of entropy and redundancy and the necessary balance between them for efficient communication while offsetting noise in a channel. Briefly, the more noise in a channel the greater the need for redundancy, which reduces the relative entropy of the message (e.g., the wireless telegrapher transmitting in a noisy channel repeats key portions of the message to insure their reception. By using redundancy to overcome the noise in the channel the amount of information which can be transmitted in a given time is reduced). More will be said about these points in Chapter 4, including the application of Information Theory to the mass media.

Osgood's Models

Osgood (1954) contended that the technical communication model of Shannon and Weaver, developed for application to engineering problems, was never intended for human communication. His own model is developed from his theory of meaning and from psycholinguistic processes in general.

Osgood provides for both the sending and receiving function within one individual and he takes into account the "meaning" of symbols. (We shall see later that the Shannon and Weaver model specifically excludes meaning from the definition of information.) The Shannon and Weaver model implies separate sources and destinations and transmitters and receivers. While this is usually true of mechanical systems it is not true of human communication systems. An individual functions both as a source and a destination, as both a transmitter and a receiver by decoding the messages he or she encodes through a number of feedback mechanisms.

In this model the "input" is some form of physical energy or a "stimulus" coded in a form which is converted (decoded) to sensory impulses.

The receiver operates upon these "stimuli" or "inputs" through processes Osgood names "reception" and "perception" and the "mediator" supplies "cognition" (the addition of meaning or attitude) and the transmitter, in Osgood's terms, performs "motor organization and sequencing" operations. The "message" or "response" in the S-R chain is both "output" of the source and "input" of the destination. Output is achieved by "encoding" while input is dealt with by "decoding." In the Osgood model the destination is similar to the source unit.

In Osgood's view each person in a "speech community" is viewed as a complete communicating system which corresponds to the Shannon and Weaver model. Osgood has rearranged the Shannon model into what he calls a "communications unit" to send and receive messages.

Osgood stresses the social nature of communication and says (1954, pp. 2–3):

> Any adequate model must therefore include at least two communicating units, a source unit (speaker) and a destination unit (hearer). Between any two such units, connecting them into a single system, is what we may call the message. For purposes of this report, we will define the message as that part of the total output (responses) of a source unit which simultaneously may be a part of the total input (stimuli) to a destination unit. When individual A talks to individual B, for example, his postures, gestures, facial expressions and even manipulations with

Figure 2
Osgood's Communication Unit

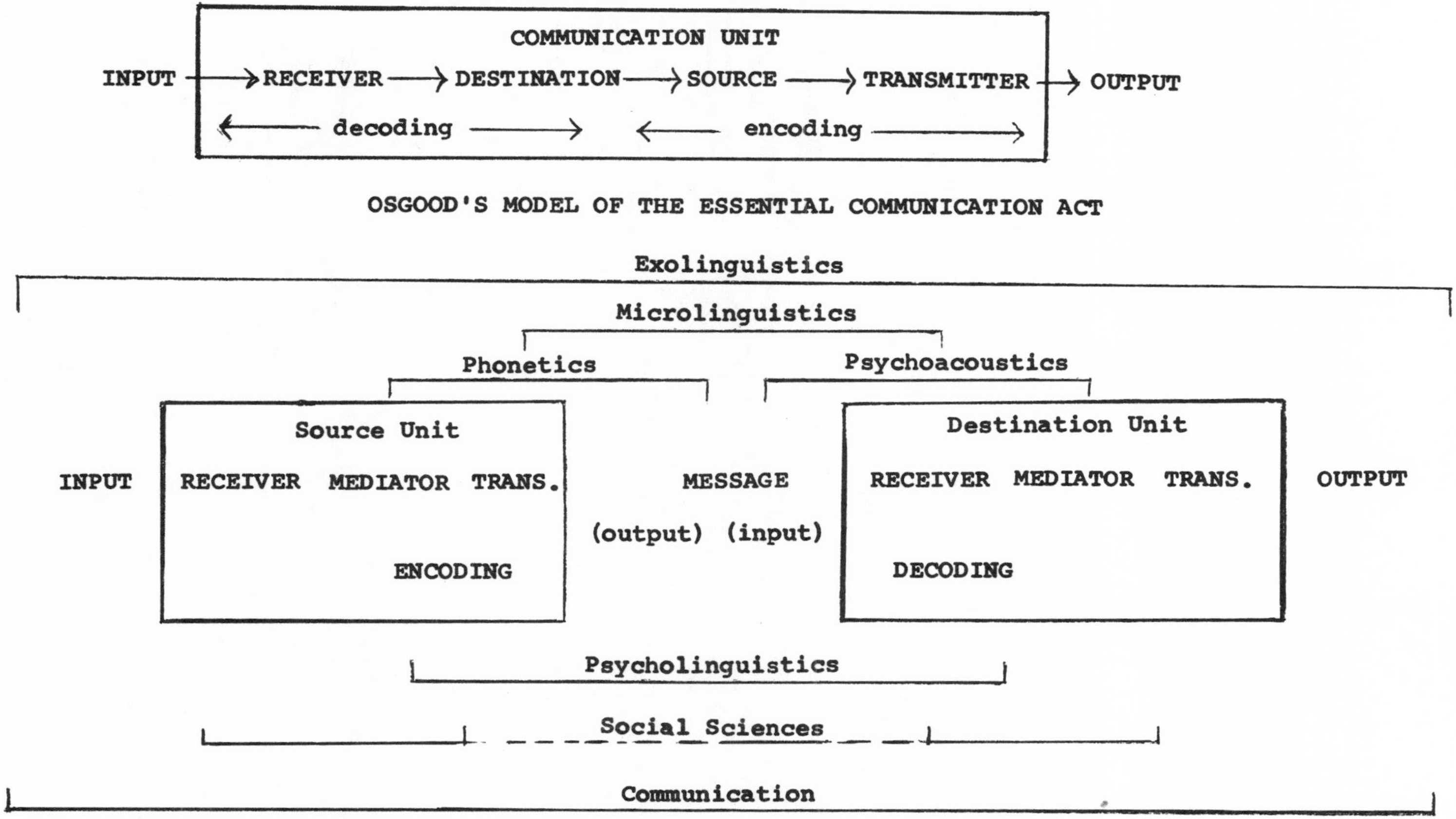

COMMUNICATION UNIT

INPUT → RECEIVER → DESTINATION → SOURCE → TRANSMITTER → OUTPUT

← decoding →   ← encoding →

OSGOOD'S MODEL OF THE ESSENTIAL COMMUNICATION ACT

Exolinguistics

Microlinguistics

Psychoacoustics

Phonetics

Psycholinguistics

Social Sciences

Communication

Source Unit

INPUT   RECEIVER   MEDIATOR   TRANS.

ENCODING

MESSAGE

(output) (input)

Destination Unit

RECEIVER   MEDIATOR   TRANS.   OUTPUT

DECODING

From Osgood (1954). Psycholinguistics: A Survey of Theory and Research Problems. *Journal of Abnormal and Social Psychology* XLIX (Morton Prince Memorial Supplement, October 1954). Copyright 1954 by the American Psychological Association. Reprinted by permission.

objects (e.g., laying down a playing card, pushing a bowl of food within reach) may all be a part of the message, as of course are events in the sound wave channel. But other parts of A's total behavior (e.g., sensations from B's own posture, cues from the reminder of the environment) do not derive from A's behavior—these events are not part of the message as we use the term. These R-S message events (reactions of one individual

Figure 3
Three of the Schramm models.

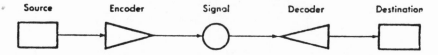

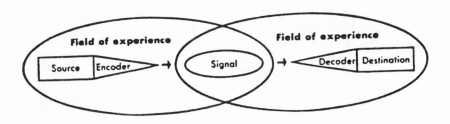

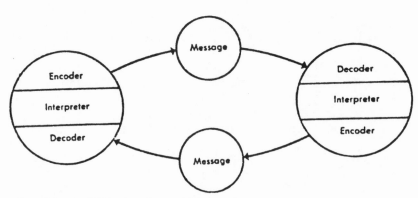

From Schramm (1954). How Communication Works. Chapter 1 in *The Process and Effects of Mass Communication.* Urbana: University of Illinois Press. Copyright 1954 by the University of Illinois. Reprinted by permission.

that produce stimuli for another) may be either immediate or mediate—ordinary face-to-face conversation illustrates the former and written communication (along with musical recordings, art objects, and so forth) illustrates the latter.

The Schramm Models

Schramm does not make the sharp distinction that Shannon and Osgood make between technical and non-technical communication, but he does acknowledge that many of his ideas are inspired by Osgood.

In an early series of models, Schramm (1954) proceeded from a simple human communication model to a more complicated model which accounted for the accumulated experiences of two individuals trying to communicate and then to a model which considered human communication with interaction between two individuals.

The first model bears a striking similarity to that of Shannon. In the second model Schramm introduces the notion that only that which is *shared* in the *fields of experience* of both the source and the destination is actually communicated, because only that portion of the signal is held in common by both source and destination.

The third model deals with communication as an *interaction* with both parties encoding, interpreting, decoding, transmitting and receiving signals. Here we see feedback and the continuous "loop" of *shared* information.

Newcomb's Symmetry Model

Theodore Newcomb's (1953) approach to communication is that of a social psychologist concerned with interaction between human beings. His model is reminiscent of the diagrams of group networks made by social

Figure 4
The basic Newcomb A–B–X model.

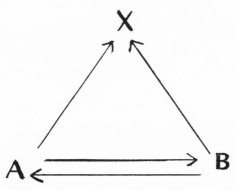

From Newcomb (1953). An Approach to the Study of Communicative Acts. *Psychological Review* 60:393–404. Copyright 1953 by the American Psychological Association. Reprinted by permission.

psychologists and is one of the early formulations of cognitive consistency. In its simplest form of the communication act a person, A, transmits information to another person, B, about something, X.

The model assumes that A's orientation (attitude) toward B and toward X are interdependent, and the three constitute a system comprising four orientations (Newcomb, 1953, pp. 393–4):

1. A's orientation toward X, including both attitude toward X as an object to be approached or avoided (characterized by sign and intensity) and cognitive attributes (beliefs and cognitive structuring).
2. A's orientation toward B, in exactly the same sense. (For purposes of avoiding confusing terms, Newcomb speaks of positive and negative attraction toward A or B as persons, and of favorable and unfavorable attitudes toward X.)
3. B's orientation toward X.
4. B's orientation toward A.

In the Newcomb model communication is the common and effective way in which individuals orient themselves to their environment. This is a model for intentional, two-person communicative acts. Newcomb derives the following postulates from his model:

1. The stronger the forces toward A's co-orientation in respect to B and X, (a) the greater A's strain toward symmetry with B in respect to X; and (b) the greater the likelihood of increased symmetry as a consequence of one or more communicative acts.
2. The less the attraction between A and B, the more nearly strain toward symmetry is limited to those particular X's co-orientation toward which is required by conditions of association.

Newcomb's model implies that any given system may be characterized by a balance of forces and that any change in any part of the system will lead to strain toward balance or symmetry, because imbalance or lack of symmetry is psychologically uncomfortable and generates internal pressure to restore balance.

Symmetry has the advantage of a person (A) being able to readily calculate another person's (B's) behavior. Symmetry also validates one's own orientation toward X. This is another way of saying we have social and psychological support for the orientations we hold. When Bs we hold in esteem share our evaluations of Xs, we tend to be more confident of our orientations. It follows that we communicate with individuals we hold in esteem about objects, events, people and ideas (Xs) which are important to us to try to reach consensus or co-orientation or, in Newcomb's term, symmetry. Asymmetry also is included in Newcomb's model when people "agree to disagree." (Chapter 11 deals with Newcomb's model further.)

The Westley-MacLean Model

Westley and MacLean, in the process of reviewing and classifying research in journalism and mass communications, felt the need for a different model (Westley, 1976, p. 28). Because of their interest in news they realized that the communication process can be started by an event as well as by an individual. The linear and noninteractive nature of both Shannon's and Lasswell's models were also sources of concern. Although neither of these models was satisfactory for their purposes, they do acknowledge the influence both had on their own model.

Westley had been influenced by the Newcomb model while a student of Newcomb's at Michigan. It provided a starting point for the Westley-MacLean (1957) model of the mass communication process. They took the Newcomb model, added an infinite number of events, ideas, objects and people (X's from X_1 through $X\infty$), which are "objects of orientation," placed a C role between A and B, and provided for feedback.

The Westley-MacLean model provides for As and Xs outside the immediate sensory field of B. The new role, C, allows these additional As and Xs to contribute to B's orientation of the environment. The C role functions to:

a. select the abstractions of object X appropriate to B's need satisfactions or problem solutions;
b. transform them into some form of symbol containing meanings shared with B;
c. transmit such symbols by means of some channel or medium to B.

They acknowledge their indebtedness to Newcomb for his emphasis on the shared symbol system.

In effect, C observes, selects, encodes, and transmits a limited portion of Xs to fulfill B's information needs. This is the "gatekeeper" role played by the media. In this model B can be a person, a group, or an entire social system.

Unlike the Newcomb model, in the Westley-MacLean model messages can be purposive (with the intent of modifying B's perception of X) or non-purposive (an absence of any intent on the part of the communicator to influence B). Feedback can also be purposive (e.g., a letter or call to the editor) or non-purposive (e.g., a purchase or a subscription which becomes a part of a statistic which indicates the effect of a commerical or liking for a publication).

In the Westley-MacLean model As become advocacy roles ("the communicator"). As can be a personality or a social system which selects and transmits messages purposively.

Bs (Behavioral system roles, to use the authors' term) are what is usually meant by "the receiver," or "the public." These are individuals, groups or social systems which need and use information about their enviroment to help satisfy needs and help solve problems.

Figure 5

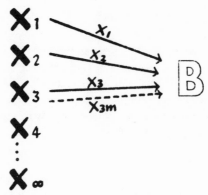

Objects of orientation (X_1 . . . X_∞) in the sensory field of the receiver (B) are transmitted directly to him in abstracted form (X_1 . . . X_3) after a process of selection from among all Xs, such selection being based at least in part on the needs and problems of B. Some or all are transmitted in more than one sense (X_{3m}, for example).

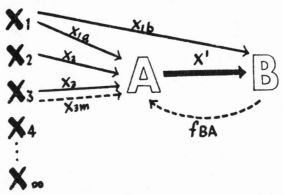

The same Xs are selected and abstracted by communicator (A) and transmitted as a message (X') to B, who may or may not have part or all of the Xs in his own sensory field (X_{1b}). Either purposively or non-purposively B transmits feedback (f_{BA}) to A.

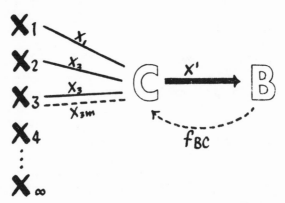

What Xs B receives may be owing to selected abstractions transmitted by a non-purposive encoder (C), acting for B and thus extending B's environment. C's selections are necessarily based in part on feedback (f_{BC}) from B.

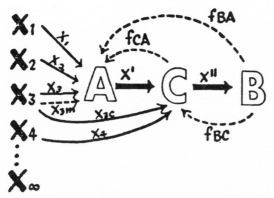

The messages C transmits to B (X″) represent his selections from both messages to him from As (X′) and C's selections and abstractions from Xs in his own sensory field (X_{3c}, X_4), which may or may not be Xs in A's field. Feedback not only moves from B to A (f_{BA}) and from B to C (f_{BC}) but also from C to A (f_{CA}). Clearly, in the mass communication situation, a large number of Cs receive from a very large number of As and transmit to a vastly larger number of Bs, who simultaneously receive from other Cs.

Steps in the progression of the Westley-MacLean model. From Westley and MacLean (1957). A Conceptual Model for Communication Research. *Journalism Quarterly* 34:31–8. Reprinted by permission.

Cs (Channel roles) serve as agents of Bs by selecting and transmitting nonpurposively the information B's need, especially that information which is not readily available to B.

Xs are the objects and events which are "out there." X′s are these objects and events in message form (abstractions of X in a form which can be transmitted.)

Channels are the means by which X′s (messages) are transmitted through As to Bs. Channels include Cs who may alter messages (acting as "gatekeepers").

Encoding is the process by which As and Cs abstract from Xs the messages (X′) which are transmitted in channels. Decoding takes place when Bs receive the message and interiorize it.

Feedback provides As and Cs information about the effect of their messages on Bs.

Westley and MacLean took the Newcomb model and extended it to include mass communication.

The Gerbner Model

Gerbner (1956) elaborates on Lasswell's model and provides a verbal model which implies ten basic areas of communication research as follows:

Verbal Model	Areas of Study
1. Someone	Communicator and audience research
2. perceives an event	Perception research and theory
3. and reacts	Effectiveness measurement
4. in a situation	Study of physical, social setting
5. through some means	Investigation of channels, media, controls over facilities
6. to make available materials	Administration; distribution; freedom of access to materials
7. in some form	Structure, organization, style, pattern
8. and context	Study of communicative setting, sequence
9. conveying content	Content analysis, study of meaning
10. of some consequence	Study of over-all changes.

These ten aspects represent shifts in emphasis only, rather than tight compartments for the study of communication.

Gerbner (p. 175) also provides a pictorial model which he discussed in detail.

Gerbner's model appears to be an extension of the Lasswell model, but Gerbner includes the following comparison with the Shannon model:

Figure 6

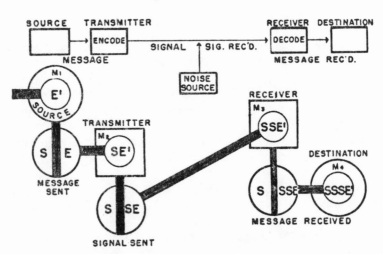

Shannon's diagram of a general communication system (top) compared with the progress of a signal in the same system as illustrated on Gerbner's graphic model. From Gerbner, G. (1956). Toward a General Model of Communication. *AV Communication Review* 4:171–99. AECT, 1126 16th Street, Washington, D.C., 20036. Reprinted with permission.

Once again we see the influence of Shannon, here in the later model proposed by Gerbner.

CONCLUSIONS

In addition to the models discussed here, there are a number of other models used in communication research and theory building. Several of them will be introduced in other chapters of this book.

As we said earlier, each model emphasizes certain points its creator feels are relevant in the communication process or structure. By selecting certain aspects of communication to be included in a model, the originator of a model implies judgments of relevance, and a theory about the process or structure which is modeled.

No one model can "do it all." Even if it could, it would defeat the purpose of a model—a simplified representation of the real world. Therefore, we select the model which best fits our purposes for the immediate problem at hand. If none is available to do the job required, the researcher might well be forced to modify an existing model, as we have seen in this chapter, or even invent a new one, as we have also seen.

REFERENCES

Deutsch, K. (1952). On Communication Models in the Social Sciences. *Public Opinion Quarterly* 16:356–80.

Gerbner, G. (1956). Toward a General Model of Communication. *Audio-Visual Communication Review* 4:171–99.

Johnson, F. and G. Klare (1961). General Models of Communication Research: A Survey of the Developments of a Decade. *Journal of Communication* 11:13–26.

Lasswell, H. D. (1948). The Structure and Function of Communication in Society. In Lyman Bryson (ed.) *The Communication of Ideas* New York: Harper & Bros. Also reprinted in W. Schramm (1960). *Mass Communications* Urbana: University of Illinois Press, pp. 117–30.

Newcomb, T. M. (1953). An Approach to the Study of Communicative Acts. *Psychological Review* 60:393–404.

Osgood, C. E. (ed., 1954). Psycholinguistics: A Survey of Theory and Research Problems. *Journal of Abnormal and Social Psychology* XLIX (October 1954) Morton Prince Memorial Supplement.

Schramm, W. (ed., 1954). How Communication Works. Chapter 1 in *The Process and Effects of Mass Communication.* Urbana: University of Illinois Press. Also see revised edition, 1971, W. Schramm, and D. Roberts, (eds.).

Schramm, W. (1955). Information Theory and Mass Communication. *Journalism Quarterly* 32:131–46. Also in B. Berelson and M. Janowitz (eds., 1953) *Reader in Public Opinion and Communication,* Second Edition. New York: The Free Press. Also in A. Smith (ed., 1966) *Communication and Culture.* New York: Holt, Rinehart and Winston.

Shannon, C. and W. Weaver (1949). *The Mathematical Theory of Communication.* Urbana: University of Illinois Press.

Westley, B. H. (1976). MacLean and I and "The Model" In Manca, L. (ed.) *The Journal of Communication Inquiry* (Spring 1976) Essays in Honor of Malcolm S. MacLean, Jr.

Westley, B. H. and M. MacLean (1957). A Conceptual Model for Communication Research. *Journalism Quarterly* 34:31–8.

Wiener, N. (1948). *Cybernetics.* New York: John Wiley and Sons.

Chapter 4

Information Theory

IN the previous chapter it was observed that the Mathematical Theory of Communication has been the most important single stimulus for the development of other models and theories in communication. This chapter will deal in greater detail with that theory and some of its many implications without, however, taking a mathematical approach. The student who is interested in pursuing the mathematics of Information Theory is directed to the references which conclude this chapter.

Claude Shannon developed the mathematical theory of communication while he was a research mathematician at the Bell Telephone Laboratories and a professor of science at the Massachusetts Institute of Technology. However, the theory has important and far ranging applications outside the engineering field for which it was developed, including the social sciences and communications theory. Warren Weaver, then a consultant on scientific projects at the Sloan Foundation, summarized the main concepts of Shannon's mathematical theory and delineated important applications of the theory to the whole problem of communications in society. The Philosophical Review called it, ". . . a beautiful example of a theory that unifies hitherto separate branches of physical science, and Dr. Weaver makes important suggestions as to how this unity may be extended . . ."

Information Theory, as the Mathematical Theory of Communication has become known, is ". . . exceedingly general in its scope, fundamental in the problems it treats, and of classic simplicity and power in the results it reaches." (Shannon and Weaver, p. 114). The theory is general enough that it can be applied to written language, musical notes, spoken words, music, pictures and many other communication signals. The term "communication" is used in "a very broad sense to include all of the procedures by which one mind may affect another." (Weaver, p. 95). The purpose of communication is defined as an attempt to influence the conduct of the destination with a broad definition of conduct (Weaver, p. 97).

The concepts of Information Theory provide insight and they fit intuitively in mass communication situations. As has already been noted, the theory has provided the impetus for many other models of the communication process. The theory is deep enough to reveal relationships within many forms of communication. It is so imaginative that it deals with the core of communication—relationships which exist no matter what form communication may take.

Information Theory is essentially a theory of signal transmission. At first it may seem disappointing to the student of the mass media because it has nothing to do with meaning and perhaps even a bit bizarre because Information Theory equates information with uncertainty. As we shall see, these are two of the theory's greatest assets in that they provide a new and fruitful way of viewing the communication process.

Figure 1

A schematic diagram of Shannon's general communication system.

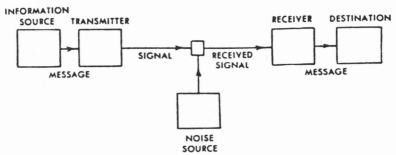

From Shannon and Weaver (1949). *The Mathematical Theory of Communication.* Urbana: University of Illinois Press. Copyright 1949 by the Board of Trustees of the University of Illinois. Reprinted by permission.

The communication process begins with a *source* selecting a message out of all the messages which would be possible to communicate. This *message* can be in the form of spoken or written words, musical notations, the music itself, pictures, mathematical notations, symbolic logic, body movements, facial expression, or a host of other forms we have available. The *transmitter* operates on the message to produce a *signal* suitable for transmission over a *channel*. When we use the telephone the channel is the wire, the signal is the electrical current passing over the wire and the transmitter (mouthpiece) transforms the sound pressure of the spoken word into varying electrical current. In oral speech the source is the brain, the transmitter is the human voice mechanism or vocal system, the channel is the air and the signal is the varying pressure passing from the vocal system of one person to the ear of another. The transmitter functions to encode the message and when it is received the receiver (in this case the ear) must *decode* the message (convert the varying sound waves coming through the air into neural impulses for the brain).

The *signal,* of course, takes different forms, depending upon the communication system we are examining. We have seen that in speech the signal is varying sound pressure traveling through the air (the channel). In radio and television the signal is the electromagnetic wave which is transmitted while newspapers, magazines and books utilize the printed word and illustrations as the signal on a page (the channel). The *channel* is, as implied, the medium used to transmit the signal from the transmitter to the receiver.

Channel capacity, in Information Theory terms, is not the number of symbols a channel can transmit, but rather the information a channel can transmit, or, a channel's ability to transmit what is produced out of a source of information (Weaver, p. 106). Of course, all channels, be they electronic, mechanical or human, have an upper limit of capacity. For example, the human eye can resolve and transmit far more information in a period of time than the brain can process and store. As we shall see, all communications are composed of chains of systems and, as with any chain, they are no stronger than their weakest link. In most communication chains it is the human which is the weakest link. Channel capacity is also limited by the space or time available to the editor or newscaster and by the time available the receiver to spend with the media.

Once a transmitter has encoded a message for transmission over a channel a *receiver* must reconstruct the message from the signal transmitted. Ordinarily the receiver performs the inverse operation of the transmitter. That is, the receiver changes the transmitted signal back into a message and passes this message on to a *destination.* In broadcasting the receiver is, as the term implies, the radio or television set. In speech the receiver is the ear and that part of the nervous system associated with the ear. With print material it is the eye and its associated nervous system.

The *destination* is the person or thing for whom the message is intended. With the mass media the destination is, of course, the member of the audience—the reader, listener, or viewer. The destination can also be a thing. A thermostat communicates with a heating system or cooling system, a governor communicates with a motor or the fuel supply to an engine. Computers can be programmed to communicate with one another.

The thermostat or governor provides *feedback* to allow a system to make corrections in its own operation. The concept of feedback was first introduced by Norbert Wiener of M.I.T. in his book *Cybernetics.* In the mass media we have many forms of feedback from the destination back to the source which help the communicator correct subsequent output. Letters and telephone calls from readers and listeners are a form of feedback, as are responses to advertising campaigns, audience ratings in broadcasting and increases or decreases in newsstand sales or subscriptions. Feedback in the classroom can take many forms including puzzled looks or signs of boredom which inform the lecturer that a point needs to be clarified or that it is time to move on to another topic.

Up to this point the reader probably has had little difficulty with Information Theory. But its most unique feature and most valuable contribution to our understanding of the communication process is its approach to what constitutes *information*. In this theory the term information is used in a very special way. It is most important that the reader not confuse information with meaning, as is commonly the case. We, each one of us, add our own meaning to the information which we receive, as we shall see in subsequent chapters. Information, in terms of the Mathematical Theory of Communication or Information Theory, " . . . relates, not so much to what you do say, as to what you could say." (Weaver, p. 100). Information becomes a measure of our freedom of choice in selecting a message to transmit. In information theory terms, information is very similar to *entropy* in the physical sciences—it is a measure of the degree of randomness. Entropy is the uncertainty or disorganization of a situation. In information theory it is associated with the amount of freedom of choice one has in constructing a message.

A highly organized message does not have a high degree of randomness, uncertainty or choice. In such a case the entropy or information is low because any parts of the message which are missing when it is received have a high probability of being supplied by the receiver. For example, because of the organization (redundancy) of the English language a receiver who is familiar with it can correct most misspellings. Individuals familiar with a given subject matter can provide missing elements in a passage. We shall see how this has been applied to measure the "readability" of a passage.

The part of the message which is not entropy or information is called, as we might expect, *redundancy*. Redundancy is defined as that portion of the message which is determined by the rules governing the use of the symbols in question or that which is not determined by the free choice of the sender. Redundancy is unnecessary in that if it were missing the message would be essentially complete or could be completed (Weaver, p. 104). When we use the English language about half of our choices are controlled by the nature of the language and the rules for its usage.

Redundancy can be used to offset *noise* in a communication channel. The fact that English is about 50% redundant makes it possible, as has been noted, to correct errors in a message which has been received over a noisy channel. However, key or important items are often repeated in transmission (a form of redundancy) to ensure their reception when transmitting through a noisy channel (e.g., " . . . will arrive Tuesday, REPEAT TUESDAY").

Redundancy is a measure of certainty or predictability. The more redundant a message is, the less information it is carrying. Sometimes, however, increased redundancy will increase the efficiency of a communication system.

Noise is defined as anything which is added to the signal which is not intended by the information source. Noise can take many forms. Probably the example that comes most readily to mind is that of static on the radio. In Information Theory terms, noise can also be distortions of sound in telephony, radio, television or film, distortions of shape or shading in a television image, a smudged reproduction of a printed photo, or errors of transmission in telegraphy. Noise can also take the form of a speaker's distracting mannerism—added to the signal, but not intended by the information source.

Noise increases uncertainty, and technically, in an information theory sense, increases information. Information as used in Information Theory can have good or bad connotations. Noise is spurious information. For the sender or source a high degree of uncertainty or freedom of choice (entropy) is desirable but from the destination's point of view uncertainty because of errors or noise is undesirable. To get useful information the destination must subtract the spurious information (noise) from the received message.

From the standpoint of the destination, noise can also be competing stimuli from outside the channel. An obvious example is the low flying aircraft which blocks out the sound of a newscast, or the crying baby, barking dog or fighting children. It can also take the form of the couple alongside of you at the cinema who are whispering or the co-ed who habitually arrives late for class wearing revealing attire. She is obviously communicating information, but from the standpoint of the lecturer it is information not intended by the communicator. The communicator must then increase the level of redundancy in the lecture (usually by repeating a point) in order to offset the noise introduced by a competing source.

The mass communicator usually tries to reduce noise as much as possible in his or her own transmission and expects noise to be present when the message is received. As has been pointed out, this noise can be offset through increased redundancy. The art of the right balance between entropy and redundancy is much of what makes a good editor—striking a balance between predictability and uncertainty. This, in turn, becomes a function of how an editor defines what his or her audience wants, what it can absorb and what he or she feels it should have, all, of course, within the limits or constraints of the medium used to communicate.

When rates of transmission are at less than channel capacity, noise can be reduced to any desired level through improved coding of the message. However, if the rate of transmission of information exceeds channel capacity then noise cannot be reduced below the amount the rate of transmission exceeds channel capacity. In most communication situations it is the capacity of the individual to process information which is the limiting factor. If the channel is overloaded, error increases dramatically. A major decision for any communicator when encoding a message becomes that of finding the optimum level of redundancy.

Information Theory Applied

Any human communication consists of a series of systems coupled into chains. A *system* is defined as any part of an information chain which is capable of existing in one or more states, or in which one or more events can occur (Schramm, p. 713). A communication system can be the telephone wire, the air, or a human optic nerve. Systems include the channels of information, but also include sources, transmitters, receivers and destinations. Systems must be coupled with one another in order to transfer information, and the state of any system depends upon the state of the system adjoining it. If the coupling is broken information is not transferred (e.g., when a student's attention wanders while "reading" an assignment).

Human communication contains many coupled systems. This coupling or "interface" between two systems is a *gatekeeper* point. A "gatekeeper" determines what information is passed along the chain and how faithfully it is reproduced. This principle applies to reporters, photographers, editors, commentators and all others who decide what information to use in the media from the vast array of information available to them. How much do they filter out? How much emphasis is changed? How much distortion is there, both systematic through bias, and random distortion through ignorance or carelessness? A newspaper or a broadcasting station is a gatekeeper deciding what to present to its audience. It must select from all of the local, state, national and international news available. The human destination (reader, viewer or listener) also acts as a gatekeeper (as we shall see in Chapters 9 and 11) by selecting and interpreting material according to his or her own individual needs.

Human communication systems, however, are *functional systems,* as opposed to Shannon's structural system—that is, they can learn. When we say that the human central nervous system is a functional system because it is capable of learning we mean that its present state depends upon its own past operation. As Schramm (p. 713) pointed out very early, the mathematical formulas of Information Theory are based on probabilities and learning alters those probabilities. This prevents the direct application of Shannon's Mathematical Theory to human communication.

Communication systems may be corresponding or non-corresponding. By corresponding is meant that they can exist in identical states. The telegraph transmitter or key and the telegraph receiver or magneto coil accept and repeat the same series of dots and dashes (minus any noise introduced in transmission). Non-corresponding systems cannot exist in identical states. For example the information given the telegraph operator does not correspond with the message which is transmitted, nor does the message transmitted with the current on the wire or the radiation transmitted through the air in the case of radio-telegraphy.

In information theory terms communication takes place " . . . when two corresponding systems, coupled together through one or more non-corresponding systems, assume identical states as a result of signal transfer along a chain." (Schramm, p. 714). As has been noted, in human communication we have very long chains (e.g., foreign reporting). The reporter or photographer on the scene in the Middle East or Latin America has his or her material pass through a great many gatekeepers before it is offered to a potential audience member. At each step is can be edited, discarded, distorted or have its emphasis changed.

The mass media are usually characterized by a relatively high output compared to a low input, or to state it differently, the mass media are high amplifiers—relatively few people produce the news, entertainment, advertising and public relations which are seen, heard or read by millions. This is simply another aspect of the industrial revolution where, through the application of technology, a relatively small number of workers in an industry produces commodities for a much larger number of consumers. It is the application of corporate and industrial economic efficiency in creating and distributing the commodity called "information."

The mass media themselves are made up of groups of people, and, as with any group or groups communication *networks* must be established and maintained if the group is to function. Communication networks are equally important in all groups in society (as we shall see in Chapters 10 and 14) as well as in electronic and mechanical communications. Schramm cites a number of measures derived from information theory which suggest new ways of studying communication activity in small groups (Schramm, p. 725). Some of them are: Traffic, or who does most of the talking and how much talking is done; Closure, or how open is the group to outsiders and ideas from the outside; and Congruence, the question of whether members are equal participants in group communication or are some mainly the originators of communications while others are mainly the recipients of communications?

Information Theory Applied to Readability

A direct and practical application of Information Theory's concepts of entropy and redundancy to message content is "Cloze Procedure" developed by Wilson Taylor. This procedure provides us with a useful way of estimating the entropy or redundancy of a passage of writing for a given audience. As we shall see in Chapter 6, Taylor's procedure deletes every nth word in a passage and then asks readers to supply the missing word. The frequency with which words are provided for the various deletions and the number of different words provided for a particular deletion indicate the predictability of the passage for a given audience. The concepts of entropy and redundancy are here put to work to measure a specific audience's familiarity with a specific content and also the difficulty of the level of writing for a specific audience.

CONCLUSIONS

Shannon's Mathematical Theory of Communication is the most important single contribution to the communication models in use today. It has not only stimulated much of the later research in this area but his schematic diagram of the communication process has been the impetus for many subsequent diagrams of communication models.

Shannon provides a concept of information as entropy or uncertainty. Messages are composed of entropy and redundancy, the latter which can be used to offset noise which may enter the channel upon transmission. The theory is very general in its scope, treats fundamental problems, and attains results with a classic simplicity and power.

As we have seen, this concept of information which has nothing to do with meaning is not only NOT disappointing but highly fruitful in the paths it leads to. Upon close inspection a concept of information which is identified with uncertainty is hardly bizarre.

If we evaluate Information Theory with the criteria given in Chapter 3 we find that it does allow one to organize, order and relate data and shows similarities and connections which had previously not been perceived. It implies predictions which can be verified with physical tests. It has been heuristic in that it has led to new, unknown facts and methods. It provides formulas for the measurement of phenomena of central interest to communication researchers.

Information Theory is general enough to organize a great deal of material, much of which is strategic or central to the concerns of communication researchers. While it is a model of simplicity or parsimony it is also highly original and provides many new insights.

The student who wishes to examine the theory more fully, especially the mathematical bases, is directed to the following references.

REFERENCES

Shannon, C. and W. Weaver (1949). *The Mathematical Theory of Communication.* Urbana: University of Illinois Press.

Schramm, W. (1955). Information Theory and Mass Communication. *Journalism Quarterly* 32:131–46. Reprinted in B. Berelson and M. Janowitz (eds.) (1966) *Reader in Public Opinion and Communication,* Second Edition. New York: The Free Press. Also in A. Smith (ed.) (1966) *Communication and Culture.* New York: Holt, Rinehart and Winston.

Taylor, W. (1953). Cloze Procedure: A New Tool for Measuring Readability. *Journalism Quarterly* 30:415–33.

Weaver, W. (1949). Recent contributions to the Mathematical Theory of Communication. In C. Shannon and W. Weaver (1949). *The Mathematical Theory of Communication.* Urbana: University of Illinois Press.

Wiener, N. (1948). *Cybernetics.* New York: John Wiley and Sons.

Chapter 5

General Semantics
— A Look at Encoding

E NCODING is the translation of purpose, intention or meaning into symbols or codes. Often these symbols are the letters, numbers, and words that make up a language such as English. But of course encoding can also take place through photographs, musical notes or images on motion picture film.

ENCODING is in many ways a mysterious process. How do the "preverbal tensions" (or whatever you want to call the feelings that precede words) become converted into words? It is not an easy process even to describe.

Some help in understanding encoding is provided by the work of a group of students of language called General Semanticists. These thinkers have not explained all the mysteries of encoding, but they have identified some characteristics of language that make encoding (at least in language) difficult. They have succeeded very well in pointing out some common misuses of language that cause people problems.

The General Semanticists

The founder of General Semantics was Alfred Korzybski, a Polish Count who came to live in the United States. Korzybski was born in Warsaw in 1879. As a young man, he was a brilliant swordsman and survived several duels in various parts of Europe (Haslam, 1970). He trained as an engineer at the Polytechnic Institute of Warsaw (Winters, 1974). During World War I, he served as an intelligence officer in the Russian Army General Staff. He was wounded in battle and was assigned to the United States in 1915.

When he was ordered to return to Russia, he refused, and he remained thereafter in the United States. He later studied mental illness with Dr. William Alanson White at St. Elizabeth's Hospital in Washington, D.C. (Hayakawa, 1962, p. ix). His later work showed the combined influences of his scientific training and mental health study.

During the 1930's and 1940's, Korzybski was offering off-campus seminars in General Semantics near the University of Chicago. The academic community rejected him and he apparently never belonged to the faculty of a college or university in the United States (Rapoport, 1976, pp. 355–356). This was probably because his writings crossed over traditional disciplines and dealt with topics as diverse as logic, the foundations of mathematics, colloidal chemistry and psychotherapy.

Korzybski's masterwork was the book *Science and Sanity: An Introduction to Non-Aristotelian Systems and General Semantics.* The book, which is large and difficult to read, presents a case that mental illness is caused by misuses of language. Korzybski argued that people should use language in everyday life the way the scientist uses language. In science, language refers to things that can be observed. This connection between the scientific way of thinking and mental health is stressed in the title of the book, *Science and Sanity.*

Korzybski's book was important, but it was so ponderous and difficult a volume that few people would ever have discovered the ideas of General Semantics through that book alone. Like some other bold and original thinkers, Korzybski needed disciples or translators to make his thinking available to others. A number of these popularizers showed up at the right time and place to help spread Korzybski's ideas. Two of the most effective were Wendell Johnson and S. I. Hayakawa.

Wendell Johnson had a problem of stuttering from his early childhood, and as a young man he traveled in 1926 to the State University of Iowa for treatment (Sies, 1968, p. 267). He stayed on to earn a Ph.D. in clinical psychology and speech pathology and to work in a speech clinic. Johnson had tried all kinds of treatments for his stuttering, including psychoanalysis. One theory suggested that stuttering was related to which hand a person used, and Johnson wore a cast on his right arm for part of ten years to try to change from being right-handed to being left-handed. Apparently none of these treatments were very effective. One night in 1936 a friend who had a book to review gave it to Johnson. On the following day, Johnson was hospitalized for an appendectomy, and he spent the next two weeks reading the book. It was *Science and Sanity.* Johnson said, "There was something new in the point of view of this book that changed my views on stuttering. I finished *Science and Sanity,* and I've never been the same since." (Sies, 1968, p. 268).

A few years later, in 1938, Johnson attended one of Korzybski's General Semantics seminars. Some of these were marathon efforts, in which Korzybski apparently lectured for as much as nine hours a day. Johnson later referred to the one he attended as "Korzybski's twenty-five hour lecture."

Johnson was tremendously influenced by Korzybski, and for much of his career referred to himself as a General Semanticist. He taught university courses in General Semantics, and thus, along with Hayakawa, gave the topic the academic respectability that Korzybski had not been able to provide. Johnson took Korzybski's theme of the connection between the use of language and mental health, and he wrote a popular book spreading this message titled *People in Quandaries: The Semantics of Personal Adjustment.* The book became widely known. Luther F. Sies, a colleague of Johnson's at the State University of Iowa, tells of getting into taxi cabs in New York City and Washington, D.C., telling the drivers he was from Iowa City and having them ask immediately whether he knew Wendell Johnson (Sies, 1968, pp. 263–264).

Johnson also had an interest in mass communication, and became one of the early critics of television. This criticism has been continued by his son, Nicholas Johnson, who served as a Federal Communication Commissioner, wrote the book *How to Talk Back to Your Television Set,* and became publisher of *Access* magazine, a publication aimed at helping the consumer of television.

Hayakawa was teaching in Chicago at the time Korzybski was giving seminars there, and became a disciple. He could be seen in the audience at Korzybski's seminars (Rapoport, 1976, p. 352), and he became the first editor in 1943 of the journal *ETC.: A Review of General Semantics.* One of Hayakawa's first books presenting the ideas of General Semantics for popular consumption was *Language in Action,* published in 1941. The book appeared in a revised edition as *Language in Thought and Action* in 1949.

Hayakawa was a professor at San Francisco State University in the late 1960's when student demonstrations were prevalent at the campus. He showed himself to be a man of action rather than words when he was made acting president of the university and had to deal with demonstrators. A famous news photograph distributed nationally showed Hayakawa wearing his trademark tam-o'-shanter and ripping the wires out of a public address system on a sound truck the demonstrators were using to urge a student strike. This kind of action made Hayakawa popular with California conservatives, and in 1976 he was elected to the U.S. Senate, running on the Republican ticket and defeating Democratic incumbent John Tunney.

Characteristics of Language

The General Semanticists have been concerned with language and how it relates to our success in everyday living and our mental health. They argue that we run into many of our problems because we misuse language. They say we would misuse language less if we used it more the way scientists use it. Scientists use language in such a way that it constantly refers to the realities it represents.

The General Semanticists point out several characteristics of language that make it difficult to use it carefully. These characteristics cause difficulty in *encoding* and make communication difficult.

1. *Language is static; reality is dynamic.* Words themselves do not change over a period of time, and yet the world around us is full of change. Modern science has shown that *matter* is ultimately made up of small particles moving very rapidly. A wooden table that appears to be solid is actually decaying and oxidizing. Twenty years from now it might not be a table at all, but a pile of firewood. Einstein's formula of $E = MC^2$ brought out that even matter and energy are not distinct, but can be converted one into the other.

Modern biology shows the same pattern of constant change. The caterpillar becomes a butterfly. The hard shell crab loses its shell and becomes temporarily a soft shell crab because it is the only way it can grow bigger. The theory of evolution brought out that even the species are not permanent and distinctive, but are changing and developing through time.

Reality is a process, and yet the language we must use to describe it is fixed and static. Another example of the process nature of reality is the cycle of the day. The sun is constantly moving, and its position in the sky changes throughout the day. The words we have to describe that everchanging process are primarily two—*night* and *day.* Anyone who has watched a sunset and tried to say exactly when it has become night recognizes the difficulty of fitting those two words to reality in an exact way. People have invented a few other words to help deal with that problem: twilight, dusk and dawn. But we still have only a handful of words to refer to an ever-changing process.

Towns and people change also, and yet the words (names) we have to refer to them usually remain the same. The fact that the word does not change over time can blind us to the fact that the reality is changing. A man might spend twenty years dreaming of retiring in Pleasant Valley, a town he visited as a young man, only to go there and find that it has become a busy city. Eldridge Cleaver in 1968 was a militant who was critical of almost everything American. Eldridge Cleaver in 1976 was a converted Christian who said things were better in the United States than they were in Communist countries. The name stayed the same, although the behavior of the person being referred to changed drastically. The General Semanticists recommend a technique of *dating* to help remind ourselves of this kind of change. Putting a date after the name would help remind us which Eldridge Cleaver we are referring to: Eldridge Cleaver $_{1968}$ or Eldridge Cleaver $_{1976}$.

2. *Language is limited; reality is virtually unlimited.* Wendell Johnson (1972, p. 306) points out that there are 500,000–600,000 words in the English language, and that they must represent millions of individual facts, experiences and relationships. The vocabularies that people ordinarily use are much smaller. In telephone conversations, people typically use a vocabulary of about 5,000 words, and the average novel uses a vocabulary of about 10,000 different words (Miller, 1963, p. 121). This might suggest that our vocabularies are normally sufficient for everyday communication, but it is not difficult to think of cases in which our vocabularies begin to appear limited.

Suppose someone was to place a dozen oranges on a table before you and randomly pick one of them and ask you to describe it in words. Could you describe it in such a way that someone else who had not been present could later pick that orange out of the dozen? Unless by luck the orange had some obvious deformity, the task would probably be difficult. The point is that we can make more distinctions in reality than we have words to describe easily.

The same kind of problem shows up on a more practical level in giving physical descriptions of people. Sometimes it seems as if people are only a little easier to describe than the oranges in the example above. The problem shows up frequently in law enforcement work, where people have to describe another person so exactly that the person can be recognized by other people. Many people often aren't very good at this, partly because they don't observe carefully but also because only a limited number of words exist for describing people.

Or think of the problem of describing in words some continuous process, such as playing a violin, riding a bicycle or even tying a shoe. Most people would find these acts difficult to convey in words, and they are the kinds of things that are typically taught by one person showing another. Just something as simple as the correct way to hold a guitar might be almost impossible to express in words, and a beginning guitar book will usually contain a picture to get the message across. The writer of a beginning guitar manual has a similar problem in communicating what certain guitar effects are supposed to sound like when they are done correctly. Such a writer might be forced to describe a certain rhythm pattern by inventing words such as "*boom*-chicka, *boom*-chicka". Even these invented words would only approximate the desired sound.

Because of the limited nature of language, General Semanticists stress, you can never say *all* about anything. They recommend a technique of putting *etc.* at the end of any statement to remind yourself that more could be said about anything. (If you don't actually say or write the *etc.*, you can at least *think* it.) The General Semanticists also named their journal *ETC.*, stressing the importance of this idea.

3. *Language is abstract. Abstraction* is a process of selecting some details and leaving out other details. Any use of language involves some abstraction. And indeed, abstraction is one of the most useful features of language. It allows us to think in categories, and this gives us the ability to generalize.

In classifying a number of fruits into categories such as apple, pear, orange and peach, for instance, we are selecting some details, such as their color, shape and texture, and ignoring others, such as their weight. We could classify them another way, into categories such as 6-ounce fruits, 7-ounce fruits, 8-ounce fruits and so forth, and we would be selecting a different detail, their weight, and ignoring the details we paid attention to at first.

Much of human knowledge is intimately bound up in the process of categorizing or classifying; we learn that certain red, round objects are good to eat, and giving those objects a name makes it easier to remember that knowledge and pass it on to others.

Abstraction is a useful characteristic of words, but it is also one that can lead to problems, particularly when people are not aware of abstraction.

All words involve some abstraction, or leaving out of details, but some words are more abstract than others. And as words become more and more abstract, their correspondence to reality becomes less and less direct. S. I. Hayakawa (1964, p. 179) has developed a useful diagram to show the way words can have differing degrees of abstraction. His diagram is called an "abstraction ladder," and it is based on a concept developed by Korzybski (1958, p. 397) called "the structural differential." An example of an abstraction ladder appears in Figure 1. The abstraction ladder in Figure 1 takes a particu-

Figure 1
The Abstraction Ladder

8	transportation
7	land transportation
6	motor vehicle
5	car
4	Volkswagen
3	"Old Black" or "Jim Tankard's VW"

Verbal Levels

Non-verbal Levels

2	Object Level	The black 1964 VW in the parking lot that we can see and touch.
1	Process Level	The car as atomic process.

lar object, an automobile belonging to one of the authors of this text, and shows how it can be referred to at different levels of abstraction. The lowest level of abstraction, at which no details are left out, is the process level, the level at which scientists using instruments can observe the car. The second level is the car as the object that we can experience with our senses. Notice that even at this level, the level of everyday observation, some details are being left out. This is partly because the eye can process more information than the brain (See Chapter 4). But it is also because we can only observe from one point at a time. When we observe the car from the front, we do not see the details at the back. And we see only the surface, not the internal structure of the car. Even in *observation,* some abstraction or leaving out of details takes place. The third level is the first verbal level, or the first level involving the use of words. At this level there is one word or phrase that refers uniquely to the one car being described. This could be the phrase "Old Black" that the car's owner uses to refer to it. Or, to other people, it could be the phrase "Jim Tankard's VW." At this level, the word being used refers to the one particular object. At the fourth level, we can use the word "Volkswagen" to refer to the same object. We have then assigned the object to a category, the category of all Volkswagens. We have left out the detail that would distinguish that particular Volkswagen from all other Volkswagens. At the next level, that of the word "car," we would be including Volkswagens but also Hondas, Fords, Cadillacs and so forth, so still more distinguishing detail would be left out. At the sixth level, we could refer to the car as a "motor vehicle," putting it into a category that also includes trucks and jeeps and leaving out still more detail. At the seventh level, we could use the term "land transportation," categorizing the car with railroad trains and snowmobiles. And at the eighth level, we could refer to the car with the word "transportation," putting it in a class that would also include airplanes and ships. Notice that at each level more detail is left out until at the eighth level we come to a very abstract word, "transportation." This word does not suggest a particular picture to the mind the way the word "Volkswagen" does. Some people might hear the word "transportation" and visualize a boat, while others might visualize a truck, and many others undoubtedly would have no clear picture of anything. That is one of the characteristics of very abstract words: they do not suggest a clear picture of something in reality, and people often have very different meanings in mind for them.

Misuses of Language

Because of the static, limited and abstract nature of language, certain misuses of language are likely to occur. One of the great contributions of the General Semanticists has been to identify some of these for us. Four common misuses are dead-level abstracting, undue identification, two-valued evaluation and unconscious projection.

1. *Dead-level abstracting.* This concept was described by Wendell Johnson (1946, p. 270), and it refers to getting stuck at one level of abstraction. The one level could be a high level or a low level.

High level abstractions are words like justice, democracy, freedom, mankind, Communism, "peace with honor" and "law and order." When words like these are used in a message that does not also contain words at lower levels of abstraction, it is difficult to know what the message is saying. Words at a high level of abstraction that are not accompanied with more concrete words are sometimes referred to as "words cut loose from their moorings" (Hayakawa, 1964, p. 189). They are not anchored at lower levels of abstraction.

Much political rhetoric gets stuck on a high level of abstraction. When the words "law and order" were used in a Presidential campaign several years ago, it was not clear what they referred to at a less abstract level. Did they mean a police officer would be placed on every street corner? Did they mean a 6 p.m. curfew would be enforced in major cities? Did they mean demonstrators in the streets would be arrested and placed in jail without being charged (as actually happened in Washington, D.C. in May, 1971)?

It was hard to know, because we were given the high level abstractions but not the translation at a concrete level to go with them.

The motion picture *Cabaret* contained an example of the way high level abstractions can be baffling. In one scene some Germans are sitting around a living room at the time the Nazis were rising in power and one of them says, "If all the Jews are bankers, how can they be Communists too?"

Language can also get stuck at a low level of abstraction in one message, and this is another type of dead-level abstracting. An example of this might be someone telling in great detail of everything that happened during that person's day. A message that stays at a low level of abstraction usually does not come to a general conclusion, and it is often difficult to see the point of what is being said. Receiving a message stuck at a low level of abstraction can be something like reading a Sears Roebuck catalog.

The General Semanticists say the most effective communication ranges up and down the ladder of abstraction. An effective message contains generalizations at a high level of abstraction, but there are also specific details at a low level of abstraction. One effective technique for doing this that many skilled teachers use is to give lots of *examples*.

2. *Undue identification*. This is the failure to see distinctions between the members of a category or class. The term points out that they are seen as "identical," or *identified*. Another term for this is *categorical thinking*. In everyday discourse, it is sometimes referred to as *overgeneralization*. One common kind of undue identification is *stereotyping*.

The following statements all show a failure to see distinctions between members of a class:

"If you've seen one tree, you've seen them all."
"I'll never trust another woman."
"You can't believe a thing you read in the newspapers."
"Statistics don't prove anything."

The stereotyping of mothers-in-law as "interfering" and "critical" or of Italians as "great lovers" are other examples of undue identification.

At an emotional meeting of the general faculty of the University of Texas, a historian said, "After hearing Dr. Schild speak, I have come to think less of the physics department." The historian was willing to condemn the entire physics department on the basis of what he heard one of its members say.

Feminist writer Germain Greer once said on the William Buckley program "Firing Line" that "advertising is universally depraving." Buckley asked her about a message telling people to get a chest X-ray, pointing out that her statement was probably an over-generalization.

A person who goes around saying, "I can't spell" is showing a similar kind of over-generalization (Stoen, 1976, p. 324). Indeed, the person can spell some words but not others; the remark is an overstatement. It may be a remark with important consequences, too, if it makes people think they are worse spellers than they are and leads to a defeatist attitude.

General Semanticists sometimes recommend the use of *index numbers* to prevent undue identification. If we were to attach an index number to a word like "student" each time we used it, we might be less likely to think of all students as alike. This would remind us that student$_1$ is not student$_2$, or, to take another example, that Jew$_1$ is not Jew$_2$. Of course the important thing is not so much actually to use index numbers like that in our writing and talking but to *think* them—to be aware that members of a class share some characteristics but are different in terms of many others.

3. *Two-valued evaluation.* This misuse is also known as *either-or thinking,* or *thinking with the excluded middle.* It involves thinking that there are only two possibilities when there are actually a range of possibilities. Language contributes to this tendency because there are often only two words that are opposites available to describe a situation. Familiar examples are words like "night" and "day," "black" and "white," "right" and "wrong." As we discussed earlier, "night" and "day" are two words that do not begin to reflect the many different states that occur during the cycle of the day. Many people would say that the same is true of the other pairs of opposites—"black" and "white" and "right" and "wrong." This is reflected in the commonplace statement when referring to moral questions: "It's not a matter of black and white; there are shades of gray."

Some examples of two-valued evaluation can be found in the rhetoric of student demonstrators and their critics during the late 1960s. The demonstrators who were critical of society sometimes said, "You're either part of the problem or part of the solution." The statement leaves no room for a middle ground. But there must have been some people—children, perhaps, or people in iron lungs in hospitals—who even the protesters would say were neither part of the problem nor part of the solution.

Critics of the demonstrators would sometimes reply with two-valued evaluation of their own in bumper stickers reading "America—Love it or leave it." This excludes the existence of other possibilities, such as "staying and changing it." In such times of confrontation it is also common to hear people speaking of "them" and "us," another example of either-or thinking.

Shortly before he resigned as CIA director, William Colby appeared on a television news program and said, "Are we going to acknowledge our place in the world or go on an isolationist binge as we did in the twenties?" In this case we not only see two-valued evaluation, but we also see one of the choices being given a negative label in an effort to make the other choice more attractive—a common rhetorical device.

The same technique can be seen in this statement from a document of the Symbionese Liberation Army, the group that kidnapped Patty Hearst: "The choice is yours alone, to be and show yourselves as lovers of the people and our children and true to your word revolutionaries or as egotistic opportunists and lovers of the group and organization and enemies of the people."

Wendell Johnson (1946, pp. 9–10) points out that applying two-valued evaluation to ourselves can lead to mental health problems. If a person begins to think "I am either a failure or a success" and takes the statement too seriously, some major problems can develop. The next line of thinking is liable to be, "Boy, I sure don't feel like a success. Then I must be a failure!" This is a kind of thinking that could in some cases lead to suicide, when the person to a large extent is being deluded by language. *Family Weekly* (Treffert, 1976) recently told of a 15-year-old girl who had received straight A's and hanged herself when she got her first B. She wrote in her suicide note, "If I fail in what I do, I fail in what I am."

In reality, most of us have some small successes and some small failures every day. Summing it all up with a general conclusion about whether one is a success or a failure is not necessary and does not reflect reality accurately.

The cure the General Semanticists suggest for two-valued evaluation is *multi-valued evaluation,* or thinking in terms of a range of possibilities instead of two.

4. *Unconscious projection.* Unconscious projection is a lack of awareness that one's statements are to a degree statements about oneself. Wendell Johnson (1972, p. 304) went so far as to claim that "Basically we always talk about ourselves." An example is the statement "The room is hot." It is a statement about the room, but it is also a statement about the condition of the nervous system of the person making the statement. The same is true of the statement "The orange is sweet." It might be sweet to one person, but sour to another. Many people might be aware of their own projection when they say something is "hot" or "sweet." But people seem less aware that their statement is about themselves when they say something like "The art exhibit is ugly." That sounds like a factual statement about the art exhibit, when actually it is a statement that involves a great deal of personal reaction. And we can see how unconscious projection can lead to problems when we recall that people sometimes get into fights over whether or not an art exhibit is ugly.

The statement "Who cares?" is usually one that is high in projection; it implies that "Nobody cares" but can really be translated as "I don't care."

We are all familiar with the "Pollyanna optimist" who always sees the world through rose-colored glasses, or the chronic pessimist who has a sour view of the world. These people are involved in projection: their own moods and opinions influence the way they see and describe the world.

Novelist Erica Jong once said on the "Today" show on television that "Marriage is an invention for making lawyers rich." Since she had recently been through a divorce, we can assume that the statement was high in projection (although it may not have been *unconscious* projection, since Ms. Jong appears to be a careful user of language).

Unconscious projection can become dangerous when it occurs in government leaders or other persons with great responsibility. President Nixon once complained during a televised news conference that television coverage of his administration had been "outrageous, vicious [and] distorted." When the National News Council asked the White House to supply the specific details that supported the charge, it was never given them. President Nixon was apparently not aware that his statement was to a large degree an expression of his own personal reaction. When such statements become the basis of official and unofficial actions—and there is evidence that the Nixon administration was taking steps against the television networks (Whiteside, 1975)—we begin to see the seriousness of the consequences of unconscious projection by government leaders.

The General Semanticists suggest that a cure for unconscious projection is to add "to me" to the end of any statement you make. Again, it might not be necessary to write or say the words "to me," but it should help to at least think them. And occasionally it will be appropriate to actually say "It appears to me . . ."

Three Kinds of Statements

A major debate in journalism has concerned objectivity—whether it is good or bad, and whether it is even possible to achieve it. Some well-known journalists, including Hunter Thompson, Bill Moyers and David Brinkley, have described objectivity as a myth, while other well-known journalists, such as Clifton Daniel and Herbert Brucker, have defended objectivity as essential to reporting.

Some concepts introduced by S. I. Hayakawa can help the journalist to make some sense out of the controversy over objectivity. Hayakawa (1964) discusses three kinds of statements people can make—*reports, inferences* and *judgments* (and the related issue of *slanting*).

A report is a statement capable of verification and which excludes inferences and judgments. An example is the statement "The low temperature last night in Durham, N.C., was 47 degrees." This statement is capable of verification, or of being checked out. You could go to the weather station in Durham and examine the records or interview the meteorologist there. Other examples or reports would be these statements: "The City Council approved a budget of $237 million for the fiscal year 1976–77." (Either they did or they didn't, and the action can be verified by checking with council members, eyewitnesses attending the meeting, and the official minutes of the meeting.) "Robbery suspect Larry Joe Smith was seen at Municipal Airport Saturday afternoon." (This would be more difficult to verify, and it might not be verified until Smith is apprehended and identified in court or in a line-up by an eyewitness, but the statement is still capable of verification.)

An *inference* is a statement about the unknown made on the basis of the known. Any statement about another person's thoughts or feelings is an example of an inference. You might observe a person pounding her fist on the table, raising her voice and becoming red in the face. These would be the known aspects. If you then made the statement "She is angry," you would be making a statement about the unknown, the person's emotions. You would be making an inference. In many cases, the safest course is to stick to what is known and report it—the pounding of the fist, the raising of the voice and the reddening of the face. Statements about these observable characteristics are verifiable and are reports.

Any statement about the future is an inference, since the future is unknown. The statement "The President will go into the hospital Thursday for a checkup" is an inference, since it deals with the future. The safer statement in this case would be "The press secretary said the President will go into the hospital Thursday for a checkup." That is capable of verification—a report.

A Texas delegate to the 1976 Democratic National Convention in New York who was mugged said of his assailant: "He must have been six-feet-two and probably high on something." The conclusion that the mugger was "high on something" was an inference, although it might be most accurate to refer to it as a *labeled inference* since the word "probably" was used.

Inferences sometimes appear in news articles. A wire service story contained this sentence: "The hearing room was crowded and judging from the number of yellow legal pads seen, many in the audience were lawyers." A statement about the unknown—the number of lawyers in the room—was being made on the basis of the known—the number of legal pads. This was also a labeled inference, since the word "judging" was included to let the reader know an inference was being made.

In another example of a labeled inference, a television correspondent describing Congress's failure to override a Presidential veto of an emergency job bill said: "The Democrats seemed bewildered by what happened."

A *judgment* is an expression of approval or disapproval for an occurrence, person or object. For example, students sometimes use words like "great" (approval) or "terrible" (disapproval) to describe a teacher.

Letters to the editor of a newspaper sometimes contain judgments, as did the letter commenting on the television series "Roots" which described it as an "ethnic hatemongering diatribe" and "overdone fiction."

In an unusual departure from wire service objectivity, United Press International filed a news story with the following lead sentence: "Elizabeth Ray, the secretary whose intimate services led to the resignation of former Rep. Wayne Hays, has launched an acting career with a shoddy performance that nearly ruined the show."

The last phrase—"with a shoddy performance that nearly ruined the show"—is clearly a judgment. In defense of UPI, however, the show did contain some specific detail supporting the evaluation later in the story.

Sometimes the source of a news story will state a judgment, and it might be necessary for an alert journalist to challenge it. During some textbook hearings in Texas, a feminist critic of sexism in books told a television interviewer: "This year there are some books we almost like, and there are a lot of bad books."

The interviewer said, "What's a bad book?"

The critic was ready with an answer, however, and said, "A bad book is one that shows 75 per cent or more of males in the working roles." This shifted the interview out of the realm of judgments and into the realm of reports.

A journalist can do a great deal toward being objective by eliminating inferences and judgments and sticking as much as possible to reports. But this alone will not guarantee objectivity. Another factor must be considered, as Hayakawa points out. That factor is slanting. *Slanting* is selecting of details favorable or unfavorable to the subject being described.

In describing large outdoor demonstrations, for example, a newspaper often has available several different estimates of crowd size from which to choose. Leon Mann (1974) studied coverage of an anti-war rally in Washington, D.C., in October, 1967, and found that anti-war newspapers were more likely to choose a large estimate of the crowd size while pro-war newspapers were most likely to choose a small estimate.

Time magazine showed some slanting in 1974 in its description of Dr. Lorene Rogers when she was appointed acting president of the University of Texas. Dr. Rogers had served previously as a vice president of the university and as associate dean of the graduate school, and had been a member of the national Graduate Record Examination Board. *Time* referred to her only as "Lorene Rogers, 60, a professor of home economics."

Absolute objectivity might not be possible, but in fact the journalist (or any other communicator) can go a long way toward being objective by sticking as much as possible to reports (and excluding inferences and judgments) and by making a conscious effort to avoid slanting. Furthermore, these concepts provide some specific terms for discussing the ways in which reporting might or might not be objective.

Studies of Objectivity

Journalism professor John Merrill (1965) used General Semantics concepts as well as concepts of his own in his study of "How *Time* Stereotyped Three U.S. Presidents." He set up the following six categories of bias: attribution bias (for example, "Truman snapped"); adjective bias (Eisenhower's "warm manner of speaking"); adverbial bias ("Truman said curtly"); outright opinion (equivalent to Hayakawa's judgments—for example, "Seldom has a more unpopular man fired a more popular one."); contextual bias (bias in whole sentences, whole paragraphs or the entire story; six judges had to agree), and photographic bias ("What overall impression does the photograph give? How is the President presented in the picture—dignified, undignified; angry, happy; calm, nervous; etc.? What does the caption say/imply?").

Merrill examined a sample of ten issues of *Time* for each president— Truman, Eisenhower and Kennedy—and counted the occurrences of bias in each of the six categories. The results, summarized in Table 1, showed a

Table 1
Instances of Bias Shown by *Time* Magazine
in 10-Issue Samples for Each of Three Presidents

	Truman	Eisenhower	Kennedy
Total Bias	93	82	45
Total Positive Bias	1	81	31
Total Negative Bias	92	1	14

Adapted from Merrill, J.C. (1965). How *Time* Stereotyped Three U.S. Presidents. *Journalism Quarterly* 42:563–570. Reprinted by permission.

strong negative bias toward Truman, a strong positive bias toward Eisenhower, and a rather balanced portrayal of Kennedy. The portrayals of Truman and Eisenhower are good examples of *slanting*—over a period of time the details selected almost overwhelmingly added up to either a favorable or an unfavorable impression of these presidents.

Another journalism professor, Dennis Lowry (1971), used the Hayakawa categories of reports, inferences and judgments as the basis for a study of whether Vice President Spiro Agnew's famous Des Moines speech had an intimidating effect on television newscasters. Lowry studied a random sample of network newscasts before and after the Agnew address. He looked only at statements dealing with the Presidential administration, and he sorted them into these nine categories: attributed reports, unattributed reports, labeled inferences, unlabeled inferences, attributed favorable judgments, attributed unfavorable judgments, unattributed favorable judgments, unattributed unfavorable judgments and others. Lowry found an increase in the percentage of attributed reports, the safest kind of statement, after the Agnew speech. There were hardly any judgments in the newscasts before or after the Agnew speech, indicating that critics who accused the networks of being biased against the Nixon administration apparently were not noticing judgments. The critics may have been objecting to unlabeled inferences, the category with the highest percentage before and after the Agnew speech (49 per cent each time). The critics might also have objected to slanting, but that would be difficult to study since it involves omission of material.

Other Applications

Occasionally the mass media have called directly on a General Semanticist to help analyze some language. Four days after Patricia Hearst was kidnapped, a radio station received a letter from the Symbionese Liberation Army stating that they had taken her. Journalists became interested in analyzing that message and some others received previously from the SLA to get information about her captors. The *New York Times* quoted Dr. S. I. Hayakawa as saying that the writings showed "a high grade of intellect devoted to revolutionary ideology" (Turner, 1974). A few weeks later, CBS News brought in a similar kind of language expert. A tape recorded message was received from Cinque, the leader of the SLA. The CBS Morning News for Feb. 26, 1974, featured a psycholinguist as a guest. He analyzed the message and pointed out the categorical thinking in phrases such as "The Hearst empire" and "I am the nigger that you fear in the night."

Implications for Encoding

Now we can return to our original question of what can General Semantics tell us about *encoding*, or the translating of purpose, intention or meaning into symbols or codes. The lesson from General Semantics is that encoding is a difficult task often fraught with pitfalls. There are only a limited number of words available in the English language, and often these words correspond to the real world in only a rough way. Any writer facing the common problem of trying to find "the right word" to express an idea is aware of the difficulty of encoding.

Furthermore, it is possible to encode in such a way that one is actually saying very little about the real world. This is true when language stays at a high level of abstraction.

Finally, the concept of projection makes us aware of the difficulty of being objective. Any statement is to some degree a statement about ourselves, and is thus subjective. The best way to overcome the problem of subjectivity is to stick to verifiable statements, or reports.

CONCLUSIONS

General Semantics deals with the relationship between language and reality, and with the ways language influences our thinking.

General Semantics has a number of implications for the practitioner of mass communication. First, it points out the difficulty of encoding, or of expressing meaning in symbols or codes. Second, it provides a basis for analyzing and talking about objectivity—a major communications concept. Third, it can help the mass communicator—or anyone else—in sorting out information and misinformation. The General Semanticists have identified some misuses of language—dead level abstracting, undue identification, two valued evaluation, and unconscious projection—that are widespread. Knowledge of these misuses could be very beneficial to the reporter interviewing a news source. Such knowledge could also help the consumer of mass communication—the ordinary citizen trying to cope with the daily barrage of information and misinformation from the mass media.

REFERENCES

Haslam, G. (1970). Korzybski's Quest. *ETC: A Review of General Semantics* 27:67–80.

Hayakawa, S. I. (1962). Foreword. In S. I. Hayakawa (ed.) *The Use and Misuse of Language.* Greenwich, Conn.: Fawcett Publications.

Hayakawa, S. I. (1964). *Language in Thought and Action.* 2nd ed. New York: Harcourt, Brace and World.

Johnson, N. (1970). *How to Talk Back to Your Television Set.* Boston: Little, Brown and Company.

Johnson, W. (1946). *People in Quandaries: The Semantics of Personal Adjustment.* New York: Harper & Row.

Johnson, W. (1972). The Communication Process and General Semantic Principles. In W. Schramm (ed.) *Mass Communications.* 2nd ed., pp. 301–315. Urbana: The University of Illinois Press.

Korzybski, A. (1958). *Science and Sanity: An Introduction to Non-Aristotelian Systems and General Semantics.* 4th ed. Lakeville, Conn.: The International Non-Aristotelian Library Publishing Co.

Lowry, D. T. (1971). Agnew and the Network TV News: A Before/After Content Analysis. *Journalism Quarterly* 48:205–210.

Mann, L. (1974). Counting the Crowd: Effects of Editorial Policy on Estimates. *Journalism Quarterly* 51:278–285.

Merrill, J. C. (1965). How *Time* Stereotyped Three U.S. Presidents. *Journalism Quarterly* 42:563–570.

Miller, G. A. (1963). *Language and Communication.* New York: McGraw-Hill Book Company.

Rapoport, A. (1976). What I Think Korzybski Thought—And What I Think About It. *ETC.: A Review of General Semantics.* 33:351–365.

Sies, L. F. (1968). Wendell Johnson—An Appreciation. *ETC.: A Review of General Semantics* 25:263–269.

Stoen, D. (1976). Stuttering Pencils. *ETC.: A Review of General Semantics* 33:323–325.

Treffert, D. A. (September 19, 1976). Five Dangerous Ideas Our Children Have About Life. *Family Weekly* pp. 26–27.

Turner, W. (February 9, 1974). Release of 2 May be Kidnapping "Price." *The New York Times.*

Whiteside, T. (March 17, 1975). Annals of Television (The Nixon Administration and Television). *The New Yorker* pp. 41–91.

Winters, W. (1974). Korzybski in the Shadow of War. *ETC.: A Review of General Semantics* 31:425–427.

Chapter 6

The Measurement of Readability

MASS communication, which by definition is attempting to reach the largest audience possible, should be committed to writing and other forms of expression that are as easy to understand as possible.

A newspaper editorial might be making the most important statement in the world, but if it is written so that a person needs a college education to understand it, it will go right over the heads of 88 per cent of the population. The same principles apply to a magazine advertisement, a news story, and editorial page column, and even to spoken messages on the broadcast media, although the evidence is less clear here.

What factors make writing easy to understand or difficult to understand? Can a method be developed to measure how easy or difficult it is to understand a piece of writing? The area of research that attempts to answer these questions is known as readability research.

The study of readability is important for two reasons. First, it may give us a way to measure the *readability* of written material. Readability refers to "ease of understanding or comprehension due to the style of writing" (Klare, 1963, p. 1). Ideally, one would like to find a simple *formula* for measuring readability. A useful formula of this type might involve making some simple counts in a book or news story and then doing some simple computations to get some kind of score. Of course, such a formula should be *reliable* and *valid*. There should be evidence that different applications of the formula (by different people, for instance) would give the same readability score, and there should be evidence that the score really measures ease or difficulty of understanding.

Second, the search for a formula could provide some information about the most important aspects of style influencing ease of understanding. This could lead to some helpful advice for writers. We would be in a position to say that we know certain factors make a real difference in understanding, and therefore a writer should pay some attention to them in his or her writing.

Some researchers have also been interested in measuring whether or not a piece of writing is interesting, but that turns out to be a different question from whether or not a piece of writing is easy to understand. For a while, researchers were trying to deal with both of these aspects at the same time, but eventually they sorted them out. In the end, separate formulas were developed for measuring readability and interest.

History of Readability Measurement

The term *readability formula* is used here, following Klare, to mean "a method of estimating the probable success a reader will have in reading and understanding a piece of writing" (p. 34).

Although some interest in counting words can be traced back to Biblical times, the first attempts to develop a readability formula were by educators involved in selecting reading material for both children and adults.

The first readability formula is usually attributed to Lively and Pressey (1923), although some earlier work by Sherman (1888) and Kitson (1921) dealt with factors that would later be important in formulas. Sherman and Kitson did not take the step of constructing a predictive formula, however.

Sherman published what appears to be the first investigation of sentence length, one of the elements often included in later readability formulas. He pointed out an interesting decline in the average sentence length of authors as one moves through the centuries from Chaucer to Emerson. Sherman did not relate sentence length to difficulty of understanding, however.

Kitson's work is significant because he came up with the very two elements later used by Flesch and others in the modern readability formulas. Kitson was writing an advertising textbook, and he presented a measure of the "psychological differences" between periodicals. He compared publications on number of syllables per word and sentence length, the elements later used by Flesch and others. Kitson found that the percentage of words over two syllables long was 13.2 in the *Chicago Evening Post*, 7.7 in the *Chicago American*, 13.5 in *Century* magazine and 9.9 in *American* magazine. He found that the percentage of sentences longer than 20 words was 49.0 for the *Post*, 43.4 for the *Chicago American*, 45.4 for *Century* magazine and 33.5 for *American* magazine. Kitson was primarily interested in estimating the intellectual level of the public that a periodical served in order to help an advertiser choose a medium. He was not interested in measuring the reading difficulty of the material except as that was a measure of something else, and he did not develop a predictive formula.

The Lively and Pressey study—a frequent choice for the first readability formula—was based on the assumption, common among educators at that time, that vocabulary difficulty was a key factor in determining the difficulty of understanding for written material. They were concerned with the practical problem of selecting junior high school science textbooks. Many of these textbooks were so heavily laden with technical vocabulary that the teaching of the course almost became the teaching of vocabulary. They argued that it would be useful to have a means of measuring this "vocabulary burden." They also suggested that such a technique might be useful in measuring the vocabulary difficulty of supplementary reading, such as novels that might be assigned in addition to texts.

The Lively and Pressey formula rests on the key assumption that word difficulty is directly related to word frequency, with the most frequent words in the English language being the easiest to understand. The technique is based on E. L. Thorndike's *The Teacher's Word Book*, which rests on the same key assumption. Thorndike's book lists the 10,000 most common words in the English language with an index number beside each one. The more common the word, the higher the index number it was given. For instance, the word "and" had an index number of 210 and the word "atom" had an index number of 4. Words that were so rare that they did not appear in the 10,000 most common were considered zero-value words.

The first step in the Lively and Pressey procedure—it is not really quite a formula—is to select 1,000 words in samples evenly distributed throughout the book. Then a number of measures are computed: the total number of different words per thousand (called the vocabulary range), the total number of zero-value words per thousand (a measure of rare words) and the median Thorndike index number with zero-value words counted twice (called the weighted median index number).

Lively and Pressey applied their method to 16 different samples of reading matter, including three second grade readers, three fourth grade readers, several science textbooks, some novels, a newspaper front page and a medical school physiology text. They took two different 1,000-word samples from each work, and found that the two samples agreed closely enough to call the method "fairly reliable." Some evidence for the validity of the method came from the way different materials were ranked. For instance, the second grade readers scored lowest in number of zero-value words and the physiology text scored highest. Likewise, the second grade reader scored highest on the weighted median index number (with a higher number indicating more common words) and the physiology text scored lowest. These findings indicate the Lively and Pressey method is correctly identifying difficult materials. The range measure seemed to discriminate least: the fourth grade reader and the physiology text were quite close on that measure, and the newspaper front page showed the highest vocabulary range of all.

Lively and Pressey did not combine their three measures into a single formula, and in fact suggested that the weighted median index number alone was probably the best measure of vocabulary burden. They pointed out one way the method could be used: Robert Louis Stevenson's *Kidnapped* scored very close to the fourth grade readers, suggesting that it could be used as supplementary reading at the fourth or fifth grade level. They also suggested that further data be gathered so that norms could be established for evaluating texts or other kinds of reading matter. They were obviously thinking of some kind of a scale that would allow any weighted median index number that might be found to be translated into a grade level or other standard level of difficulty. This kind of scale was to be developed with later formulas.

The Lively and Pressey method was a good beginning, but it rested on the assumption that word frequency was the key element in determining difficulty of reading, and it did not provide much of a scale for interpreting scores. The scores were mostly interpretable in relation to other scores. If you studied two or more books, you could show that one scored as more difficult than another, but you couldn't give much meaning to a single score taken alone.

A study a few years later by Vogel and Washburne (1928), employees of the public school system of Winnetka, Illinois, considered several elements instead of just one, and apparently was the first study to develop an actual prediction formula. They presented a four-element equation using the number of different words in 1,000, the number of prepositions in 1,000 words, the number of uncommon words in 1,000 and the number of simple sentences in 75.

A still more comprehensive look at the elements that might influence readability was published in 1935 by Gray and Leary under the title *What Makes A Book Readable*. These authors were particularly interested in the problem that many American adults were not reading widely and apparently found much of the available reading material too difficult.

Rather than assuming that any one element was an adequate measure of difficulty of understanding of writing, Gray and Leary began their research with an exhaustive search aimed at finding all the possible elements that might influence readability. They began by surveying a number of librarians, publishers, and other persons interested in adult education. These experts were asked what elements they thought contributed to readability for adults of limited education. This produced a list of 289 elements. Some of these had to do with format, content, and general organization rather than style. When these were eliminated, the list had been pared down to 82 style elements. Some of these were elements which could not be objectively measured, such as "poetic and highly literary words." When these were eliminated, there were 64 elements still on the list. A preliminary investigation showed that only 44 of these occurred frequently enough to appear at least once in half the passages studied.

The next step of the research was to see which of these 44 elements correlated with a measure of the difficulty of various passages. Measures of the difficulty of several passages were available from paragraph meaning comprehension tests given to adults. These tests involve giving a person a paragraph to read and then immediately asking multiple choice questions about the paragraph. If a paragraph is easy to read, more people will give the correct answer. This can be used to assign a difficulty score to each paragraph. The correlations would show which of the 44 style elements vary systematically with the difficulty of the paragraph. For example, a correlation coefficient would express in one number whether or not there was a tendency for longer sentences to appear in paragraphs that are more difficult to understand. This stage of the research showed that 21 of the elements had significant correlations with difficulty as measured by paragraph meaning comprehension scores.

The final step was to boil these 21 down to a few that could be used in a mathematical formula that would measure difficulty. The most useful elements were selected on this basis: they had to correlate closely with average reading score, correlate relatively little among themselves, be readily recognizable, and give an adequate representation of known measures of difficulty.

The final Gray and Leary formula used five elements and looked like this:

$$X_I = -.01029\ X_2 + .009012\ X_5 - .02094\ X_6 - .03313\ X_7 - .01485\ X_8 + 3.774$$

The elements in the formula are the following:

X_I = reading score

X_2 = number of different hard words (words not on a list of 756 easy words) in a passage of 100 words

X_5 = number of first-, second- and third-person pronouns

X_6 = average sentence length in words

X_7 = percentage of different words

X_8 = number of prepositional phrases

Gray and Leary applied their formula to samples from 350 books. The scores ranged from a high of 2.06 for a rewritten version of *Robinson Crusoe* to a low of −.26 for the original *Robinson Crusoe*. The mean score for all books was .676.

The authors provided a scale for interpreting their scores by arranging them in a normal distribution and dividing the range of scores into five equal units. Area A, including scores from 1.15 to 1.46 and beyond, was labeled "very easy." Area B, from .84 to 1.15, was labeled "easy." Area C, from .53 to .84, was labeled "average." Area D, from .22 to .53, was labeled "difficult." And Area E, from -.09, or below, to .22, was labeled "very difficult."

Gray and Leary also studied 81 textbooks at varying grade levels, and found that their reading scores discriminated between the texts in the expected way except in the upper grades. Books for grades seven, eight and nine scored about the same on the reading score. Gray and Leary speculated that the elements not included in their formula become more important in determining difficulty of reading materials at the junior high level and beyond.

These factors might include the number and quality of ideas or the degree of directness with which ideas are presented.

The Readability Laboratory of Teachers College, Columbia University, became the scene of the next two important developments in readability measurement. This lab was set up by the American Association for Adult Education and focused on the problem of assessing reading materials for adults. Two of the researchers who worked there were Irving Lorge and Rudolf Flesch.

Lorge (1939) paved the way for the modern, streamlined formulas by suggesting that a two-element formula might work. He studied a number of two-element combinations and found a higher multiple correlation with reading comprehension scores for some of them than Gray and Leary had with their five-element formula. Combinations that worked well included: number of prepositional phrases and number of different hard words (giving a multiple correlation of .7456), average sentence length and number of different hard words (.7406) and number of prepositional phrases and average sentence length (.6949).

Flesch set forth in his doctoral dissertation to develop a still better formula. He took as his starting point the finding that the Gray and Leary formula failed to indicate clear differences in readability beyond a certain level of difficulty. Research at the Readability Laboratory found that the Gray and Leary formula could not distinguish between mature English prose and what is known as "light reading." Flesch undoubtedly was influenced also by the finding of Lorge that a formula using only two elements could predict difficulty as well as a formula with five or more elements.

Flesch (1943) reasoned that the Gray and Leary formula did not measure readability at the adult level better because it relied too heavily on the use of uncommon words as a measure, and that this element is not really that important with adults. Flesch turned to linguistic theory and other research on reading ability for some clues about other elements that might be important. These theories suggested that "seeing verbal relationships, logic, ideas, meaning" might be an important element in adult reading that was left out of earlier formulas. Flesch interpreted this as "abstract reasoning," and tried to find a way to measure it. One method he tried was to count the number of abstract words. This had been considered by Gray and Leary, but they had dropped it because of the difficulty of getting agreement on whether or not a word is abstract. Flesch came up with a solution by creating his own list of 13,918 abstract words. However, he found in further research that counting the number of affixes (additions placed at the beginning or end of words) was just as good a measure of abstraction, so he dropped the abstract word count.

Flesch kept the sentence length measure that had been used by Gray and Leary and others because it appeared to be a good measure of readability at both the children's level and the adult level. And he included a count of personal words because Lyman Bryson, the director of the Readability Laboratory, said that "appeal" was an important part of readability. Gray and Leary had included a count of personal pronouns in their formula. Flesch decided to disregard all neuter pronouns and count all words referring to people either by names or by words meaning people. He was assuming that human interest was the most important part of appeal, and that the types of words he classified as "personal references" would correlate with human interest.

The result of this research was the first Flesch readability formula: $X = .133 X_S + .0645 X_M - .0659 X_H - .7502$

The elements in the formula are the following:

X = reading score
X_S = average sentence length in words
X_M = number of affixes within a 100-word sample
X_H = number of personal references within a 100-word sample

The resulting score could be looked up on a chart which would supply either a verbal description of style such as "very easy" or a school grade level of the potential audience.

Flesch showed that his formula produced a multiple correlation coefficient of .7358 with paragraph meaning comprehension test scores, an improvement over the multiple correlation coefficient of .6435 that Gray and Leary obtained with five elements.

Flesch went on to popularize and publicize his formula probably more than any other readability researcher. His dissertation, *Marks of a Readable Style,* was published as a book. Flesch himself said that since it was a Ph.D. dissertation it "was not a very readable book." He rewrote it in a simplified version, and the result was published in 1946 as *The Art of Plain Talk.*

Soon after the publication of *The Art of Plain Talk,* two psychologists applied the Flesch readability formula to a group of standard psychology textbooks (Stevens and Stone, 1947a). Their results indicated an unexpectedly high readability score for Koffka's *Gestalt Psychology,* a book regarded by graduate students as notoriously difficult. In fact, Koffka scored higher than William James, a textbook author that students thought relatively easy. Stevens and Stone explained that this appeared to be true because of the high number of personal pronouns used by Koffka. Flesch was apparently provoked to action by the results concerning Koffka and James, for he wrote Stevens and Stone that he was working on revising his formula (Stevens and Stone, 1947b). Flesch indicated that he was working on a new formula element which was the "percentage of non-declarative sentences," and that this element correctly indicated that James was more readable than Koffka.

Flesch did come out with a revised formula the following year, but it did not contain the "percentage of non-declarative sentences." Instead, Flesch (1948) had dropped the count of "personal references" from the readability formula and used it to create a new Human Interest formula. Another change was that the count of affixes in the readability formula had been replaced

Table 1

Chart for Interpreting Flesch Reading Ease Scores

Reading Ease Score	Description of Style	Estimated Reading Grade
90–100	Very Easy	5th grade
80–90	Easy	6th grade
70–80	Fairly Easy	7th grade
60–70	Standard	8th and 9th grade
50–60	Fairly Difficult	10th to 12th grade
30–50	Difficult	13th to 16th grade (college)
0–30	Very Difficult	college graduate

After figure on p. 177 from *The Art of Readable Writing,* revised and enlarged edition by Rudolf Flesch. Copyright 1949, 1974 by Rudolf Flesch. By permission of Harper & Row, Publishers, Inc.

by a measure of word length—the number of syllables per 100 words. The results were two formulas—the Reading Ease formula and the Human Interest formula—and these are the two forms of the Flesch formulas used today.

The Reading Ease formula takes this form: $R.E. = 206.835 - .846\ w1 - 1.015\ s1$

The elements in the formula are the following:

$R.E.$ = reading ease score.
$w1$ = number of syllables per 100 words
$s1$ = average number of words per sentence

The resulting score should range between 0 and 100 and can be looked up in a chart such as the one presented in Table 1.

The Human Interest formula takes this form: $H.I. = 3.635\ pw + .314\ ps$

The factors in the formula are the following:

$H.I.$ = human interest score
pw = number of personal words per 100 words
ps = number of personal sentences per 100 sentences

The resulting score should fall between 0 and 100 and can be looked up in a chart such as the one in Table 2.

The Flesch Reading Ease formula has proved to be the most widely used readability formula (Klare, 1963). It was popularized in a book published in 1949—*The Art of Readable Writing.*

The Flesch Reading Ease formula has produced a number of useful offshoots.

The Gunning Fog Index, developed by Robert Gunning (1952), is based

Table 2

Chart for Interpreting Flesch Human Interest Scores

Human Interest *Score*	*Description* *Of Style*
0–10	Dull
10–20	Mildly Interesting
20–40	Interesting
40–60	Highly Interesting
60–100	Dramatic

After figure on p. 179 from *The Art of Readable Writing,* revised and enlarged edition by Rudolf Flesch. Copyright 1949, 1974 by Rudolf Flesch. By permission of Harper & Row, Publishers, Inc.

on two elements: average sentence length in words and number of words of three syllables or more per 100 words. These two numbers are added and multiplied by .4, and the resulting number is the approximate grade level at which the material can be read. When Gunning began his consulting work with newspapers, he was using the original Flesch formula that counted affixes (Gunning, 1945), and the formula that he developed later resembles the Reading Ease formula. At the earlier stage in Gunning's career, the term "Fog Index" also had a different meaning—it referred to "a measure of uselessly long and complex words" (p. 12). The main advantage of the Gunning Fog Index over the Flesch Reading Ease formula is that the former gives a grade level immediately while a Reading Ease score has to be looked up in a table to produce a grade level.

Dr. Edward Fry, director of the Reading Center at Rutgers University, has developed a slide rule type device that essentially takes the computation out of using a readability formula (Fry, 1977). It is based on average sentence length and average number of syllables per 100 words, the same two elements used in the Flesch Reading Ease formula. To use the device, you slide a moveable part along a scale until a black square is beside the average number of syllables per 100 words that you found in your sample. Then you look at another place on the instrument where average sentence lengths are indicated, and beside the average sentence length for your sample will be the approximate grade level for reading that material.

In another step of simplification, Wayne Danielson and Sam Dunn Bryan (1963) have developed a computerized readability formula in which the computer does the *counts* and the *computations* and gives you a readability score. The formula is based on two elements that are similar to the two in the Flesch Reading Ease formula except that they are defined in units that the computer can recognize easily. They are: average number of characters per space (essentially a measure of word length) and average number of characters per sentence (essentially a measure of sentence length). The resulting score is very much like a Reading Ease score and in fact can be looked up on the Flesch Reading Ease chart.

In order to use the Danielson and Byran computerized formula, you must have the written material you want to analyze punched on cards, paper tape, or some other means of input that the computer can read. In some cases, this would require hand punching. But in the case of wire copy such as that provided by the Associated Press, the hand punching is not necessary. Wire copy is normally available in the form of punched paper tapes that can be used to operate a Linotype machine in a newspaper building. Danielson discovered that it was only necessary to modify the tape punching machine slightly and the paper tapes could be read directly into a computer. This allowed him to study the readability of the Associated Press output for a week without repunching all of that material.

Tables are also available that eliminate the computation necessary to apply the Flesch Reading Ease and Human Interest formulas (Farr and Jenkins, 1949). To determine the Reading Ease score of a sample, you simply look up the average sentence length on the side of the table and the number of syllables per 100 words across the top of the table. Where the row and the column intersect can be found the Reading Ease score. A similar table for the Human Interest score has per cent of personal sentences on the side and per cent of personal words across the top.

Using a Formula

An example will help to bring out exactly how the Flesch Reading Ease formula can be applied to a piece of writing. We will take a sample of writing and make the necessary counts and do the computations to come up with a Reading Ease score.

Before we begin, we need to present exact definitions of some of the things we will be counting. Flesch defines a word as a letter, number, symbol or group of letters, numbers or symbols surrounded by white space. Thus, 1949, C.O.D. and vice-chairman would all be counted as words. Flesch defines a sentence as a unit of thought grammatically independent and usually marked by a period, question mark, exclamation point, semicolon, colon or dash. Syllables are counted the way you would pronounce the word. For example, 1916 would count as a four-syllable word. Since you need to find the number of syllables per 100 words, one short cut that is sometimes useful is to start by writing down 100 and then count only the words of two syllables or more, writing down a 1 for a two-syllable word, a 2 for a three-syllable word, and so forth. Then you simply add all the numbers you have written down, including the 100. This can often save time because many words are one-syllable words. The writing down of the number of syllables for each word is a good idea so you can go back and check your work.

Now we are ready to apply the Reading Ease formula to the following sample—the beginning paragraphs of a news story written by a student:

The Texas Water Rights Commission (TWRC) voted Tuesday to allow the South Texas Nuclear Project the use of Colorado River water despite a warning from Atty. Gen. John Hill that such action could result in state instituted court proceedings against TWRC.

Hill's warning came at the commission's meeting, after he advised it that the Lower Colorado River Authority (LCRA) had no control over the unallocated waters involved in a debate between LCRA and TWRC and should not be paid for the use of them.

The debate stemmed from a dispute between TWRC, which controls all the unallocated water in the state, and LCRA, which has power over all Colorado River water within a 10-county area, over who would profit from sale of the water.

This sample is more than 100 words so it is adequate to illustrate the workings of the formula, although you would probably measure the entire story if you were seriously attempting to determine its readability.

First, it is necessary to determine the average sentence length (sl). Remember that LCRA, TWRC and 10-county should count as one word each. The sample contains three sentences and 124 words. Dividing 124 by three gives an average sentence length of 41.33 words.

Next, it is necessary to determine the number of syllables per 100 words (wl). The easiest way to determine this is to count the syllables in the first 100 words. The 100th word is the word "the" before the word "state" in the third paragraph. The only tricky parts in counting the syllables might be the word TWRC, which includes six syllables when it is pronounced, and the words Atty. and Gen., which include three syllables each when the full words are pronounced. The number of syllables in the first 100 words is 189.

Next, we substitute these numbers for *sl* and *wl* in the Reading Ease formula, and obtain the following:

R.E. = 206.835 − .846 (189) − 1.015 (41.33)

Doing the two multiplications gives the following:

R.E. = 206.835 − 159.894 − 41.950

And doing the final subtractions gives 4.991, the Reading Ease score.

This is a very low Reading Ease score. It can be looked up in the Reading Ease chart in Table 1, and it falls in the "Very Difficult" category, where the estimated reading grade is "college graduate." This is understandable when we look at the long sentences used, the acronyms (LCRA and TWRC) and the use of complicated terms (unallocated water). Of course, if the entire story had been analyzed, the Reading Ease score might have been lower. News writers often attempt to pack a great deal of information into the beginning of a news story, and this can make the beginning less readable than the rest of the story. This practice can be questioned, however; if the beginning of the story is not readable, people might not get to the later sections.

Applications of Readability Formulas

Readability measurement has been used in a number of areas, including textbook evaluation, analysis of mass communication, writing for new literates, improving income tax forms and other government writing, and rewriting insurance policies. We turn now to some of these applications.

Textbook Evaluation

The main reason Lively and Pressey and some of the other pioneers developed their measures of readability was to help in textbook selection. Gray and Leary had a similar purpose—the selection of suitable books for adult readers.

Extending the idea of textbook evaluation to college texts, Stevens and Stone (1947) used Flesch's first formula to study 18 psychology textbooks. They found that most of the ratings agreed pretty well with student assessments of difficulty, except for the problem we have discussed of Koffka receiving a score of higher readability than William James.

Researchers following in the footsteps of Stevens and Stone have used Flesch formulas to study the readability of psychology texts (Gillen, 1973; Cone, 1976), educational psychology texts (Hofmann and Vyhonsky, 1975), and journalism texts (Tankard and Tankard, 1977). The latter study of nine books using the Reading Ease formula showed five were in the "difficult" range, two were in the "fairly difficult" range, and two were in the "standard" range. The Human Interest formula placed one journalism text in the "dull" category, three in the "mildly interesting" category and five in the "interesting" category.

Readability formulas are also being used by a number of college textbook publishers to make sure texts are not being written at too difficult a level. McGraw-Hill Book Co. does its own in-house readability checks, while John Wiley and Sons and Oxford University Press hire readability specialists to do the checks for them.

Mass Communication

Soon after Flesch's first formula was published in 1943, Robert Gunning began applying it to consulting work for newspapers (Gunning, 1945). He studied the readability of eight newspapers in 1944 and concluded, "Today's newspapers are offering the public some of the most difficult reading material published" (p. 2).

Several readability experts—including Gunning, Flesch and Danielson—have served as consultants to the major wire services. Gunning worked with United Press in the 1940s and reported that "within three weeks the reading difficulty of UP copy had been cut by five grade levels" (p. 2).

Flesch and Danielson have served at different times as consultants to the Associated Press. Flesch studied the AP news report during 1948–50. In keeping with his formulas, Flesch recommended that AP writers use short sentences, short words and human interest writing.

Readability studies going back to some of the earliest (Lively and Pressey, 1923; Gray and Leary, 1935) have often included newspapers as a base of comparison. Typically the newspapers have not scored as the easiest material being considered. In the Lively and Pressey study, for instance, the newspaper studied had the largest vocabulary range of all materials studied. Gray and Leary found that newspapers contained a longer median sentence length (measured in syllables) than general magazines or books.

Charles Seib, the ombudsman of *The Washington Post,* conducted a non-scholarly but informative study of sentence length, one of the two elements in the popular readability formulas. Seib found the average sentence length on the front pages of three newspapers on a Sunday were the following: *The Washington Star,* 31 words; *The New York Times,* 33 words; *The Washington Post,* 38 words. By contrast, he found the average sentence length for several popular books to be the following: Saul Bellow's *Humboldt's Gift,* just under 12 words; Woody Allen's *Without Feathers,* just over 12 words; Jimmy Breslin's *How the Good Guys Finally Won,* under 11 words.

Seib concluded, "News stories can't be judged on the same basis as fiction or even Breslin's free-style journalism. But an average of over 30 words per sentence is too much for comfortable reading. Particularly when the tube is waiting just across the room."

As Seib's analysis points out, readability research can be used to formulate some advice for journalists. That advice would be: Use short sentences and short words. Flesch has been even more specific in his advice about sentence length—he has recommended to the AP that newswriters use an average sentence length of 19 words. Several popular magazines are already doing a good job of following his advice—the average sentence length a number of years ago in *Time* and *Reader's Digest* was 17 words or less (Gunning, 1952).

Research has also shown that the readability level of a newspaper article has a definite effect on how much of the article will be read. Swanson (1948) conducted a controlled field experiment to determine the effect of readability on readership. Two versions of the same story were produced—one with a Flesch Reading Ease score of 49.84 (difficult) and the other with a Reading Ease score of 84.94 (easy). Then two versions of an experimental campus newspaper were produced—one with the difficult story and one with the easy story. In a "trailer village" where married students lived, one version was delivered to odd-numbered trailers and the other to even-numbered trailers. Interviewers arrived within 30 hours to ask the adult male at each trailer about his readership of every paragraph in the paper. The mean number of paragraphs read was 13.087 for the "difficult" story and 23.969 for the "easy" story.

New Literates

The problem of illiteracy in the world is still a huge one. UNESCO figures indicate about half the world's population is illiterate. Even if people are given some initial training in reading, they are likely to lose their ability if they don't practice it. Thus, there is an important need for material especially written for "New Literates." This material must be written at the easiest levels possible. Readability formulas can be used to achieve this goal. It is not surprising, then, that a book such as Laubach and Laubach's *Toward World Literacy: The Each One Teach One Way* should contain a chapter on readability formulas and another on Flesch's Human Interest formula.

Government Regulations

A study done for the Commission on Federal Paperwork indicated that a person needed the reading skills of a college graduate to understand the 1976 short form of the income tax (Quinn, 1978). Only 12 per cent of the population 25 years and over had completed four years of college in 1972. In the same year, the percentage of the U.S. population 20 years old and over that had at least a high school education was 61.5. This means that if an important piece of writing from the government is written so that it takes a high school education to understand it, nearly 40 per cent of the adult population will not understand it. Since the percentage of people with a high school education drops to 43.7 per cent for blacks and other minority groups, the government prose will be understandable to even fewer of them.

These figures suggest that many kinds of important government documents—including the standard tax forms—might be difficult for most people to understand.

Some government officials, including President Jimmy Carter, are aware of this problem and are trying to do something about it. The Internal Revenue Service has conducted a readability study of its 1971 IRS form 1040 instructions using the Dale and Chall readability formula (Pyrczak, 1976). It identified a list of almost 800 "unfamiliar" words and many overly long sentences. On the basis of this analysis, several steps were taken to improve readability of the instructions, including having a panel of teachers review the instructions and hiring a consultant to help with analysis and rewriting.

Are tax forms getting easier or harder to read and understand? Jan Costello (1977), an undergraduate honors student, attempted to answer this question by determining Reading Ease and Human Interest scores for 1040 instructions over a period of years. She applied the formulas to the instructions for odd numbered years from 1943 to 1975 (except for 1945, which she couldn't locate). Costello modified the Flesch procedures slightly. When she came to a paragraph with a large dose of symbols and numbers, she went to the next paragraph. When the paragraph had a few symbols and numbers, she treated them as one syllable each instead of counting every syllable. These procedures led to more generous Reading Ease scores, but she did it

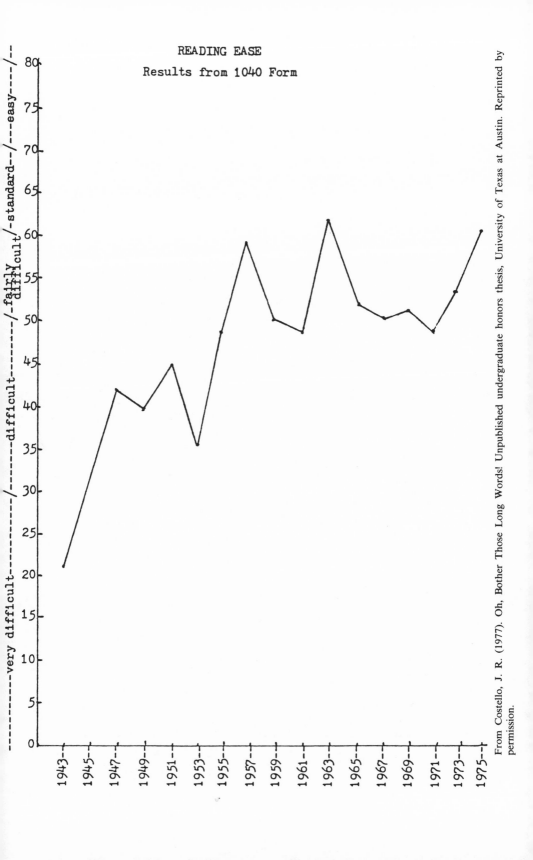

READING EASE

Results from 1040 Form

From Costello, J. R. (1977). Oh, Bother Those Long Words! Unpublished undergraduate honors thesis, University of Texas at Austin. Reprinted by permission.

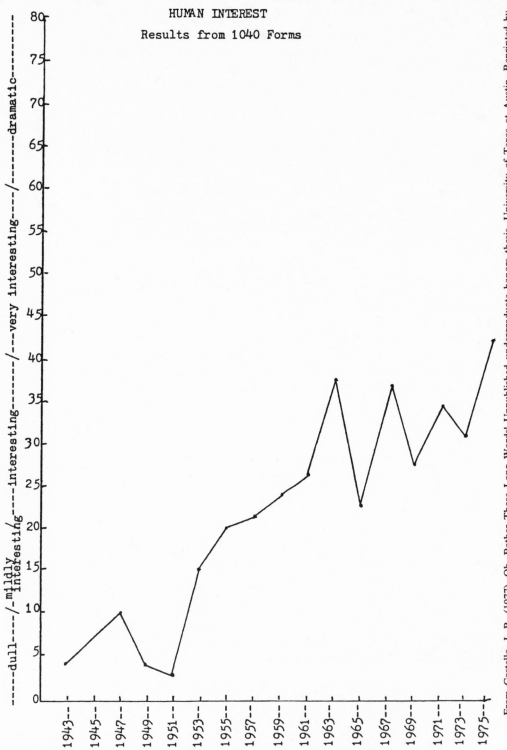

HUMAN INTEREST
Results from 1040 Forms

From Costello, J. R. (1977). Oh, Bother Those Long Words! Unpublished undergraduate honors thesis, University of Texas at Austin. Reprinted by

to allow for the fact that a tax form must naturally use many symbols and numbers. Costello's results (see Tables 3 and 4) show a fairly regular increase in Reading Ease and Human Interest for 1040 instructions over a period of 30 years.

Insurance Policies

In 1976, the State Insurance Board of Texas hired Rudolf Flesch as a consultant to assist in simplifying the language used in insurance policies. The result was a set of rules designed to make accident and health insurance policies easier to read. Flesch has also helped the St. Paul Fire and Marine Insurance Co. rewrite its policies.

Also in 1976, a new home owner's insurance policy written in easy-to-understand language was being tried in six states—Colorado, Georgia, Illinois, Nevada, Ohio and Vermont (Anonymous, Winter 1975–76). The rewritten policy eliminated awkward terminology and shortened overlong sentences. Throughout the policy, the company is referred to as "we" and the insured person is referred to as "you." Flesch formulas were used to test the readability.

The old policy used to begin with a 307-word section that opened with a 247-word first sentence. That sentence began this way: "In Consideration of the Provisions and Stipulations Herein or Added Hereto and of the Premium Above Specified (or special endorsements made a part hereof) the Company, for the term shown above from inception. . . ."

In the rewritten policy, the entire 307-word section becomes the following: "We will provide the insurance described in this policy in return for the premium and compliance with all applicable provisions of this policy."

Cloze Procedure

A very different approach to measuring readability has been introduced by communication scholar Wilson L. Taylor (1953). He noticed that readability formulas had a weakness in that their basic assumptions could be contradicted. Most of the formulas are based on the assumption that a short word is easier to understand than a long word. And yet one can easily think of examples in which that would not be true. The word "erg" is shorter than the word "respectability," and yet most people would not know the meaning of "erg" but would know the meaning of "respectability." If a sample of writing had a lot of words of this type that violated the assumptions of the formulas, then the formulas would give very misleading readability scores.

Taylor invented another procedure for measuring readability which he says measures *all* the potential elements influencing readability. He called this method "Cloze Procedure." The name is based on the word *closure,* which stands for the human tendency to complete a familiar but incomplete pattern.

To use Cloze Procedure, you take the sample of writing you are interested in and "mutilate" it by replacing some of the words with blanks. This can be done in different ways, but a common way is just to replace every fifth word with a blank. Then the mutilated passage is given to a test group of subjects who are asked to fill in the missing words. The Cloze score becomes the number or percentage of blanks that are filled in correctly. The simplest scoring procedure is to count only the exact word and not synonyms. Attempting to count synonyms introduces a subjective element into the scoring and slows it down considerably.

The theory behind Cloze Procedure is, in its simplest form, the notion that the simpler a piece of writing is, the easier it will be for a test reader to replace the missing words. Putting it another way, Cloze Procedure measures the extent to which a sample of prose is written in the patterns that a reader is naturally anticipating. And these patterns can involve all the different factors that might influence readability—overall organization, sentence structure, appropriateness of vocabulary, simplicity of vocabulary, and so forth.

We can also think of Cloze Procedure as a measure of *redundancy* (see Ch. 4). The more redundant a piece of writing is, the easier it will be for someone to fill in the blanks.

Taylor did not just assume that his method measured readability, but provided some evidence of its validity. First he showed that his procedure ranked passages very similarly to the Flesch Reading Ease formula and other orthodox formulas when the passages studied were "standard."

Then Taylor devised an "acid test" for Cloze Procedure—could it give a more trustworthy rating of readability for material that might fool the readability formulas? The kind of material he needed was written prose that might violate a lot of the assumptions basic to the formulas. Taylor decided that this kind of material could be found in two novels recognized by literary critics as being highly experimental—James Joyce's *Finnegan's Wake* and Gertrude Stein's *Geography and Plays*. Taylor set up a test in which both Flesch Reading Ease scores and Cloze Procedure scores would be determined for passages from these two experimental novels and six other more standard books. Taylor predicted that the Reading Ease scores would indicate that the Joyce and Stein were easy reading because they contain short words and short sentences, even though critics find both books difficult to read. Cloze Procedure, in contrast, was expected to rank the two experimental novels as more difficult than the other six books. In the Cloze Procedure for this test, Taylor deleted every seventh word in a passage from each book until he had 25 deletions for each book. Each passage was read by 18 subjects, giving a possible total Cloze score for each book of 18 times 25, or 450. The results of the test are summarized in Table 5.

The Flesch Reading Ease scores indicate that the Stein passage is the easiest of the eight, and that the Joyce is somewhere in the middle. These scores fall in the "very easy" and "fairly easy" categories. In contrast, the Cloze scores rank the Stein and Joyce selections as the two most difficult. This supports Taylor's argument that in the case of written material that violates the assumptions of the formulas, Cloze Procedure would give a truer indication of reading difficulty than the formulas.

Table 5

Comparisons of Flesch Reading Ease Scores and Cloze Procedures Scores for Samples from Eight Books

	Reading Ease Score	Rank by R.E. Score	Cloze Score	Rank by Cloze Score
Stein—*Geography and Plays*	96	1	123	7
Boswell—*Life of Johnson*	89	2	186	3
Swift—*Gulliver's Travels*	80	3	170	4
Caldwell—*Georgia Boy*	79	4.5	336	1
Joyce—*Finnegan's Wake*	79	4.5	49	8
Dickens—*Bleak House*	69	6	263	2
Huxley—*Man Stands Alone*	68	7	155	5
James—*The Ambassadors*	47	8	135	6

Adapted from Taylor, W. L. (1953). "Cloze Procedure": A New Tool for Measuring Readability. *Journalism Quarterly* 30:415–433. Reprinted by permission.

Cloze scores are probably easiest to interpret when two or more samples of writing are being compared. Then the several passages can be tested on the same group of subjects, and the passages can be ranked according to difficulty. The passages with the highest average Cloze scores are the easiest ones and the passages with the lowest Cloze scores are the most difficult.

Meaning can also be assigned to individual Cloze scores. Rankin and Culhane (1969), extending earlier work by Bormuth (1968), have developed a scale for interpreting Cloze scores. Their research indicates that a Cloze score of 61 per cent or higher shows the material is at the "independent level" of reading, a score of 41 per cent or higher shows the material is at the "instructional level" of reading, and a score below 41 per cent indicates the material is too difficult to be used with that particular class.

Cloze Procedure is coming into some general use, although it is not yet being used as widely as the formulas. Kincaid and Gamble (1977) used Cloze to study automobile insurance policies rewritten by the Nationwide and Sentry companies to be more readable. The Cloze scores showed that the rewritten policies were easier to understand than standard policies used by the same companies.

Future Research

Research on readability will undoubtedly continue. Further research is needed on factors that are known to affect readability but which are not included in formulas—factors such as organization, directness of approach, and conceptual difficulty.

Further research is needed on the "listenability" of spoken messages. Klare (1963) points out that most of the studies of listenability have produced negative results so far.

CONCLUSIONS

The most obvious use for readability formulas is in measuring the difficulty of samples of writing. They do this quickly and with a fairly high degree of accuracy, and they are being used in many different fields.

The following general guidelines might help in selecting a readability formula. The Flesch Reading Ease formula is the most widely used formula. The easiest formula to apply, according to Klare (1963), is the Farr, Jenkins and Paterson (1951). This formula is based on average sentence length and number of one-syllable words per 100 words. The most accurate formula, also according to Klare, is the Dale and Chall (1948a, 1948b). This formula is based on average sentence length and the percentage of words outside the Dale list of 3,000 easy words. Klare reports that the Dale and Chall formula predicts reading comprehension scores more reliably than any of the other popular formulas.

Readability formulas are also useful in providing us with some solid evidence about which elements make writing easy or difficult to understand. The two most important elements, identified through a series of studies building on one another, are vocabulary burden and sentence complexity. We can translate this into advice for writers and editors and recommend that they use short words and short sentences.

Flesch has recommended that newswriters use an average sentence length of 19 words. That does not mean that every sentence has to be exactly that length. Some variety in sentence length is usually more pleasing than having all sentences the same length. But it means that 19 words is a good average length to aim for over a number of sentences.

Everyone who reads this chapter does not have to become a champion of readability formulas. But we hope that not many readers will take on the attitude of the distinguished newspaper writer visiting a department of journalism. He bragged that he used to write 70-word sentences as a protest because the newspaper he worked for "was enamored of this guy Rudolf Flesch." This kind of attitude may be appropriate if you are interested in writing only for the elite in our society, but if you are attempting to reach the largest audience possible, it is foolhardy.

REFERENCES

Anonymous. (Winter, 1975–76). Easy Reader: A New Insurance Policy for Homeowners. *Journal of American Insurance* 51, no. 4:12–15.

Bormuth, J. R. (1968). Cloze Test Readability: Criterion Reference Scores. *Journal of Educational Measurement* 5:190–196.

Cone, A. L. (1976). Six Luxury Models. *Contemporary Psychology* 21:544–48.

Costello, J. R. (1977). Oh, Bother Those Long Words! Unpublished undergraduate honors thesis, University of Texas at Austin.

Dale, E., and J. S. Chall. (1948a). A Formula for Predicting Readability. *Educational Research Bulletin* 27:11–20.

Dale, E., and J. S. Chall. (1948b). A Formula for Predicting Readability: Instructions. *Educational Research Bulletin* 27:37–54.

Danielson, W. A., and S. D. Bryan. (1963). Computer Automation of Two Readability Formulas. *Journalism Quarterly* 40:201–206.

Farr, J. N., and J. J. Jenkins. (1949). Tables for Use with the Flesch Readability Formulas. *Journal of Applied Psychology* 33:275–78.

Farr, J. N., J. J. Jenkins and D. G. Paterson. (1951). Simplification of Flesch Reading Ease Formula. *Journal of Applied Psychology* 35:333–337.

Flesch, R. (1943). *Marks of a Readable Style: A Study in Adult Education.* New York: Teachers College, Columbia University.

Flesch, R. (1948). A New Readability Yardstick. *Journal of Applied Psychology* 32:221–233.

Flesch, R. (1962a). *The Art of Plain Talk.* New York: Collier Books.

Flesch, R. (1962b). *The Art of Readable Writing.* New York: Collier Books.

Fry, E. (1977). Fry's Readability Graph: Clarification, Validity, and Extension to Level 17. *Journal of Reading* 21:242–252.

Gillen, B. (1973). Readability and Human Interest Scores of Thirty-Four Current Introductory Psychology Texts. *American Psychologist* 28:1010–11.

Gray, W. S., and B. E. Leary. (1935). *What Makes a Book Readable with Special Reference to Adults of Limited Reading Ability: An Initial Study.* Chicago: The University of Chicago Press.

Gunning, R. (May 19, 1945). Gunning Finds Papers too Hard to Read. *Editor & Publisher,* p. 12.

Gunning, R. (1952). *The Technique of Clear Writing.* New York: McGraw-Hill.

Hofmann, R. J., and R. J. Vyhonsky. (1975). Readability and Human Interest Scores of Thirty-Six Recently Published Introductory Educational Psychology Texts. *American Psychologist* 30:790–92.

Kincaid, J. P., and L. G. Gamble. (1977). Ease of Comprehension of Standard and Readable Automobile Insurance Policies as a Function of Reading Ability. *Journal of Reading Behavior* 9, no. 1:85–87.

Kitson, H. D. (1921). *The Mind of the Buyer: A Psychology of Selling.* New York: The Macmillan Company.

Klare, G. R. (1963). *The Measurement of Readability.* Ames, Iowa: Iowa State University Press.

Laubach, F. C., and R. S. Laubach. (1960). *Toward World Literacy: The Each One Teach One Way.* New York: Syracuse University Press.

Lively, B. A., and S. L. Pressey. (1923). A Method for Measuring the "Vocabulary Burden" of Textbooks. *Educational Administration and Supervision* 9:389–398.

Lorge, I. (1939). Predicting Reading Difficulty of Selections for Children. *Elementary English Review* 16:229–233.

Pyrczak, F. (1976). Readability of 'Instructions for Form 1040.' *Journal of Reading* 20:121–127.

Quinn, J. B. (February, 1978). How to Cope with Your 1977 Federal Income Tax Form. *Reader's Digest*, pp. T1-T16.

Rankin, E. F., and J. W. Culhane. (1969). Comparable Cloze and Multiple-Choice Comprehension Test Scores. *Journal of Reading* 13:193–98.

Sherman, L. A. (1888). Some Observations upon the Sentence-Length in English Prose. *University Studies of the University of Nebraska* 1, no. 2:119–130.

Stevens, S. S., and G. Stone (1947a). Psychological Writing, Easy and Hard. *American Psychologist* 2:230–235.

Stevens, S. S. and G. Stone. (1947b). Further Comment. *American Psychologist* 2:524–525.

Swanson, C. (1948). Readability and Readership: A Controlled Experiment. *Journalism Quarterly* 25:339–345.

Tankard, J. W., and E. F. Tankard. (1977). Comparison of Readability of Basic Reporting Texts. *Journalism Quarterly* 54:794–97.

Taylor, W. L. (1953). "Cloze Procedure": A New Tool for Measuring Readability. *Journalism Quarterly* 30:415–433.

Vogel, M., and C. Washburne. (1928). An Objective Method of Determining Grade Placement of Children's Reading Material. *Elementary School Journal* 28:373–81.

Chapter 7

Measuring Connotative Meaning: The Semantic Differential

How do we accurately measure the "image" of a product, political candidate, organization or an idea for a specific group or audience? How
do we communicate to someone else what a concept means to us? How do
we accurately compare the "meaning" of two different concepts, issues, products or candidates? How do we compare the image of a political candidate
held by two different groups? How can we determine if people in different
cultures judge things in the same way?

For *denotative* meanings of words we turn to a dictionary. Here we
find the history and law of the language—how words have been used in
the past and their "proper" usage now. But language, as everything else,
changes or evolves.

Language is a living thing, and the meaning of words and concepts
change with time, location and individuals—we have *connotative* as well as
denotative meanings.

We all know that nouns are modified by adjectives and verbs are modified
by adverbs, but we use expressions such as "The now generation," in complete
violation of the rules.

Besides that, a dictionary is of little help when we want to know how
a given audience or population sees the "image" of a newspaper, a TV program, an organization, a political candidate or a deodorant.

In other words, can we use the scientific method to measure that elusive
human trait of assigning meaning to certain sounds and symbols—language—
be it words, spoken or written, pictures, music, etc.?

What we need is a measuring tool which is accurate enough for our purposes but at the same time highly adaptable to an infinite variety of situations and needs.

The Semantic Differential Technique of Charles Osgood is such a tool. However, we should stress that there is no one Semantic Differential. The Differential is constructed for each concept with each audience or group. Not to do so is to lose much of its power and value. For this reason it behooves the student and the practitioner to understand a few basic underlying premises. Otherwise, as one of its originators has observed, it remains the most misunderstood and misused measuring tool we have today.

The Cumulative Nature of Science

The development of the Semantic Differential Technique is a good example of the cumulative nature of science as discussed earlier.

Osgood recalls his boyhood when he played many kinds of word games with his grandfather, a Harvard graduate and a successful Boston dentist who regretted not having become a college professor. Grandfather Osgood developed a feeling for language in his now famous grandson by teasing out subtle distinctions in meanings, giving him lists of rare words to memorize and rewarding their spontaneous and correct use. As a birthday gift, his aunt, Miss Grace Osgood, gave him a thesaurus, the exploration of which became the object of hours of aesthetic pleasure.

Osgood's recollection of his visual representation of the thesaurus was that of words as clusters of stars in an immense space. Already an avid reader of fantasy, horror and science fiction, the young man soon turned his thoughts to a career as a writer. In high school he was the editor of both the weekly newspaper and the monthly magazine and he also began submitting articles to short-story magazines.

At Dartmouth College, where he went to study English literature and creative writing, Osgood took introductory and advanced psychology courses with Professor Theodore Karwoski and found a combination of rigor and creativity which appealed to him. At that time Karwoski was experimenting with color-music synesthesia (a process in which one type of stimulus produces a secondary, subjective sensation sometimes referred to as neural short-circuiting). Later Osgood was to incorporate this, along with other earlier experiences, into his semantic differential technique.

In 1949 Osgood accepted an invitation from the University of Illinois to teach and do research half-time in the new Institute for Communication Research. At Illinois he drew upon earlier background he had acquired in learning theory to develop a behavioral theory of meaning, upon his background in attitude scaling from psychology to devise a measurement model which he coupled with new developments in multivariate statistics (Illinois was a center of activity in developing multivariate statistics at that time), and upon his childhood conception of words as clusters in space for his image of semantic space. (Snider and Osgood (1969) pp. vii–ix; and Osgood (1976) pp. 1–5.)

Semantic Space

Osgood (1963) requires us to begin by imagining an impossibility, a "semantic space" with an unknown number of dimensions. The origin of semantic space is at its center and represents complete meaninglessness. Words or concepts become points to be located in this space. It follows that the farther a point is in this space from the center, or meaninglessness, the more

Figure 1

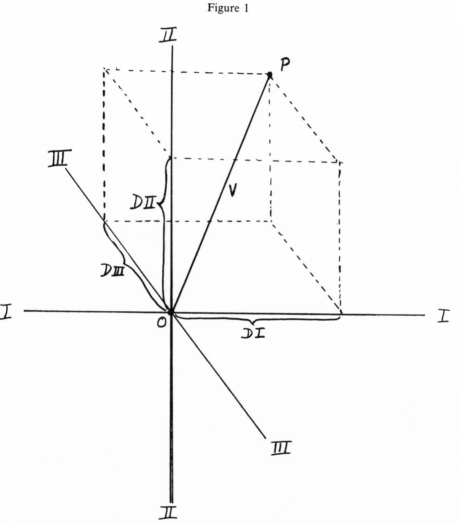

I, II, III = Dimensions (Coordinates) of Semantic Space
O = The Origin of Semantic Space (Meaninglessness)
P = A Point in Semantic Space (Location of a Concept)
V = A Vector in Semantic Space (Intensity of Meaning of Concept)
DI, DII, DIII = Distance of the Point from Origin on Three Dimensions in Semantic Space

meaningful the word or concept is. A straight line from the center of semantic space to the point which represents a word becomes a vector in semantic space and the longer that vector, the more meaningful the word. The direction of the vector from the center of semantic space indicates the "semantic quality" of the word. The distance between any two concepts located in a semantic space is an indicator of how similar or dissimilar in meaning those concepts are for a given audience.

As with any space, including our own physical space, we need reference coordinates. Centuries ago the geographic directions—North, South, East and West—were established. An airplane pilot must add the dimension of altitude. So too with semantic space. Here the reference coordinates depend upon the concept which is to be located and need to be defined for each concept since the dimensions of each semantic space vary according to the concept evaluated.

To construct a semantic differential for a concept, one first draws a sample of subjects from a group one is interested in. Individuals are then asked to name the adjective or adjectives which come to mind when the concept is mentioned. The most frequently mentioned adjectives (about 50)

Figure 2
Last Session's
Television Coverage of the Legislature
in Your Home District

	Extr.	Modr.	Slgt.	Neut.	Slgt.	Modr.	Extr.	
Responsible	___	___	___	___	___	___	___	Irresponsible
Vague	___	___	___	___	___	___	___	Precise
Alert	___	___	___	___	___	___	___	Dull
Weak	___	___	___	___	___	___	___	Powerful
Colorful	___	___	___	___	___	___	___	Colorless
Disreputable	___	___	___	___	___	___	___	Reputable
Important	___	___	___	___	___	___	___	Unimportant
Backward	___	___	___	___	___	___	___	Progressive
Fresh	___	___	___	___	___	___	___	Stale
Hazy	___	___	___	___	___	___	___	Clear
Wholesome	___	___	___	___	___	___	___	Unwholesome
Inaccurate	___	___	___	___	___	___	___	Accurate
Good	___	___	___	___	___	___	___	Bad
Careless	___	___	___	___	___	___	___	Deliberate
Safe	___	___	___	___	___	___	___	Dangerous
Unpleasant	___	___	___	___	___	___	___	Pleasant
Interesting	___	___	___	___	___	___	___	Uninteresting
Meaningless	___	___	___	___	___	___	___	Meaningful
Pleasing	___	___	___	___	___	___	___	Annoying

are then used on a rating sheet with their "polar" opposites, separated by a seven-step scale.

George Miller (1967) and others have observed that most persons can make absolute judgments about a stimulus in terms of a scale involving about seven categories.

These rating sheets are then given to a sample of the group to be measured and ratings of the concept to be located in semantic space are obtained against the seven step scales defined by the polar adjectives.

Factor Analysis

These ratings are then fed into a computer for a Factor Analysis. A Factor Analysis determines the extent to which the different scales are measuring an underlying set of fewer dimensions. With this relatively large number of scales on the original rating sheet, the researcher is interested in finding out if some scales overlap in their measurement, indicating that many scales may be measuring a more basic or unique factor. A Factor Analysis is a way of determining if a large number of variables have a fewer, or more basic or unique number of factors underlying them (Williams, F., 1968, Ch. 12).

Table 1
Factor Loadings of Newspaper Scales

	I	II	III	IV	V
Relaxed	.7926	.2047	−.0601	−.2218	−.0194
Impartial	.7690	−.2314	.2657	.2178	.0307
Unbiased	−.7536	.0255	−.0203	.0625	.1336
Right	−.7046	.2013	−.1382	−.1547	.4222
Fair	.6336	−.2123	.2197	.0647	−.4702
Accurate	−.5342	.3015	−.3043	−.0937	.5401
Good	.4901	−.4472	.0558	−.2397	−.4338
Active	−.0915	−.8062	.2244	.1506	−.0172
Strong	−.1706	.8061	.0811	.2480	.1111
Progressive	−.3773	.7061	−.0772	.1206	.2498
Complete	.0439	.5784	−.0382	.3318	.3413
Truthful	.1237	−.1035	.9000	−.0723	−.0838
Pleasant	.2068	−.0676	.8458	−.0611	−.2191
Colorful	−.0307	.1398	−.0017	.8345	.0320
Interesting	−.0551	−.1274	.4938	−.6748	.0029
Careful	.2947	−.2431	.0053	.1181	−.7545
Balanced	.0528	−.0152	−.4913	.1925	.7155
Superior	.3928	−.4597	.2249	−.0963	−.4991
Attractive	.4431	−.3720	.0382	−.3332	−.4524

The computer provides a factor matrix which lists the factors in columns. The numbers within the matrix tell us the correlation or relationship between each of the original measurements and each of the underlying hypothetical variables. These numbers are called loadings. The researcher's creativity comes to play in the interpretation of each factor, which is a subjective valuation and is sometimes open to differences of opinion. Because of this, studies employing the Semantic Differential Technique usually present the final factor loadings so that the reader can evaluate the factor interpretations for himself.

Table 2
Factor Loadings of Television Scales

	I	II	III	IV	V
Safe	.8351	−.0436	−.1409	.1908	−.0609
Reputable	−.7438	−.0944	.1955	−.0952	.1794
Responsible	.7359	.2615	−.3460	.0484	.0454
Wholesome	.7268	.2090	−.0663	.2359	−.0113
Pleasant	−.6738	−.2343	.1928	−.0912	.2737
Pleasing	.6719	.2543	−.2068	.1345	−.1560
Good	.5151	.4591	−.2425	.4843	−.0506
Strong	.0274	−.8392	.3104	−.1403	.0531
Alert	.3498	.7852	−.1567	.0597	−.0012
Colorful	.0770	.7565	.0171	.2268	−.2283
Progressive	−.3619	.6519	.1799	−.1765	.1998
Deliberate	−.3306	−.0312	.7993	.0019	−.0073
Precise	−.1338	−.3788	.7298	−.0886	.0743
Accurate	−.3144	.0566	.6558	−.4280	.2712
Clear	.2390	−.4346	.6122	−.1805	−.0277
Fresh	.2812	.3794	−.0699	.7739	.0130
Meaningful	−.1503	−.1374	.5294	−.6971	.0990
Interesting	.3626	.3823	.0670	.4011	−.2731
Important	.2341	.2364	−.0591	.0358	−.8939

After the pre-test of semantic differential ratings has been factor analyzed, the number of scales is reduced to those which load most heavily on the dominant factors in the analysis. Usually three or four scales are used for each of as many as five factors or dimensions of the semantic space within which a concept is to be located. This leaves the researcher with from ten to twenty adjectival pairs defining the end points of as many seven-step scales for the final rating of the concept. It is this shortened semantic differential rating sheet which is then used to locate the given concept in "semantic space." Because of the procedures outlined, the scales and dimensions of semantic space are custom tailored to fit the concept the researcher is interested in locating in semantic space.

Comparisons

It follows that if the investigator is interested in comparing the similarities and differences between two concepts (e.g., between two products, or between a candidate and the "ideal" candidate) they must both be located in the same semantic space (i.e., a space defined by the same dimensions or factors which are measured by the same scales or adjectival pairs). This means that dimensions and scales which are common to both concepts must be chosen,

Figure 3

**Opinion Leader Profile on Black Student,
at Elgin High, for Two Different Peer Groups**

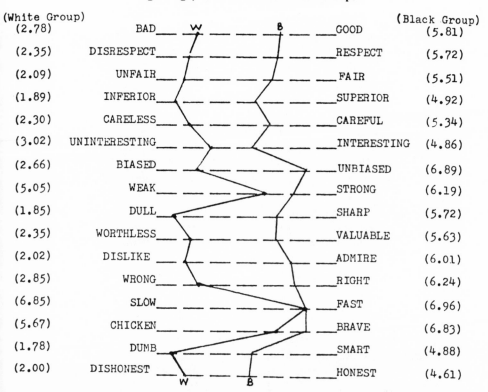

(White Group)			(Black Group)
(2.78)	BAD	GOOD	(5.81)
(2.35)	DISRESPECT	RESPECT	(5.72)
(2.09)	UNFAIR	FAIR	(5.51)
(1.89)	INFERIOR	SUPERIOR	(4.92)
(2.30)	CARELESS	CAREFUL	(5.34)
(3.02)	UNINTERESTING	INTERESTING	(4.86)
(2.66)	BIASED	UNBIASED	(6.89)
(5.05)	WEAK	STRONG	(6.19)
(1.85)	DULL	SHARP	(5.72)
(2.35)	WORTHLESS	VALUABLE	(5.63)
(2.02)	DISLIKE	ADMIRE	(6.01)
(2.85)	WRONG	RIGHT	(6.24)
(6.85)	SLOW	FAST	(6.96)
(5.67)	CHICKEN	BRAVE	(6.83)
(1.78)	DUMB	SMART	(4.88)
(2.00)	DISHONEST	HONEST	(4.61)

otherwise the investigator is comparing apples with oranges, so to speak. The distance between the location of two concepts in the same semantic space then becomes a measure of their similarity or dissimilarity. In the same way, one concept can be evaluated by two groups as shown in Figure 3.

Generality of Findings

As Osgood and his colleagues measured many concepts against large numbers of adjectival pairs with many different groups it became apparent that three factors or dimensions of semantic space were dominant. These are an Evaluative dimension (with scales like good-bad, pleasant-unpleasant and positive-negative), a Potency dimension (strong-weak, heavy-light, hard-soft) and an Activity dimension (slow-fast, active-passive and excitable-calm). This system of judging concepts, Evaluative, Potency and Activity, has been found to be remarkably stable across people in many different cultures using many different languages. However, this does not indicate that the meanings of specific concepts (their location in semantic space) were the same across cultures, only that the same dimensions were used to evaluate particular concepts. It means that the semantic frame in which judgments are made is constant across cultures, that is, the scales correlate with each other in the same ways for people who differ widely in culture and language.

Osgood contends that various peoples are very similar in the major ways in which they evaluate experiences, objects and events. Many cross cultural studies with the semantic differential indicate that people the world over share a common meaning system. This is contrary to Benjamin Lee Whorf's "psycholinguistic relativity" which holds that people who use different languages and are of different cultures perceive the world differently, think differently and hold differing philosophies because of their different languages and cultures (Whorf, 1952).

When one examines the findings of the semantic differential technique across *concepts* however, one finds a much different situation. The relationship of scales and factors or dimensions of semantic space across concepts is quite unstable. We do not use the same dimensions for judging all concepts, nor do the same scales (adjectival pairs) "load" on the same factors. Because of this it is necessary to construct a specific semantic differential for every new concept to be located in semantic space. This means that the practitioner must begin by gathering adjectives describing the concept from a sample of the population of interest and carry out the process already described.

Newspaper Research

The Semantic Differential Technique was developed at the Institute for Communication Research at the University of Illinois during the 1950's, and as might be expected, media research was one of the early areas to which it was applied. In 1960 Jack Lyle published findings from research he had done at Stanford applying the technique to newspaper research. His intent was to measure reader attitudes toward newspapers without having to select adjectives in an arbitrary way. In order to get adjectives which would be meaningful to readers when applied to newspapers, Lyle had journalism students at Stanford write comparisons of the *New York Times,* the *Palo Alto Times, Time* magazine and their hometown paper. *Palo Alto Times* subscribers were also asked to compare this paper with any other they were familiar with.

All descriptive adjectives were extracted from these comparisons as well as from other published newspaper reader attitudes, including those in a newspaper criticism contest. The 32 most frequently mentioned adjectives, along with their antonyms as given in a dictionary, were used in a pre-test. Added to these 32 adjectival pairs were 25 from Osgood's original semantic differential, for a total of 57 adjectival pairs pre-tested with undergraduate students at Stanford and Michigan State University.

A short form of a Stanford newspaper attitude scale, the most reliable and carefully constructed one existing, was also administered with the pre-test to test the "face validity" of this semantic differential for newspaper images. The correlation for face validity between the 57-item semantic differential and the 14-item newspaper attitude scale was .90. Two weeks later the original group of Stanford students was re-tested and the reliability coefficient was .93.

The final semantic differential was reduced to 20 scales which would provide a wide range of response and assess five main areas: Osgood's potency and activity factors; the bias and accuracy factors from the Stanford newspaper attitude scale; and an evaluative factor from both Osgood and the Stanford scale. This reduction from 57 scales to 20 eased the computational burden while retaining a correlation of .98 between the long and short forms. Reliability for the 20 items moved up slightly to .94.

The 20-item semantic differential was then administered to a random sample of 200 male subscribers to the *Palo Alto Times* and the data obtained were factor analyzed.

The major portion of the variance was extracted in the first factor which Lyle named "newsworthiness." Adjectives fresh-stale, complete-incomplete, strong-weak, balanced-unbalanced, interesting-uninteresting, along with sharp-dull and fast-slow "loaded" heavily on this factor. The last two adjectival pairs are from Osgood's activity factor and as Lyle noted, this should not be surprising since speed is considered important in newsgathering.

Lyle named the second factor "bias" because the adjectival pairs unbiased-biased, impartial-partial and fair-unfair loaded heavily on it. Factor III he named "accuracy" although this was not readily apparent. Two scales, accurate-inaccurate and careful-careless fit easily. Three other scales which loaded heavily on Factor III came from the general evaluative group: good-bad; interesting-uninteresting and fair-unfair. Lyle reasoned that being "fair" can be regarded as being "accurate" and it is not illogical to see an "accurate" paper as a "good" one.

The fourth factor caused problems in interpretation. Seven scales loaded above the arbitrary .40 criterion level Lyle had set. Four scales came from the general evaluation group, and one each from the potency, activity and accuracy groups. They were superior-inferior, attractive-unattractive, good-bad, fair-unfair, strong-weak, active-passive, and right-wrong. Lyle interpreted this factor to measure the "general quality" of the newspaper and named it so. He considered right-wrong and fair-unfair in a moral sense rather than in the sense of measuring accuracy and bias. He interpreted strong-weak and active-passive as a measure of the newspaper as a force within the community.

Because the fifth, and last, factor could not be logically interpreted, Lyle left it unnamed.

The original Stanford Test for newspaper attitudes, a relatively long list of items, resulted in three factors, while the Semantic Differential resulted in five. Two of the five, Bias and Accuracy, are among those on the Stanford Test. Instead of the third general factor of the original Stanford test, Lyle extracted factors on Newsworthiness and General Quality and another factor which he left uninterpreted.

Lyle argued that by using a 20-scale semantic differential a publisher can get a picture of his reader's attitude toward the paper. From a profile of scores on 20 scales he can see where his paper is strong and weak in the eyes of his public. By comparing scores from various sub-groups in his readership, political, religious, ethnic, etc., he might identify differences in the way various sub-groups see his newspaper.

The semantic differential technique is an easily administered and quickly analyzed way to measure the attitudes readers have toward a newspaper.

Newspaper Image Study

Percy Tannenbaum, one of the originators of the Semantic Differential Technique, directed a study in early 1961 at the University of Wisconsin Mass Communication Research Center to ascertain the image of the *Milwaukee Journal* in three Wisconsin communities. The survey also gathered data on the images of other Wisconsin newspapers which would serve as a baseline for comparison.

The data gathering instrument consisted of a questionnaire of demographic items (age, education, sex, race, etc.), a series of items regarding general media use, questions about specific newspaper use, specific questions for *Milwaukee Journal* readers, and newspaper image ratings utilizing the semantic differential technique.

According to the report, of the 22 scales used to rate the *Journal,* three other newspapers, and the "ideal" newspaper, 21 scales were selected on the basis of previous findings in applying the semantic differential to measuring newspaper images and one scale, Democratic-Republican, was added to determine how respondents judged the political leaning of the various newspapers.

A factor analysis of the scales used in judging the newspapers' images produced the following factors (in order of importance) and the scales which "loaded" on the factors:

Factor	*Scales Loading Heavily*
General Evaluative:	pleasant; valuable; important; interesting.
Ethical:	fair; truthful; accurate; unbiased; and responsible.
Style:	exciting; fresh; easy; neat; and colorful.
Activity:	relaxed; and active.
Potency:	bold; and powerful

Tannenbaum and his research associate, Bradley Greenberg, observed that "a newspaper can rarely if ever please all of the people all of the time," because it must strike a balance in servicing a mass audience with a diversity of preferences and interests. It also has an obligation to both reflect a community and lead it, while providing both fact and opinion on controversial issues.

Because of these obligations, some individuals will be highly pleased and others equally displeased, especially on specific issues on which feeling can become quite intense. The researchers observed that because of this a newspaper's image will always fall short of the ideal, but concluded that, here at least, "the data from this survey add up to a very favorable image of the *Milwaukee Journal.*"

Media Images

In the late winter of 1959, Scripps-Howard Research conducted field work in ten metropolitan U.S. cities on the comparative images of newspapers, radio, television and magazines. The study consisted of 550 respondents who rated each of the four media on 24 semantic differential scales. Following Scripps-Howard's analysis the data were turned over for further analysis to Dr. Paul Deutschmann, then director of the Communication Research Center at Michigan State University. Deutschmann (1960) and his associate Donald Kiel analyzed the semantic differential ratings of the four media in ten cities, divided it into three age levels, and subjected it to a series of factor analyses.

All Media Combined

Upon analyzing the ratings for all media on all scales the following appeared. Listed are the scales which loaded most heavily on each factor.

I. Ethical Factor

Responsible-Irresponsible
Reputable-Disreputable
Orderly-Disorderly

II. Potency Factor

Important-Unimportant
Powerful-Weak

III. Pleasant-Veracity Factor

Pleasant-Unpleasant
Good-Bad
Truthful-Untruthful

IV. Informative-Vitality Factor

Progressive-Backwards
Alert-Dull
Fresh-Stale
Meaningful-Meaningless

V. Entertainment Factor

Interesting-Boring
Pleasing-Annoying
Relaxed-Tense

The researchers noted the similarity of the Potency factor to that of Osgood's. The Entertainment and Informative vitality factors have many of the characteristics of Osgood's Activity factor and the Pleasant-Veracity factor appears to be Osgood's evaluative factor. The Ethical factor is a new dimension.

On the basis of the factor analysis of the semantic differential data the authors speculate that users of the mass media discriminate in making judgments about the media in at least five ways: 1) to be responsible or irresponsible; 2) to be strong or weak; 3) to be pleasantly truthful or unpleasantly untruthful; 4) to be freshly informative or stale and meaningless; 5) to be entertaining or boring and annoying.

Newspapers

While the newspapers analyses corresponded roughly to the patterns for all media, there were some differences. No separate Ethical factor appeared for newspapers. Several of the scales with ethical connotations clustered with others which were earlier identified as Informative-Vitality, so the factor was named Ethical Informative for newspapers. A Careful Dynamism factor appeared for newspapers which did not have a clear relationship to the all-media results. This factor included "precise," "alert," and "progressive." A final factor for newspapers, "Honesty," included in the cluster, "safe," "honest," and "relaxed."

Radio and Television

The Ethical factor for radio contained only three scales in the cluster, "responsible," "honest," and "truthful." There was no evidence of a separate Potency dimension for Radio. "Powerful" and "important" cluster in what the researchers called an Approved Dynamism factor which included "alert," "interesting," "progressive," and "good," "honest," and "clear," all suggesting an evaluation of activity in one dimension or factor. Other Radio factors which emerged from analysis were: Accuracy; Approved Precision; Entertainment and Drabness. The first two factors (Accuracy and Approved Precision) might well be combined.

The five factors which emerged from the factor analysis of semantic differential ratings of television in the ten cities were named: Ethical; Vitality; Triviality; Indulgence; and Clarity.

Magazines

There was considerable difficulty in identifying factors for magazines. Four clusters were produced which the researchers tentatively named: Ethical-Evaluative; Vitality; Informativeness (which they linked with Drabness); and Sensationalism.

As can be readily seen the dimensions upon which the media were judged varied from medium to medium and the scales which loaded on each dimension also varied somewhat from medium to medium. This serves to underscore the need to tailor the semantic differential technique to the specific problem at hand. There is no *one* Semantic Differential—there is *one technique* called the Semantic Differential. In this case, when people look at an individual medium we find that they look at it with what appears to be a somewhat different set of criteria than when they judge the media as a whole. They also appear to judge different media by different criteria.

The report concludes that the semantic differential technique, when compared with opinion survey findings, allows for an analysis which permits more subtle differentiation among media, with a variety of dimensions of attitude. After factor analyzing the data the semantic differential allows considerable simplification in the number of scales used to represent dimensions upon which the media are judged. Key opinions can be elicited in a much more economical interview and scales can be selected so that they will be comparable across media.

Opinion Measurement and the Semantic Differential

The question has been raised, "To what extent does the semantic differential measure what an opinion researcher wants to measure?" As we have seen, the differential was developed to determine the dimensions of "semantic space" in order to measure meaning. Opinion researchers seek accurate descriptions of respondents' orientations to elements in their environment. Three researchers, Carter, Ruggels and Chaffee (1968), argue that such an instrument should be structured enough to be comparable from one respondent to another, but not so structured as to force the respondent to distort his orientation or fabricate responses. They point out that with opinions it is assumed that the respondent knows what he thinks and is able to describe it, while in research on meaning the object is to get judgments from respondents that they may not ordinarily make or be aware of.

The researchers hypothesize that only the evaluative component of semantic differential scales is of interest for most opinion research. They feel that in opinion research the "activity" and "potency" factors, often a single factor of "dynamism," (the capacity of an object to act) affects an individual's evaluation of an object and is highly correlated to the evaluative dimension.

The authors asked 135 teachers attending a summer conference to evaluate twelve concepts connected with schools (four each: human, inanimate and relational) by using the fifteen semantic differential scales Osgood found to load highest on his three dominant dimensions. However, in this application several departures from traditional semantic differential use were introduced.

Subjects were allowed to modify the semantic differential in several ways. First, only one adjective was provided for each scale and the subject was asked to provide the appropriate polar opposite for the concept being rated. Subjects were also allowed not to use a particular scale to rate a given concept.

Beyond this, subjects were allowed to indicate a "don't know" for any given scale on a given concept.

It was concluded that respondents can more accurately indicate their attitudes to objects when one end of the scale is left to them to define. The authors suggest that if a researcher wants to obtain comparable results, a pre-test should be made to ascertain the most appropriate polar opposite for a given scale (that most frequently supplied on the pre-test) in judging a concept. These scales are then incorporated into a more structured, traditional semantic differential.

The researchers infer from their findings that in opinion research, as in other uses of the semantic differential, the first, overwhelming factor is a general evaluative one. The main affective response someone gives for an object is its total utility for that person.

It is possible to get a more accurate report of a person's attitudes toward objects, the authors contend, when, to some extent, dimensions for the scales can be selected by that person. Error is minimized by allowing the respondents to ignore scales with which they would not or could not evaluate a given object.

While the modified device suggested probably results in what is no longer a semantic differential in its strict sense, the authors contend that it is "probably the best brief opinion measure yet devised."

The Semantic Differential in Advertising and Marketing

Soon after the development of the semantic differential technique, William Mindak (1961) saw the application of this tool to the problem of quantifying data which deals with consumers' images of products, brands and companies. Mindak observed that this data is often highly subjective and difficult to verbalize, and that the semantic differential technique is well suited to the task.

In an article reporting research in this area, the author observes that the technique is a quick, efficient way of obtaining direction and intensity of attitudes and opinions toward a concept—be it a brand, product or company. And, the differential will obtain data for large samples in a readily quantifiable form. He also notes that it is a standardized technique for getting at the multitude of factors which go to make up a brand or product "image" and so it provides a comprehensive picture of the "image" or meaning of a product or personality.

Among other advantages Mindak cites for the semantic differential technique in advertising and marketing research are: it is easily repeatable and highly reliable so it can be used to record consumer reactions over time; it encourages quick, "top-of-mind" responses allowing for individual frames of reference which avoid stereotyped responses; it eases the task of interviewing respondents who may not be too articulate in reacting to products, brands or company images.

Mindak lists several modifications suggested by researchers to make the differential more sensitive to subtle distinctions in the images of products which are physically similar. A major modification is the use of descriptive nouns and phrases to increase the shades of meaning through the use of longer, more involved scale definitions. Also suggested is the use of tailor-made scales because of the lack of flexibility and appropriateness to specific problems by standardized lists. Suggested sources of tailor-made scales are advertising copy, word association tests with consumers and individual and group interviews.

Because respondents often refuse to "play the game" or balk at using negative sides of scales, or refuse to judge a concept negatively, the author suggests the use of "connotative" and "non-polar" opposites. This, he says, avoids the clustering about the middle of the scales which makes it difficult to differentiate among concept profiles. Examples of non-polar opposites he gives are: "really modern—sort of old fashioned" and "high-quality product—so-so quality product."

By rating concepts such as "the ideal company" or "my favorite brand" there are built in controls for comparisons. Mindak claims that respondents do not use the extremes on all scales to differentiate an "ideal" or "favorite."

The researcher reports the findings of a brand-image study which applies these suggestions. He concludes that the semantic differential technique allows one to quantify what has often been considered abstract, mysterious and qualitative material about consumers' opinions, tones, and emotional reactions. He suggests using the differential not only as a simple, large sample, counting device, but also as a source to indicate areas in need of further, more intensive probing using other qualitative projective techniques.

Politicians Rate Media Coverage

Following Vice-President Spiro Agnew's attacks on the news media John Merwin (1971) sought to discover how one group of politicians, Texas legislators, viewed newspaper and television coverage of their work. Agnew charged that approximately a dozen television journalists and a few influential newspapers shape our view of the day's events.

The investigator observed that "The press continuously comments upon and evaluates the activities of governmental officials, but rarely are government officials able to evaluate the press' performance collectively." Here the author provided government officials the opportunity to do just that.

The researcher used the semantic differential technique to get legislators' ratings of "Home District Newspaper Coverage of the Legislature" and "Home District Television Coverage of the Legislature." The newspaper scales were from sets developed by Lyle, Tannenbaum and Deutschmann and the television scales were taken from Deutschmann's study (all discussed earlier).

The Merwin questionnaire also included four sets of variables to be checked by the respondent: political leaning (conservative, mildly conservative, moderate, mildly liberal or liberal); number of years in the legislature; largest city in the home district; and primary occupation. The variables were analyzed to insure that the sample did not vary significantly from the entire population of legislators and no significant departures were found.

The newspaper factors, in order of appearance in Table 1 were labelled Ethical, Potency, Style, Appearance and Quality. The television factors, in order of appearance in Table 2 were called Quality, Potency, Accuracy, Attractiveness and Importance. Their scale and factor mean scores are shown in Table 3.

Table 3

Scale and Factor Scores

Legislative Coverage by Home District Newspapers		*Legislative Coverage by Home District Television*	
Ethical Factor	3.84	*Quality Factor*	2.78
Relaxed-Tense	3.86	Safe-Dangerous	2.60
Impartial-Partial	4.36	Reputable-Disreputable	2.57
Unbiased-Biased	4.40	Responsible-Irresponsible	2.68
Right-Wrong	3.50	Wholesome-Unwholesome	2.80
Fair-Unfair	3.50	Pleasant-Unpleasant	2.75
Accurate-Inaccurate	3.54	Pleasing-Annoying	3.03
Good-Bad	3.72	Good-Bad	3.00
Potency Factor	3.93	*Potency Factor*	3.31
Active-Passive	3.92	Powerful-Weak	3.48
Strong-Weak	3.81	Alert-Dull	3.23
Progressive-Backward	3.93	Colorful-Colorless	3.40
Complete-Incomplete	4.07	Progressive-Backward	3.14
Style Factor	4.32	*Accuracy Factor*	3.37
Truthful-Untruthful	4.47	Deliberate-Careless	3.12
Pleasant-Unpleasant	4.17	Precise-Vague	3.55
		Accurate-Inaccurate	3.23
Appearance Factor	4.24	Clear-Hazy	3.57
Colorful-Colorless	4.07	*Attractiveness Factor*	2.97
Interesting-Uninteresting	4.42		
		Fresh-Stale	3.00
Quality Factor	3.95	Meaningful-Meaningless	3.03
		Interesting-Uninteresting	2.89
Careful-Careless	4.06		
Balanced-Unbalanced	3.86	*Importance Factor*	2.70
Superior-Inferior	4.24		
Attractive-Unattractive	3.65	Important-Unimportant	2.70

Although each concept comprises 19 rating scales, only seven are common to both concepts. The most desirable answer, such as "extremely accurate," received a value of one; thus the lower the score the more "accurate," etc.

It was found that lawyers saw newspapers to be more potent than non-lawyers. Those serving in the legislature more than two years judged newspapers to be significantly more potent than those serving two years or less. Non-lawyers saw television as being more potent than the lawyers.

Respondents with no large city in their home districts rated television as more accurate than did respondents from a district with a large city.

While all scales were not common to both concepts, the legislators assigned generally higher ratings to television news coverage of the Legislature than to newspaper coverage. Not only was the overall average higher, but 17 of the 19 scale ratings for television were higher than the single highest average newspaper scale rating.

Merwin notes however that the two concepts cannot be equated because of the way the two media differ. He points out that legislative news is treated more briefly on television than in newspapers, while newspapers editorialize far more than television, especially with formal endorsements of candidates. As with other researchers, he notes that the difference might be due to the fact that newspapers simply offer more material for criticism than does television.

Merwin found the most distinct departure from the average newspaper scale ratings on the "bias," "partial," "untruthful," and "uninteresting," scales. (Table 3). This later set of judgments was an interesting contrast to the remarks made by Vice President Agnew.

The finding that lawyers judged newspapers significantly more potent than non-lawyers and that non-lawyers judged television to be significantly more potent than lawyers is not unprecedented, as Merwin observes. Greenberg (1966) and Westley and Severin (1964) found that the percentage of persons who assigned more credibility to newspapers than television increased with education, with the reversal from television to newspapers occurring in the college educated bracket. Westley and Severin also found that men in the professions, such as law, assign greater credibility to newspapers than do those in managerial positions.

Considering that the Texas State Legislature is often referred to as beating the zoo any day of the week and "the finest free entertainment in Texas," (c.f., Ivins, 1975) the ratings of the legislature seem high indeed, contrary to what one would expect from views expressed by Agnew.

Selling the President

In his book *The Selling of the President 1968,* Joe McGinniss (1969, pp. 77–8) tells how the "Semantic Differential Test" was used in the Nixon campaign. He relates how leading campaign strategists received the results of a national sample of evaluations of the presidential candidates and the qualities an "ideal" President should have.

John Maddox, at the New York advertising agency, Fuller and Smith and Ross, explained, "The semantic differential is the most sensitive instrument known to modern marketing research." Maddox projected charts of semantic differential scales which rated Nixon, Humphrey, Wallace and the "Ideal." The charts showed the national mean scores for each scale with a line connecting the points on each scale to make individual profiles for candidates. Gaps between the Nixon profile and the "Ideal" profile indicated the personality traits Nixon needed to move toward the "Ideal" to become more acceptable in the eyes of the voters.

Maddox is reported to have later written that Nixon's image on the "cold-warm" scale was the widest and most in need of improvement. He speculated "that if the real personal warmth of Mr. Nixon could be more adequately exposed," it would make other inhibitions about him disappear and make him more attractive to large numbers of the electorate leaning toward Humphrey.

McGinniss reports that Maddox divided the semantic differential data into various geographic regions and ethnic groups so that Nixon's image in different parts of the country and among various people could be studied. This would enable television commercials to be tailored to fit specific problem areas to make Nixon appear a warmer person.

The Image of the Air Force

In the Fall of 1970, at a time of considerable dissent over the U.S. role in Vietnam, a U.S. Air Force colonel, working for a Ph.D. in Mass Communication (Public Relations) at the University of Texas in Austin, pretested a semantic differential to ascertain attitudes toward the U.S. Air Force by University of Texas faculty (Williams, J., 1970).

He reasoned that the USAF may be expending too much effort on those who already hold favorable attitudes toward the USAF, while devoting little attention to those who may be either neutral or hostile. He perceived professors as influentials for their students because they exhibit many of the characteristics of opinion leaders—they are viewed as credible, trustworthy and prestigious sources of information. Their forum, college students, and student opinions, are as much a concern to the Air Force as are the professors, for their support can be a critical factor in areas such as recruitment, budget requests, etc. The colonel noted that personal observation led him to believe that college professors could not be characterized as having a pro-Air Force bias.

A research design was devised to determine what college professors' attitudes toward the Air Force actually were. This was done with several purposes in mind. First the data would aid the Air Force in devising "appropriate information programs related to the academic community." Second, "one may assume that this research design may have the potential for broader applications."

The colonel gave two reasons for selecting college professors as being likely to be neutral or hostile to the Air Force—their tendency to be politically liberal, and the fact that it is from the liberal side of the political spectrum that the U.S. military has traditionally drawn opposition, and because of personal experiences with professorial comments about the military.

Another reason, already given, was the professors' supposed influence with students, "whose good opinions and support the Air Force covets."

A questionnaire was mailed to a 10 per cent sample (151) of the 1,507 voting members of the general faculty of the University of Texas at Austin in the Fall of 1970. A cover letter requesting participation and promising anonymity was included. This letter stated that the research was part of an "investigation of attitudes held by groups of influentials toward various institutions and establishments in our society." It also added, "This study will be part of a doctoral dissertation." The researcher signed his name only and did not identify himself as a colonel in the U.S. Air Force.

The second page of the packet listed five groups of variables to be checked by the respondent—age, college or school in which the respondent teaches, military service information, political leanings, and sources of information about the Air Force. It was hoped that the study would yield information on the attitudes toward the Air Force held by professors of varying ages, political inclinations, prior military service, etc.

The third page of the packet was a semantic differential sheet which requested ratings on one of the "various institutions and establishments in our society"—the concept "The United States Air Force."

Of the 151 questionnaires mailed out, 85 (or 56 per cent) were returned. Of those returned 20 were improperly or incompletely filled out and could not be used. The remaining 65 valid returns represented 43 per cent of the sample.

Because of the small number of valid returns and the comments that faculty provided on returns, the researcher concluded that future investigators who plan to seek responses from professors should have a professor sign the cover letter which is sent with the questionnaire.

After preliminary tabulation, the author found that nearly all of the valid responses came from three schools or colleges, with only one to three respondents from each of the eight other schools on the campus. Almost two-thirds of the respondents checked more than one source of information about the Air Force, some checked three, four and even five responses. For these reasons no analysis was made on these two variables.

The information provided by respondents about age, military service and politics was divided into two categories each. The respondents were divided into the 28 who were 40 or over, and the 37 who were under 40. They were divided nearly evenly on prior military service, 33 veterans and 32 without military service. Only nine faculty respondents at the University of Texas saw themselves as either politically conservative or mildly conservative, 16 termed themselves moderate, and 40 as slightly liberal or liberal. The assumption that more professors would consider themselves liberal than conservative was supported in this sample.

In rating the U.S. Air Force the usual three factors were extracted in the factor analysis—evaluative, activity, and potency. Respondents were then divided into two groups for each of three variables, age, prior military service and political self-identification. Statistically significant differences were found between the two age groups on both the evaluative and activity factors, between veterans and non-veterans on the activity factor, and between conservative-moderates and liberals on both the evaluative and potency factors.

The researcher concluded that younger, non-veteran, liberal professors held less favorable attitudes toward the Air Force than older, veteran, conservative professors. Because the potency factor scale scores were significantly higher than those in the evaluative factor the researcher drew the inference that for this "public" (professors), the "USAF should expend more persuasive effort in shoring up its ethical and moralistic images and less in flexing its jet powered muscle." The researcher added that such Air Force "potency" programs as the Thunderbirds (a touring aerobatics team) and firepower demonstrations might well be reduced and the emphasis placed elsewhere.

Identifying High School Opinion Leaders

With the end of the military draft, the armed forces are totally dependent upon voluntary enlistments to fill their ranks. A major area of recruitment is among high school students. With this view in mind, the armed forces have funded research on the factors which relate to acceptance or rejection of military service by potential recruits (McCleneghan, 1974).

One study in this area was for the U.S. Air Force Directorate of Advertising to devise a method for identifying opinion leaders in high schools for Air Force recruiting and advertising purposes. The study was intended to develop a method to aid recruiters in identifying "influentials" or "opinion leaders" in high schools anywhere in the country. Beyond identifying the opinion leaders, the problem was to learn the best channels and the right questions to ask in order to ascertain pro and anti-Air Force attitudes.

These high school opinion leaders, both faculty and student, could then be used for a variety of purposes, including to "review advertisements, advise on regional differences regarding attitudes, etc., and participate in such advising activities that would have the effect of cultivating their pro-Air Force bent, which should find expression in any opinion leading they do. . . . By initiating face-to-face communication. . . . recruiters can cultivate pro-Air Force attitudes among those opinion leaders, who in turn, can encourage other prospects within their sphere of influence about the benefits the USAF has to offer."

The program was designed to begin with recruiting personnel obtaining opinion leader nominations from any general high school population desired through the use of a questionnaire asking for names of persons who are seen as having certain qualities. The recruiting sergeant is then to follow up with interviews on predispositions about the U.S. Air Force, and select from the named influentials those with whom they wish to work to further recruiting goals.

In the words of the Air Force research report, "These individuals can then be used for whatever purposes local recruiting offices deem necessary. . . . Alert sergeants will be able to use any leader to good advantage." Among the suggested uses are: to evaluate different advertising campaigns; to help select media channels to reach a certain target audience; to give oral presentations; and to talk to individuals.

The semantic differential technique was used to measure the "profiles" of those individuals named as "influential" on 16 adjectival scales.

Prior to receiving the questionnaire the students were told:

> You are participating in a national study administered by the University of Texas School of Communication. There are no right or wrong answers. To the best of your ability fill out the questionnaire given to you.

The report does not indicate that either students or school officials were ever informed that the purpose of the study was to facilitate military recruiting in high schools.

The first part of data gathering consisted of a series of twelve questions to discover individuals in the school with the qualities of opinion leaders. These questions were designed to elicit names of school personnel in various specific capacities who the individual surveyed might consider fair, superior, active, attractive, careful and impartial. There followed several questions aimed at locating student leaders.

The semantic differential technique was used to evaluate the opinion leaders nominated by the subjects in the questionnaire, to compare the strengths and weaknesses of leadership qualities of each and to compare changes over time. According to the report, the scales were adopted from Osgood (1957), but no further information is given.

The study concluded that student opinion leaders: "hold strategic or advantageous social positions or leadership roles in their respective high school environments," (e.g., many held office in school organizations or class offices); "they tended to be social norm supporters rather than deviants," (e.g., they admire authority and respect discipline). However, the study found that in one high school opinion leading minority students were social deviants and did not support the social norm and they exhibited a lack of respect toward authority and discipline.

These findings are in general agreement with the findings of other studies dealing with opinion leadership in many walks of life.

Misunderstandings and Misuse

As has been repeatedly stressed, there is no *one* semantic differential, the differential must be tailored to every new concept to be located in semantic space. This means gathering descriptive adjectives from the group the researcher is interested in, obtaining their polar opposites, making a pre-test with a random sample from the group, factor analyzing the data, and then obtaining ratings on those scales which load highest on the dominant factors obtained from the pre-test factor analysis. To simply take scales which have loaded most frequently on the factors found to be most dominant in many applications of the semantic differential puts into serious question the validity of the data generated. The same *factors* do not appear when judging *every* concept, nor do the *same* scales load on the *same* factors for every concept judged.

In the study of faculty members' judgments of the U.S. Air Force, the researcher did not report having gone through the described procedures. Presumably he simply went to the "back of the book" and took those scales which were most frequently found to load on given dimensions in past research. As stated, this approach jeopardizes the validity of the data, unless the researcher is able to find factors and scales which have already been well substantiated for a given concept—as was the case in the study done by Merwin of legislators' views of media coverage of their activities.

Another mis-application involved the alumni association of a large state university which attempted to ascertain former students' "images" of the association. The alumni organization had heard that the semantic differential technique could be used to obtain this information from ex-students. Once the data were gathered and analyzed, an advertising and public relations campaign could then be put into effect to make the image of the organization more favorable. This would then facilitate membership drives—and donations.

Either the association did not fully understand the theoretical concepts which underlie the semantic differential technique, or decided to do a "quick and dirty" study. The association simply went to the "back of the book" for its scales, and additionally, the data were gathered by calling former students on the telephone. It is difficult to imagine what images respondents conjured up when semantic differential rating sheets were described to them *verbally* over the telephone, especially those ex-students who had never encountered one before. This would have been a good opportunity for follow-up tests for both reliability and validity of the data gathered.

The association then took the analysis, and, reportedly, on that basis spent considerable time, effort and money to increase membership. The campaign was less successful than the association officials had hoped, and it was concluded that the semantic differential technique was "just a lot of baloney."

CONCLUSIONS

Charles Osgood (1963, p. 34) has expressed his hope that the semantic differential would demonstrate a shared semantic framework across cultures and that the application of the technique would contribute to better international communication and understanding.

The behavioral scientist has no more control over the uses of his findings than does the atomic physicist or any other scientist. Science, as noted, is non-ethical. Science is concerned with what is, what exists, or did exist, not what should be. The scientist is concerned with verifying reality—with empirically testing hypotheses about the nature of the world we live in. The uses to which the findings of science are put remain the concern of all of us—as members of the society in which we live. The scientist, as a member of society, shares these concerns, but the decisions of how research findings are used do not remain with the researcher alone—they are the responsibility of all of us.

Herbert Schiller (1972), in an article, "Polls are Prostitutes for the Establishment," discusses the subversion of public opinion polling in terms of their use to manipulate public opinion rather than to ascertain public opinion for policy making decisions, which is often their stated purpose.

At the time of widespread student dissent in the late 1960's and early 1970's, some government agencies took an official interest in attitudes and opinions held by American youth. One federal agency made grants to a research "think tank" to develop a simple and reliable test which would identify high school students who held "negative" or "anti-establishment" attitudes. Presumably the data obtained would be included in an individual's files to be used later when recommendations were sought for jobs or college entrance. In 1970, the American Civil Liberties Union entered into a lawsuit to prevent the use of secret data files by a government agency for such purposes (Waldron, 1970). An earlier example of the attempt to use social science research data for similar purposes is found in Irving Louis Horowitz's book, "The Rise and Fall of Project Camelot" (Horowitz, 1967).

We have discussed the application of the semantic differential technique in measuring media images, in marketing and advertising, public opinion, political and institutional image modification, in locating "favorable" opinion leaders, and in locating individuals with "unacceptable" attitudes.

However, our topic here is communication theory, not ethics. How scientific findings are applied in a society is outside the realm of science, it is the domain of ethics, philosophy, law and religion. Suffice it to say that these are issues to be decided by all of us—they are neither the burden nor the responsibility of the scientist alone.

REFERENCES

Carter, R., L. Ruggels and S. Chaffee (1968). The Semantic Differential in Opinion Measurement. *Public Opinion Quarterly* 32:666–74.

Deutschmann, P. and D. Kiel (1960). *A Factor Analytic Study of Attitudes Toward the Mass Media.* Scripps-Howard Research.

Greenberg, B. (1966). Media Use and Believability: Some Multiple Correlates. *Journalism Quarterly* 43:665–70.

Horowitz, I. (1967). *The Rise and Fall of Project Camelot.* Cambridge, Mass.: The M.I.T. Press.

Ivins, M. (March, 1975). Inside the Austin Fun House. *Atlantic Monthly,* pp. 48–55.

Lyle, J. (1960). Semantic Differential Scales for Newspaper Research. *Journalism Quarterly* 37:559–62; 646.

McCleneghan, J. (1974). *Method of Identification of Opinion Leaders in High Schools for Air Force Recruiting/Advertising Purposes: Two Case Studies.* Report No. 4 Of the Sponsored Research Program on The Function of Advertising in the All-Volunteer Military Services. Austin, Texas: School of Communication.

McGinniss, J. (1968). *The Selling of the President 1968.* New York: Pocket Books.

Merwin, J. (1971). How Texas Legislators View News Coverage of Their Work. *Journalism Quarterly* 48:269–74.

Miller, G. (1967). The Magical Number Seven, Plus or Minus Two: Some Limits on Our Capacity for Processing Information. In Miller, G. *The Psychology of Communication: Seven Essays.* New York: Basic Books.

Mindak, W. (1961). Fitting the Semantic Differential to the Marketing Problem. *Journal of Marketing,* April 1961, 25–33.

Osgood, C., G. Suci and P. Tannenbaum (1957). *The Measurement of Meaning.* Urbana: University of Illinois Press.

Osgood, C. (1963). An Exploration into Semantic Space. In Schramm, W. *The Science of Human Communication.* New York: Basic Books.

Osgood, C. (1976). *Focus on Meaning, Volume 1: Explorations in Semantic Space.* The Hague: Mouton.

Schiller, H. (July, 1972). Polls are Prostitutes for the Establishment. *Psychology Today,* pp. 20–26; 91.

Snider, J. and C. Osgood (Eds.) (1969). *Semantic Differential Technique.* Chicago: Aldine, Atherton.

Tannenbaum, P. (1961). *Newspaper Image Study.* Madison: University of Wisconsin Mass Communications Research Center.

Waldron, M. (November 1, 1970). "Oklahoma Suit Challenges Secret Files on Activists." *New York Times,* p. 48.

Westley, B. and W. Severin (1964). Some Correlates of Media Credibility. *Journalism Quarterly* 41:325–35.

Whorf, B. (1952). Language, Mind, and Reality. *ETC.,* Vol. IX, No. 3, Spring.

Williams, J. (1970). A Study of University of Texas Professors Attitudes Toward the United States Air Force. Austin: University of Texas. Unpublished seminar paper.

Williams, F. (1968). *Reasoning With Statistics: Simplified Examples in Communication Research.* New York: Holt, Rinehart and Winston, Inc.

Chapter 8

Propaganda

W HEN Harold Lasswell's doctoral dissertation on the use of propaganda
in World War I was published as a book in 1927, one reviewer called
it "a Machiavellian textbook which should promptly be destroyed" (Dulles,
1928, p. 107).

The reviewer's reaction indicates the kind of fear with which the techniques of propaganda were viewed following World War I. Propaganda was
thought to have great power. Another book on American propaganda in
World War I even had the title *Words that Won the War* (Mock and Larson,
1939). In this climate, it is no wonder that people were concerned about
the effects of propaganda as World War II began to draw near.

Propaganda was the topic of a number of books between the World
Wars. This analysis of propaganda included some of our first theoretical
thinking about the effects of mass communication. As we look back on it
now, much of it appears to be rather primitive theory. Nevertheless, two
important areas of communication theory have their roots in this early thinking about propaganda. One of these is attitude change, traditionally one of
the major areas of communication research. What are the most effective
methods of changing people's attitudes? The study of propaganda provided
some tentative answers to this question. The second area is theoretical thinking
about the general effects of mass communication. What effects does mass
communication have on individuals and society? How do these effects take
place? The early thinking about propaganda also provided one of the first
general answers to these questions concerning effects.

Definitions of Propaganda

Lasswell's classic work, *Propaganda Technique in the World War* (1927), presented one of the first careful attempts to define propaganda: "It refers solely to the control of opinion by significant symbols, or, to speak more concretely and less accurately, by stories, rumours, reports, pictures and other forms of social communication" (p. 9).

Another definition by Lasswell (1937) presented a few years later is slightly different: "Propaganda in the broadest sense is the technique of influencing human action by the manipulation of representations. These representations may take spoken, written, pictorial or musical form" (pp. 521–522).

Both of Lasswell's definitions would include most of advertising, and in fact, would appear to include all of what is often referred to as *persuasion.* In fact, Lasswell (1937) has stated that "both advertising and publicity fall within the field of propaganda" (p. 522).

Lasswell's definitions would include a teacher influencing a class to study, an act many people would not want to call propaganda. Thus Lasswell's definitions may be too broad for some purposes.

Psychologist Roger Brown (1958) has attempted to deal with this problem by making a distinction between propaganda and persuasion. Brown defines *persuasion* as "symbol-manipulation designed to produce action in others" (p. 299). He then points out that persuasive efforts are labeled *propaganda* "when someone judges that the action which is the goal of the persuasive effort will be advantageous to the persuader but not in the best interests of the persuadee" (p. 300). In other words, there are no absolute criteria to determine whether an act of persuasion is propaganda—that's a judgment that someone makes. And as far as the techniques used are concerned, persuasion and propaganda are identical. It's only someone perceiving that the source is benefiting and not the receiver that leads to something being called propaganda.

Propaganda—as defined by both Lasswell and Brown—would include much of advertising (where the aim is not the good of the receiver but greater sales for the advertiser), much of political campaigning (where the aim is not the good of the receiver, but to get the candidate elected), and much of public relations (where the aim is often not the good of the receiver but to present the most favorable image of a corporation).

Lasswell (1927) also discussed four major objectives of propaganda:

1. To mobilize hatred against the enemy; 2. to preserve the friendship of allies; 3. to preserve the friendship and, if possible, to procure the cooperation of neutrals; 4. to demoralize the enemy (p. 195).

These are obviously wartime objectives that would not apply to advertising or other peacetime types of persuasion.

History of Propaganda

The term *propaganda* comes from the *Congregation de propaganda fide,* or Congregation for the Propagation of Faith, established by the Catholic Church in 1622. This was the time of the Reformation, in which various groups were breaking away from the Catholic Church, and the Congregation was part of the Church's Counter-Reformation. One of the great issues of this period was the struggle between science and religion as the source of knowledge about the world. One of the principal figures in this struggle was Galileo, who argued on the basis of observations through a telescope that the earth revolved around the sun. This idea ran directly against the teachings of the Catholic Church, and in fact was one of the Church's forbidden propositions. Galileo was tried and convicted by the Inquisition in 1633 and was made to renounce his statements that the earth revolved around the sun. The Church was left in the position of defending an indefensible idea. Perhaps the term propaganda picked up some of its negative associations or its connotations of untruth from this major incident in which the Church was left arguing for a position that was scientifically demonstrable as false.

Wartime propaganda can be traced back to *The Art of War,* a book written by Sun Tsu before the birth of Christ (Read, 1941). But it came into its own in World War I, when it was used on a scale and with an effectiveness that had never been seen before. This was in large part because people were naive about propaganda. One expert has pointed out that the 1913 edition of the *Encyclopaedia Britannica* did not even have an article on "propaganda" (Read, 1941). One of the most effective techniques, particularly in achieving Lasswell's first objective of mobilizing hatred for the enemy, was the atrocity story. These were spread by both sides. The Allies were very successful in whipping up hatred for the Germans with a widely reported story that German soldiers in Belgium were cutting the hands off Belgian children. Atrocity stories were often part of speeches given in movie theaters in the United States by "Four-Minute Men," speakers with talks carefully timed to four minutes (Mock and Larsen, 1939). Most of these atrocity stories were false, but they did a great deal to make World War I propaganda effective because people believed them.

Propaganda education became a major concern in the United States in the period prior to World War II. Perhaps some Americans were worried that the techniques the United States had used so effectively in World War I were about to be used against them.

Social psychologist Hadley Cantril (1965) has described how sometime during the 1930s he gave a radio talk over a Boston radio station on the subject of propaganda. The next day, he received a telephone call from Edward A. Filene, the successful merchant who organized the credit union movement in the United States and founded the Twentieth Century Fund. Filene wanted to finance an undertaking to teach people how to think, and he asked Cantril to spend an evening with him talking over the idea. They finally decided that they might not be able to teach people how to think, but that they might have some success in teaching people how *not* to think. The result was the establishment in 1937 of the Institute for Propaganda Analysis, with Cantril as its first president. The advisory board of the Institute included names of several other persons who later made various contributions to communication theory, including Edgar Dale and Leonard Doob.

The Institute was concerned about the rise of the Nazis to power in Germany and the effects that Nazi propaganda might have in the United States. Hitler and his propaganda minister, Joseph Goebbels, seemed to be having great success with propaganda in Germany. The Institute was concerned about the possibility of a Hitler figure rising to power in the United States. This may seem unlikely now, but we should remember that Nazi rallies were being held in New York's Madison Square Garden and across America in the 1930s. Furthermore, there was even a fairly likely candidate to become the American Hitler. This was Father Charles E. Coughlin, a Catholic priest who was broadcasting over a 47-station radio network and became known as the "Radio Priest." Coughlin's radio program every Sunday was reaching 30 million listeners, or as many as some television programs reach today. This audience was proportionately much greater than most audiences reached by mass communication today. Coughlin was apparently a colorful individual: his church in Royal Oak, Michigan, was called The Shrine of the Little Flower and he had set up on the corner of the property The Shrine Super-Service and Hot Dog Stand. His radio talks, however, seemed to present a fascist philosophy. In fact, his magazine *Social Justice* was eventually banned from the U.S. mail because it mirrored the Nazi propaganda line. Coughlin's radio career finally came to a stop when he was reprimanded by the Church.

Perhaps the most famous publication of the Institute for Propaganda Analysis was a book edited by Alfred McClung Lee and Elizabeth Briant Lee (1939) called *The Fine Art of Propaganda*. The book presented seven common devices of propaganda, and it used examples from Coughlin's speeches to illustrate the devices. These devices were given catchy names and they were simple enough to be taught in the public schools.

The Propaganda Devices

The seven propaganda devices are: Name Calling, Glittering Generality, Transfer, Testimonial, Plain Folks, Card Stacking and Band Wagon. Each will be defined and discussed below, with examples from contemporary society—political campaigns, advertisements, newspaper columns and statements by extremist groups.

1. *"Name Calling*—giving an idea a bad label—is used to make us reject and condemn the idea without examining the evidence" (Lee and Lee, 1939, p. 26).

Name Calling doesn't appear much in advertising, probably because there is a reluctance to mention a competing product, even by calling it a name. Its use in politics and other areas of public discourse is more common, however.

The White Knights of the Ku Klux Klan of Mississippi were using Name Calling in their publication *The Klan Ledger* when they referred to civil rights demonstrators as "Communist-led black savages." No evidence was presented linking the demonstrators to Communism. The same publication used Name Calling again when it stated: "Please remember: Support your local police. We must stand behind our local officers of law and against *the scummy disciples of dictatorship* such as Bobby Kennedy . . . ." (italics added).

A conservative newspaper columnist was using the device of Name Calling when he referred to an abortion clinic as "a baby-killing factory." This is certainly a bad label; no one would be in favor of killing babies, but in fact, the courts have ruled that an abortion, at least during the first six months of pregnancy, is not killing a person. Legally, abortion is not baby-killing.

Mac Wilkins, the winner of the Gold Medal for the discus throw at the 1976 Olympics, drew a Name Calling reaction after he criticized the U.S. Olympic Committee. Philip O. Krumm, the president of the committee, was asked by a reporter whether disciplinary action might be taken against Wilkins. He replied, "I don't think so. We have learned to put up with jerks like that." Krumm did not bother to go into the charges of inefficiency that Wilkins had made against the committee.

Lester Maddox, the former governor of Georgia, waged a campaign against his fellow Georgian Jimmy Carter when Carter was running for President. The campaign consisted largely of Name Calling. Among the names Maddox used, according to Carter, were liar, thief, atheist, Communist, Socialist and dictator. At one press conference, Maddox was pressed by a black reporter to prove that Carter was an extreme liberal. Maddox's reply was to defend Name Calling by additional Name Calling. He said, "You're real stupid, you're naive." He also told the reporter he should be on a farm growing peanuts, rather than covering a Presidential election.

During the 1978 coal strike, television news programs showed films of John L. Lewis, the president of the United Mine Workers in the 1940s, discussing the Taft-Hartley Act. Lewis was using Name Calling when he referred to it as "that infamous Taft-Hartley slave statute."

A member of a group of Congressmen touring the United States to speak against the Panama Canal treaty was using some mild Name Calling when he said the purpose of their tour was to clear up the "confusing rhetoric from Washington."

Former President Richard Nixon got into a little Name Calling during one of his television interviews with David Frost when the topic came up of Daniel Ellsberg, the man who stole and published the Pentagon Papers.

"I didn't want to discredit the man as an individual," Nixon said. "I couldn't care less about the punk."

Other examples of Name Calling include President Jerry Ford calling Fidel Castro an "international outlaw" while speaking to newly naturalized Cuban refugees during the presidential campaign of 1976, and President Jimmy Carter referring to large automobiles as "gas guzzlers" during his major energy address to Congress in 1977.

2. *"Glittering Generality*—associating something with a 'virtue word'— is used to make us accept and approve the thing without examining the evidence" (Lee and Lee, 1939, p. 47).

The use of Glittering Generalities is so pervasive that we hardly notice it. One of the common uses of virtue words is in the very names of products, such as Gold Medal Flour, Imperial Margarine, Wonder Bread, Southern Comfort, Super Shell and Superior Dairy. Some cereals are given names that will particularly appeal to children—Cheerios, Cap'n Crunch, and Froot Loops. A new cigarette that was going to be made from lettuce and therefore nicotine-free was going to be called "Long Life."

Or the Glittering Generality can appear in a statement about the product. Commercials for Kellogg cereals say they bring "the best to you each morning"—quite a glowing phrase for a bowl of cold cereal. Commercials for United Air Lines invite people to "fly the friendly skies" of United, but they don't offer any evidence that the skies of United are any more friendly than the skies of any other airline. Another claim of the same type is the statement that "Coke adds life." It sounds as if they've found the fountain of youth and started bottling it.

Sometimes these Glittering Generalities used by advertisers can involve deception to such a degree that legal action is taken. Some shampoo manufacturers were requested by the Federal Trade Commission to document the statement that their products contained "natural ingredients," a claim played up in advertising. The "natural ingredients" turned out to be things like coconut oil and plain water.

Wheaties has for a long time been advertised as the "breakfast of champions." The claim was finally challenged in a lawsuit after the company started using Olympic decathlon champion Bruce Jenner in commercials in which he said he "downed a lot of Wheaties" on his way to winning the gold medal. The suit was brought by the consumer fraud crime unit of the district attorney's office in San Francisco, which charged false advertising. In a later press conference, Jenner indicated that he had eaten Wheaties for breakfast for many years, but that he often supplemented the cereal with steak and homemade granola.

The makers of Listerine got into trouble for stating on the bottle label: "For relief of colds symptoms and minor sore throats due to colds." The Federal Trade Commission found that research on the product did not substantiate that claim, and ordered the company to run corrective advertising.

The Glittering Generality device shows up in areas other than advertising, such as politics. Calling a proposed law a "right to work" law might be an effective way to get the law passed; who would oppose the right to work? In a similar use, the group of Congressmen that toured the United States to speak against the Panama Canal treaty called itself a "truth squad." Franklin D. Roosevelt's decision to call his program "the New Deal" was an effective choice of a Glittering Generality; it sounded good and it suggested that he was correcting a misdeal.

Economist Daniel Bell (1976) has brought out what a tricky public relations job it was to introduce installment buying in the United States, where the Protestant Ethic, with its emphasis on saving and abstinence, prevailed. The key to the campaign was to avoid the word "debt" and emphasize the word "credit."

A Glittering Generality was used to persuade the citizens of Wilsonville, Ill., to allow in their town a waste disposal center for PCB-contaminated sludge and other poisons. They were told only that "industrial residues" would be kept there.

3. *"Transfer* carries the authority, sanction, and prestige of something respected and revered over to something else in order to make the latter more acceptable" (Lee and Lee, 1939, p. 69).

Transfer works through a process of association, but instead of guilt by association it's usually something more like "admiration by association." The communicator's goal is to link his or her idea or product or cause with something that people like or have favorable attitudes toward.

Sometimes the association can be merely verbal. During the Bicentennial in 1976, it was common to link all kinds of products, from ice cream to toilet seats and coffins, to the Bicentennial. More recently, after the popularity of the movie *Star Wars,* a book appeared with the title *War Stars,* and Subaru put out commercials referring to its "star cars." In a more nonverbal type of transfer, a number of television commercials began to roll their messages back into the screen in big letters, an imitation of the opening titles of *Star Wars.*

Sometimes the transfer takes place through the use of music. Father Coughlin used to begin his Sunday radio broadcasts with churchlike music from an organ, thus transferring to himself and his message the prestige of the church. The Ku Klux Klan plays the hymn "The Old Rugged Cross" at its rallies, thus associating itself with Christianity. Music also appears in a television commercial for the telephone company. The words are "Hello, America, how are you?" but the tune is the hit song "The City of New Orleans," which was written by Steve Goodman and made popular by Arlo Guthrie. This allows the telephone company to associate itself with the nostalgia for the vanishing railroads as well as youth and the counterculture.

Transfer can also take place through the use of symbolic objects. Ku Klux Klan rallies feature a burning of a cross, another Christian symbol. A minor presidential candidate from Chicago named Lar Daley used to campaign in an Uncle Sam suit. President Richard Nixon used to wear an American flag on his lapel, and some of his television addresses to the nation during the last days of Watergate showed a bust of Lincoln in the background.

Sometimes the Transfer can take place just through two people appearing together. President Nixon might have received some favorable association with religion when he appeared at a prayer breakfast with evangelist Billy Graham. Jimmy Carter might have picked up some votes during the presidential campaign of 1976 when he appeared on stage at a concert with rock star Gregg Allman. This kind of Transfer can be distributed to a large number of people through a news photograph of the event showing the two people together.

Many advertisements and commercials are built primarily around the Transfer device. The Marlboro cigarette campaign, thought by some experts to be the most successful advertising campaign in 30 to 40 years, is based on transferring the ruggedness and virility of the cowboys in the ads and commercials to the cigarette and to the people that smoke Marlboros.

Many liquor ads around Christmas are designed to build strong associations between Christmas and the use of liquor. J&B Scotch has used the song title "Jingle Bells" in ads of this type with the "J" and the "B" in the title emphasized in such a way that there appears to be an intimate connection between the old familiar song and their product. The goal seems to be to make it so you can't think of "Jingle Bells" without thinking of their product. A Seagram's 7 advertisement in magazines showed a young couple baking Christmas cookies. A couple of glasses of whiskey were prominent in the picture. If one looked more closely, there was an even more subtle tie-in between Christmas and their product—each of the cookies being baked was in the shape of a "7" with a crown on it.

4. "*Testimonial* consists in having some respected or hated person say that a given idea or program or product or person is good or bad" (Lee and Lee, 1939, p. 74).

Testimonial is a common technique in advertising and political campaigning.

Examples from political campaigning include John Wayne speaking for presidential candidate Richard Nixon and Paul Newman appearing on behalf of candidate George McGovern.

Examples from advertising include Olympic decathlon champion Bruce Jenner doing television spots for Wheaties, race driver A. J. Foyt appearing in magazine ads for Rolex watches, actress Angie Dickinson and her husband, songwriter Burt Bacharach, doing a commercial for Martini & Rossi Vermouth, comedian Don Rickles doing National Car Rentals commercials, actress Catherine Deneuve doing television spots for Chanel No. 5, comedian Bob Hope doing Texaco commercials, actor Jason Robards doing television ads for Commercial Credit, and football player Joe Namath appearing for shaving cream, popcorn poppers, pantyhose, and almost anything else you can name.

It is not only establishment figures that get lured into doing Testimonials.

Members of the counterculture must have been surprised when Euell Gibbons, the author of *Stalking the Wild Asparagus* and other books on natural foods, began appearing on television for Grape Nuts Flakes.

How true are testimonials? Writer Barry Farrell (1975) did some checking on Peter Ustinov's commercials for Gallo wines. Ustinov was praising the company's new line of varietal wines, but Gallo also makes Ripple, Boone's Farm and Thunderbird—wines unlikely to appear on Peter Ustinov's table. In the commercials, Ustinov speaks of "my friends Ernest and Julio Gallo" and their passion for making fine wines. Farrell found out that Ustinov never knew the Gallos until he was hired to do the commercials.

5. *"Plain Folks* is the method by which a speaker attempts to convince his audience that he and his ideas are good because they are 'of the people,' the 'plain folks' " (Lee and Lee, 1939, p. 92).

The Plain Folks device is more common in politics than it is in advertising, although campaigns such as the Butter Krust Bread series of commercials stressing "down home" scenes and featuring a jingle about a "land of gingham blue" are clearly using the approach.

A good example of the Plain Folks approach a few years ago appeared in television spots shown in Arkansas when Senator William J. Fulbright was running for re-election. The ads showed Fulbright appearing without a necktie and whittling on a piece of wood. This is an unlikely image for Fulbright, a Rhodes scholar and probably one of the most erudite persons who ever served in the Senate, but it was an image that would be appealing in rural Arkansas.

Nelson Rockefeller threw in a touch of the Plain Folks approach when he appeared at a Senate hearing considering his appointment as Vice President of the United States. Rockefeller stressed that his grandfather had sold turkeys. This was from a man whose net worth has been reported at $62 million.

Richard Nixon used a similar strategy in his famous Checkers speech when he pointed out that he had worked in the family grocery when he was young and that his wife Pat had a "respectable Republican cloth coat."

Nixon also used the Plain Folks device in subtle ways during the time he was defending his Presidency against the charges of Watergate. During a trip to Houston, he had coffee at a lunch counter in a drug store and chatted with the waitress. Photographs of this scene were published all over the country.

What could be more "Plain Folks" than a peanut? A candidate for governor of Texas in 1972 was described in at least one newspaper editorial as having risen "from the obscurity of a peanut farm." And of course the "peanut farm" theme was a prominent part of Jimmy Carter's successful campaign for the Presidency in 1976.

6. *"Card Stacking* involves the selection and use of facts or falsehoods, illustrations or distractions, and logical or illogical statements in order to give the best or worst possible case for an idea, program, person or product" (Lee and Lee, 1939, p. 95).

Card Stacking is basically identical to the General Semantics technique of *slanting* (see Ch. 5). It is a selecting of the arguments or evidence that support a position and ignoring the arguments or evidence that do not support the position. The arguments that are selected can be true or false. The device probably operates most effectively when the arguments are true, but other equally true arguments are ignored, because then it is hardest to detect.

Some of the clearest examples of Card Stacking can be found in movie ads that present quotations from movie reviews. These quotations are highly selected to be only the most favorable. An ad for *The Sugarland Express,* for instance, quoted critic Vincent Canby of *The New York Times* as saying it was "first rate and very funny," critic Judith Crist of *New York Magazine* as saying it was "a triumph," and critic Rex Reed of the New York *Daily News* as saying, "Never a dull moment in *The Sugarland Express.*" These critics no doubt said these things, but they probably said some negative or less positive things also, and these were not brought out.

Ralph Ginzburg's *Fact* magazine used Card Stacking in an article dealing with presidential candidate Barry Goldwater, and ended up losing a libel suit because of it. The article was based on interviews with psychiatrists and reached the conclusion that Goldwater had a "severely paranoid personality" and was psychologically unfit to be president. The article did not bring out, however, that a large number of psychiatrists had been interviewed, and that many had indicated that Goldwater was psychologically normal. By reporting only the negative opinions on Goldwater, the magazine article was engaging in Card Stacking.

A television spot for a U.S. Senator seeking re-election in 1964 contained a similar kind of Card Stacking. Senator Clair Engle had undergone brain surgery, had a paralyzed arm, and could barely walk or talk. His campaign staff was able to produce a television commercial that showed a picture of health by repeatedly filming the Senator and selecting only the best shots (Nimmo, 1970). Engle died before the primary election; if he had not, the voters might have re-elected a nearly incapacitated man to serve in the U.S. Senate.

A use of Card Stacking in wartime communication occurred during the Israeli attack on Palestine guerilla bases in Lebanon in 1978. Dr. Fathi Arafat, the brother of PLO commander Yasir Arafat, showed an Associated Press reporter sacks containing the bodies of two children killed in rocket attacks by the Israelis. There was undoubtedly a lot of information Arafat could have made available to the reporter; he selected the information that would make the Israelis look bad in the eyes of the world. This incident was strikingly similar to the use of atrocity stories in World War I, although in this case the information was probably true.

Many television commercials that show interviews with ordinary citizens are also using the Card Stacking technique. This is the type of commercial in which a television interviewer comes across a person in a shopping center and asks her if she would like a free cup of coffee. After she tastes it, she is asked, "Would you say it tastes as rich as it looks?" The person then says "It tastes as rich as it looks," or perhaps something even more favorable. These commercials show the people who were interviewed who praised the product, but they don't show or even report the number of interviews in which people did not praise the product. One interviewer for this kind of commercial has said, "The bulk of the answers in those things is indifference. People will say, 'Oh, it's all right.' " (Grant, 1978, p. 65).

7. *"Band Wagon* has as its theme, 'Everybody—at least all of *us*—is doing it'; with it, the propagandist attempts to convince us that all members of a group to which we belong are accepting his program and that we must therefore follow our crowd and 'jump on the band wagon' " (Lee and Lee, 1939, p. 105).

Many examples of *Band Wagon* appeals appear in advertising. A deodorant is described as "The People's Choice." A recruitment ad for the U.S. Army shows a group of smiling young people in uniform and says, "Join the people who've joined the Army." A jingle for Sara Lee bakery products states, "But nobody doesn't like Sara Lee." McDonald's brags about 2½ billion hamburgers sold. A soft drink argues that "It's the Pepsi generation," suggesting that a whole generation is drinking the product. Other advertisements state "Acme's got Americans wearing Denims on their feet," "Here's the Early Times drink they're all making," and "What a lot of people have been waiting for." And a kind of blend of Band Wagon and Testimonial appears in the statement that "Nine out of ten doctors use Crest."

Effectiveness of the Devices

The Institute for Propaganda Analysis identified the seven propaganda devices, but it did not do research on the effectiveness of the devices. The Institute seemed to assume that the devices were effective, and leave it at that.

Scientific evidence is now available on the effectiveness of some of the propaganda devices. Most of it comes from experiments done by social psychologists investigating how attitudes can be changed. Several of these experiments are essentially tests of the propaganda devices of Card Stacking, Testimonial and Band Wagon (Brown, 1958). These experiments are discussed briefly here and in greater detail in later chapters on attitude change and the role of groups in communication.

Evidence on the effectiveness of Card Stacking comes from experiments on the effectiveness of one-sided versus two-sided messages (Hovland, Lumsdaine and Sheffield, 1949; Lumsdaine and Janis, 1953). The one-sided message is essentially a card-stacking message. Only the arguments on one side of a controversy are presented. In the two-sided message, some of the arguments that can be raised on the other side are mentioned briefly. In general, this research has shown that the one-sided messages works best on some kinds of people (those initially tending to agree with the argument of the message, or those lower in education) and a two-sided message works best on other kinds of people (those initially tending to oppose the argument of the message, or those higher in education).

Evidence on the effectiveness of Testimonial comes from experiments on the effects of the credibility of the source (Hovland and Weiss, 1951). In general, these experiments show that the high credibility source produces more attitude change than the low credibility source, but that even the high credibility source typically changes the attitudes of fewer than half the people who receive messages attributed to it.

Evidence on the effectiveness of Band Wagon comes from experiments on the effects of group pressure and conformity (Asch, 1958; Sherif, 1958). These experiments demonstrate that in a rather contrived situation most people can be influenced in their judgment when a group of other people present a different view. This effect is strongest when there is a unanimous majority against the person. If one other person breaks the unanimous majority, then the influence is not nearly as strong. And even with a unanimous majority against them, one-third of the people put through these experiments remain independent on their judgments.

This evidence on three of the propaganda devices indicates that in general the devices can be effective, but only on some people. And whether a device will be effective or not depends on some other factors. These include characteristics of the persons getting the message, such as their education level and their initial attitude on the topic. They also include characteristics of the setting, such as whether the group holding a different view from a person is unanimous or not. Psychologist Roger Brown (1958) has summed up this research by saying that the evidence indicates that the propaganda devices are "contingently rather than invariably effective" (p. 306).

It appears from the scientific evidence that the Institute for Propaganda Analysis exaggerated the effectiveness of these devices. Nevertheless, they can be effective enough to increase the sales of a product by a meaningful amount, and that is why they are so widespread in advertising. The seven propaganda devices are also important because they can be viewed as an early attempt to state a theory of attitude change. Some of the devices that the Institute was only guessing about have turned out to be key variables in later attitude change experiments.

Effectiveness of Nazi Propaganda

The Institute for Propaganda Analysis and others who were concerned may have over-reacted when they began flooding the country with pamphlets presenting the seven propaganda devices. It now appears unlikely that a person using these methods could have successfully introduced Nazism to the United States or become an American Hitler. But if this is the case, how does one explain the apparent success of Nazi propaganda in Germany prior to World War II?

There were some important differences in the situations in the United States and Germany prior to World War II. One important difference is that the Nazis in Germany had essentially a communication monopoly (Bramsted, 1965). Dissenting views were not permitted, and that is very different from the situation in the United States. Perhaps the most important difference, however, is that propaganda in Germany was wedded to terror and backed up by force. If your neighbor expressed a dissenting view, he could disappear from his home during the middle of the night never to be seen again. Joseph Goebbels, the Nazi minister of propaganda, is reported to have said that "a sharp sword must always stand behind propaganda, if it is to be really effective" (Bramsted, 1965, p. 450). A book on Nazi radio propaganda written during World War II expressed a similar thought: "Political propaganda in Nazi Germany is a form of coercion; while it lacks the bluntness and irrevocability of physical violence, it derives its ultimate efficacy from the power of those who may, at any moment, cease talking and start killing" (Kris and Speier, 1944, p. 3).

The "Bullet Theory"

We have seen that there was a widespread notion after World War I of propaganda being extremely powerful. This notion was certainly held by some book authors and some book reviewers, and to some extent it was held by people working at the Institute for Propaganda Analysis. This idea of mass communication having great power can be considered one of the first general theories of the effects of mass communication. Sometimes this theory is known as the "Bullet Theory" (Schramm, 1971), the "hypodermic-needle" theory (Berlo, 1960) or the "Stimulus-Response" theory (DeFleur and Ball-Rokeach, 1975). The theory suggests that people are extremely vulnerable to mass communication messages. It suggests that if the message "hits its target," it will have its desired effect.

We now know that this theory of mass communication is oversimplified. A mass communication message does not have the same effect on everyone. Its effect on anyone is dependent on a number of things, including various personality characteristics of the person and various aspects of the situation and the context. Nevertheless, the "Bullet Theory" is a conceivable theory of mass communication, and it even appeared a likely one after the effectiveness of propaganda in World War I. In a sense, the "Bullet Theory" was an accurate description of mass communication effects in World War I. It was accurate partly because people were naive and they believed lies, and it will probably never work as well again, but for a time it was accurate.

And the "Bullet Theory" may not be dead yet. It appears in a somewhat revised form in the writings of the French philosopher Jacques Ellul (1973). Ellul argues that propaganda is much more effective than recent analysis by Americans has shown. He particularly rejects the evidence from experiments, stating that propaganda is part of a total environment and cannot be duplicated in a laboratory setting. Ellul argues that propaganda is so pervasive in American life that most of us are not even aware of it, and yet it is controlling our values. The central one of these values is, of course, "the American way of life." This thinking is not completely different from the ideas of some American communication scholars. As we shall see, sociologists Paul Lazarsfeld and Robert Merton have discussed the tendency of mass communication to reinforce the economic and social status quo, and communication theorist Joseph Klapper has suggested that the general effect of mass communication is reinforcement of attitudes.

CONCLUSIONS

The analysis of propaganda after World War I expressed certain thinking about the effects of mass communication that we can regard as one of the first general theories about the effects of mass communication. In essence, this theory was what has come to be known as the "Bullet Theory."

The work of the Institute for Propaganda Analysis led to what we can consider a primitive theory of attitude change. Several of the propaganda devices the Institute identified are quite similar to techniques later studied more carefully in scientific research on persuasion. Scientific research shows that these devices have some ability to change attitudes, but that it is limited.

Even though their effectiveness is limited, the seven propaganda devices can still serve their initial purpose of giving us a checklist of techniques commonly used in mass communication. In one way or another, all the propaganda devices represent faulty arguments. Knowledge of the devices can make people better consumers of information.

REFERENCES

Asch, S. E. (1958). Effects of Group Pressure Upon the Modification and Distortion of Judgments. In E. E. Maccoby, T. M. Newcomb and E. L. Hartley (eds.) *Readings in Social Psychology,* 3rd ed., pp. 174–183. New York: Holt, Rinehart and Winston.

Bell, D. (1976). *The Cultural Contradictions of Capitalism.* New York: Basic Books.

Berlo, D. (1960). *The Process of Communication: An Introduction to Theory and Practice.* San Francisco: Rinehart Press.

Bramsted, E. K. (1965). *Goebbels and National Socialist Propaganda: 1925–1945.* East Lansing, Mich.: Michigan State University Press.

Brown, R. (1958). *Words and Things.* New York: The Free Press.

Cantril, H. (1965). Foreword. In M. Choukas, *Propaganda Comes of Age.* Washington, D.C.: Public Affairs Press.

DeFleur, M., and S. Ball-Rokeach. (1975). *Theories of Mass Communication,* 3rd ed. New York: David McKay.

Dulles, F. R. (1928). Problems of War and Peace. *The Bookman* 67:105–107.

Ellul, J. (1973). *Propaganda: The Formation of Men's Attitudes.* New York: Vintage Books.

Farrell, B. (December, 1975). Celebrity Market. *Harper's,* pp. 108–110.

Gordon, G. N. (1971). *Persuasion: The Theory and Practice of Manipulative Communication.* New York: Hastings House, Publishers.

Grant, M. N. (1978). I Got My Swimming Pool by Choosing Prell Over Brand X. In R. Atwan, B. Orton and W. Vesterman (eds.), *American Mass Media: Industries and Issues,* pp. 61–67. New York: Random House.

Hovland, C. I., A. A. Lumsdaine and F. D. Sheffield. (1949). *Experiments on Mass Communication.* New York: John Wiley & Sons.

Hovland, C. I., and W. Weiss. (1951). The Influence of Source Credibility on Communication Effectiveness. *Public Opinion Quarterly* 15:635–650.

Kris, E., and H. Speier. (1944). *German Radio Propaganda: Report on Home Broadcasts During the War.* London: Oxford University Press.

Lasswell, H. D. (1927). *Propaganda Technique in the World War.* New York: Peter Smith.

Lasswell, H. D. (1937). Propaganda. In E. R. A. Seligman and A. Johnson (eds.) *Encyclopaedia of the Social Sciences,* vol. 12, pp. 521–528.

Lee, A. M. and E. B. Lee (eds.) (1939). *The Fine Art of Propaganda: A Study of Father Coughlin's Speeches.* New York: Harcourt, Brace and Company.

Lumsdaine, A. A., and I. L. Janis. (1953). Resistance to "Counterpropaganda" produced by One-sided and Two-sided "Propaganda" Presentations. *Public Opinion Quarterly* 17:311–318.

Mock, J. R., and C. Larson. (1939). *Words that Won the War: The Story of The Committee on Public Information 1917–1919.* Princeton: Princeton University Press.

Nimmo, D. (1970). *The Political Persuaders: The Techniques of Modern Election Campaigns.* Englewood Cliffs, N. J.: Prentice-Hall.

Read, J. M. (1941). *Atrocity Propaganda: 1914–1919.* New Haven: Yale University Press.

Schramm, W. (1971). The Nature of Communication Between Humans. In W. Schramm and D. Roberts (eds.) *The Process and Effects of Mass Communication,* rev. ed., pp. 3–53. Urbana: University of Illinois Press.

Sherif, M. (1958). Group Influences Upon the Formation of Norms and Attitudes. In E. E. Maccoby, T. M. Newcomb and E. L. Hartley (eds.) *Readings in Social Psychology,* 3rd ed., pp. 219–232. New York: Holt, Rinehart and Winston.

Chapter 9

Perception and Communication

D URING the 1972 presidential campaign, a television spot for candidate George McGovern showed him chatting with a group of disabled veterans.

One viewer of the commercial expressed this reaction:

> He really cares what's happening to disabled vets. They told him how badly they've been treated and he listened. He will help them.

Another viewer of the same commercial expressed this reaction:

> McGovern was talking with these disabled vets. He doesn't really care about them. He's just using them to get sympathy (Patterson and McClure, 1976, p. 89).

These viewers were demonstrating *selective perception,* or the tendency for people's perception to be influenced by wants, needs, attitudes and other psychological factors. The first viewer was a 37-year-old McGovern supporter; the second was a 33-year-old Nixon fan.

Selective perception plays an important role in communication. Selective perception means that different people can react to the same message in very different ways. The communicator cannot assume that his or her message will have the meaning he or she intended for all receivers, or even that it will have the same meaning for all receivers. This complicates our models of mass communication. Perhaps mass communication is not just a matter of hitting a target with an arrow, as some models suggest. The message

128

can reach the receiver (hit the target) and still fail to accomplish its purpose because it is subject to the interpretation of the receiver.

The process of receiving and interpreting a message is referred to in many communication models as *decoding*. The process involves perception, or the taking in of information through the senses, an area that psychologists have studied in considerable detail. Before we consider the operation of perception in the decoding of a mass communication message, we will discuss some of the research findings about perception in general.

Modern psychology has shown perception to be a complex process, and rather different from the naive view that many people probably had a century ago. This old view—which we might refer to as the common sense view— saw human perception as largely a physical or mechanical process. The human eye and the other sense organs were thought to work much like a camera, or a tape recorder. This view of perception held that there was a quite direct correspondence between an "external reality" and a person's perception, or what was in the mind. This view would hold that everybody perceives the world in essentially the same way.

Psychologists have found perception to be a more elaborate process than that. A recent definition (Berelson and Steiner, 1964) states that perception is the "complex process by which people select, organize and interpret sensory stimulation into a meaningful and coherent picture of the world" (p. 88). This definition brings out the active role that a person plays in perception. The person doing the perceiving brings something to the act of perception, just as does the object being perceived. Putting it another way, perception is influenced by a number of psychological factors, including assumptions based on past experience (that often operate at an almost unconscious level), cultural expectations, motivation (needs), moods, and attitudes. A number of experiments have demonstrated the effects of these factors on perception.

Assumptions and Perception

Much of the research showing that perception is influenced by assumptions has come from a group of researchers working at one time or another at Princeton University. These researchers have presented what has been called the "transactional view" of perception. These scholars have included Adelbert Ames, Jr., Hadley Cantril, Edward Engels, Albert Hastorf, William H. Ittelson, Franklin P. Kilpatrick and Hans Toch. Exactly what these thinkers mean by the transactional view of perception is abstract and somewhat philosophical, but essentially it means that both the perceiver and the world are active participants in an act of perception (Toch and MacLean, 1962).

The transactional thinkers have developed a number of convincing demonstrations that perception is based on assumptions. One of the most striking, invented by Adelbert Ames, Jr., is called the "monocular distorted room." This room is constructed so that the rear wall is a trapezoid, with the vertical distance up and down the left edge of the wall longer than the vertical distance up and down the right edge of the wall. In addition, the rear wall is positioned at an angle so that the left edge is further back than the right edge. This angle is carefully selected so that the room will appear to be an ordinary rectangular room to an observer looking through a small hole at the front of the room. If two people walk into the room and stand in the rear corners, something interesting happens. The one on the right appears to a viewer looking through the hole to be very large because he or she is closer to the viewer and fills most of the distance from the floor to the ceiling. The one on the left appears to be very small because he or she is further away and fills less of the distance from the floor to the ceiling. This illusion takes place because the mind of the viewer is assuming that the rear wall is parallel to the front wall of the room. This assumption is based on prior experience with other rooms that looked similar. The illusion is so strong that if the two people in the corners switch places one will appear to grow larger right before the viewer's eye and the other will appear to get smaller.

Cultural Expectations and Perception

Some of the most striking evidence for cultural expectations influencing perception comes from research on binocular rivalry (Bagby, 1957). It is possible to construct a device which has two eyepieces like a pair of binoculars, but which can be used to present a different picture to each eye. When this is done, people seldom see both pictures. They more often see one picture and not the other or one picture coming first and then being replaced by the other. Sometimes they see a mixture of some elements of each picture, but this usually occurs after seeing one picture alone first. Bagby used this instrument to investigate the effect of cultural background on perception.

Subjects were 12 Americans (6 males and 6 females) and 12 Mexicans (6 males and 6 females). Except for one matched pair made up of a person from each country, the subjects had not traveled outside their own country. Bagby prepared ten pairs of photographic slides, with each pair containing a picture from the American culture and a picture from the Mexican culture. One pair, for instance, showed a baseball scene and a bullfight scene. Subjects were exposed to each slide for 60 seconds and asked to describe what they saw. The assignment of the Mexican or the American picture to the left or right eye was randomized to eliminate the effect of eye dominance. The first 15 seconds of viewing for each slide were scored for which scene was dominant—the Mexican or the American. Dominance was determined by which scene was reported first or which was reported as showing up for the longest period of time.

The results (see Table 1) indicate a strong tendency for subjects to see the scenes from their own culture rather than the scenes from an unfamiliar culture.

Toch and Schulte (1961) used the binocular rivalry procedure to investigate whether training in police work led a person to perceive violent scenes

Table 1

**Perceptual Predominance in Ten Pairs of Pictures
for Mexican and American Subjects**

	No. Where Mexicans Dominated	No. Where Americans Dominated	Total Number of Trials
Mexican males (6)	44	16	60
Mexican females (6)	45	15	60
American males (6)	7	53	60
American females (6)	12	48	60

From Bagby, J. W. (1957). A Cross-Cultural Study of Perceptual Predominance in Binocular Rivalry. *Journal of Abnormal and Social Psychology* 54:331–334. Copyright 1957 by the American Psychological Association. Reprinted by permission.

more readily. Subjects who received training were advanced students in a three-year law enforcement course. Control groups were beginning students in the same course and introductory psychology students. Subjects were given one-half second exposures through a binocular instrument presenting a picture of a violent scene (such as a man with a gun standing over a body) to one eye and a picture of a neutral scene to the other eye. There were nine pairs of pictures. Subjects were asked to describe the objects they saw. The violent pictures were alternately presented to the left and right eyes, to control for eye dominance. In a second run of the experiment each violent scene was presented to the eye it was not presented to the first time.

The results (see Table 2) showed that the advanced students saw the violent scenes about twice as frequently as people in either control group. Training apparently increased the expectation of seeing violent scenes.

Table 2

Perception of Violent Pictures by Different Groups

	Average Number of "Violent" Pictures Perceived (out of 18 presentations)
Control Group 1 (27 psychology students)	4.03
Control Group 2 (16 beginning trainees)	4.69
Experimental Group (16 advanced trainees)	9.37

Toch, H. H., and R. Schulte. (1961). Readiness to Perceive Violence as a Result of Police Training. *British Journal of Psychology* 52:389–393. Reprinted by permission of Cambridge University Press.

Motivation and Perception

One of a number of experiments that show the effect of motivation on perception has been done by McClelland and Atkinson (1948). The type of motivation being investigated was hunger. Subjects were Navy men waiting for admission to a submarine training school. One group had been 16 hours without food, a second had been 4 hours without food and the third had been 1 hour without food. All subjects were told they were participating in a test of their ability to respond to visual stimulation at very low levels. The men went through 12 trials in which a picture was supposedly projected, but actually nothing was projected at all. To make this realistic, during the instructions they were shown a picture of a car and then the illumination was turned down until the car was only faintly visible. In some of the trials subjects were given clues such as: "Three objects on a table. What are they?"

Table 3
Mean Number of Food-Related Responses
out of Possible 14

Hours of Food Deprivation	Mean Number of Food Related Responses
1	2.14
4	2.88
16	3.22

Adapted from McClelland, D.C., and J. W. Atkinson. (1948). The Projective Expression of Needs: I. The Effect of Different Intensities of the Hunger Drive on Perception. *Journal of Psychology* 25:205–222. Reprinted by permission.

The results (see Table 3) showed that the frequency of food-related responses increased reliably as the hours of food deprivation increased. Furthermore, in another phase of the experiment food-related objects were judged larger than neutral objects by hungry subjects but not by subjects who had recently eaten.

Mood and Perception

An experiment using hypnosis has demonstrated that mood has an effect on perception. Leuba and Lucas (1945) hypnotized subjects, suggested to them that they were experiencing a certain mood and then asked them to tell what they saw in a picture. Each subject was put in a happy mood and then shown six pictures. Then the subject was told to forget the pictures and what had been said about them and was put in a critical mood and again shown the same six pictures. Finally the subject was given the same treatment once more except that the suggested mood was anxious.

The descriptions of the pictures that people gave were drastically different depending on the mood the person was in. They differed not only in the train of thoughts the pictures suggested but in the details noticed.

One picture showed some young people digging in a swampy area. Here is one subject's description of that picture while in a happy mood:

> It looks like fun; reminds me of summer. That's what life is for: working out in the open, really living—digging in the dirt, planting, watching things grow.

Here is the same subject describing the same picture while in a critical mood:

> Pretty horrible land. There ought to be something more useful for kids of that age to do instead of digging in that stuff. It's filthy and dirty and good for nothing.

Here is the same subject describing the same picture while in an anxious mood:

> They're going to get hurt or cut. There should be someone older there who knows what to do in case of accident. I wonder how deep the water is.

Attitude and Perception

The effects of attitude on perception have been documented in a study of perception of a football game by Hastorf and Cantril (1954). The 1951 football clash between Dartmouth and Princeton was an exciting and controversial one. Princeton's star player Dick Kazmaier was taken out of the game in the second quarter with a broken nose. In the third quarter, a Dartmouth player received a broken leg. Discussion of the game continued for weeks, with editorials in the two campus newspapers charging the other school with rough play. Hastorf and Cantril took advantage of this situation to conduct a study of perception. They showed a film of the game to two groups: two fraternities at Dartmouth and two undergraduate clubs at Princeton. Students from the two schools saw about the same number of infractions by the Princeton team. But Princeton students saw an average of 9.8 infractions by the Dartmouth team, while Dartmouth students saw an average of 4.3 infractions by the Dartmouth team. That is, the Princeton students saw more than twice as many violations by the Dartmouth team as did the Dartmouth students. Hastorf and Cantril state, "It seems clear that the 'game' actually was many different games and that each version of the events that transpired was just as 'real' to a particular person as other versions were to other people" (p. 132).

Perception and Mass Communication

So far this discussion of research has shown that perception in general is influenced by assumptions (often unconscious), cultural expectations, needs, moods and attitudes. The same kinds of forces are at work when people respond to mass communication messages, as the following examples show.

A Time *Magazine Cover*

The issue of *Time* magazine for July 21, 1975, had a cover picture showing a hand with American flag patterning on it shaking hands with a red hand with a Russian hammer and sickle on it. The cover story was called "Space Spectacular" and dealt with the Apollo-Soyuz orbital linkup and cooperation in space.

Not everyone perceived this theme of cooperation, however. A few weeks later, the following letter to the editor from D. Vincent O'Connor of North Adams, Mass., appeared in *Time:* "The cover illustrates very well that the Russians have got us."

The Carter-Ford Debate

The New York Times and CBS News conducted a poll of 1,167 respondents after the first televised debate between presidential candidates Jimmy

Table 4

**How Supporters of Ford and Carter
Perceived the First Debate**

	Ford Supporters	*Carter Supporters*
Who won the first debate?		
Ford	66%	14%
Carter	6	40
Tie	24	42
Don't Know	4	4
	100%	100%

Carter and President Jerry Ford (Apple, 1976). Overall, 37% of the respondents thought Ford had won, 24% thought Carter had won, 35% called it a draw and 4% were unwilling to express an opinion. If the results are examined separately for Carter supporters and Ford supporters, however, some striking differences in reaction show up (see Table 4).

The table shows that Ford supporters were most likely to see the debate as a victory for Ford, while Carter supporters were most likely to see the debate as a tie. All viewers were exposed to the same televised debate, and yet people came away with very different views depending on their own initial attitudes. Similar evidence of selective perception was found in studies of the earlier Kennedy-Nixon debates (Kraus, 1962).

Anti-Prejudice Cartoons

Satire is a familiar journalistic device. It has been used in works ranging from Jonathan Swift's *Gulliver's Travels* to Garry Trudeau's "Doonesbury" comic strip. But how is satire perceived?

The American Jewish Committee was interested in studying the effects of satire in reducing prejudice. They sponsored a study by Eunice Cooper and Marie Jahoda (1947) which investigated the effects of anti-prejudice cartoons. The cartoons featured an exaggerated figure named "Mr. Biggott" who appeared in situations designed to make prejudice appear ridiculous. For instance, one cartoon showed Mr. Biggott lying in a hospital bed and dying. He is saying to the doctor, "In case I should need a transfusion, doctor, I want to make certain I don't get anything but blue, sixth-generation American blood!" The intention was that people looking at the cartoon would see how ridiculous prejudice is and would lessen their own feelings of prejudice.

Cooper and Jahoda tested the cartoons on 160 white, non-Jewish working class men. About two-thirds of the sample misunderstood the cartoons. Some said the purpose of the cartoons was to legitimize prejudice. These people explained that the cartoons showed that other people had attitudes of prejudice, so the viewer should feel free to have those attitudes also. The cartoons were most likely to be understood by respondents low in prejudice and most likely to be misunderstood by respondents high in prejudice. Cooper and Jahoda suggested that fear of disapproval by a social group was one of the factors leading to this evasion of propaganda. They argued that accepting the anti-prejudice message threatened the individual's security in groups the individual valued.

This study suggests that making fun of prejudice is not an effective way of reducing it. People tend to view satiric cartoons differently depending on their own attitudes. Both prejudiced and unprejudiced people tended to see elements in the cartoons which confirmed their existing attitudes.

All in the Family

When the television program "All in the Family" appeared in 1971, some television critics began immediately to suggest that the program might have a harmful effect of reinforcing bigotry. They pointed out that the main character, Archie Bunker, was portrayed as a "lovable bigot," and that this condoned and perhaps even encouraged bigotry. They also pointed out that the program was teaching racial slurs such as "coon," "chink," and "wop," some of which might have been fading from the American scene at the time.

Producer Norman Lear replied that the program actually reduced prejudice by bringing bigotry out into the open and showing it to be illogical. He said the program showed Archie to be a fool, and that the program was a satire on bigotry. He claimed that the program shows Archie losing at the end to Mike, who makes more sense. Carroll O'Connor, the actor who played Archie, also defended the program. He stated in a *Playboy* interview that the effect of the program was to help reduce prejudice. The Los Angeles chapter of the NAACP agreed with this favorable evaluation, and gave the program an award in 1972 for its contribution to racial relations.

Neil Vidmar and Milton Rokeach (1974) conducted a study to determine how the program was being perceived by viewers. They conducted surveys of a sample of U.S. adolescents and a sample of Canadian adults. Contrary to the opinion of Lear, neither sample indicated that Archie was the one seen as being made fun of. U.S. adolescents were most likely to pick Mike as the one most often being made fun of, and Canadian adults were most likely to pick Edith as the one most often being made fun of. In another question, respondents were asked whether Archie typically wins or loses at the end of the program. People low in prejudice were most likely to say Archie loses, but people high in prejudice were most likely to say Archie wins. The Vidmar and Rokeach study shows the operation of selective perception in viewing "All in the Family." Viewers high in prejudice and viewers low in prejudice were likely to perceive the program in line with their existing attitudes.

These findings that viewers tend to exercise selective perception in viewing "All in the Family" have been supported in other studies. For instance, Brigham and Giesbrecht (1976) found that whites who were high in prejudice showed a strong tendency to like and agree with Archie and to see Archie's racial views as valid.

In recent years, producer Norman Lear has changed his tune about the effects of "All in the Family." "To think about what the show might accomplish is to defeat the creative process," Lear said recently (Gross, 1975). "I seriously question what a half-hour situation comedy can accomplish when the entire Judeo-Christian ethic has accomplished so little in the same area."

Other Selective Processes

Two other processes that are similar to selective perception sometimes come into play in mass communication. These are selective exposure and selective retention.

Selective exposure (or *selective attention*) is the tendency for a person to expose himself or herself to those communications that are in agreement with the person's existing attitudes and to avoid those communications that are not.

The notion of selective exposure follows nicely from Festinger's theory of cognitive dissonance, which suggests that one way to reduce dissonance after making a decision is to seek out information that is consonant with the decision.

Selective retention is the tendency for the recall of information to be influenced by wants, needs, attitudes, and other psychological factors.

Some evidence for selective retention comes from studies of rumor transmission by Allport and Postman (1947), in which they found that details were frequently left out when people passed on stories or descriptions of pictures. In another study supporting selective retention, Jones and Kohler (1958) found that people in favor of segregation learned plausible prosegregation and implausible antisegregation statements more easily than they learned plausible antisegregation and implausible prosegregation statements. The reverse was true for antisegregationists. Both groups learned most easily the information that would be useful in protecting their own attitudinal positions. In a third study supporting selective retention, Levine and Murphy (1958) found that subjects confronted with pro- or anti-Soviet material learned it more slowly and forgot it more quickly when it conflicted with their own attitudes.

The three selective processes can be thought of as three rings of defenses, with selective exposure being the outermost ring, selective perception coming in the middle, and selective retention being the innermost ring. Undesirable information can sometimes be headed off at the outermost ring. A person can just avoid those publications or programs that might contain contrary information. If this fails, the person can then exercise selective perception in decoding the message. If this fails, the person can then exercise selective retention, and just not retain the contrary information.

Sometimes one of these selective mechanisms will be more appropriate or more possible to use than the others. For instance, in watching a televised debate between two presidential candidates, you might find it difficult to practice selective exposure. If you want to see and hear the candidate you agree with, you will also be exposed to some degree to the other candidate. In this case, a person can fall back on the second and third defenses—selective perception and selective retention.

In another study of "All in the Family," this one conducted in Holland, selective exposure seemed to be the mechanism preferred over selective perception. Wilhoit and de Bock (1976) found a tendency for selective exposure among persons who might not like to see a bigoted, rigid person being made fun of. That is, persons high in parental authoritarianism or lifestyle intolerance tended to avoid watching "All in the Family." There was less of a tendency for people to practice selective perception. Contrary to the selective perception hypothesis, persons high in parental authoritarianism or lifestyle intolerance who did watch the program often perceived the satiric intent.

In general, the research evidence supporting selective perception and retention has been stronger than the evidence supporting selective exposure. Sears and Freedman (1967) reviewed a large number of studies attempting to investigate selective exposure and found very little convincing evidence of a general psychological preference for supportive information.

Subliminal Perception

One other topic involving perception and mass communication is the controversial and rather dubious technique known as *subliminal perception.* This is the notion that people can be influenced by stimuli of which they are not aware.

Subliminal perception first came to public attention in 1957 when James M. Vicary of the Subliminal Projection Co. began attempting to sell a special projector. The machine was reported to flash a message on a motion picture screen every five seconds at the same time that a regular motion picture projector was showing a film on the same screen. The message flashes were for $\frac{1}{3000}$ of a second.

Vicary reported that he had conducted an experiment in a New Jersey movie house in which subliminal messages stating "Eat Popcorn" and "Drink Coca-Cola" were flashed on the screen. He said he achieved a 57.5% increase in popcorn sales and an 18.1% increase in Coca Cola sales. Vicary said subliminal advertising would be a boon to the consumer because it would eliminate bothersome commercials and allow more entertainment time (Anonymous, Sept. 16, 1957, p. 127).

Vicary's claims provoked quite a negative reaction. Norman Cousins, the editor of *Saturday Review,* wrote an editorial that began with the sentence "Welcome to 1984.' Some people were worried that subliminal ads would be used to force people to drink alcohol against their will. Subliminal advertising was banned in Australia and Great Britain, and in the United States it was prohibited by the National Association of Broadcasters.

Vicary's theater study was never described fully enough that researchers could evaluate it. Other researchers began to look into the phenomenon, however. Much of the research on subliminal perception was undertaken by the advertising industry. It was concerned because the controversy about subliminal perception was giving the advertising industry a bad name.

Researchers attempting to study subliminal perception immediately ran into some problems. Subliminal perception is supposed to be perception that takes place below the threshold of awareness. One of the first problems is that there is no sharp threshold of awareness (Wiener and Schiller, 1960). At one moment a person might be able to identify a stimulus shown for $\frac{1}{25}$ of a second, but a short time later the same person might be able to identify a stimulus shown for $\frac{1}{100}$ of a second. Psychologists have typically solved this problem by defining the threshold as the point where the subject identifies the stimulus 50% of the time. But this is essentially an arbitrary definition. Also, thresholds differ from person to person and for the same person depending on tiredness, etc. These factors make it difficult to apply subliminal perception. It is not clear which of the various thresholds should be used.

In addition to the threshold problem, there are other difficulties. A number of studies of subliminal perception have shown that people can respond to a stimulus below the threshold of awareness. For instance, a person who has been given a shock when he or she is exposed to certain nonsense words will sometimes show a galvanic skin response reaction indicating fear when these nonsense words are flashed so briefly that the person still cannot recognize them (Lazarus and McCleary, 1951). But essentially no studies have shown the next step, that this kind of subliminal perception leads to persuasion.

In fact, there is some evidence that no magic change in perception occurs just because you cross the "threshold" of awareness. The main effect may be that you have taken a chance that your message will not be perceived at all, because it is of lower impact (Klass, 1958). Interestingly enough, it appears that selective perception may operate even in subliminal perception. That is, instead of the subliminal message stimulating a need or want, the message is interpreted in terms of existing needs or wants. Some indication of this comes from a study in which the word "beef" was flashed subliminally in an attempt to make people hungrier for beef sandwiches (Byrne, 1959). The test audience was made up of college students, and two of them reported later they thought they had seen the word "beer."

Berelson and Steiner (1964), in their summary of scientific findings about human beings, drew this conclusion about subliminal perception:

> There is no scientific evidence that subliminal stimulation can initiate subsequent action, to say nothing of commercially or politically significant action. And there is nothing to suggest that such action can be produced "against the subject's will," or more effectively than through normal, recognized messages (p. 95).

Claims for the effectiveness of subliminal perception continue to be made, despite the absence of scientific research for the phenomenon. Wilson Bryan Key has presented a variation on the old idea in his books *Subliminal Seduction* (1972) and *Media Sexploitation* (1976). Key claims that many advertisements contain within them subtle printings of the word "sex" as well as disguised representations of male and female sex organs. These hidden words and symbols are called "embeds." According to Key's theory, which is loosely based on Freudian theory, the viewer perceives these "embeds" unconsciously and is influenced by them to desire the advertised product, whether it is a bottle of perfume or an automobile tire. Key's books contain little in the way of scientific documentation. His proof rests more on the reproduction of advertisements supposedly containing embeds. Most of these are ambiguous at best. In keeping with perception theory, one begins to wonder if the fact that Key sees these pictures as filled with sexual references does not tell us something about Key rather than something about the advertisements!

Subliminal perception popped up in still another form in 1978. Newspapers reported that Hal Becker of Metairie, La., had developed a system for preventing theft in department stores by putting hidden messages deep in the background of a music system similar to Muzak (Garvin, 1978). Two of the messages were "I am honest" and "I will not steal." Becker claimed that he had conducted an experiment in a store in an Eastern city for six months and had cut the annual theft rate from $1.6 million to less than $900,000.

CONCLUSIONS

There is a great deal of scientific evidence for selective perception, or the tendency for people's perception to be influenced by their wants, needs, attitudes and other psychological factors. Selective perception occurs in the receiving of the messages of mass communication just as it does in other areas. This complicates our models of mass communication. The communicator cannot be sure that the meaning he or she intended in a message will also be seen there by members of the audience. The receiver of the message has a very active role in assigning meaning to that message. As communication scholar Dean C. Barnlund (1970) has put it, "It should be stressed that meaning is something 'invented,' 'assigned,' 'given,' rather than something 'received' " (p. 88).

Communication scholar Franklin Fearing (1970) has put the same idea another way: *"All communications contents are in some degree ambiguous. This may be termed the Principle of Necessary Ambiguity, and is basic to the understanding of all communications effects"* (p. 50).

The ambiguity that Fearing was talking about is perhaps most obvious in a rich and complicated television program like "All in the Family," where some viewers can identify with one character while other viewers identify with another character. But the ambiguity is also present in a presidential State of the Union address, a newspaper editorial or the 6 o'clock television news.

REFERENCES

Allport, G. W., and L. Postman. (1947). *The Psychology of Rumor.* New York: Henry Holt.

Anonymous. (Sept. 16, 1957). "Persuaders" Get Deeply "Hidden" Tool: Subliminal Projection. *Advertising Age* 28, no. 37:127.

Apple, R. W. (Sept. 27, 1976). Voter Poll Finds Debate Aided Ford and Cut Carter Lead. *The New York Times,* p. 1.

Bagby, J. W. (1957). A Cross-Cultural Study of Perceptual Predominance in Binocular Rivalry. *Journal of Abnormal and Social Psychology* 54:331–334.

Barnlund, D. C. (1970). A Transactional Model of Communication. In K. K. Sereno and C. D. Mortensen (eds.) *Foundations of Communication Theory,* pp. 83–102. New York: Harper and Row.

Berelson, B., and G. A. Steiner. (1964). *Human Behavior: An Inventory of Scientific Findings*. New York: Harcourt, Brace & World.

Brigham, J. C., and L. W. Giesbrecht. (1976). "All in the Family": Racial Attitudes. *Journal of Communication* 26, no. 4:69–74.

Byrne, D. (1959). The Effect of a Subliminal Food Stimulus on Verbal Responses. *Journal of Applied Psychology* 43:249–252.

Cooper, E., and M. Jahoda. (1947). The Evasion of Propaganda: How Prejudiced People Respond to Anti-Prejudice Propaganda. *Journal of Psychology* 23:15–25.

Cousins, Norman. (Oct. 5, 1957). Smudging the Subconscious. *Saturday Review* 40:20.

Fearing, F. (1970). Toward a Psychological Theory of Human Communication. In K. K. Sereno and C. D. Mortensen (eds.) *Foundations of Communication Theory*, pp. 40–54. New York: Harper and Row.

Garvin, G. (April 14, 1978). Mind Over Muzak? *Austin American-Statesman*, pp. B1–B2.

Gross, L. (Nov. 8, 1975). Do the Bigots Miss the Message? *TV Guide*, pp. 14–16, 18.

Hastorf, A. H., and H. Cantril. (1954). They Saw a Game: A Case Study. *Journal of Abnormal and Social Psychology* 49:129–34.

Jones, E. E., and R. Kohler. (1958). The Effects of Plausibility on the Learning of Controversial Statements. *Journal of Abnormal and Social Psychology* 57:315–320.

Key, W. B. (1972). *Subliminal Seduction: Ad Media's Manipulation of a Not So Innocent America*. Englewood Cliffs, N.J.: Prentice-Hall.

Key, W. B. (1976). *Media Sexploitation*. Englewood Cliffs, N.J.: Prentice-Hall.

Klass, B. (1958). The Ghost of Subliminal Advertising. *Journal of Marketing* 23:146–150.

Kraus, S. (1962). *The Great Debates: Background, Perspective, Effects*. Bloomington: Indiana University Press.

Lazarus, R. S. and R. A. McCleary. (1951). Autonomic Discrimination Without Awareness: A Study of Subception. *Psychological Review* 58:113–122.

Leuba, C., and C. Lucas. (1945). The Effects of Attitudes on Descriptions of Pictures. *Journal of Experimental Psychology* 35:517–524.

Levine, J. M., and G. Murphy. (1958). The Learning and Forgetting of Controversial Material. In E. E. Maccoby, T. M. Newcomb and E. L. Hartley (eds.), *Readings in Social Psychology*, 3rd ed., pp. 94–101. New York: Holt, Rinehart and Winston.

McClelland, D. C., and J. W. Atkinson. (1948). The Projective Expression of Needs: I. The Effect of Different Intensities of the Hunger Drive on Perception. *Journal of Psychology* 25:205–222.

Patterson, T. E., and R. D. McClure. (July, 1976). Political Campaigns: TV Power Is a Myth. *Psychology Today* 10, no. 2:61, 62, 64, 88–90.

Sears, D. O., and J. L. Freedman. (1967). Selective Exposure to Information: A Critical Review. *Public Opinion Quarterly* 31:194–213.

Toch, H., and M. S. MacLean, Jr. (1962). Perception, Communication and Educational Research: A Transactional View. *Audio Visual Communication Review* 10, no. 5:55–77.

Toch, H. H., and R. Schulte. (1961). Readiness to Perceive Violence as a Result of Police Training. *British Journal of Psychology* 52:389–393.

Vidmar, N., and M. Rokeach. (1974). Archie Bunker's Bigotry: A Study in Selective Perception and Exposure. *Journal of Communication* 24, no. 1:36–47.

Wilhoit, G. C., and H. de Bock. (1976). "All in the Family" in Holland. *Journal of Communication* 26, no. 4:75–84.

Wiener, M., and P. H. Schiller. (1960). Subliminal Perception or Perception of Partial Cues. *Journal of Abnormal and Social Psychology* 61:124–137.

Chapter 10

Groups and
Communication

THE Dutch philosopher Baruch Spinoza pointed out 300 years ago that
human beings are social animals. His statement has been strongly reinforced by modern psychology, which has shown that other people have a
great influence on our attitudes, behavior and even our perceptions.

The other people that influence us are found in the groups that we
belong to, whether large or small, formal or informal. These groups can
have a great influence on the way we receive a mass communication message.
This has already been hinted at in the previous chapter, in which we reported
Cooper and Jahoda's suggestion that group membership can make attitudes
of prejudice hard to change. Groups influence people's communication behavior in other ways, as we shall see.

The scientific study of the influence of groups on human behavior began
in the 1930s, primarily with the work of social psychologist Muzafer Sherif.
Solomon Asch, another social psychologist, did some noteworthy work on
group pressures and conformity. Another important name in the study of
groups was Kurt Lewin, the founder of the field known as "Group Dynamics."
The importance of groups in the formation of political attitudes and the
making of voting decisions was brought out in some classic election studies
conducted in the 1940s by sociologist Paul Lazarsfeld and his associates.

Some of the more important types of groups are the following:

A *primary group* is a group (two or more persons) involving long lasting,
intimate, face-to-face association. Examples are a family, a work group, a
team, a fraternity or a military unit.

A *reference group* is a group identified with and used as a standard of

143

reference, but not necessarily belonged to. For instance, a student wishing to belong to a certain fraternity might begin to dress like members and adopt their attitudes even though he is not a member.

A *casual group* is a one-time group of people who didn't know each other before they were brought together. Examples are people riding in an elevator, people riding a bus, or strangers sitting together at a football game.

Sherif's Research on Group Norms

Groups often share certain rules or standards, and these can be referred to as *norms*. Norms operate in almost every area of human behavior. Some everyday examples of areas for the operation of norms are hair style, skirt length, taste in popular music, courtship behavior (such as whether or not to kiss on the first date), style of greeting, form of handshake, and so forth. Some norms are shared by an entire society. Many people may not realize that the norms of their society are somewhat arbitrary until they see that different norms operate in a different culture. In some countries, the evening meal is served much later than it is in the United States. In some countries, it is customary to take a mid-day siesta—not an American habit. Many other differences in food preferences and habits, sexual mores, conversational styles, gestures, clothing choices, and even values show up between cultures. All these things can be thought of as norms.

Sherif (1936, 1937) wanted to study the process of the formation of norms. He found a laboratory situation that was ideal for this purpose. Sherif built his research around a phenomenon known as the *autokinetic light effect*. When a person is seated in a completely darkened room and a tiny stationary point of light is made to appear, the person usually sees the light begin to move. The light appears to move because the nervous system is over-compensating for the dim light, and in doing so it sends the same type of impulses to the brain that are normally sent when the eye is following a moving object (McBurney and Collings, 1977). This gave Sherif a situation that was high in ambiguity and which therefore would work well for the study of norms. Almost everyone sees the light move, but since it really isn't moving, no one can really know how far it moves.

Sherif set up an experimental situation in which a subject was placed in a darkened room with a telegraph key in a convenient place. Five meters away was a device for presenting a point of light. The person was given these instructions: "When the room is completely dark, I shall give you the signal ready, and then show you a point of light. After a short time the light will start to move. As soon as you see it move, press the key. A few seconds later the light will disappear. Then tell me the distance it moved. Try to make your estimates as accurate as possible."

When the subject pressed the key, a timer began ticking off. It ticked for two seconds, and then the light went off.

Sherif first ran this experiment with an individual alone in the room.

After repeated trials, a person usually settles on a norm. The estimates might range between 4 and 6 inches but generally be around 5 inches. Other people would settle on very different norms, however. One person might have a norm of one-half an inch and another might have a norm of two feet.

In the next stage of the experiment, Sherif took several people who had been in the room alone and had established their own norms and put them in the room together. They went through the experiment together and could hear one another giving their estimates. The usual finding in this situation was that as trials were repeated, the different estimates became closer and closer together. Eventually the group adopted a norm of its own, which often would be somewhere around the average of the separate standards of the individuals.

In the third stage of the experiment, Sherif took individuals who had been in the group situation and put them back in the room alone for further trials. In this situation, the individual usually stayed with the norm that he or she had formed previously in the group.

Sherif's experiment shows that in a situation of uncertainty, people are dependent on other people for guidance. It also shows that the influence of the group can extend to situations in which the group is not present. Many norms in society must develop through the process that Sherif has isolated. After all, many situations in life are full of uncertainty. In some of the most important areas of human concern—politics, religion, morality—there is little that is certain. On the basis of Sherif's work, we might expect to find that groups have a great deal of influence on attitudes in these and other ambiguous areas.

Asch's Research on Group Pressure

Sherif's research dealt with groups in a situation with high ambiguity; Asch (1955, 1956) investigated similar forces at work in a situation with little ambiguity. Asch wanted to investigate group pressure and the tendency for people to either conform to the pressure or be independent of it.

Asch set up an experimental situation that appeared to be an investigation of a subject's ability to judge the length of some drawn lines. Subjects were shown two cards. One of them had a single line. The other card had three lines of different lengths labeled 1, 2 and 3. The task for the subject was to call out the number for the one of the three that was the same length as the single line. There were twelve different sets of cards. This is a relatively easy perceptual task that people can do quite well in the absence of group pressure. A control group of 37 included 35 people who made no errors, 1 who made 1 error and 1 who made 2 errors.

Asch was really interested in what happens when group pressure is introduced into the situation. In this phase of the experiment, he had subjects participating in the line judging task in groups of eight. Actually only one of these eight was a true subject, and the others were allies of the experimenter who were instructed to begin giving wrong answers after a couple of trials with correct answers. They all would give the same incorrect answer, so the subject would hear everyone else appear to agree on a single answer, but one that his or her senses indicated was the wrong one. What would a person do in this situation?

The results for 123 subjects (see Table 1) showed 76 per cent of them yielding to the group pressure and giving the wrong answer at least one

Table 1
**Error Rates on 12 Trials for 123 Subjects
in the Asch Experiment**

Error Rate	Number of Subjects	Percentage of Subjects
0 errors	29	24%
1–7 errors	59	49
8–12 errors	35	27
	123	100%

time. In the total number of answers given, the subjects were influenced by group pressure to give the wrong answer in 36.8 per cent of their answers.

Asch modified his experiment in several ways, and came up with additional findings of interest. The size of the group giving the incorrect judgment was varied from 1 to 15. The striking finding here was that a group of three giving a unanimous opinion was essentially as effective in producing conformity to wrong answers as were larger groups.

Asch also investigated the effect of having one other person give the correct answer in addition to the subject. He found that having one supporting partner of this type eliminates much of the power of group pressure. Subjects answered incorrectly only one-fourth as often as they did when confronted with a unanimous majority.

Asch also attempted to make the physical difference in the length of lines so great that no one would still be susceptible to group pressure. He was not able to do this. Even with a difference between the correct and incorrect lines of seven inches, some people still gave in to the group response.

Asch's research gives a striking demonstration that some people will go along with the group even when it means contradicting information derived from their own senses.

Group pressures have also been shown to have strong effects in decision-making in politics and government. Psychologist Bertram H. Raven (Anonymous, Sept. 1, 1974) has described how a particular kind of group pressure called the "risky-shift" led former President Richard Nixon and his aides to questionable actions. The "risky-shift" refers to the tendency for a group to take greater risks than any of its members would endorse individually.

This can happen in a group like the Nixon inner circle, which shared norms of being tough and taking bold positions. Raven points out as an example the meeting in which G. Gordon Liddy presented a plan of using high-paid prostitutes, kidnappings, blackmail and burglaries to help defeat the Democrats. Even though people were apparently shocked at this plan, no one said anything stronger than indicating that it was not exactly what they had in mind.

One further point should be made about the Sherif and Asch studies. Their experiments show group influences having a strong effect even with casual groups, people who had never seen each other before. It seems likely that the power of groups would be even greater when we are dealing with primary groups such as families or work groups.

Lewin's Food Habits Studies

Kurt Lewin made a number of contributions that have been important in the study of communication, including the idea of the gatekeeper, the statement that "there is nothing so practical as a good theory," and the founding of the Group Dynamics movement. Lewin was a brilliant scholar and teacher whose students, including Leon Festinger, Alex Bavelas, Ron Lippitt and Dorwin Cartwright, went on to make additional major contributions to psychology.

During World War II, Lewin participated in a program designed to use communication to get people to change some of their food habits. He became involved in this work through his friendship with anthropologist Margaret Mead. Mead was helping M. L. Wilson, Director of Extension in the U.S. Department of Agriculture. Wilson wanted to apply social science to problems of social change. He appointed Mead to be secretary for the Committee on Food Habits of the National Research Council (Marrow, 1969).

In one group of experiments, Lewin (1958) and his associates were attempting to get housewives as part of the war effort to increase their use of beef hearts, sweetbreads and kidneys—selections of meat not frequently served. Assisted by Bavelas, Lewin set up two experimental conditions—a lecture condition and a group decision condition. In the three groups in the lecture condition, oral presentations were given describing the nutrition, economics and methods of preparation of the unpopular cuts of meat, and mimeographed recipes were handed out. In the three groups in the group decision conditions, people were given some initial information but then a discussion was begun of the problems "housewives like themselves" would face in serving these cuts of meat. Techniques and recipes were offered but only after the groups became sufficiently involved to want to know whether some of the problems could be solved.

At the end of the meeting, the women were asked to indicate with a show of hands who was willing to try one of the cuts of meat in the next week. A follow-up showed that only 3% of the women who heard the lectures served one of the meats they hadn't served before, while 32% of the women in the group decision condition served one of them.

A number of factors were at work in this experiment, including group discussion, public commitment, coming to a decision on future action, and perception of group consensus. A subsequent experiment by Edith Bennett Pelz (1958) indicates that the first two did not have much of an impact and that the latter two alone were sufficient to cause differences as large as those found by Lewin and his associates.

Groups and Political Attitudes

In the 1940s, researchers did some of the first careful studies of how people decide who to vote for in an election. These studies were conducted by Paul Lazarsfeld and his associates at the Bureau of Applied Social Research at Columbia University. They studied voters in Erie County, Pa., during the 1940 election between Roosevelt and Willkie (Lazarsfeld, Berelson and Gaudet, 1968), and voters in Elmira, N.Y., during the 1948 election between Truman and Dewey (Berelson, Lazarsfeld, and McPhee, 1954). Both studies were sample surveys of the panel type, in which the same respondents are interviewed at several points of time.

Both studies made a point of looking at the mass media as important factors in the election decision-making process. Both studies came up with the surprising finding that the mass media played a weak role in election decisions compared with personal influence, or the influence of other people. In fact, it is sometimes said that these studies rediscovered personal influence, a factor communication researchers had tended to overlook as they began to think along the lines of the "Bullet Theory."

These studies showed a strong tendency for people to vote the same

Table 2

Percentage of Respondents Who Intend to Vote Republican Tabulated by the Vote Intentions of Their Three Closest Friends

	Vote Intentions of Their Three Closest Friends			
	Republican *Republican* *Republican*	*Republican* *Republican* *Democrat*	*Republican* *Democrat* *Democrat*	*Democrat* *Democrat* *Democrat*
Percentage of Respondents Who Intend to Vote Republican	88%	74%	48%	15%

Adapted from Berelson, B. R., P. F. Lazarsfeld and W. N. McPhee. (1954). *Voting: A Study of Opinion Formation in a Presidential Campaign.* Chicago: The University of Chicago Press. Copyright 1954 by The University of Chicago. Reprinted by permission.

way the members of their primary groups voted. The family is one of the most important of these primary groups. The influence of the family is indicated by the fact that 75 per cent of the first voters in the Elmira study voted the same way their fathers did. People also tend to vote like their friends and co-workers. Table 2 reports data from the Elmira study which show a strong tendency for people to vote like their three best friends, particularly when the three best friends are unanimous. Table 3 reports additional data from the Elmira study showing a strong tendency for people to vote like their three closest co-workers.

Table 3

Percentage of Respondents Who Intend to Vote Republican Tabulated by the Vote Intentions of Their Three Closest Co-Workers

	Vote Intentions of Their Three Closest Co-Workers			
	Republican *Republican* *Republican*	*Republican* *Republican* *Democrat*	*Republican* *Democrat* *Democrat*	*Democrat* *Democrat* *Democrat*
Percentage of Respondents Who Intend to Vote Republican	86%	75%	53%	19%

Adapted from Berelson, B. R., P. F. Lazarsfeld and W. N. McPhee. (1954). *Voting: A Study of Opinion Formation in a Presidential Campaign.* Chicago: The University of Chicago Press. Copyright 1954 by The University of Chicago. Reprinted by permission.

Berelson, Lazarsfeld and McPhee refer to this strong consistency as the "political homogeneity of the primary group" (p. 88). The findings are strikingly parallel to the Asch research on group pressure, which showed that a unanimous majority of three was sufficient to influence many people's judgments.

This homogeneity of opinion in the political area could be explained by two different processes. One is that the group exerts pressure on and influences the individual's judgment, just as it did in the Asch experiments. The other is that people might select friends whose political attitudes agree with their own. Both of these probably go on to some extent. But the second explanation would not be sufficient alone. People have a great deal of choice in selecting their friends. But they have less choice in selecting their co-workers. And of course they have no choice in selecting their families.

People also belong to certain larger groups just because of their sex, age, race, occupation, religious preference, and so forth. People in these types of very broad groups also tend to vote alike. This is shown in Table 4, based on data from the Elmira study. Just knowledge of two factors—religion and socio-economic status—makes a person's vote predictable with a fairly

Table 4

**Percentage of Respondents Who Voted Republican Tabulated by
Religious Affiliation and Socioeconomic Status**

	High Socioeconomic Status		Middle Socioeconomic Status		Low Socioeconomic Status	
	Prot	Cath	Prot	Cath	Prot	Cath
Percentage of Respondents Who Voted Republican	98	50	83	31	66	31

Adapted from Berelson, B. R., P. F. Lazarsfeld and W. N. McPhee. (1954). *Voting: A Study of Opinion Formation in a Presidential Campaign.* Chicago: The University of Chicago Press. Copyright 1954 by the University of Chicago. Reprinted by permission.

high degree of accuracy. Using several more factors—say five or six—makes a person's vote even more predictable. This tendency of people in certain broad categories to vote alike is also the basis of the election night projections that the television networks use to announce the winners of elections on the basis of as little as 5% of the vote (Skedgell, 1966).

Groups As Instruments of Change

Because of the power of social influence, groups can sometimes be used as agents or instruments of change.

Group structure and group dynamics are very much a part of the process at work in organizations such as Alcoholics Anonymous, Weight Watchers, and some kinds of groups aimed at helping people stop smoking. The principles of group norms and group pressure can often be seen at work in these kinds of efforts. Alcoholics Anonymous, for instance, has a group norm that permits and encourages people to talk about their problems with alcohol. This is a reversal of the norm in the culture at large, which discourages talking about an individual's alcohol problem and almost makes such discussion a taboo. A.A. members also share other norms, such as the willingness to be available to talk to another member any time of night or day. Similar forces are at work in stop-smoking groups, whose members often are encouraged to select a "Quit Day" and publicly announce it to the group. This then generates group pressure for the individual actually to quit on that day and then stick by the decision.

The writings of Alcoholics Anonymous, which describe the 12 steps and the 12 traditions of A.A., bring out the importance of the group as part of the process.

Bill W., one of the founders of A.A., wrote in *The A.A. Way of Life* (Anonymous, 1967):

The moment Twelfth-Step work forms a group, a discovery is made—that most individuals cannot recover unless there is a group. Realization dawns on each member that he is but a small part of a great whole; that no personal sacrifice is too great for preservation of the Fellowship. He learns that the clamor of desires and ambitions within him must be silenced whenever these could damage the group.

It becomes plain that the group must survive or the individual will not (p. 9).

Bill W.'s belief that the group was more important than the individual was once put to a severe test—he was offered the chance to have his picture on the cover of *Time* magazine as the co-founder of Alcoholics Anonymous. He thought about it a while and turned it down.

Group dynamics can also be applied to fund drives, such as the United Way or United Appeal. DeFleur and Ball-Rokeach (1975) have described the way this process often works. First a quota is set for the community as a whole. This quota is sometimes displayed in the middle of town on a big thermometer, so everyone can see it. This quota is in fact somewhat arbitrary, being set by the fund drive organizers, but it begins to take on the appearance of a community norm. This approach is carried further by distributing pledge cards to individuals which indicate the "fair share" that they are supposed to pay for the community to meet the quota. This is a tactic of group pressure, in that the individual is made to feel that he or she will be letting down others if a donation isn't made. Personal influence is also brought into the process. Often the pledge cards are distributed and collected by an important co-worker, such as the boss's secretary. Some of these fund drives also use door to door collections, in which the person doing the collecting is a neighbor or a person living on the same block—an effective use of social influence.

Groups and Mass Communication

The importance of group influence has been well understood by many people involved in mass communication. Father Coughlin, the "Radio Priest" who was such a skillful user of propaganda, used to ask his audience to listen to him in groups. He would also begin his broadcasts with music, and tell audience members to take that time to call a friend and ask the person to listen to the program.

Many advertisements and commercials attempt to incorporate some form of group influence. For instance, a television commercial for a dye for gray hair makes the statement, "I bet a lot of your friends are using it and you don't even know it." Basically, this type of commercial is using the old propaganda device of "Band Wagon."

In politics, the mass media campaigns are often supplemented by various types of interpersonal communication, including door to door visits, telephone calls and neighborhood coffees.

CONCLUSIONS

Groups have impact on mass communication in a number of ways:

1. Groups serve to anchor attitudes and make them hard to change. This was suggested by the Cooper and Jahoda study of the Mr. Biggott cartoons and also documented in the area of politics by the election studies of Lazarsfeld and his associates.
2. Knowledge of the groups that a person belongs to or identifies with can often help us predict the person's behavior. This is particularly true in the area of political preferences, where knowledge of five or six broad group categorizations about a person will often give a high degree of accuracy in predicting an election vote.
3. Effective programs of communication often involve a combination of mass communication and interpersonal communication. This is true of many of the well-organized charity fund drives and many election campaigns. There is also some evidence that it is an effective approach in health education (Maccoby and Farquhar, 1975, 1976).
4. Sometimes ways can be found to obtain some of the advantages of interpersonal communication *through* mass communication. Television programs in which a candidate answers questions telephoned in by viewers would be an example. So would President Jimmy Carter's citizens press conferences, in which he answered questions phoned in by citizens over a national radio broadcast. Some of the same advantages can be obtained by having a panel of typical citizens in the studio to question a political candidate in a kind of "town meeting" format.

REFERENCES

Anonymous. (1967). *The A.A. Way of Life: A Reader by Bill.* New York: Alcoholics Anonymous World Services, Inc.

Anonymous. (Sept. 1, 1974). Group Pressure Led Nixon Aides Astray. *Austin American-Statesman,* p. A12.

Asch, S. E. (November, 1955). Opinions and Social Pressure. *Scientific American* 193, no. 5:31–35.

Asch, S. E. (1956). Studies of Independence and Conformity: I. A Minority of One Against a Unanimous Majority. *Psychological Monographs* 70, no. 9:1–70.

Berelson, B. R., P. F. Lazarsfeld and W. N. McPhee. (1954). *Voting: A Study of Opinion Formation in a Presidential Campaign.* Chicago: The University of Chicago Press.

DeFleur, M., and S. Ball-Rokeach. (1975). *Theories of Mass Communication,* 3rd ed. New York: David McKay.

Lazarsfeld, P. F., B. Berelson and H. Gaudet. (1968). *The People's Choice: How the Voter Makes Up His Mind in a Presidential Campaign,* 3rd ed. New York: Columbia University Press.

Lewin, K. (1958). Group Decision and Social Change. In E. E. Maccoby, T. M. Newcomb and E. L. Hartley (eds.), *Readings in Social Psychology,* 3rd ed., pp. 197–211. New York: Holt, Rinehart and Winston.

Maccoby, N., and J. W. Farquhar. (1975). Communicating for Health: Unselling Heart Disease. *Journal of Communication* 25, no. 3:114–126.

Maccoby, N., and J. W. Farquhar. (1976). Bringing the California Health Report Up to Date. *Journal of Communication* 26, no. 1:56–57.

Marrow, A. J. (1977). *The Practical Theorist: The Life and Work of Kurt Lewin.* New York: Teachers College Press.

McBurney, D. H., and V. B. Collings. (1977). *Introduction to Sensation/Perception.* Englewood Cliffs, N. J.: Prentice-Hall.

Pelz, E. B. (1958). Some Factors in "Group Decision." In E. E. Maccoby, T. M. Newcomb and E. L. Hartley (eds.), *Readings in Social Psychology,* 3rd ed., pp. 212–219. New York: Holt, Rinehart and Winston.

Sherif, M. (1936). *The Psychology of Social Norms.* New York: Harper & Brothers.

Sherif, M. (1937). An Experimental Approach to the Study of Attitudes. *Sociometry* 1:90–98.

Skedgell, R. A. (1966). How Computers Pick An Election Winner. *Trans-action* 4, no. 1:42–46.

Chapter 11

Cognitive Consistency and Mass Communication

THE general notion of consistency underlies all of science. It is the notion that phenomena are ordered (or consistent) which allows predictability. Predictability, in turn, allows the scientist to formulate and test hypotheses, make generalizations from them, build theory and predict future outcomes. The purpose of the communication researcher and theorist is, to a great measure, to predict the effect or future outcomes of messages.

The concept of consistency in human behavior is an extension of the general notion from the physical world to the area of human behavior. Various theorists contend that humans strive for consistency in a number of ways— between attitudes, between behaviors, between attitudes and behaviors, in our perception of the world, and even in the development of personality. In short, we try to organize our world in ways which seem to us to be meaningful and sensible.

The concepts of human consistency are based upon the notion that human beings act in rational ways. However, we also have a term, rationalization— the attempt by humans to explain in a rational or consistent way their irrational behavior. Rationalization emphasizes that in our attempts to appear rational or consistent to ourselves we often employ means which may seem to others to be irrational or inconsistent.

The notions of consistency assume that inconsistency generates "psychological tension" or discomfort within human beings, which results in internal pressure to eliminate or reduce the inconsistency, and, if possible, achieve consistency.

Examples of the consistency principles in everyday affairs are widespread.

Defenders of our involvement in Vietnam are often forced to resort to a number of psychological mechanisms to reduce inconsistency when they are confronted with the information that as early as 1966 the former Commandant of the U.S. Marine Corps and former chairman of the Joint Chiefs of Staff spoke out strongly against our Vietnam involvement (Shoup, 1966).

Students at a large Southern university which is widely referred to by its alumni and students as *The* University resort to many of the same defensive psychological mechanisms when confronted with the information that in a nationwide poll of deans and directors of professional schools (e.g., law, architecture, business, communication, engineering, etc.) not one professional school at that large Southern campus was ranked among the top ten in its field in the nation (*The National Observer,* Feb. 1, 1975).

A university board of regents rejects a three-semester appointment as a visiting professor and the gift of a collection of personal papers of an individual who was a high-ranking official in Marshall Tito's Communist government. This rejection comes after the appointment was approved by the departments of history and comparative studies and by the university provost (*New York Times,* 1971).

A first-ranked football team in an area where football reigns supreme suffers a humiliating defeat at the hands of a long standing rival and the following day both the media and individual conversations are filled with rationalizations and justifications.

As noted, the consistency theories recognize human attempts at rationality but in the ways in which we achieve it we often display striking irrationality. The concept of rationalization assumes both rationality and irrationality— we often use irrational means to achieve understanding or to justify painful experiences.

Mass communication research is concerned, in part, with how individuals deal with discrepant or inconsistent information, which is often presented with the purpose of bringing about attitude change. This attitude change is one of the many ways in which we can reduce or eliminate the discomfort or psychological pressure of inconsistency.

While there are a number of consistency theories of interest to behavioral researchers (Kiesler, *et al.,* 1969; Abelson, et al., 1968) for the purposes of this book only four major ones will be discussed.

Heider's Balance Theory

Most writers usually credit Heider with the earliest articulation of a consistency theory although the informal concept can be traced back to earlier work (c.f., Kiesler, *et al.,* p. 157). As a psychologist, Heider was concerned with the way an individual organizes attitudes toward people and objects in relation to one another within his or her own cognitive structure. Heider postulated that unbalanced states produce tension and generate forces to restore balance. He says "the concept of a balanced state designates a situation in which the perceived units and the experienced sentiments co-exist without stress" (Heider, 1958, p. 176).

Heider's paradigm focused upon two individuals, a person (P), the object of the analysis, some other person (O), and a physical object, idea or event (X). Heider's concern was with how relationships between these three entities are organized in the mind of one individual (P). Heider distinguished two types of relationships between these three entities, liking (L) and unit (U) relations (such as cause, possession, similarity, etc.). In Heider's paradigm, "a balanced state exists if all three relations are positive in all respects or if two are negative and one is positive." All other combinations are unbalanced.

Figure 1

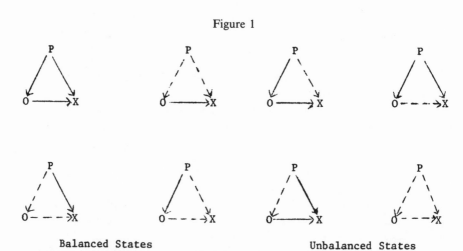

Balanced States   Unbalanced States

Examples of balanced and unbalanced states according to *Heider's* definition of balance. Solid lines represent positive, and broken lines negative relations.

From Zajonc, R. B. (1960). The concepts of balance, congruity and dissonance. *Public Opinion Quarterly* 24:280–96. Reprinted with permission.

In Heider's conception degrees of liking cannot be represented; a relation is either positive or negative. It is assumed that a balanced state is stable and resists outside influences. An unbalanced state is assumed to be unstable and is assumed to produce psychological tension within an individual. This tension "becomes relieved only when change within the situation takes place in such a way that a state of balance is achieved" (Heider, 1958, p. 180). This pinpoints the communicator's interest in the theory for it implies a model of attitude change and resistance to change. Unbalanced states, being unstable states, are susceptible to change toward balance. Balanced states, being stable states, resist change. Data supporting Heider's Balance Theory are discussed in Zajonc (1960); Kiesler, *et al.* (1969) and Abelson, *et al.* (1968).

Newcomb's Symmetry Theory

Social psychologist Theodore M. Newcomb took Heider's idea of balance out of the head of one person and applied it to communication between people. He uses the term "symmetry" to distinguish it from Balance Theory and contends that we attempt to influence one another to bring about symmetry (or balance or equilibrium). As discussed in some detail in Chapter 3, Newcomb postulates that attempts to influence another person are a function of the attraction one person has for another. In this respect Newcomb's theory is more of a theory of interpersonal attraction than one of attitude change. If we fail to achieve symmetry through communication with another person about an object important to both of us we may then change our attitude toward either the other person or the object in question in order to establish symmetry.

Because Newcomb's model (see Chapter 3, Figure 4) deals with two people and the communication between them, he labels them A and B (rather than Heider's P and O) and retains X to represent the object of their attitudes. As with Heider, he assumes a human need for consistency which he calls a "persistent strain toward symmetry." If A and B disagree about X, the amount of this strain toward symmetry will depend upon the intensity of A's attitude toward X and upon A's attraction to B. An increase in A's attraction for B and an increase in A's intensity of attitude for X will result in: 1) an increased strain toward symmetry on the part of A toward B about their attitudes toward X; 2) the likelihood that symmetry will be achieved; and 3) the probability of a communication by A and B about X. The last item, of course, is the focus of our concern.

Newcomb says, "the likelihood of a symmetry—directed A to B re X varies as a multiple function of the perceived discrepancy (i.e., inversely with perceived symmetry), with valence toward B and with valence toward X" (Newcomb, 1953, p. 398).

Newcomb, in contrast to Heider, stresses communication. The less the symmetry between A and B about X, the more probable that A will communicate with B regarding X. Symmetry predicts that people associate with or become friends of people with whom they agree ("Birds of a feather flock together.").

However, for attitude change to take place a person must come into contact with information which differs from his or her present attitudes. Newcomb's Symmetry Model predicts that the more A is attracted to B (a person or a group), the greater the opinion change on the part of A toward the position of B.

Osgood and Tannenbaum's Congruity Theory

The Congruity model is a special case of Heider's Balance Theory. While it is similar to Balance Theory, it deals specifically with the attitudes persons hold toward sources of information and the objects of the source's assertions. Congruity theory has several advantages over Balance Theory including the ability to make predictions about both the direction and the degree of attitude change. The Congruity model assumes that "judgmental frames of reference tend toward maximal simplicity." Because extreme judgments are easier to make than refined ones (c.f. Chapter 5, either-or thinking and two valued evaluation) valuations tend to move toward the extremes, or, there is "a continuing pressure toward polarization." In addition to this maximization of simplicity the assumption is also made that identity is less complex than the discrimination of fine differences (see Chapter 5 on either-or thinking and categorization). Because of this, related "concepts" are evaluated in a similar manner.

In the congruity paradigm a person (P) receives an assertion from a source (S) toward which he has an attitude about an object (O) toward which he also has an attitude. In Osgood's model how much P likes S and O will determine if a state of congruity or consistency exists.

Figure 2

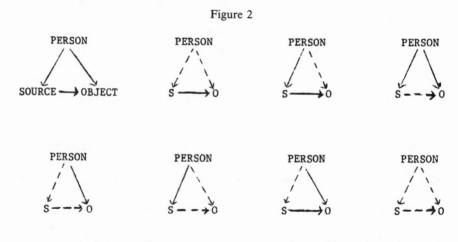

CONGRUITY   INCONGRUITY

Examples of congruity and incongruity. Heavy lines represent assertions, light lines attitudes. Solid heavy lines represent assertions which imply a positive attitude on the part of the source, and broken heavy lines negative attitudes. Solid light lines represent positive, and broken light lines negative attitudes.

From Zajonc, R. B. (1960). The concepts of balance, congruity and dissonance. *Public Opinion Quarterly* 24:280–96. Reprinted with permission.

According to Congruity Theory, when a change occurs it is always toward greater congruity with prevailing frames of reference. Osgood uses his Semantic Differential (Chapter 7) to measure the amount of liking a person may have for a source and the object of an assertion.

In essence the definitions of balance and congruity are identical. Incongruity exists when the attitudes toward the source and the object are similar and the assertion is negative, or when they are dissimilar and the assertion is positive. An unbalanced state has either one or all negative relations.

Tannenbaum had 405 college students evaluate three sources, labor leaders, the Chicago Tribune and Senator Robert Taft and three objects, gambling, abstract art and accelerated college programs. Some time later the students were presented with newspaper clippings which contained assertions attributed to the sources about the objects. The entire range of predicted changes was supported by Tannenbaum's data, as summarized on the following page. The direction of change is indicated by either a plus or minus sign, while the extent of change is indicated by one or two such signs.

A graphic example of this phenomena in the media world occurred when Walter Cronkite and CBS news covered the Democratic convention in Chicago in August 1968. CBS news reported at the same time what the Walker Commission later called a "police riot" on the streets of Chicago. Walter Cronkite expressed the opinion on the air that the convention floor seemed to be in the control of a "bunch of thugs" after Dan Rather was floored while "on camera" when attempting to interview delegates from a Southern state being removed from the convention floor. CBS news (the source) had made negative assertions about objects (Mayor Richard Daley and the Chicago police) which apparently were held in high esteem by many persons in the television audience. Feedback to CBS news expressed considerable dissatisfaction on the part of audience members with the news coverage. Presumably their attitude toward the source became more negative. If, in a democracy, we cannot behead the messenger who brings unpleasant news as supposedly was the case in ancient Persia, then congruity theory predicts that we can come to dislike the bearer of information which does not agree with our view of the world. We have incorporated this into the folk saying, "Don't confuse me with the facts, I have already made up my mind."

Incongruity does not always produce attitude change. There is some basis for the belief that much material in the media which would produce incongruity in an individual never does so. In the process of selecting what we will pay attention to we may well avoid those messages which we suspect will not agree with our concept of the world. This is selective exposure or selective attention, on which the findings are as yet inconclusive (see Chapter 9).

If we do receive a message which causes incongruity we may misperceive the message (selective perception) and make it fit our view of reality. If we are unable to misperceive the message we may attack the credibility of the communicator. Students confronted with the national rankings of professional schools (cited earlier in this chapter) often counter by asking if the deans and directors of professional schools at Southern universities were included in the survey—implying bias in the survey to attack the credibility of the findings.

Denial or incredulity is another means of dealing with incongruity. Many

Table 1

Change of Attitude Toward the Source and the Object When Positive and Negative Assertions Are Made by the Source

Original Attitude toward the source	Positive Assertion about an object toward which the attitude is		Negative Assertion about an Object toward which the Attitude is	
	Positive	Negative	Positive	Negative
CHANGE OF ATTITUDE TOWARD THE SOURCE				
Positive	+	- -	- -	+
Negative	+ +	-	-	+ +
CHANGE OF ATTITUDE TOWARD THE OBJECT				
Positive	+	+ +	- -	- -
Negative	- -	-	+	+ +

From Zajonc, R. B. (1960). The concepts of balance, congruity and dissonance. *Public Opinion Quarterly*, 24:280–96. Reprinted with permission of the publisher.

individuals simply do not believe that a former Marine Corps Commandment, holder of the Congressional Medal of Honor and former Chairman of the Joint Chiefs of Staff, made strong public statements against our Vietnam intervention as early as 1966, even when copies of the Congressional Record in which those remarks were reprinted at the time are shown to them.

If, indeed, an incongruous message does reach an individual there is still no guarantee of attitude change. Selective retention (see Chapter 9) may enter the picture and we may well remember only that which supports our "prevailing frame of reference."

The communicator who believes that reaching the intended audience member with material designed to change attitudes is sufficient to guarantee change in laboring under the assumption that the "bullet" or "hypodermic" approach is valid. (See Chapters 8 and 17). By ignoring the "phenomenistic" approach (where a great many factors interact with the media to bring about an effect), the communicator risks repeated disappointment.

Festinger's Theory of Cognitive Dissonance

The most general of all the consistency theories and, as one might expect, the one which has generated the largest body of empirical data, is Leon Festinger's theory of Cognitive Dissonance. It is also a theory which has generated considerable controversy in the field of social psychology.

Dissonance theory holds that two elements of knowledge ". . . are in dissonant relation if, considering these two alone, the obverse of one element would follow from the other." (Festinger, 1957, p. 13). As with other consistency theories it holds that dissonance ". . . being psychologically uncomfortable, will motivate the person to try to reduce dissonance and achieve consonance" and ". . . in addition to trying to reduce it the person will actively avoid situations and information which would likely increase the dissonance." (Festinger, 1957, p. 3).

In Cognitive Dissonance the elements in question may be: 1) irrelevant to one another; 2) consistent with one another (or in Festinger's terms consonant); or 3) they may be inconsistent with one another (or dissonant in Festinger's terms). Relationships need not be logically related for consistency or inconsistency.

A relationship may be logically inconsistent to an observer while psychologically consistent to an individual who holds these obverse beliefs. In the earlier example of the university board of regents' refusal of a visiting professorship for a former high government official from a Communist country the decision was probably logically inconsistent with what most people would regard as the duty of a University to deal openly with all ideas. However, since the individual was obviously a staunch Communist, the refusal was probably psychologically consistent with the beliefs of a majority of the board of regents and perhaps many of their constituency.

Several rather interesting consequences follow from dissonance theory especially in the areas of decision making and role playing. The focus of this book is on how people use information and dissonance theory is important in that respect.

Decision Making

Upon making a decision, dissonance is predicted to follow to the extent that the rejected alternative contains features which would have resulted in its acceptance and that the chosen alternative contains features which could have caused its rejection. In other words, the more difficult a decision is to make, the greater the predicted dissonance is after the decision (post-decision dissonance). It also follows that the post-decision dissonance is greater for more important decisions. A number of studies report evidence to support these hypotheses.

One researcher reports that purchasers of new cars were more apt to notice and read ads about the cars they had just bought than other cars (Ehrlich, *et al.,* 1957). Since ads are supposed to stress "benefits" of the products they promote, presumably the new car buyers were seeking reinforcement for their decisions by reading ads for the cars they had just purchased.

Evidence has also been cited for a change in the attractiveness of alternatives once a decision has been made. In other words, after a decision has been made between alternatives which are ranked as nearly equal in desirability the chosen alternative is later seen as more desirable than it had been before the decision while the rejected alternative is ranked as less desirable than it was before the decision was made (Brehm, 1956). The authors of one book on attitude change state, "The postdecision process involves cognitive change not unlike that of attitude change; indeed the effects of this process may legitimately be referred to as attitude change." (Kiesler, *et al.,* 1969, p. 205)

Forced Compliance

An interesting area, even if not directly related to the mass media, is attitude change following forced compliance. Dissonance theory postulates that when an individual is placed in a situation where he or she must behave publicly in a way which is contrary to that individual's privately held beliefs or attitudes the individuals experiences dissonance from knowledge of that fact. Such situations often occur as the result of a promise of a reward or the threat of punishment, but sometimes it may be simply as the result of group pressure to conform to a norm an individual does not privately agree with. Role playing is one such example.

If a person performs a public act which is inconsistent with his or her beliefs, it is predicted that dissonance will follow. One way of resolving this dissonance is to change the privately held beliefs to conform with the public act. The least amount of pressure necessary (promise of reward or threat of punishment) to induce an individual to act publicly in a way contrary to his or her privately held beliefs will result in the greatest dissonance. The greater the dissonance, the greater the pressure to reduce it, hence the greater the chance for attitude change in the direction of the public act or behavior. In the case of a relatively large promised reward or threatened punishment the individual can always rationalize his or her public behavior which was contrary to the privately held beliefs or attitudes (e.g., "I did it for the money." or, "Anybody would do the same under such a threat.").

Dissonance theory is of greatest interest to us in the areas of information seeking and avoidance. The theory predicts that individuals will avoid dissonance producing information. In a summary of research in this area, two authors conclude, ". . . while subjects sought out dissonance-reducing information, they did not necessarily avoid dissonance-increasing information." (Brehm and Cohen, 1962, p. 93). Some researchers and theorists contend that individuals seeking novelty will not necessarily avoid dissonance producing information and that perceived utility of information (e.g., the learning of "implausible" counter-arguments to one's position cited in Chapter 9) may impel an individual to pay attention to dissonance producing information. For two differing positions on this issue see Freedman and Sears (1966) who conclude people do not avoid dissonant information and Mills (1968) who argues that under some circumstances they do. Both are included in Abelson, *et al.* (1968) which provides an extended, in-depth treatment of consistency theories.

CONCLUSIONS

As should be obvious by now, consistency theories have many implications for how humans perceive the world, communicate and use, distort, ignore or forget the contents of the mass media. In their generality and scope they apply to both media practitioners and media consumers—from the reporter at the scene of the news or the producer of an advertisement to the final destination of the message.

REFERENCES

Abelson, R. P., E. Aronson, W. J. McGuire, T. M. Newcomb, M. H. Rosenberg and P. H. Tannenbaum (eds.), (1968), *Theories of cognitive consistency: a sourcebook.* Skokie, Ill.: Rand-McNally.

Brehm, J. W. (1956) Post-Decision changes in the desirability of alternatives. *Journal of Abnormal and Social Psychology* 52:384–9.

Brehm, J. W. and A. R. Cohen (1962) *Explorations in Cognitive Dissonance.* New York: John Wiley and Sons.

Ehrlich, D., I. Guttman, P. Schonbach and J. Mills (1957) Post-decision exposure to relevant information. *Journal of Abnormal and Social Psychology,* 54:98–102.

Festinger, L. A. (1957) *A theory of cognitive dissonance.* Stanford, Calif.: Stanford University Press.

Freedman, J. L., and D. Sears. (1966) Selective exposure. In L. Berkowitz (Ed.), *Advances in experimental social psychology.* New York: Academic Press, 1966.

Heider, F. (1958) *The psychology of interpersonal relations.* New York: John Wiley and Sons.

Kiesler, C. A., B. E. Collins, and N. Miller (1969). *Attitude change.* New York: John Wiley & Sons.

Mills, J. (1968) Interest in supporting and discrepant information. In Abelson, et al. (eds.), *Theories of cognitive consistency: a sourcebook.* Skokie, Ill.: Rand-McNally.

The National Observer (February 1, 1975) Ranking universities, p. 9.

Newcomb, T. M. (1953) An approach to the study of communicative acts. *Psychological Review,* 60:393–404.

New York Times (June 20, 1971) U. of Texas Bars Former Tito Aide. p. 19.

Osgood, C. E. and P. H. Tannenbaum (1955). The principle of congruity in the prediction of attitude change. *Psychological Review,* 62:42–55.

Shoup, D. M. (1966) Former Marine Commandment Questions Vietnam. In *Congressional Record—Senate* (February 20, 1967) p. S2279–82.

Zajonc, R. B. (1960) The concepts of balance, congruity and dissonance. *Public Opinion Quarterly,* 24:280–96

Chapter 12

Beginnings of Attitude Change Research

PERSUASION is only one type of mass communication, but it is a type in which many people are interested. The advertiser using mass communication to sell soft drinks, headache remedies or automobiles is engaged in persuasion. So is the oil company that hires public relations experts to convince the public that it is not making excessive profits. So are the political candidate who buys newspaper ads, the public health organization that prepares radio spots designed to make people stop smoking, and the religious group that puts evangelical messages on television. All of these people are attempting to use mass communication messages to produce some kind of behavior change in other people.

Persuasion has probably always been a part of human life. It seems inevitable that people will try to influence other people, even their closest friends and family members. For centuries, people must have operated on the basis of intuition and common sense in their attempts to persuade. Aristotle was one of the first to try to analyze and write about persuasion, in his works on rhetoric. Years later, particularly when mass communication became more widespread, people began to study persuasion even more systematically. The Institute for Propaganda Analysis, with its identification of seven techniques of propaganda, was doing some of this early work. Part of the motive for this more careful study of persuasion was obviously fear—the war-inspired fear that propaganda could win the hearts and minds of people. The Institute was operating in that panicky period just before World War II. A few years later, the same war was to produce the first careful scientific studies of persuasion, or attitude change, as it became known. This work was done by a psychologist named Carl Hovland and his associates, all of whom were working for the Research Branch of the U.S. Army's Information and Educational Division. This work was so original and influential that it has been called "the most important fountainhead of contemporary research on attitude change" (Insko, 1967, p. 1). The Hovland work was based on controlled experiments in which variables were carefully manipulated in order to observe their effects.

Some earlier work on attitude change was done before Hovland, but it was rather poorly done. A study sometimes cited as the first attitude change study was an investigation by Rice and Willey of the effects of William Jennings Bryan's address on evolution at Dartmouth College in 1923 (described in Chen, 1933). A group of 175 students indicated their acceptance or rejection of evolution on a five-point scale. The students were asked to give their attitudes after hearing the speech, and, from retrospection, their attitudes before hearing the speech. They found that more than one-quarter of the students showed substantial change in attitude, but the use of the retrospective report makes the finding highly questionable.

The Concept of Attitude

The concept of attitude has been described by psychologist Gordon Allport (1954) as "probably the most distinctive and indispensable in contemporary American social psychology" (p. 43). Allport points out that the term came to replace in psychology such vague terms as *instinct, custom, social force,* and *sentiment.*

A number of investigators agree that the concept of attitude was first used in a scientific way in 1918 in a study by Thomas and Znaniecki (1927). They defined the concept this way: "By attitude we understand a process of individual consciousness which determines real or possible activity of the individual in the social world" (p. 22). This is not too different from more recent definitions, although the word "consciousness" is one that contemporary researchers would avoid.

The following are some more recent definitions of attitude:

"Attitude is primarily a way of being 'set' toward or against certain things." (Murphy, Murphy and Newcomb, 1937, p. 889).

"A mental and neural state of readiness, organized through experience, exerting a directive or dynamic influence upon the individuals' response to all objects and situations with which it is related." (Allport, 1954, p. 45)

"An enduring, learned predisposition to behave in a consistent way toward a given class of objects." (English and English, 1958, p. 50)

"An enduring system of positive or negative evaluations, emotional feelings and pro or con action tendencies with respect to a social object." (Krech, Crutchfield and Ballachey, 1962, p. 177)

Some other scholars, such as Rosenberg and Hovland (1960), have suggested that an attitude has three components: an affective component (evaluation of something or feeling toward something), a cognitive component (perceptual responses or verbal statements of belief) and a behavioral component (overt actions). This approach is logical, since most of us would agree that an attitude can manifest itself in several different ways. However, this approach may be unnecessarily complicated, and it may be blurring the distinction between attitude and behavior in an unfortunate way. Other scholars say it is best to restrict attitude to the affective component and leave the relationship between attitude and behavior open for investigation through research.

Part of the problem in defining attitude is that it is basically an internal state, and thus not available for direct observation. This leads to some obvious difficulties in measuring attitudes, and in being sure that your measure, once you have developed it, is a meaningful one.

The problem of defining attitude has shown up again recently in the question of the relationship between attitude and behavior. That is a problem we will take up in the next chapter, after we have discussed Carl Hovland's pioneering work on attitude change.

Hovland's Army Work

During World War II, the U.S. Army began using films and other forms of mass communication on an unprecedented scale. Most of this material was used in the training and motivation of U.S. soldiers. The Experimental Section of the Research Branch of the War Department's Information and Education Division was given the task of evaluating the effectiveness of these materials. This Section was directed by Carl Hovland and was made up mostly of psychologists, including Irving Janis, Nathan Maccoby, Arthur A. Lumsdaine and Fred D. Sheffield. Other prominent names in psychology were also involved. Samuel Stouffer was civilian head of the Research Branch professional staff, and Lt. Col. Charles Dollard was one of the officers in charge of the Branch. This bringing together of some of the brightest people in psychology in a large scale program is recognized as the beginning of modern attitude change research, and as the source of some of the major contributions to mass communication theory.

Hovland's background in psychology was learning theory. He had studied with one of the major figures in that field, Clark Hull (who had also been a teacher of Charles Osgood's). This had a considerable influence on Hovland's approach to attitude change research, and his is sometimes referred to as a "learning theory" approach. This is most clearly shown in Hovland's thinking of an attitude as a learned habit. But it also shows up in the importance attached to motivation, intellectual ability, incentive and reward, and variables such as attention, comprehension and retention.

Much of the research of the Experimental Section is reported in the volume *Experiments on Mass Communication,* first published in 1949 (Hovland, Lumsdaine and Sheffield, 1965). The Section did two basic types of research; evaluation studies of existing films, and experimental studies in which two different versions of the same film (or message) were compared. The section had to do much of the first type of research because it suited the practical purposes of the Army. However, it soon became apparent that the second type of research was more useful from a scientific point of view because it led to generalizations. It was these experimental studies in which certain variables were manipulated that really constituted the beginning of attitude change research. The evaluation studies of existing films also made some interesting contributions to communication theory, however.

One of the first tasks the Section took on was to evaluate the first four films of the "Why We Fight" series. This series was produced by Frank Capra, the famous Hollywood director who had made *It Happened One Night* (1934) and *Mr. Deeds Goes to Town* (1936) and who would go on to make *It's a Wonderful Life* (1946). The "Why We Fight" films were essentially indoctrination films to be used in orientation of American soldiers. They were based on the assumptions that many draftees did not know the national and international events that led to America's entrance in World War II, and that a knowledge of these events would lead men to more easily accept their transition from civilian life to that of a soldier.

One of the films studied in great detail was "The Battle of Britain," a 50-minute film that had the purpose of instilling greater confidence in America's British allies. Hovland and his associates designed research to determine the film's effects in three main areas: specific factual knowledge gained from the film, specific opinions on the Battle of Britain and acceptance of the military role and willingness to fight. The research procedure was simply to have an experimental group which saw the film and a control group which did not, and then one week later to give both groups a questionnaire that appeared unrelated but which measured knowledge and opinions on subjects related to the film. These Army studies were conducted with "captive" audiences of subjects and therefore ended up with large sample sizes—the "Battle of Britain" study involved 2,100 people.

The results showed the film was quite effective in conveying factual information about the air war over Britain in 1940, that it was somewhat effective in changing specific opinions about the conduct of the air war, and that it had essentially no effect at all on motivation to serve or building increased resentment of the enemy. Thus the film failed in its ultimate objective—increasing soldiers' motivations. Similar results showed up for the other "Why We Fight" films studied.

This research on the "Why We Fight" series became part of the growing body of evidence indicating that a single mass communication message is unlikely to change strongly held attitudes. Similar evidence comes from other studies as different as the Cooper and Jahoda investigation of anti-prejudice cartoons and the research by Lazarsfeld and his associates on political campaigns.

The research on the "Battle of Britain" produced another interesting result. In one study, subjects were tested for opinion change five days after seeing the film and then again nine weeks later. On some opinion items, there was a greater amount of opinion change after nine weeks than there had been after five days. The authors called this a "sleeper" effect. They suggested a number of possible explanations for it, none of which they were really able to test. One was that the source for the items that showed the sleeper effect might have been one that was regarded as untrustworthy, but that this source could have been forgotten after the passage of time.

One-Sided and Two-Sided Messages

Hovland and his associates turned to the second type of research, in which the same message is produced in two versions that differ in only one variable, in an experiment on the effectiveness of one-sided and two-sided messages. On many issues, there are arguments on both sides. Which is the better strategy—to mention only the arguments on the side you are trying to present, or to mention the arguments on both sides but focus on the ones on the side you are trying to present? This is essentially the old question of the effectiveness of Card Stacking, one of the propaganda devices identified by the Institute for Propaganda Analysis.

Hovland and his associates were trying to answer this question because they faced a real communication problem. After the defeat of Germany in 1945, many soldiers apparently felt the war was almost over. The Army wanted to get across the idea that there was still a tough job ahead in defeating the Japanese.

The researchers realized that there were arguments for each strategy. A one-sided presentation can be defended on the basis that a two-sided presentation raises doubts in the minds of people unfamiliar with the opposing arguments. A two-sided presentation can be defended on the basis that it is more fair and that it will help prevent people who are opposed to a message from rehearsing counterarguments while being exposed to the message. A specific purpose of the study was to measure the effectiveness of the two kinds of message presentation on two kinds of audience members—those initially opposed to the message and those initially sympathetic to the message.

Two versions of a radio message were prepared. Both presented the general argument that the war would take at least two more years. The one-sided message was 15 minutes long and brought out arguments such as the size of the Japanese army, the determination of the Japanese people, and so forth. The two-sided message was 19 minutes long and brought out arguments on the other side, such as the advantage of fighting only one enemy, but it focused mostly on the arguments that the war would be a long one.

One week before the presentation of the radio message, subjects were given a preliminary questionnaire in which they expressed their estimates of how long the war in the Pacific would take. Then one group made up of eight platoons heard the one-sided message, a second group of eight platoons heard the two-sided message, and a third group heard neither message and served as a control group. Then all three groups received another questionnaire differing from the first one in its form and its announced purpose, but again asking for an estimate of how long the war in the Pacific would take. All questionnaires were anonymous, but the before and after questionnaires for the same person could be matched on the basis of the answers to questions about date of birth, schooling, etc.

Looked at in general for all groups (see Table 1), the results indicated that both kinds of presentations produced clear opinion change in comparison

Table 1

**Results of Experiment on One-Sided and Two-Sided Messages
Showing Percentages Who Estimated a War
of More than 1 1/2 Years**

	Group 1 (8 platoons)	Group 2 (8 platoons)	Control Group (8 platoons)
Preliminary Survey	37%	38%	36%
Exposure to Message	1-sided	2-sided	none
Follow-Up Survey	59%	59%	34%

From *Experiments on Mass Communication,* by Carl I. Hovland et al., Vol. III *Studies in Social Psychology in World War II* (copyright 1949 © 1977 by Princeton University Press) sponsored by Social Science Research Council: Table 1, p. 210. Reprinted by permission of Princeton University Press.

with the control group, but that neither presentation was more effective than the other. The researchers had anticipated that the two-sided presentation might work better with an audience initially opposed to the message, however, and so they proceeded to check out this possibility. They did this by dividing each test group into those subjects initially opposed to the message and those initially favorable to the message. The men who had given initial estimates that the war would take 1½ years or less were considered to be initially opposed to the message, while those who gave initial estimates of more than 1½ years were considered to be initially favorable to the message. Results of this analysis are shown in Table 2. Results are presented in terms of *net effect,* or the percentage in a group who increased their estimate minus the percentage in that group who decreased their estimate.

This examination of results according to initial attitude shows the one-

Table 2

**Effects of One-Sided and Two-Sided Messages on Men Who
Initially Opposed the Message and Men Who Were
Initially Favorable to the Message**

	Initially Opposed *To the Message*	*Initially Favorable* *To the Message*
One-Sided	36%	52%
Two-Sided	48%	23%

The number in the table is the *net effect,* or the percentage in a group who increased their estimate minus the percentage in that group who decreased their estimate.

From *Experiments on Mass Communication,* by Carl I. Hovland et al., Vol. III *Studies in Social Psychology in World War II* (copyright 1949 © 1977 by Princeton University Press) sponsored by Social Science Research Council: Figure 1, p. 213. Reprinted by permission of Princeton University Press.

sided message is most effective with persons initially favorable to the message and the two-sided message is most effective with persons initially opposed to the message. This is what the researchers had predicted in advance.

Hovland and his associates also investigated whether one type of message—one-sided or two-sided—might work better with a more educated or a less educated audience. One might expect that better-educated audience members would be less affected by a clearly one-sided presentation. To check out this possibility, the researchers divided each test group into those subjects who graduated from high school and those who did not (see Table 3).

The results of this analysis by education level showed that the one-sided message is most effective with people of less education and the two-sided message is most effective with people of greater education.

Table 3

**Effects of the One-Sided and Two-Sided Messages on
Men Who Graduated from High School
and Men Who Did Not**

	Didn't Graduate *From High School*	*Did Graduate* *From High School*
One-Sided	46%	35%
Two-Sided	31%	49%

The number in the table is the *net effect,* or the percentage in a group who increased their estimate minus the percentage in that group who decreased their estimate.

From *Experiments on Mass Communication,* by Carl I. Hovland et al., Vol. III *Studies in Social Psychology in World War II* (copyright 1949 © 1977 by Princeton University Press) sponsored by Social Science Research Council: Figure 2, p. 214. Reprinted by permission of Princeton University Press.

Both of these additional analyses—the one by initial opinion and the one by educational level—show that the kind of presentation that is most effective depends on the characteristics of the audience. These results brought out the complexity of attitude change—that variables in the message sometimes interact with other variables, such as personal characteristics of the audience. This is part of the evidence that led psychologist Roger Brown (1958) in his analysis of propaganda to conclude that the propaganda devices are "contingently rather than invariably effective."

The Yale Communication Research Program

After the war, Hovland returned to Yale University, where he had been a faculty member, and continued his research on attitude change. A number of his fellow workers in the research for the Army, including Irving Janis, Arthur Lumsdaine, and Fred Sheffield, also went to work at Yale. The researchers received funding from the Rockefeller Foundation and set up the Yale Communication Research Program. This program had the purpose of "developing scientific propositions which specify the conditions under which the effectiveness of one or another type of persuasive communication is increased or decreased" (Hovland, Janis and Kelley, 1953, p. v). The project had three characteristics: 1. It was primarily concerned with theoretical issues and basic research; 2. It drew upon theoretical developments from diverse sources, both within psychology and related fields; 3. It emphasized testing propositions by controlled experiment (Hovland, Janis and Kelley, 1953).

This program was to produce a number of important volumes on attitude change, which are sometimes known as "the Yale series." It included these books:

> *Communication and Persuasion* (Hovland, Janis and Kelley, 1953). *The Order of Presentation in Persuasion* (Hovland, et al., 1957). *Personality and Persuasibility* (Janis, et al., 1959). *Attitude Organization and Change* (Rosenberg, et al., 1960). *Social Judgment* (Sherif and Hovland, 1961)

The first volume, *Communication and Persuasion,* was the most general. It dealt with a number of topics that would later receive entire volumes in the Yale series or else become topics investigated extensively by later researchers. Two of these topics—source credibility and fear appeals—are particularly important because they led to many later studies. The book also reported a replication and extension of the one-sided versus two-sided message study done earlier for the Army. Rather than attempt to summarize the entire Yale research program, we will describe these three studies in some detail.

Source Credibility

One of the variables in a communication situation that the communicator frequently has some control over is the choice of the source. An advertiser can hire a movie star or a well known athlete to endorse a product. Similarly, the federal government can choose a minor official or the Secretary of Health, Education and Welfare to release a national health report. The selection of an effective source to speak for your idea or product is essentially the propaganda device of Testimonial. But does the choice of source really make a difference in the amount of attitude change produced? Hovland and Weiss designed an experiment to answer this question.

Hovland and Weiss apparently were led to study this variable not by the Institute for Propaganda Analysis's selection of Testimonial as one of its seven devices but by a phenomenal radio program involving entertainer Kate Smith. In an 18-hour program during World War II, Kate Smith received pledges for an astounding $39 million worth of War Bonds. In comparison, the Jerry Lewis muscular dystrophy telethon for 1977 went on for 20 hours and only received pledges for $27 million. Studies by other researchers indicated that key elements in Kate Smith's success were her perceived *sincerity* and *trustworthiness.*

Hovland and Weiss designed an experiment in which the same messages would be presented to some people as coming from a high credibility source and to other people as coming from a low credibility source. This would allow them to determine the effect of the source variable alone.

The experiment was done with four messages on four different topics. Each subject received a booklet containing four articles. Each article was on a different topic. The subjects' opinions on the four topics were measured with questionnaires before getting the communication, immediately after getting it and four weeks after getting it. Each article was presented with a high credibility source for half of the subjects and a low credibility source for the other half. The four topics were controversial ones at the time, and revolved around the following opinion questions:

1. Should antihistamine drugs continue to be sold without a doctor's prescription? The high credibility source on this issue was the *New England Journal of Biology and Medicine.* The low credibility source is identified in the research report as "a mass circulation monthly pictorial magazine."
2. Can a practicable atomic-powered submarine be built at the present time? The high credibility source was Robert J. Oppenheimer, the father of the atomic bomb. (This was before his security clearance investigation, which undoubtedly damaged his credibility.) The low credibility source was *Pravda,* the Russian newspaper.
3. Is the steel industry to blame for the current shortage of steel? The high credibility source was the *Bulletin of National Resources Planning Board.* The low credibility source is identified as an "antilabor, anti-New Deal, 'rightist' newspaper columnist."
4. As a result of TV, will there be a decrease in the number of movie theaters in operation by 1955? The high credibility source was *Fortune* magazine. The low credibility source was identified as "a woman movie-gossip columnist."

The design was counterbalanced so that every source argued both pro and con on his or her topic, although each subject would see only the pro or the con message.

The results for the immediate after test (see Table 4) show that the high credibility source did produce more opinion change on three of the four topics. The exception is the topic of the future of movies, and for some reason the woman movie-gossip columnist was apparently seen as a slightly more credible source on this topic than *Fortune* magazine.

Table 4

**Net Percentage of Cases in Which Subjects Changed
Opinion in Direction of Communication for
High and Low Credibility Sources**

	High Credibility	Low Credibility
antihistamines	23%	13%
atomic submarines	36%	0%
steel shortage	23%	−4%
future of movies	13%	17%

The number in the table is the net percentage of cases who changed their opinions in the direction of the communication, or the percentage who changed in the direction of the communication *minus* the percentage who changed in the opposite direction.

Adapted from Hovland, C. I., I. L. Janis and H. H. Kelley. (1953). *Communication and Persuasion.* New Haven: Yale University Press. Reprinted by permission.

The retest of opinion after four weeks produced an interesting finding. These results are presented in Figure 1 for all four topics combined.

The figure shows that when the subjects were retested after four weeks, the amount of opinion change retained was approximately equal for the high credibility and low credibility sources. For the low credibility source, there appeared to be *greater* opinion change after four weeks than there was immediately after receiving the communication. This was a second finding of what Hovland, Lumsdaine and Sheffield earlier had called the "sleeper" effect. Hovland and Weiss did some further research and found that this was not due to the forgetting of the source, as Hovland, Lumsdaine and Sheffield had suggested, but to a tendency after the passage of time not to associate the source and the opinion.

More recent research has cast substantial doubt on the sleeper effect as a general phenomenon. Gillig and Greenwald (1974) were unable to produce a sleeper effect—that is, a statistically significant increase in opinion change for a group exposed to a low credibility source—in seven replications of an experiment designed to show the effect. Furthermore, their review of

Figure 1

**Changes in Extent of Agreement With High Credibility and Low Credibility Sources
After Four Weeks**

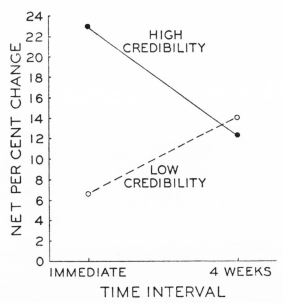

From Hovland, C. I., and W. Weiss. (1951). The Influence of Source Credibility on
Communication Effectiveness. *Public Opinion Quarterly* 15:635–650. Reprinted by
permission of the publisher.

the literature indicated no previous study had really shown that kind of
sleeper effect. What the earlier studies, including that of Hovland and Weiss,
had shown was a significant difference in the effects of high and low credibility
sources over time, but that is not the same as a significant increase in opinion
change for a group exposed to a low credibility source. Gillig and Greenwald
also point out a limitation on the very first sleeper effect found by Hovland,
Lumsdaine and Sheffield—it occurred for only a subset of a large group of
opinion items, and there was no apparent means of predicting beforehand
which items would show the change and which would not. In light of their
research, the most appropriate verdict on the sleeper effect at this time would
seem to be "not proved."

Fear Appeals

Another common tactic in mass communication is to threaten or arouse
some fear in the audience. Films shown to teenagers to promote safe driving
sometimes show terrible traffic accidents and what they do to people. A
television commercial for an insurance company arouses fear by saying, "You

need something to help keep these promises, even if you're not there." How effective are such methods? *Communication and Persuasion* reports an experiment by Janis and Feshbach designed to answer this question.

On the basis of learning theory—a key element in the Hovland approach—it can be predicted that a strong fear appeal would lead to increased attitude change because it would increase arousal and bring about greater attention and comprehension. Motivation to accept the recommendations of the communication would also be increased. On the other hand, the researchers realized that a high degree of emotional tension could lead to spontaneous defensive reactions and the possibility of the audience distorting the meaning of what is being said. Part of their research purpose was to investigate this potentially adverse effect of a strong fear appeal.

Janis and Feshbach designed an experiment that was based on three different messages with three different levels of fear appeal. They selected dental hygiene as their topic. The subjects were the entire freshman class of a large Connecticut high school. The class was randomly divided into four groups, three of which were to get the different fear messages and one of which was to be a control group.

The basic message, common to all three fear levels, was a standard lecture on dental hygiene. The level of fear was varied primarily through changing the material used to illustrate the lecture. In the minimal fear appeal message, the illustrative material used X-rays and drawings to represent cavities, and any photographs used were of completely healthy teeth. In the moderate fear appeal version, photographs were used of mild cases of tooth decay and oral diseases. In the strong fear appeal version, the slides used to illustrate the lecture included very realistic photographs of advanced tooth decay and gum diseases. The strong fear condition also contained some personalized threats, such as the statement, "This can happen to you." The control group received a lecture on the structure and function of the human eye.

Subjects were given a questionnaire asking specific questions about their dental hygiene practices one week before the lecture and one week after. Comparison of these questionnaires would show whether subjects changed their dental hygiene behavior after being exposed to the various types of messages.

The results in Table 5 show that the minimal fear appeal was the most effective in getting the students to follow the dental hygiene recommendations in the lecture. The strong fear appeal was the least effective. This was definite evidence that a fear appeal can be too strong and can evoke some form of interference which reduces the effectiveness of the communication. This experiment had several strengths that have not always been present in later attitude change studies. One is that the message was shown to have an effect on reported behavior, and not just on a paper and pencil measure of a hypothetical attitude. The field of attitude change research was involved in a controversy a few years later in which many studies were criticized for producing

Table 5

Increased or Decreased Conformity to Dental Hygiene Recommendations for Subjects Receiving Messages with Different Levels of Fear

	Strong Fear Appeal	*Moderate Fear Appeal*	*Minimal Fear Appeal*	*Control Group*
Increased Conformity	28%	44%	50%	22%
Decreased Conformity	20	22	14	22
No Change	52	34	36	56
	100%	100%	100%	100%

Adapted from Hovland, C. I., I. L. Janis and H. H. Kelley. (1953). *Communication and Persuasion.* New Haven: Yale University Press. Reprinted by permission.

slight changes in unimportant attitudes. Second, the persuasive messages used by Janis and Feshbach were shown to have produced long term attitude change. Another criticism of some later attitude change studies is that they dealt only with short term attitude change, often measured immediately after the message. Janis and Feshbach went back to their subjects a year later and still found the differences in attitude change between their experimental groups.

The Janis and Feshbach study was the first of a large number of studies on fear appeals. Some of the later studies have found that a minimal fear appeal was most effective in producing attitude change, as did the Janis and Feshbach study, but some have found that a strong fear appeal was most effective. One explanation for these opposite findings could be that there is a curvilinear relationship between the amount of fear and the amount of attitude change. That is, increasing the amount of fear could lead to an increase in attitude change up to a certain point, but increasing the fear beyond that point could lead to defensive avoidance and less attitude change. Some evidence for this comes from a study by Krisher, Darley and Darley (1973), which found that subjects in a moderate fear condition were more likely to get a mumps vaccination than subjects in either the high fear condition or the low fear condition.

Another line of research on fear appeals has investigated whether certain types of persons are more likely to have negative reactions to strong fear appeals. Goldstein (1959) studied personality types called *copers* and *avoiders* and showed that it is the avoiders who are most likely to have a defensive reaction to a strong fear appeal.

Resistance to Counterpropaganda

It is one thing to produce a temporary attitude change; it is something else to produce attitude change that is long lasting and permanent. One way to measure the permanance of an attitude change is to determine how resistant the new attitude is to change. Lumsdaine and Janis report a study in *Communication and Persuasion* that deals with resistance of a new attitude to change. Their experiment builds on the earlier work on one-sided and two-sided communications by Hovland, Lumsdaine and Sheffield.

Lumsdaine and Janis produced one-sided and two-sided messages arguing that Russia would be unable to produce large numbers of atomic bombs for at least five years. This was a realistic issue for differences of opinion in the early 1950s. The one-sided message argued that the Russians lacked some crucial secrets, that their espionage was not effective, and that Russia was lacking in industry. The two-sided message added brief mentions of the arguments that Russia had uranium mines in Siberia, that it had many top scientists and that its industry had grown since the war. Several weeks before the messages were presented, all subjects were given a questionnaire to determine their initial opinions. One group received the one-sided message and another received the two-sided message. A week later, half of each group was exposed to a countercommunication from a different communicator arguing that Russia had probably already developed the A-bomb. This counterpropaganda brought out some new arguments not included in the two-sided message. Both the initial messages and the counterpropaganda were presented in the form of recorded radio programs. Finally, all subjects were given a last questionnaire.

The key question, asked in both the initial and final questionnaires, was this: "About how long from now do you think it will be before the Russians are really producing *large numbers* of atomic bombs?"

Figure 2 presents the net opinion change from initial to final questionnaire

Figure 2

Comparison of the Effectiveness of Programs I and II: Changes in Opinions Concerning the Length of Time before Russia Produces Large Numbers of A-bombs.

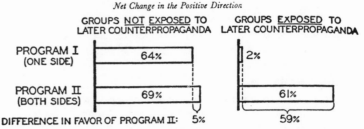

From Lumsdaine, A., and I. Janis. (1953). Resistance to "Counterpropaganda" produced by One-Sided and Two-Sided "Propaganda" Presentations. *Public Opinion Quarterly* 17:311–318. Reprinted by permission of the publisher.

for those who received counterpropaganda and those who did not in both the one-sided and two-sided message groups. The results show that for those receiving no counterpropaganda, the one-sided and two-sided messages were about equally effective. This replicates the finding of the earlier study by Hovland, Lumsdaine and Sheffield. The results show a striking difference for those receiving counterpropaganda, however. Those receiving a one-sided message showed almost no remaining attitude change after they were exposed to counterpropaganda. Those receiving a two-sided messasge showed almost as much attitude change remaining after counterpropaganda as they did when they weren't exposed to counterpropaganda.

One of the advantages of the two-sided message over the one-sided message, then, is that it is more effective in building resistance to later persuasive efforts. Lumsdaine and Janis speak of the recipient of the two-sided message as becoming "inoculated." This is a medical analogy that William McGuire would later draw upon in developing his "inoculation theory."

Hovland and his associates went on to produce the four other classic volumes on attitude change that were listed earlier in this chapter. One of particular interest is *Attitude Organization and Change,* because it reports work by Hovland's group on attitude consistency, an area more strongly identified with researchers such as Heider, Festinger, Osgood and Tannenbaum. Rosenberg reported in this volume an interesting experiment using hypnosis which showed that when you change a person's feelings toward an attitude object, the person's beliefs about that attitude object will tend to change to agree with the feelings. The experiment provides striking evidence for the psychological process of rationalization. We begin with our feelings about something, then find the beliefs that are consistent with those feelings.

CONCLUSIONS

This chapter has described the beginnings of contemporary attitude change research in the work Carl Hovland and his associates did for the U.S. Army during World War II. This work developed a paradigm or approach that has been used in many attitude change studies since. It also contributed a number of classic studies, several of which we have described in some detail.

These experiments are important both for their own results and because most of them led to many later experiments by other researchers. Hovland and his coworkers were an outstanding group, and many of them have gone on to do further research in the communication area. Feshbach has been a prominent researcher on the topic of the effects of television violence. Janis has extended his fear appeal research by developing techniques to help people stop smoking and has done research on "groupthink" processes in politics and government. Maccoby has applied attitude change theory to the problems of health communication in the Stanford Heart Disease Prevention Program.

William McGuire developed his "inoculation theory" and became an important synthesizer and critic of attitude change research in general. Hovland himself died an untimely death in 1961.

REFERENCES

Allport, G. W. (1954). The Historical Background of Modern Social Psychology. In G. Lindzey (ed.), *Handbook of Social Psychology,* vol. I, pp. 3–56. Reading, Mass.: Addison-Wesley.

Brown, R. (1958). *Words and Things.* New York: The Free Press.

Chen, W. (1933). The Influence of Oral Propaganda Material Upon Students' Attitudes. *Archives of Psychology* 150:1–43.

English, H. B., and A. C. English. (1958). *A Comprehensive Dictionary of Psychological and Psychoanalytical Terms: A Guide to Usage.* New York: Longmans, Green.

Gillig, P. M., and A. G. Greenwald. (1974). Is It Time to Lay the Sleeper Effect to Rest? *Journal of Personality and Social Psychology* 29:132–139.

Goldstein, M. I. (1959). The Relationship Between Coping and Avoiding Behavior and Response to Fear-Arousing Propaganda. *Journal of Abnormal and Social Psychology* 58:247–252.

Hovland, C. I., I. L. Janis and H. H. Kelley. (1953). *Communication and Persuasion.* New Haven: Yale University Press.

Hovland, C. I., A. A. Lumsdaine and F. D. Sheffield. (1965). *Experiments on Mass Communication.* New York: John Wiley and Sons.

Hovland, C. I., W. Mandell, E. H. Campbell, T. Brock, A. S. Luchins, A. R. Cohen, W. J. McGuire, I. L. Janis, R. L. Feierabend, and N. H. Anderson. (1957). *The Order of Presentation in Persuasion.* New Haven: Yale University Press.

Insko, C. A. (1967). *Theories of Attitude Change.* New York: Appleton-Century-Crofts.

Janis, I., C. I. Hovland, P. B. Field, H. Linton, E. Graham, A. R. Cohen, D. Rife, R. P. Abelson, G. S. Lesser and B. T. King. (1959). *Personality and Persuasibility.* New Haven: Yale University Press.

Krech, D., R. S. Crutchfield and E. L. Ballachey. (1962). *Individual in Society: A Textbook of Social Psychology.* New York: McGraw-Hill.

Krisher, H. P. III, S. A. Darley and J. M. Darley. (1973). Fear-Provoking Recommendations, Intentions to Take Preventive Actions, and Actual Preventive Actions. *Journal of Personality and Social Psychology* 26:301–308.

Murphy, G., L. B. Murphy and T. M. Newcomb. (1937). *Experimental Social Psychology: An Interpretation of Research Upon the Socialization of the Individual,* rev. ed. New York: Harper and Brothers.

Rosenberg, M. J., and C. I. Hovland. (1960). Cognitive, Affective and Behavioral Components of Attitudes. In M. Rosenberg, C. Hovland, W. McGuire, R. Abelson and J. Brehm, *Attitude Organization and Change,* pp. 1–14. New Haven: Yale University Press.

Rosenberg, M. J., C. I. Hovland, W. J. McGuire, R. P. Abelson and J. W. Brehm.

(1960). *Attitude Organization and Change: An Analysis of Consistency Among Attitude Components.* New Haven: Yale University Press.

Sherif, M. and C. I. Hovland. (1961). *Social Judgment: Assimilation and Contrast Effects in Communication and Attitude Change.* New Haven: Yale University Press.

Thomas, W. I., and F. Znaniecki. (1927). *The Polish Peasant in Europe and America,* 2nd ed, vol. I. New York: Alfred A. Knopf.

Chapter 13

Further Developments in Attitude Change

S INCE Carl Hovland and his associates did the first scientific studies of attitude change for the Army during World War II, there have been hundreds if not thousands of other attitude change studies conducted. Hovland's approach was primarily a learning theory approach which viewed attitude change as a type of learning. The Hovland approach and the consistency theory approach, dealt with in Chapter 11, have been the two major approaches to attitude change research.

This chapter will go beyond these two approaches to discuss some further developments in attitude change research. These include two other theoretical approaches—Daniel Katz's functional approach and William McGuire's Inoculation Theory. They also include the important issue of whether attitude change produced by persuasive messages is accompanied by change in behavior. And finally, they include Otto Lerbinger's taxonomy of persuasive designs for the practical communicator.

Katz's Functional Approach

The two major theoretical approaches to attitude change—the learning theory approach, primarily associated with Hovland, and the consistency theory approach, primarily associated with Festinger, Newcomb, Heider, and Osgood and Tannenbaum—existed side by side and with little apparent relation to one another for some time. Is there any way to reconcile these rather different theoretical approaches, or at least bring them together under a common umbrella? This is apparently the line of thinking that led Daniel Katz and his colleagues Irving Sarnoff and Charles McClintock to develop the functional approach to attitude change. These authors were trying to bring together two different models of human beings that have been presented over the years—the irrational model and the rational model. The irrational model suggests that human beings are nonthinking creatures whose beliefs are easily influenced by people around them and whose perception of reality can even be influenced by their own desires. The rational model suggests that human beings are intelligent and critical thinkers who can make wise decisions when given ample information. How can both of these models be true? Katz and his associates suggest that the answer to this dilemma is that human beings are both rational and irrational, depending on the particular person, the situation, the motivations operating at the time, etc. And they argue that this kind of thinking has important implications for problems of attitude change.

A principal assumption they make is that both attitude formation and attitude change must be understood in terms of the functions which attitudes serve for the personality. As these functions differ, so will the conditions and techniques of attitude change. Katz and his colleagues point out that much earlier research on mass communication has dealt with factors which are not really psychological variables, such as exposure to a motion picture. Since being exposed to a motion picture can serve different functions for different individuals, they argue that the researcher dealing only with exposure to a film is in a poor position to understand or predict attitude change. Katz makes the key point that the same attitude can have a different motivational basis in different people. He suggests that "unless we know the psychological need which is met by the holding of an attitude we are in a poor position to predict when and how it will change" (Katz, 1960, p. 170).

Katz identifies the following four major functions that attitudes can serve for the personality:

1. *The instrumental, adjustive or utilitarian function.* Some attitudes are held because people are striving to maximize the rewards in their external environments and minimize the penalties. For instance, a voter who thinks taxes are too high might favor a political candidate because that candidate promises to reduce taxes.

2. *The ego-defensive function.* Some attitudes are held because people are protecting their egos from their own unacceptable impulses or from knowledge of threatening forces without. Feelings of inferiority are often projected onto a minority group as a means of bolstering the ego. This would be an example of an attitude of prejudice serving the ego-defensive function.

3. *The value-expressive function.* Some attitudes are held because they allow a person to give positive expression to central values and to the kind of person the individual feels he or she is. For instance, a teenager who likes a particular rock and roll group is expressing his or her individuality through this attitude.

4. *The knowledge function.* Some attitudes are held because they satisfy

a desire for knowledge or provide structure or meaning in what would otherwise be a chaotic world. Many religious beliefs serve this function, as do other attitudes such as the shared norms of a culture.

Katz has presented a table (see Table 1) summarizing the origin and dynamics, the arousal conditions, and the change conditions for attitudes serving each of the four functions.

Katz warns that an attempt to change an attitude may backfire if it is not based on an understanding of the functions the attitude is serving. For instance, an attempt to change attitudes of prejudice by presenting factual information on the accomplishments of minority group members is not going to succeed if the attitudes of prejudice are held for ego defense reasons.

Katz and his associates have conducted some research supporting the functional approach and showing that understanding the motivations underlying attitudes can be important in trying to change attitudes.

One experiment (Katz, Sarnoff and McClintock, 1956) investigated the effectiveness of two types of messages in changing attitudes of prejudice toward blacks. Their subjects were white female students at a Northern college. The authors theorized that attitudes of prejudice toward blacks could be caused by three different underlying motives: 1. Reality-testing and the search for meaning. 2. Reward and punishment, including social acceptance. 3. Ego defense, or the need to defend against inner conflict. It is apparent that these are similar to three of the four basic functions described by Katz. The authors speculated that number 1 should not apply for their sample of Northern college girls because in such a sample misinformation based on old stereotypes should not be common. They speculated that number 2 should not apply for their sample because in a Northern college setting, social rewards for prejudice had been relaxed. Therefore they assumed that number 3 should be the major motivation for prejudice in their population. On that basis, they predicted that a message explaining the ego defense process (which they called an interpretation message but which can also be called an insight message) should be more effective in producing attitude change than an informational message. They also predicted that the people highest in ego defense should resist change on the basis of the insight message because it is too threatening for them. Finally, they predicted that people lowest in ego defensiveness would be most easily influenced by the informational message.

Their experiment involved three sessions. In an initial session, subjects were given several attitude scales to measure their racial prejudice and were given a test of their ego defensiveness. In a second session one week later, one group got the insight message, which dealt with psychological concepts such as scapegoating and discussed a case history of a college girl. A second group got the informational message, which discussed blacks in a setting of cultural relativity and which brought out the achievements of blacks in various fields. A control group received no message. After the message presentations, the subjects filled out the same attitude measures again. They did so a third time at a session six weeks later.

Table 1

**Determinants of Attitude Formation, Arousal, and Change
in Relation to Type of Function**

Function	Origin and Dynamics	Arousal Conditions	Change Conditions
Adjustment	Utility of attidinal object in need satisfaction. Maximizing external rewards and minimizing punishments	1. Activation of needs 2. Salience of cues associated with need satisfaction	1. Need deprivation 2. Creation of new needs and new levels of aspiration 3. Shifting rewards and punishments 4. Emphasis on new and better paths for need satisfaction
Ego defense	Protecting against internal conflicts and external dangers	1. Posing of threats 2. Appeals to hatred and repressed impulses 3. Rise in frustrations 4. Use of authoritarian suggestion	1. Removal of threats 2. Catharis 3. Development of self-insight
Value expression	Maintaining self identity; enhancing favorable self-image; self-expression and self-determination	1. Salience of cues associated with values 2. Appeals to individual to reassert self-image 3. Ambiguities which threaten self-concept	1. Some degree of dissatisfaction with self 2. Greater appropriateness of new attitude for the self 3. Control of all environmental supports to undermine old values
Knowledge	Need for understanding, for meaningful cognitive organization, for consistency and clarity	1. Reinstatement of cues associated with old problem or of old problem itself	1. Ambiguity created by new information or change in environment 2. More meaningful information about problems

From Katz, D. (1960). The Functional Approach to the Study of Attitudes, *Public Opinion Quarterly* 24: 163–204. Reprinted by permission of the publisher.

The attitude measurements taken immediately after the messages showed no significant differences between the two approaches. However, results after six weeks showed the interpretative message having a greater effect than the informational message on both measures of attitude. In addition, the prediction was supported that people highest in ego defense should resist the insight approach because it was too threatening. Finally, the prediction that people lowest in ego defensiveness would be most easily influenced by the informational message was not confirmed. The people high in ego defensiveness were just as influenced by the informational message as the people low in ego defensiveness. The authors speculate that this was due to the pressure for conformity produced in the experiment.

Further evidence giving at least partial support to the functional approach was found in subsequent studies by Katz, McClintock and Sarnoff (1957) and McClintock (1958).

McGuire's Inoculation Theory

While some researchers have concentrated on finding the most effective means of changing attitudes, others have concentrated on finding the most effective means of making attitudes resistant to change. One application of this research would be to make military personnel more resistant to brainwashing. During the Korean War, many Americans who were captured apparently surrendered some of their basic beliefs rather quickly under prison camp conditions. If we wanted to make these beliefs more resistant to change, what would be the best way to do it?

The main workers on this problem have been William McGuire and his associate Demetrios Papageorgis. Their work on Inoculation Theory built on the research on one-sided and two-sided messages by Lumsdaine and Janis, who first used the word "inoculation" in relation to attitude change.

McGuire's theory rests on the medical analogy that is suggested by its name. He points out that most people have many unchallenged beliefs, and that these beliefs can often be easily swayed once they are attacked because the person is not used to defending them. The situation is similar to that in the medical field of a body that is brought up in a germ-free environment and is suddenly exposed to germs. The body is vulnerable to infection because it has not developed any resistance. Such a person can be given resistance either by supportive treatment—good diet, exercise, rest, etc.—or by inoculation, a deliberate exposure to a weakened form of the germ that stimulates the development of defenses. In the medical area, the inoculation approach has been more effective in producing resistance. The word immunization can be applied to either of these methods of building immunity—the supportive approach or the inoculation approach.

McGuire and Papageorgis have conducted a number of experiments to test this theory. One of the first (McGuire and Papageorgis, 1961) tested the basic prediction that the supportive approach of pre-exposing a person to arguments supporting basic beliefs would have less immunizing effectiveness than the inoculation approach of pre-exposing the person to weakened, defense-stimulating forms of the counterarguments. It also tested a second hypothesis that active participation during exposure to a defense should be less effective than passive participation in producing immunity to later persuasion. The authors made this prediction because they theorized that subjects would not be used to active participation in defending their basic beliefs and so would not do it very well. Furthermore, they thought that active participation might interfere with the reception of any defensive material presented. There was also a complicated third hypothesis that need not concern us here.

McGuire and Papageorgis selected for their study some beliefs that were hardly ever attacked in our culture, which they called "cultural truisms." The four beliefs were these: "Everyone should get a chest X-ray each year in order to detect any possible tuberculosis symptoms at an early stage"; "The effects of penicillin have been, almost without exception, of great benefit to mankind"; "Most forms of mental illness are not contagious"; "Everyone should brush his teeth after every meal if at all possible." These cultural truisms were so widely believed that control groups of subjects rated them at an average level of 13.26 on a scale ranging from 1 for "definitely false" to 15 for "definitely true."

Subjects took part in two one-hour experimental sessions that were two days apart. The first exposed subjects to the two types of immunizing material designed to make the basic beliefs ("cultural truisms") resistant to change; the second exposed subjects to strong counterarguments attacking the basic beliefs. Questionnaires were administered at the end of each session to measure strength of acceptance of beliefs.

The two major types of immunizing material presented to subjects were "supportive" and "refutational." The supportive material was made up of arguments supporting the cultural truisms. The refutational material consisted of possible counterarguments against the cultural truisms together with refutations of these counterarguments. The amount of participation in the defense was primarily varied by having subjects write in a high participation condition and read in a low participation condition.

Each subject was tested on one cultural truism for which he or she received no immunization but did receive the later counterarguments. The average scale position for these beliefs after they were attacked was 6.64, compared to the average level of 13.26 prior to attack. This shows that the cultural truisms were highly vulnerable to attack if no immunization was given.

McGuire and Papageorgis found, as they had predicted, that the refutational defenses were more effective in making the cultural truisms resistant to change than were the supportive defenses. After the supportive defenses, the counterarguments were able to reduce the belief in the cultural truisms to an average scale rating of 7.39, only slightly better than the 6.64 level achieved when there was no prior preparation at all. After the inoculation defenses the counterarguments were able to reduce the beliefs in the cultural truisms only to an average scale rating of 10.33. The authors also found support for their second hypothesis; the passive (reading) conditions had a greater effect in making beliefs resistant to persuasion than did the active (writing) conditions.

The McGuire and Papageorgis experiment was limited in one respect that needed further investigation. The attacks on the cultural truisms that were presented and then refuted in the inoculation were the same attacks that were presented in the next session when the cultural truisms were assailed. It was not clear whether presenting and refuting one set of attacks would also provide later immunity to a different set of attacks. This question was investigated in another experiment by Papageorgis and McGuire (1961).

Papageorgis and McGuire (1961) predicted that a kind of generalized immunity would develop when subjects were exposed to attacks on basic beliefs and refutations of those attacks. That is, they predicted that this procedure would develop a general resistance that would make the basic belief unlikely to change even when it was exposed to attacks that were not the same. They expected this for two reasons: 1. The experience of seeing the first attacks refuted could lower the credibility of the later attacks. 2. Preexposure to attacks may make a person more aware that his or her beliefs are indeed vulnerable and motivate the person to develop additional supporting arguments.

Their results showed inoculation led to an immunity to differing counterarguments that was almost as strong as the immunity to the same counterarguments. In fact, the final attitude positions in these two conditions were not significantly different. This, of course, extends the usefulness of inoculation—the planner of the inoculation program does not have to anticipate all the attacks on a belief that a person might be exposed to later.

McGuire has extended inoculation theory in several ways, including looking at the effects of various types of immunizations over extended periods of time, and has found research support for these additional predictions. Insko (1967) has criticized McGuire's research for going beyond the biological analogy. The active and passive participation in a defense, for instance, do not have an exact parallel in medical inoculation. This criticism seems a little unfair since McGuire's theory is more extensive than many in the attitude change area. It is difficult to see why he should be faulted for bringing in additional factors that add to our understanding, when that is the purpose of science.

Attitudes and Behavior

Despite all the research on attitude change taking place, researchers neglected for a long time an important question. In its more general form, the question is whether attitudes as they are measured by social science methods have any real relation to behavior. In its more specific form, the question is whether attitude change produced by persuasive messages is accompanied by any meaningful change in behavior.

One early study had indicated that attitudes might not bear much of a relationship to behavior. A social scientist named Richard LaPiere traveled in the early 1930s around the United States with a young Chinese couple. They made 251 visits to hotels and restaurants, and in only one case were they refused service. Six months later, LaPiere sent a questionnaire to each establishment asking: "Will you accept members of the Chinese race as guests in your establishment?" He received replies from 128 of these businesses. The responses from 92 per cent of the restaurants and 91 per cent of the hotels said "No." Only one person gave a definite "Yes." This classic study, then, suggested the possibility that people's verbal reports of their attitudes might not be very good predictors of their actual behavior.

Leon Festinger, the psychologist who developed the theory of cognitive dissonance, raised some thought-provoking questions about attitude change experiments and subsequent behavior in an address he gave in 1963. Festinger (1964) said he had been reading a manuscript by Arthur R. Cohen when he came across the statement that very little work on attitude change had dealt explicitly with the behavior that may follow a change in attitudes. Festinger was intrigued by this notion and attempted to find as many studies as he could which showed an effect of attitude change on subsequent behavior. He found only three. One of these was the Janis and Feshbach study of fear appeals. Their study did not investigate actual behavior change, but it did look at verbal reports of tooth brushing behavior and other dental hygiene behavior. Festinger was willing to accept this verbal report since it did purportedly deal with actual behavior. In all three of the studies Festinger found, there seemed to be a slight inverse relationship between attitude change and behavior change. For instance, in the Janis and Feshbach study, the individuals who indicated the most concern about their teeth after receiving the persuasive messages showed the least change in their reported behavior. Festinger argued that this inverse relationship indicates that the relationship between attitude change and behavior is not a simple one.

One reason attitude change might not be automatically followed by behavior change, Festinger suggested, is that the environmental factors that had produced an original attitude would usually still be operating after that attitude was changed. Thus there would be a tendency for an attitude to revert to its original position after exposure to a persuasive message. Festinger (1964) noted:

> I want to suggest that when opinions or attitudes are changed through the momentary impact of a persuasive communication, this change, all by itself, is inherently unstable and will disappear or remain isolated unless an environmental or behavioral change can be brought about to support and maintain it (p. 415).

Festinger was suggesting to attitude change theorists the disturbing possibility that they had conducted hundreds of experiments on variables that make very little difference in terms of human behavior.

Wicker (1969) brought up again the more general issue of whether attitudes are related to behavior. He looked at more than 30 studies of attitude and behavior and reported that attitude-behavior correlations are "rarely above .30, and often are near zero" (p. 65). Wicker concluded "Taken as a whole, these studies suggest that it is considerably more likely that attitudes will be unrelated or only slightly related to overt behaviors than that attitudes will be closely related to actions" (p. 65).

A number of other studies after Wicker's review article also indicated little relationship between attitude and behavior. At this point, some researchers were beginning to suggest that the concept of attitude was proving to be worthless and should be thrown out. Others suggested that the prediction of behavior from attitudes could be improved if additional factors were considered. For instance, in certain cases, the situation can have a greater role in determining behavior than a person's attitude. The most obvious example of this is the presence of a mob, which can cause many people to become caught up in behavior they might say was wrong at another time. But in almost any case in which other people are present, the situation itself can play a great role in influencing behavior. Perhaps the prediction of behavior from attitudes could be improved if situational variables could also be taken into account.

Still other thinkers (Gross and Niman, 1975), pointed out that past studies have often been limited in that they attempted to use an attitude measurement to predict a single act of behavior. Perhaps the predictions would be improved if an attitude measuring instrument using a range of questions was then related to a range of behaviors.

These two lines of thinking have led to some of the recent research on the attitude-behavior question.

Realizing that the prediction of a specific behavior depends on a number of factors in addition to some kind of measure of attitude, Martin Fishbein attempted to develop a model that would include all the important factors (Ajzen and Fishbein, 1970). The model takes the form of the following algebraic expression:

$$B \sim BI = [A \ act]w_0 + [NB(Mc)]w_1$$

Although the model looks complicated, it can be translated into English that is not difficult to understand. The letters in the equation can be translated as follows:

B = overt behavior
BI = the behavioral intention to perform that behavior
A_{act} = attitude toward performing a given behavior in a given situation
NB = normative beliefs, or beliefs that significant others think one should or should not perform the behavior
M_c = motivation to comply with the norms
w_0 and w_1 = regression weights to be determined empirically

The equation can be rephrased in the following English sentence: A person's intention to perform a given behavior is a function of: (1) the person's attitude toward performing that behavior and (2) the person's perception of the norms governing that behavior and the individual's motivation to comply with those norms.

This model brings in some of the key situational factors, particularly the beliefs that other people have about the behavior and the individual's motivation to conform to those beliefs. If precise measurements could be made of all the variable quantities in the model, it should be possible to make rather exact predictions of behavioral intention and then of actual behavior. Fishbein (1973) reports that a number of experiments using the model to predict behavioral intention have produced multiple correlations of about .80, which are quite high. These experiments also found correlations between behavioral intention and overt behavior of .70 so all the key parts of the model seem supported. In a continuation of the Fishbein research, Ajzen (1971) has used the Fishbein model to demonstrate behavioral change as the result of persuasive communication, the phenomenon that Festinger had difficulty finding in 1963.

Weigel and Newman (1976) took the second line of thinking mentioned above. They conducted a study designed to overcome the limitation of most studies of attitude and behavior that had attempted to use a general attitude measure to predict a single specific behavior. They conducted a field study of attitudes on environmental issues using a random sample of residents of a community. People were first given an attitude scale measuring environmental concern. Then, over the next eight months, their behavior in the environmental area was determined with regard to 14 separate acts. The opportunities to engage in these acts were presented by people knocking on their doors who did not identify themselves with the earlier administration of the attitude questionnaire. The 14 acts included signing of three petitions on environmental issues (1–3), circulating these petitions to others (4), participating in a litter pick-up (5), recruiting a friend to pick up litter (6), and participating in a recycling program in eight different weeks (7–14). Correlations between attitude scale scores and these single behaviors ranged from .12 to .57. When the behaviors were summed into one index, however, the correlation was .62. The authors suggest that the comprehensive behavioral measure produces a higher correlation because it is broader and provides an adequate range of the universe of actions implied in the attitude measure.

These are two recent lines of research on attitude-behavior consistency—the Fishbein approach that incorporates norms and other relevant variables in a predictive model, and the Weigel and Newman approach that attempts to predict from attitude to a range of behaviors rather than a single act of behavior.

Another important development, which seems to have come about particularly because of Festinger's address, is that many more researchers are now including behavioral measures in their studies of attitude change. For instance, many fear appeal studies now include behavioral measures such as the "disclosing wafer" test of how well teeth are cleaned (Evans, Rozelle, Lasater, Dembroski and Allen, 1970) or the actual act of going to get a shot or vaccination (Krisher, Darley and Darley, 1973). Similarly, the Stanford project in using communication to reduce heart disease uses such behavioral measures as blood pressure, cholesterol level, weight, and number of cigarettes smoked (Maccoby and Farquhar, 1975).

Lerbinger's Five Designs

The application of attitude change research to practical communication problems can be difficult for the professional communicator. There are hundreds of experiments, many of them seem contradictory, and many of the findings are so heavily qualified that they seem difficult to apply. A useful approach that can serve as a bridge between the various theories of attitude change and the practical problems of persuasion faced by professional communicators has been presented by Otto Lerbinger (1972) in his *Designs for Persuasive Communication*. Lerbinger's book is a kind of handbook—almost a recipe book—on persuasion which draws upon the broad body of scientific research available. At the heart of the book is a set of five designs that Lerbinger has identified. Each of these is based upon a different theoretical approach to attitude change. Lerbinger's analysis owes a great deal to Katz's functional approach. Like Katz, he has identified different reasons that attitudes are held and has discussed various strategies for changing them. In fact, some of Lerbinger's five designs correspond rather directly to some of Katz's four functions. But Lerbinger has come up with a couple of designs that do not correspond to any of Katz's functions, and he has added some other details of his own.

The Stimulus-Response Design

The stimulus-response (S-R) design is based on scientific research showing that learning can take place just through association and repetition. The simple goal of this design is to establish a connection between a stimulus and a response. Most of the applications of the S-R design in mass communication involve establishing new meanings for words. These new meanings can be denotative or connotative.

The denotative meaning of a word is the object or thing in the real world that the word indicates. One clear use of the S-R design to establish denotative meaning is in popularizing brand names. There was a time when people did not associate Polaroid with cameras or Colgate with toothpaste. It was mass communication that played the major role in establishing these links, and it did it primarily through association (the name "Colgate" and the word "toothpaste" appeared together, for instance) and repetition.

The connotative meaning of a word is the associations, often of the emotional or affective type, that are attached to a word. For instance, United Airlines was the largest airline in the country and because of this largeness, it had a reputation for being indifferent. A campaign was designed to change the connotation of the airline from indifference to friendliness. The S-R design played a major role in this campaign. A crucial part of this campaign was the slogan "Fly the friendly skies of United," which brought the words "friendly" and "United" together in the same sentence and which could be repeated frequently.

The S-R design is also used extensively in political campaigns to give candidates the desired connotations. Television commercials can be structured to present a simple, repeated message that a candidate is friendly, intelligent, active, concerned, patriotic, or whatever. These favorable associations can be transmitted through music, rapid presentation of highly valued symbols such as the flag, babies, beaches, peace signs, and so forth. This is the "image" approach to political advertising—the purpose is to create a favorable image of the candidate.

The S-R design is a simple design. It rests on the principles of repetition, captivity and contiguity. It has the advantage that not much has to be known about the audience. This simple kind of learning works equally well for about all kinds of people. Because it applies to most people and not much has to be known about the audience, the S-R design is widely used in mass communication—particularly in television advertising.

The Motivational Design

The motivational design involves these two steps: identify people's motives and needs, then link your message or product to them. This design builds on the research on motivation which indicates that human beings are goal-seeking and tension-reducing animals.

Human beings have many different types of needs that could become the basis of motivational approaches. A catalog or list of these needs would be useful in trying to apply the design. Lerbinger presents Abraham Maslow's hierarchy of needs for this purpose.

Maslow (1970) identified needs at five levels: physiological (food, water, air, exercise, shelter), safety (to be free from fear, danger, etc.), social (the need for love, acceptance, belonging), ego (the need for reputation, self respect, status), and self-actualization (the need for creativity, self-expression, personal fulfillment). Maslow said these needs form a hierarchy in the sense that people strive to fulfill the lowest level needs (physiological and safety, for instance) before they strive to fulfill the higher level needs.

Mass communication messages attempting persuasion could be directed at any of these needs. For instance, during troubled times a politician could promise tax cuts, which would help many people meet their physiological needs better. A kind of mass communication aimed at safety needs is the typical insurance ad. Actually, the levels of needs most commonly addressed by mass communication messages in the United States seem to be the social and ego needs. Perhaps this is because the majority of Americans have met their physiological and safety needs but have not completely met their social and ego needs. At any rate, a large number of advertisements and commercials for products ranging from perfumes to Dentyne chewing gum are aimed at people's need for social success. Whole industries, such as those producing deodorants and mouth washes, have grown up as answers to people's fear of social failure.

Similarly, many commercials and advertisements are aimed at people's ego needs. Obvious examples are the coffee commercials in which a woman's whole self image depends on whether or not her husband likes her coffee.

Not very many mass communication messages are aimed at the need for self actualization. Perhaps this is because most Americans have not reached the level where this is their main concern, or perhaps it is because self actualization does not require many of the mass produced goods that are the mainstay of most commercial advertising.

The use of the motivational approach in advertising has been discussed in books such as Ernest Dichter's *The Strategy of Desire* and Vance Packard's *The Hidden Persuaders.* For a while, the motivational approach was strongly identified with the discovery of unconscious motives. Dichter was responsible for much of this research, including his famous study indicating that men wanted convertibles because the cars were symbolic mistresses.

The Cognitive Design

The cognitive design is a persuasion design that is based on rational argument. The design assumes that human beings are rational creatures trying to construct meaningful pictures of themselves and the world around them. The design draws particularly on the research on consistency theories.

The cognitive design can take two different approaches: 1. To attempt to persuade by presenting facts and information and a logical argument. 2. To use people's desire for consistency to produce attitude change, either by arousing or reminding people of an inconsistency or by forcing people to engage in a public behavior or make a commitment.

The type of cognitive design that is based on facts and logical argument is a common one in newspaper editorials. A message using this approach typically deals with the *issues,* in contrast with the S-R design, which typically deals with *images.* Lerbinger says the slogan for this design is, "Let the facts speak for themselves."

A recent magazine ad for Ban Basic, an anti-perspirant, illustrates the "facts and logical arguments" approach of the cognitive design. The headline said "Introducing Ban Basic, an anti-perspirant spray without aerosol propellants." This ad was responding to the criticisms by scientists that deodorant sprays using aerosol were contributing to a depletion of the ozone layer in the atmosphere. Other aspects of the ad further carried out the rational, scientific approach. A bar graph showed that Ban Basic lasts 29.1 days per ounce, while Arrid Extra Dry lasts 6.2 days per ounce. Presumably this meant you could get enough repeated applications from an ounce to last 29.1 days, but the advertiser probably would not object if some people misunderstood this and thought Ban Basic could prevent body odor for 29 days. There was even a footnote, a more common device in scholarly articles than magazine ads, which pointed out that the figures in the bar graph were based on a 2-second spray per underarm.

The type of cognitive approach that is based on presenting or reminding a person of an inconsistency can be illustrated by a telegram that Charles Osgood sent to every Senator and member of Congress about one year before President Richard Nixon resigned (Hall, November, 1973). The telegram read, "How long can we tolerate Nixon's callousness and arrogance and retain our democracy?" Since the leader in a democracy should not be callous and arrogant—characteristics that normally would be associated with a king or tyrant—the message should arouse some inconsistency.

The type of cognitive approach that involves forcing people to engage in public behavior to make a commitment can be illustrated by the use of bumper stickers and campaign buttons during political campaigns. If a person is lukewarm toward a candidate and then wears a campaign button for that candidate, the theory of cognitive dissonance would predict that the person would adopt a more favorable attitude toward the candidate because this is the primary means available to maintain consistency.

The Social Design

The social design appeals to a person as a member of a group. This approach is similar to the propaganda device of Bandwagon, although it is developed somewhat further. The theoretical basis for the social design is the research on groups that has been described in Chapter 10. The design draws particularly on the work of Sherif, Asch and Lewin.

This design is based on the idea that a person's dependence on others is greater than is often realized. It builds on the research showing that social approval serves as a generalized reinforcer of attitudes, as well as other human activities.

This approach is common in advertising, and many examples have already been brought out in the discussion of bandwagon. The commercials for Grecian Formula 16 hair coloring that state, "I bet a lot of your friends are using it and you don't even know it" are using the social design.

An example of a complex use of the social design is the United Way or United Appeal campaign common in most communities, which we have analyzed in some detail in Chapter 10.

Lerbinger points out that a social design would be a good design to use if you were trying to get soldiers to be willing to fight. You could stress the feelings of closeness within the group and of not wanting to let your buddies down. This might be more effective than the "Why We Fight" series of films, which used essentially a cognitive approach.

The Personality Design

The personality design is based on taking into account the personality needs of audience members while trying to persuade. In particular, those personality needs are the needs of value expression and ego defense. The general assumption of this design is that opinions and attitudes are in the last analysis an integral part of the personality.

This design builds directly on two of Katz's functions of attitudes— value expression and ego defense. In a sense, it is two designs in one, since each of these kinds of attitudes requires different strategies for persuasion.

Value expressive attitudes are those that are held for the purposes of self expression, or telling the world what kind of person you are. This is such a fundamental need of people that many advertisements and products are aimed directly at it. For instance, Marlboro cigarettes have created one of the most extensive and successful campaigns in advertising history by associating their product with ruggedness and masculinity. These qualities then transfer over to smokers, who can feel they are expressing their own masculinity and ruggedness by smoking Marlboros. A brand of Scotch that advertises that it is "For those who refuse to compromise" is also giving people a chance to express a quality they see in themselves. Many automobiles are advertised as a means for people to display their youth, courage and power. This is indicated in names like "Cougar," "Fury," and "Corvette." T shirts with pictures or statements on them are probably the ultimate in this kind of value expression. People who wear Beethoven T shirts, or, for that matter, Kiss T shirts, are saying a lot about who they are, or, at least, how they see themselves. So is a person who wears a shirt saying "I am single and I love it" or "A woman without a man is like a fish without a bicycle." But any product serves this function of expressing something about the personality of its user, not just T shirts. And that is why the value expression approach is so common.

Ego defensive attitudes are related to the individual's attempts to protect himself or herself from internal conflict and external dangers. Examples of attitudes that are often ego defensive are attitudes of prejudice and attitudes concerning public health issues, such as fluoridation of drinking water.

The Cooper and Jahoda study of the Mr. Biggott cartoons showed some ego defensiveness operating in the area of racial prejudice. Many people misperceived or "misunderstood" the cartoons because this let them avoid their threatening message. The Janis and Feshbach study of fear appeals suggested that a similar process occurred when a strong fear appeal was used in a message about dental hygiene.

It is difficult to create messages to address ego defensive attitudes, since most mass communicators are not psychiatrists. Even if they were, many psychiatric treatments take years. This is one of the great challenges of mass communication—what can be done to overcome ego defensive attitudes in a brief mass communication message such as a 30-second public service announcement? Many church groups and mental health organizations are taking up this challenge, and the attentive viewer of television can see a number of creative examples.

What techniques can be used to change ego defensive attitudes? One technique is to reduce the threat in the message, perhaps by using a low fear appeal rather than a high fear appeal. A second technique is to attempt to use some humor to reduce tension. This is risky; however, the Cooper and Jahoda "Mr. Biggott" study showed that humor does not always work with this kind of attitude. A third technique is to attempt to give the person some insight into his or her own ego defensive behavior. This is what Katz and his colleagues have tried to do in a number of experimental studies of methods of reducing racial prejudices, and they have reported some success. A fourth technique is to try to shift the person's thinking out of the area of ego defense and into the area of value expression. For instance, if you were developing a campaign to get people to wear seat belts, the best approach might not be to mention death or other harmful consequences which would arouse defensiveness. Instead, it might be possible to present the wearing of seat belts as a means people could use to show their love for their families. This approach is being used in some television messages attempting to get people to use medication to control their high blood pressure. The messages suggest, "Do it for them."

CONCLUSIONS

The field of attitude change research has expanded greatly since the early days when the learning theory approach and the consistency theory approach were dominant. Katz's functional approach was developed specifically to reconcile these two divergent views and fit them both into a larger picture. The Katz approach has led to research investigating various approaches to changing ego defensive attitudes, and has served as a rather direct inspiration for Lerbinger's five persuasive designs.

McGuire's inoculation theory is a nice counterbalance to the many studies of attitude change. While others have been trying to discover the best means of persuading people, McGuire has been investigating the best means of making people resistant to persuasion.

Festinger raised an important issue when he gave an address suggesting that all the many studies of attitude change might be nearly worthless. He claimed there was little evidence that attitude change produced by persuasive messages was accompanied by any real behavior change. About the same time, researchers began a serious study of whether attitudes in general as they were measured by researchers were of any use in predicting behavior.

One of the beneficial results of all this questioning is that many attitude change studies now incorporate behavioral measures as well as attitude measures.

Finally, Lerbinger has attempted to present much of the scientific knowledge of persuasion in a handbook for practical communicators. There is much of value in his book. We summarized one of his key ideas—the five persuasive designs. Each of these five designs relates to a body of scientific research and theory, most of which has been described in other parts of this book.

An interesting exercise is to attempt to apply Lerbinger's designs to some practical communication problem, such as the task of persuading the American people to obey the 55 mph speed limit. Which design or designs would be best to use, and exactly how would they be applied to this problem?

REFERENCES

Ajzen, I. (1971). Attitudinal vs. Normative Messages: An Investigation of the Differential Effects of Persuasive Communications on Behavior. *Sociometry* 34:263–280.

Ajzen, I., and M. Fishbein. (1970). The Prediction of Behavior from Attitudinal and Normative Variables. *Journal of Experimental Social Psychology* 6:466–487.

Dichter, E. (1960). *The Strategy of Desire.* Garden City, N.Y.: Doubleday.

Evans, R. I., R. R. Rozelle, T. M. Lasater, T. M. Dembroski and B. P. Allen. (1970). Fear Arousal, Persuasion and Actual Versus Implied Behavioral Change: New Perspective Utilizing a Real-Life Dental Hygiene Program. *Journal of Personality and Social Psychology* 16:220–27.

Festinger, L. (1964). Behavioral Support for Opinion Change. *Public Opinion Quarterly* 28:404–417.

Fishbein, M. (1973). Introduction: The Prediction of Behaviors from Attitudinal Variables. In C. D. Mortensen and K. K. Sereno (eds.), *Advances in Communication Research,* pp. 3–31. New York: Harper and Row.

Gross, S. J., and C. M. Niman. (1975). Attitude-Behavior Consistency: A Review. *Public Opinion Quarterly* 39:358–368.

Hall, E. (November, 1973). Aunt Grace's Thesaurus: A Sketch of Charles Osgood. *Psychology Today* 7, no. 6:57.

Insko, C. A. (1967). *Theories of Attitude Change.* New York: Appleton-Century-Crofts.

Katz, D. (1960). The Functional Approach to the Study of Attitudes. *Public Opinion Quarterly* 24:163–204.

Katz, D., C. McClintock and I. Sarnoff. (1957). The Measurement of Ego Defense as Related to Attitude Change. *Journal of Personality* 25:465–474.

Katz, D., I. Sarnoff and C. McClintock. (1956). Ego-defense and Attitude Change. *Human Relations* 9:27–45.

Krisher, H. P. III, S. A. Darley and J. M. Darley. (1973). Fear-Provoking Recommendations, Intentions to Take Preventive Actions, and Actual Preventive Actions. *Journal of Personality and Social Psychology* 26:301–308.

LaPiere, R. T. (1934). Attitudes vs. Actions. *Social Forces* 13:230–237.

Lerbinger, O. (1972). *Designs for Persuasive Communication.* Englewood Cliffs, N.J.: Prentice-Hall.

Maccoby, N., and J. W. Farquhar. (1975). Communicating for Health: Unselling Heart Disease. *Journal of Communication* 25, no. 3:114–126.

Maslow, A. H. (1970). *Motivation and Personality.* 2nd ed. New York: Harper and Row.

McClintock, C. (1958). Personality Syndromes and Attitude Change. *Journal of Personality* 26:479–593.

McGuire, W., and D. Papageorgis. (1961). The Relative Efficacy of Various Types of Prior Belief-Defense in Producing Immunity Against Persuasion. *Journal of Abnormal and Social Psychology* 62:327–337.

Packard, V. (1958). *The Hidden Persuaders.* New York: Pocket Books.

Papageorgis, D., and W. McGuire. (1961). The Generality of Immunity to Persuasion Produced By Pre-Exposure to Weakened Counterarguments. *Journal of Abnormal and Social Psychology* 62:475–481.

Weigel, R. H., and L. S. Newman. (1976). Increasing Attitude-Behavior Correspondence by Broadening the Scope of the Behavioral Measure. *Journal of Personality and Social Psychology* 33:793–802.

Wicker, A. W. (1969). Attitudes versus Actions: The Relationship of Verbal and Overt Behavioral Responses to Attitude Objects. *Journal of Social Issues* 25, no. 4:41–78.

Chapter 14

Interpersonal Communication and the Media

THE decades between the two World Wars saw an increasing concern with a fear of the all-powerful nature of the mass media. During the decade of the 1920's many people became aware of the widespread and effective use of propaganda during the First World War. After the war the use of advertising increased dramatically. The decade of the 1930's saw the rising use of radio to address huge audiences on both sides of the Atlantic. In the United States President Franklin Roosevelt overcame both a hostile press and a hostile Congress by going over their heads directly to the American people with his "fireside chats" on the radio. The impact of radio on the general public can be illustrated by the effect of a 1938 Halloween radio broadcast, H. G. Wells' "War of the Worlds," which caused panic in some communities. In Europe radio was put to far different and more sustained and dangerous uses by Adolph Hitler in his attempt to conquer the world.

Under these conditions it is no surprise that the prevalent image of the mass media was that of a hypodermic needle or a bullet. This was a concept of the media with direct, immediate and powerful effects on any individual they reached. It was parallel to the stimulus-response principle which characterized much of psychological research in the 1930's and 1940's.

The decade of the 1940's began with both Europe and Asia at war. Japanese armies were deep into China. Hitler's blitzkrieg had overrun Poland in a few weeks, then turned west, invaded Denmark and Norway, defeated France in six weeks and forced the British to evacuate the remains of their army from the beaches of Dunkirk to defend their home islands. Under these circumstances President Roosevelt announced that he would run for a third term—a move unprecedented in American history.

At Columbia University a group of social scientists at the Bureau of Applied Social Research became concerned about the apparently all pervasive direct effects of the media on individuals and what this might imply for the give and take of the democratic process.

Influences on Voting Behavior

To investigate the effects of the mass media on political behavior, the researchers from the Columbia Bureau of Applied Social Research selected four groups of registered voters from Erie County, Ohio. This was a typical county in that it had voted in every presidential election as the nation had voted up to that time. These voters were then interviewed at intervals throughout the campaign to determine what factors played the greatest influence in their decision making regarding the election.

The design used three control groups to check on any effects of the seven monthly interviews of the main panel. All four groups (with 600 registered voters in each) were interviewed in May. The panel was interviewed every month after the May interview up to the November election and then immediately after it. Each of the three control groups was interviewed once after the initial interview—one in July, one in August and one in October (Lazarsfeld, *et al.*, 1948).

Because the hypodermic model of the effects of mass media prevailed among communication researchers at the time, the 1940 Erie County study was designed to demonstrate the power of the mass media in affecting voting decisions. Two of the researchers said, "This study went to great lengths to determine how the mass media brought about such changes" (Lazarsfeld and Menzel, 1963, p. 96).

What the researchers found was that "personal contacts appear to have been both more frequent and more effective than the mass media in influencing voting decision" (Katz, 1957, p. 63). However, only eight percent of the respondents actually switched from one candidate to another between the first interview in May and the last one in November. The researchers proposed that messages from the media first reach *opinion leaders* who then pass on what they read or hear to associates or followers who look to them as influentials. This process was named the *two-step* flow of communication.

Because the design of the study did not anticipate the importance of interpersonal relations, the two-step flow concept was the one least well documented by the data. As a result, a number of other studies were later done to verify and refine the concept.

Among the conclusions of the 1940 voting study were the following:

1) Those who decided late in the campaign or changed their minds during the campaign were more likely than others to cite personal influence as having figured in their decisions.
2) "Opinion leaders" were found at every social level and were presumed to be very much like those they influenced.

3) Opinion leaders were found to be more exposed to the mass media than those who were not designated opinion leaders.

In the 1940 voting study, a panel of voters was drawn at random. Respondents were asked if they had tried to convince anyone of their political ideas or if anyone had asked their advice on political matters. Besides the question of the validity of designating opinion leaders by this method there is also another problem. The data result in only two subgroups, those who report themselves to be opinion leaders and those who do not. There is no way to compare individual opinion leaders with those specific individuals who look to them for advice.

As the 1940 voting study was being completed another study in a small New Jersey town (Rovere) was begun. A sample of 86 persons was asked to name the people from whom they sought information and advice. Those individuals named four or more times were considered opinion leaders and interviewed in depth. In Rovere there was certainly greater validity in designating individuals as opinion leaders than in the Erie County study and they were, no doubt, influential with a greater number of people. In the Rovere study the original sample was used only to locate the opinion leaders. After that all of the attention was focused on the attributes of the opinion leaders.

When the war ended the researchers were able to resume their work on opinion leadership with a study in Decatur, Ill. Here the research was ablt to compare the leader with the person who named the leader, or, more technically, to examine the advisor-advisee dyad. Do the advisor and advisee tend to be of the same social class, age and sex? Is the leader more exposed to the mass media than the follower? Is he or she more interested in the topic of influence than the follower?

It was during the Decatur research that the investigators saw the need to examine chains of influence longer than a dyad. Opinion leaders were reporting that they had been influenced by other opinion leaders. Also, opinion leaders were found to be influential only at certain times and only on certain issues. Opinion leaders are influential not only because of who they are (social status, age, sex, etc.) but also because of the structure and values of the groups they are members of.

The Adoption of an Innovation

It also became clear that while the previous research allowed for the study of individual decisions it did not permit study of decision making on a community level. The next study introduced the notion of diffusion over time of a specific item through the social structure of a community (Katz, 1957, pp. 57–8).

The diffusion study examined how medical doctors make decisions to adopt new drugs. All doctors in several specialties in four midwestern cities were interviewed. Besides the usual demographic data (age, medical school attended, etc.) and data about attitudes, prescription of drugs, exposure to information sources and influence, etc., each doctor was asked to name the three colleagues he was most apt to talk with about cases, the three he was most apt to seek information and advice from and the three he was most likely to socialize with.

These questions regarding a doctor's interactions with his colleagues allowed the researchers to "map" the interpersonal relations in the medical communities. The study also allowed focus on a specific item (a new drug) as it gained acceptance and a record over time (through prescriptions on file at pharmacies).

In the drug study, an objective record of decision making (the prescriptions) was available as an additional source of information (in addition to the self-report of the doctor). Also, inferences could be drawn about the different influences on the making of a decision. For example, early adopters were more likely to attend out-of-town medical meetings in their specialties. The mapping of interpersonal relations made possible inferences regarding the effect of social relations in decision making.

Findings about Opinion Leadership

The following conclusions were reached from the series of studies after the 1940 voting study:

1) Personal influence was both more frequent and more effective than any of the mass media, not only in politics but also in marketing, fashion decisions and movie going (the latter three were investigated in the Decatur study). In the case of the drug diffusion study, those doctors most integrated into the medical community were the ones most likely to be early adopters of the innovation. Those doctors most frequently named as discussion partners were most apt to be innovators. Extent of integration proved more important than the doctor's age, medical school, income of patients, readership of medical journals or any other factors examined.

    The researchers attributed the innovativeness of doctors who are integrated in their respective medical communities to their being in touch and up-to-date with medical developments. They also noted that these were the doctors who could count on social support from their colleagues when facing the risks of innovation in medicine.

2) Interpersonal influence in primary groups is effective in maintaining a high degree of homogeneity of opinions and actions within a group. In the voting studies those who changed their minds reported initially that they had intended to vote differently from their families or friends. Medical doctors tended to prescribe the same drugs as their closest colleagues, especially when treating the more puzzling diseases.

3) In the decision making process different media play different roles. Some

media inform or let one know about the existence of an item while others legitimate or make acceptable a given course of action.

Who will lead and who will follow is determined, to a large extent, by the subject matter under consideration. In the area of marketing, opinion leadership was concentrated among older women with larger families. In the Rovere study some individuals were opinion leaders in "local" affairs while others were influential in "cosmopolitan" affairs. In the areas of fashion and movie going the young unmarried woman was most often the opinion leader. The researchers found that an opinion leader in one area is unlikely to be an opinion leader in another unrelated area.

But, people talk most often to others like themselves. In marketing, fashions, movie going and public affairs, opinion leaders were found on every socio-economic and occupational level.

If opinion leaders are found at all levels, what then distinguishes the leaders from their followers?

The researchers concluded that the following factors differentiate leaders from their followers:

1) personification of values (who one is); 2) competence (what one knows); 3) strategic social location (whom one knows).

Strategic social location divides into whom one knows within the group in which opinion leadership is exercised and whom one knows outside of the group for information on topics salient to the group.

Personification of values is another way of saying that the influential is someone that his or her followers wish to emulate. The influencee admires the influential and wishes to become as similar as possible. On the other hand, the opinion leader must also be regarded as knowledgeable or competent in the area in which his or her leadership is sought. We seldom pay attention to the opinions of people who don't seem to know what they are talking about.

Even if one is both the type of person others want to emulate and is competent, one must also be accessible to those people who are interested in the area in which his or her leadership is sought. To be a leader one must have followers. As mentioned, an individual is also most apt to be an opinion leader if that individual maintains contacts outside of the group which, in turn, provide information and opinions of interest to the group members. This was found to be true in many diverse areas of opinion leadership (e.g., politics, medicine, farming, etc.).

Opinion leaders were found to be more exposed to media appropriate to their sphere of influence than their followers. The Rovere study found opinion leaders on "cosmopolitan" matters more likely to read national news magazines than those influential on "local" matters. In the drug study the influential medical doctors were more likely to read a large number of professional journals and value them more highly than their less influential colleagues. They also attended more out of town meetings and had more out of town contacts as well. One researcher observed, ". . . the greater exposure of the opinion leader to the mass media may only be a special case of the more general proposition that opinion leaders serve to relate their groups to relevant parts of the environment through whatever media happen to be appropriate." (Katz, 1957, p. 56).

Opinion leaders and their followers are very similar and usually belong to the same groups. It is highly unlikely that the opinion leader is very far ahead of his or her followers in level of interest in a given topic. Interpersonal relations are not only networks of communication but also sources of social pressure to conform to the group's norms and sources of social support for the values and opinions an individual holds.

Two others authors, in discussing this interaction of media, social and psychological variables in the communication process, have written:

> In more recent times it has been realized that mass media information is received, passed on, distorted, assimilated, rejected, or acted upon in ways which are in part determined by the operation of various social and social-psychological systems at various points of transmission and reception as the flow of information takes place. Therefore, for the student of mass communication the operation of primary groups, role structures, voluntary associations, personality variables, and vast complexes of other variables related to the operation of "diffusion networks" have become a new research domain. The developing model of the operation of the mass media couples the mass communication process to the social networks of family, work, play, school and community. (DeFleur and Larsen, 1958, p. xiii.).

As pointed out at the beginning of this chapter, most media researchers during the 1930's and even the 1940's employed the hypodermic needle model of communication in their thinking of media effects—direct, immediate and powerful. As more sophisticated methods were employed by media researchers the hypodermic model was recognized as far too simplistic. Throughout the 1940's and 1950's communication researchers began to recognize many psychological and sociological variables which intervene between the media and the mind of the receiver (e.g.: selective exposure, perception and retention; group memberships, norms and salience; opinion leadership, etc.).

Two of the researchers involved in the series of studies done at Columbia concluded, "The whole moral . . . is that knowledge of an individual's interpersonal environment is basic to an understanding of his exposure and reactions to the mass media." (Katz and Lazarsfeld, 1955, p. 133).

Criticisms of the Two-Step Flow

Numerous criticisms have been made of the two-step flow model. Among them are:

1) Many studies indicate that major news stories are spread directly by the mass media to a far greater extent than by personal sources. Westley

(1971, p. 726) cites several studies supporting this and discusses it briefly.

2) Findings that opinions on public affairs are reciprocal or that often there is " . . . opinion sharing rather than opinion giving." Troldahl and Van Dam (1965–66, p. 633) say that opinion givers " . . . were not significantly different (from seekers) in their exposure to relevant media content, their information level on national news, their occupational prestige, and four of five attributes of gregariousness."

3) Related to point two is the observation by Lin (1971, p. 203) that "The definition of the opinion leader versus non-opinion leader dichotomy is also unclear and the problem is further confounded by varying operationalizing methods." He adds that opinion leadership has been determined by both self-designation and nomination and it has been applied to both specific topics and to general activities.

4) The varying empirical definitions of mass media. In some instances specialized media (special bulletins, medical journals, farm journals) have been used, in other instances they have not been part of the definition of the mass media (Lin, 1971, p. 204).

5) Other investigators (Rogers and Shoemaker, 1971, p. 206) point out that opinion leaders can be either active or passive while the two-step flow model implies a dichotomy between active information seeking opinion leaders and a mass audience of passive individuals who then rely on the opinion leaders for guidance.

6) The limitation of the original model to two steps while the process may be either more or fewer. As already mentioned however, the Columbia group saw the need to investigate longer chains of influence during the Decatur study and followed this line of study in the drug diffusion research.

7) The implication that opinion leaders rely on mass media channels only. Sometimes, especially in developing countries without extensive networks of mass media, personal trips and conversations with change agents assume the information role that mass media might normally play.

8) Indications of different behavior by early knowers and late knowers of information. It has been found that early knowers of information more often rely on media sources while the late knowers are more dependent upon interpersonal sources. (Rogers and Shoemaker, 1971, pp. 259, 348).

9) In the diffusion of an innovation it has been found that mass media primarily serve to inform while interpersonal channels are most important at persuading. Rogers and Shoemaker (1971, p. 208) contend that these differences apply to both opinion leaders and followers.

The criticisms of the two-step flow model are mainly that it originally did not explain enough. As we shall see, subsequent work has considerably expanded and refined the model—as one would expect in the case of any cumulative research.

The Diffusion of Innovations

The two-step flow model has evolved gradually into a multi-step flow model which is often used in *diffusion research*. The latter is the study of how innovations (new ideas, practices, objects, etc.) become known and are spread throughout a social system. While the two-step flow model is mainly concerned with how an individual receives information and passes it along to others, the diffusion process concentrates on the final stage of the adoption or rejection of an innovation.

Probably the best known and most widely respected researcher in diffusion research today is Everett Rogers. In the book *Communication of Innovations* (Rogers and Shoemaker, 1971) the authors examine more than 1,500 publications to arrive at a paradigm of the innovation-decision process. They offer 103 generalizations about the process which are drawn from the findings of the 1,500 studies from many parts of the world.

The main theme of the book is that communication is necessary for social change. They define social change as "the process by which alteration occurs in the structure and function of a social system" (p. 38). Social change consists of three stages: the creation or development of new ideas; their communication to members of a social system; and the changes resulting from their adoption or rejection.

Diffusion is defined as a special type of communication concerned with the spread of new ideas (p. 39). In the previous discussion of the two-step flow model we have seen that opinion leaders and their followers are remarkably similar in many attributes. Diffusion research calls this similarity *homophily,* or the degree to which pairs of individuals who interact are similar in certain attributes such as beliefs, values, education, social status, etc. However, in the diffusion of an innovation, *heterophily* is most often present. Heterophily is the degree to which pairs of individuals who interact are different in certain attributes (the mirror opposite of homophily). A high degree of source-receiver heterophily, often present in the diffusion of innovations since new ideas often come from people who are quite different from the receiver, creates unique problems in obtaining effective communication.

In the conceptual model of diffusion an innovation is communicated through certain channels over time among members of a social system (Rogers and Shoemaker, 1971, p. 39).

The paradigm of the innovation-decision process over time consists of three major components:

1) *antecedents*
   a) the personality characteristics of an individual (e.g., attitude toward change, etc.)
   b) social characteristics (e.g., cosmopoliteness, etc.)
   c) the strength of perceived need for innovation
2) the *process* itself (e.g., knowledge, persuasion, etc.);

Paradigm of the Innovation-Decision Process

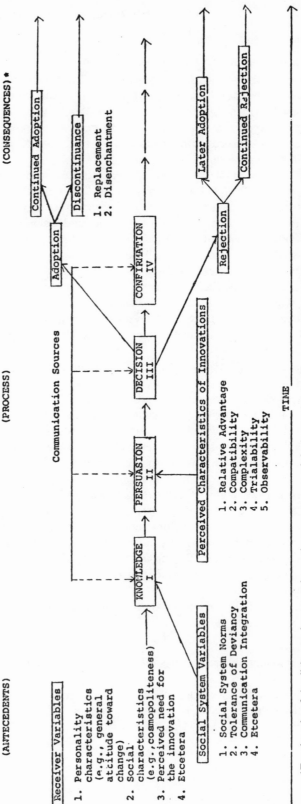

(ANTECEDENTS)

(PROCESS)

(CONSEQUENCES)*

Receiver Variables

1. Personality characteristics (e.g., general attitude toward change)
2. Social characteristics (e.g., cosmopoliteness)
3. Perceived need for the innovation
4. Etcetera

Social System Variables

1. Social System Norms
2. Tolerance of Deviancy
3. Communication Integration
4. Etcetera

Communication Sources

KNOWLEDGE I

PERSUASION II

DECISION III

CONFIRMATION IV

Adoption

Rejection

Continued Adoption

Discontinuance
1. Replacement
2. Disenchantment

Later Adoption

Continued Rejection

Perceived Characteristics of Innovations

1. Relative Advantage
2. Compatibility
3. Complexity
4. Trialability
5. Observability

TIME

*For the sake of simplicity, we have not shown the consequences of the innovation in this paradigm but only the consequences of the process.

From Rogers and Shoemaker (1971). *Communication of Innovations*. Copyright 1971 by the Free Press, New York. Reprinted by permission.

3) *consequences* (e.g., adoption or rejection, followed by the later alternatives shown in Figure 1).

An individual passes through a mental process from first awareness to the innovation to an adoption or rejection of the innovation and then a confirmation of his or her decision. Rogers and Shoemaker divide this process into four steps (p. 103):

1) *Knowledge.* The individual is exposed to the innovation's existence and gains some understanding of how it functions.
2) *Persuasion.* The individual forms a favorable or unfavorable attitude toward the innovation.
3) *Decision.* The individual engages in activities which lead to a choice to adopt or reject the innovation.
4) *Confirmation.* The individual seeks reinforcement for the innovation decision he or she has made, but may reverse the previous decision if exposed to conflicting messages about the innovation.

The rate at which an innovation is adopted (or rejected) depends upon how the members of a social system perceive five characteristics or attributes of the innovation (Rogers and Shoemaker, 1971, pp. 167–8):

1) *Relative advantage*—"the degree to which an innovation is perceived as better than the idea it supersedes."
2) *Compatibility*—"the degree to which an innovation is perceived as consistent with the existing values, past experiences, and needs of the receivers."
3) *Complexity*—"the degree to which an innovation is perceived as relatively difficult to understand and use."
4) *Trialability*—"the degree to which an innovation may be experimented with on a limited basis."
5) *Observability*—"the degree to which the results of an innovation are visible to others."

All of the attributes of an innovation except its complexity are positively related to its rate of adoption.

In their discussion of communication channels (Ch. 8), Rogers and Shoemaker point out that while mass media can reach large audiences rapidly, create knowledge and spread information and lead to changes in weakly held attitudes, the formation and change of strongly held attitudes is best accomplished by interpersonal channels.

Interpersonal channels are more effective than the media when there is apathy or resistance to a message. Interpersonal channels allow a two-way exchange of ideas. A source can add information or clarify points and perhaps surmount psychological and social barriers (e.g., selective attention, perception, retention; group norms, values, etc.).

In the Diffusion of Innovation paradigm *change agents* play key roles in the evaluation and trial stages. A change agent is a professional person who attempts to influence adoption decisions in a direction that he or she feels desirable. Change agents can be salesmen and dealers in new products (e.g., hybrid seed corn), detail men of pharmaceutical companies promoting new drugs with medical doctors, technical assistance workers in developing nations and many others who serve to link individual social systems together. The role of change agents in the evaluation and trial of innovations is especially important to advertising and public relations.

One author points out that

> . . . when a gatekeeper is a commercial change agent, his integrity is questioned by the people he seeks to change. His vulnerability is best understood by seeing him in a conflict situation: he is responsible to the bureaucracy that pays him, but he must simultaneously satisfy the need of the so-called client system—the people he seeks to influence. His credibility is impaired if he appears to execute the demands of the bureaucracy while disregarding the expectations of the client system. This happens to a commercial change agent when people feel that he promotes the 'over-adoption of new ideas to secure higher sales.' These findings suggest that a public communicator's credibility will be low when he is seen as ignoring the interests of a public in favor of his employer's interests (Lerbinger, 1972, p. 197).

In the process of innovation-decision making the mass media are at their best in providing knowledge of an innovation while interpersonal channels are more important in persuading. Mass media channels are relatively more important than interpersonal channels for earlier adopters of an innovation than for late adopters because at the early stages there are few interpersonal channels available to the early adopters. In the countries without extensive networks of mass media it has been observed that cosmopolite interpersonal channels (individuals from outside the social system) often performed the role played by media channels in the more developed societies (p. 256).

Rogers and Shoemaker contend that a "combination of mass media and interpersonal communication is the most effective way of reaching people with new ideas and persuading them to utilize these innovations" (p. 260). They cite and discuss the use of *media forums* (organized small groups of individuals who meet regularly to receive a mass media program, broadcast or print, and then discuss its content) in Canada, India, Africa, China, Latin America and Italy.

CONCLUSIONS

The available evidence indicates that the greatest effect is achieved when media messages advocating innovation or attitude change are coupled with small group discussion. Among the reasons given are: social expectations and the pressures applied by the group on individuals to attend and participate; and, the effects of group pressures on attitude change. As Rogers and Shoemaker point out "media forums serve to heighten the impact of change-oriented messages by reducing the possibility of selective exposure and selective perception" (p. 264).

REFERENCES

DeFleur, M. and O. Larsen (1958). *The Flow of Information.* New York: Harper.

Katz, E. (1957). The Two-Step Flow of Communication: An Up-To-Date Report of an Hypothesis. *Public Opinion Quarterly* 21:61–78. Also in W. Schramm (ed.) (1960). *Mass Communications.* Urbana: University of Illinois Press.

Katz, E. and P. Lazarsfeld (1955). *Personal Influence: The Part Played by People in the Flow of Mass Communications.* Glencoe, Illinois: The Free Press.

Lazarsfeld, P., B. Berelson and H. Gaudet (1948). *The People's Choice.* New York: Columbia University Press.

Lazarsfeld, P. and H. Menzel (1963). Mass Media and Personal Influence. In W. Schramm (ed.), *The Science of Human Communication.* New York: Basic Books.

Lerbinger, O. (1972). *Designs for Persuasive Communication.* Englewood Cliffs, New Jersey: Prentice-Hall, Inc.

Lin, N. (1971). *The Study of Human Communication.* Indianapolis, Indiana: Bobbs-Merrill Co., Inc.

Rogers, E. and F. Shoemaker (1971). *Communication of Innovations.* New York: The Free Press.

Troldahl, V. and R. Van Dam (1965). Face-to-Face Communication about Major Topics in the News. *Public Opinion Quarterly* 42:403–12.

Westley, B. (1971). Communication and Social Change. *American Behavioral Scientist* 14:719–42.

Chapter 15

The Mass Media
in Modern Society

M ODERN industrial and post industrial society is nearly unthinkable
without the mass media of newspapers, magazines, paperbacks, radio,
television and film. The mass media are many things to many people and
serve a variety of functions, depending on the interests and needs of specific
individuals. This chapter will examine views of how the media actually function.

For a philosophical and historical discussion of the various roles of the
media in different types of societies the reader is directed to Siebert, Peterson
and Schramm, *Four Theories of the Press.* J. S. Mill in chapter 2 of *On
Liberty* has summarized the classic arguments for the liberty of thought and
discussion in a democracy.

Functions of the Media

Harold Lasswell and Charles Wright are among the many scholars who
have seriously considered the functions and role of the mass media in society.

Harold Lasswell (1948, 1960), scholar of communication and professor
of law at Yale, noted three functions of the mass media: surveillance of the
environment; the correlation of the parts of society in responding to the
environment; and the transmission of the social heritage from one generation
to the next. To these three functions Wright (1959, p. 16) adds a fourth,
entertainment. In addition to functions, the media may also have dysfunctions,
or consequences which are undesirable for the society or its members. A
single act may be both functional and dysfunctional.

Surveillance, the first function, informs and provides news. In performing this function the media often warn us of expected dangers such as extreme or dangerous weather conditions or a threatening military situation (e.g., the Cuban missile crisis). The surveillance function also includes the news the media provide which is essential to the economy, the public and society such as stock market reports, reports about road conditions, etc. The surveillance function can also cause several dysfunctions. Panic may result through the overemphasis of dangers or threats to the society (e.g., Orson Welles' "War of the Worlds" broadcast which was mistaken by many listeners for a news broadcast). Lazarsfeld and Merton (1948, 1960) have noted a "narcotizing" dysfunction when individuals fall into a state of apathy or passivity as a result of too much information to assimilate. Besides that, too much exposure to "news" (the unusual, abnormal, unordinary) may leave many audience members with little perspective of what is the usual, normal or ordinary in a society.

Correlation, the second function, is the selection and interpretation of information about the environment. The media often include criticism and prescribe how one should react to events. It is the editorial and propaganda content of the media. The correlation function serves to enforce social norms and maintain consensus by exposing deviants, confers status by highlighting selected individuals in the media and can operate as a check on government. In carrying out the correlation function the media can often impede threats to social stability and may often monitor or manage public opinion. The correlation function can become dysfunctional when the media perpetuate stereotypes and enhance conformity, impede social change and innovation, minimize criticism, enforce majority views at the expense of minority opinions which are not aired, and preserve and extend power which may need to be checked.

One of the major dysfunctions of media correlation often cited is the creation of what Daniel Boorstin has termed "pseudo-events" or the manufacture of "images" or "personalities"—much of the stock-in-trade of the public relations industry. Products and corporations are given "images" and individuals have public "personalities" manufactured for them through the creation of "events" contrived to gain media exposure. Aspiring politicians and entertainers seek exposure for public recognition and acceptance while corporations seek a respected image and sought after products and services.

As *transmitters of culture,* the media function to communicate information, values, and norms from one generation to another or from the members of a society to newcomers. In this way they serve to increase social cohesion by widening the base of common experience. They aid the integration of individuals into a society by continuing socialization after formal education has ended as well as by beginning it during the preschool years. It has been noted that the media can reduce an individual's sense of estrangement (anomie), or feeling of rootlessness by providing a society to identify with. However, because of the impersonal nature of the mass media it has been charged that the media contribute to the depersonalization of mass society (a dysfunction). Mass media are interposed between individuals and remove personal contact in communication.

It has also been charged that the media serve to reduce the variety of subcultures and help augment mass society. This is the notion that because of the mass media we tend more and more to speak the same way, dress the same way, think the same way and act and react the same way. It is based on the idea that thousands of hours of media exposure cause millions of people to accept role models presented by the media. Along with this tendency for standardization is the charge that the mass media impede cultural growth.

Probably most media content is intended as entertainment, even in most newspapers, if one considers the many columns, features and fillers. Media entertainment serves to provide respite from everyday problems and fills leisure time. The media expose millions to a mass culture of art and music and some contend they raise public taste and preference in the arts. On the other hand there are those who argue that the media encourage escapism, corrupt fine art, lower public taste and impede the growth of an appreciation for the arts.

Harold Lasswell (1948, 1960) pointed out that in every society values are shaped and distributed which are the ideology in support of the network as a whole (1960, p. 123). He notes that in the ideological conflict of world politics "The ruling elites view one another as potential enemies . . . (and) the ideology of the other may appeal to disaffected elements at home and weaken the internal power position of each ruling class." (1960, p. 124).

Lasswell adds that ". . . one ruling element is especially alert to the other, and relies upon communication as a means of preserving power" (1960, p. 124). Discussing barriers to efficient communication in a society, Lasswell notes:

> Some of the most serious threats to efficient communication for the community as a whole relate to the values of power, wealth, and respect. Perhaps the most striking examples of power distortion occur when the content of communication is deliberately adjusted to fit an ideology or counterideology. . . . A typical instance of inefficiencies connected with respect (social class) occurs when an upper class person mixes only with persons of his own stratum and forgets to correct his perspective by being exposed to members of other classes. (1960, pp. 126–7).

Often cited as a major cause of urban riots in the 1960s were minority frustrations because of an inability to communicate their grievances to the general population.

Speaking of the flow of information within a society Lasswell says:

> When the ruling classes fear the masses, the rulers do not share their picture of reality with the rank and file. When the reality picture of kings, presidents, and cabinets is not permitted to circulate through the state as a whole, the

degree of discrepancy shows the extent to which the ruling groups assume that their power depends upon distortion. (1960, p. 129).

If the "truth" is not shared, the ruling elements expect internal conflict, rather than harmonious adjustment to the external environment of the state. Hence the channels of communication are controlled . . . in such a way that only responses will be forthcoming which are deemed favorable to the power position of the ruling classes. (1960, p. 129).

The revelations contained in the "Pentagon Papers" of truths about the Vietnam war not shared with the American people are a good example of the point Lasswell makes.

Our Mental Picture of the World

The distinguished political columnist Walter Lippmann, writing in his classic *Public Opinion,* discussed the discrepancy between the world and the "realities" we perceive and act upon. He pointed out that most of what we know of the environment we live in comes to us indirectly, but, "whatever we believe to be a true picture, we treat as if it were the environment itself." Lippmann pointed out that although we find it hard to apply this notion to the beliefs upon which we are now acting, it becomes easy to apply it to other people and other ages and to the ludicrous pictures of the world about which they were in deadly earnest.

Fictions and symbols, aside from their value to the existing social order, are important to human communication. Nearly every individual deals with events which are out of sight and hard to grasp. Lippmann observes, "The only feeling that anyone can have about an event he does not experience is the feeling aroused by his mental image of that event." He adds that at certain times we respond as powerfully to fictions as to realities, and often we help create those fictions. In every case there has been inserted between us and the environment a pseudo-environment, and it is to this pseudo-environment that we respond. If these responses are acts, they are in the real-environment, not the pseudo-environment which stimulated them. For this reason Lippmann says, ". . . what is called the adjustment of man to his environment takes place through the medium of fictions."

Lippmann does not mean that these fictions are lies, but rather that we react to a representation of an environment which is manufactured by ourselves. We do this because the real environment is too big, too complex, and too fleeting for direct experience. (See Chapter 5 on abstraction.) In order to act on the environment we must reconstruct it as a simpler model before we are able to deal with it.

The author then discusses ". . . the world-wide spectacle of men acting upon their environment, moved by stimuli from their pseudo-environments." These actions can result in commands ". . . which set armies in motion or make peace, conscript life, tax, exile, imprison, protect property or confiscate it, encourage one kind of enterprise and discourage another, facilitate immigration or obstruct it, improve communication or censor it, establish schools, build navies, proclaim 'policies,' and 'destiny,' raise economic barriers, make property or unmake it, bring one people under the rule of another, or favor one class against another."

What we do, then, is not based upon certain and direct knowledge but upon our pictures of the world, usually provided by someone else. The way we imagine the world determines what we do, our efforts, feelings and hopes, but not our achievements or results. Propaganda, Lippmann points out, is an effort to alter the pictures to which we respond.

In *Public Opinion,* Lippmann deals with the reasons why pictures inside our heads often mislead us in our dealings with the outside world. He lists among the factors which limit our access to the facts: artificial censorship; limitations of social contact; meager time available each day for paying attention to public affairs; distortions as a result of compressing events into short messages; the use of a small vocabulary to describe a complex world (see Chapter 5); and the fear of facing facts which threaten our lives (See Chapter 11).

Popular Taste and Social Action

In an article titled "Mass Communication, Popular Taste and Organized Social Action" (1948, 1960) two well known and respected communication researchers and sociologists, Paul F. Lazarsfeld and Robert K. Merton, raise several important questions about the use of the media in our society. One of the major concerns they express regarding the mass media is their use by powerful interest groups to exercise social control. They point out that organized business, which "occupies the most spectacular place" among the chief power groups, has replaced the more direct means of control of mass publics through the use of propaganda called "public relations." The authors say, "Economic power seems to have reduced direct exploitation, achieved largely by disseminating propaganda through the mass media of communication."

They add, "The radio program and the institutional advertisement serve in place of intimidation and coercion." and, ". . . media have taken on the job of rendering mass publics conformative to the social and economic status quo." (1960, pp. 493–4).

Lazarsfeld and Merton then go on to discuss several of the functions of the media: status conferral; enforcement of social norms; and the narcotizing dysfunction.

Status conferral, or recognition by the mass media, indicates that one is important enough to single out from the mass and that one's behavior and opinions are significant enough to demand media attention. By legitimizing the status of individuals and groups the media confer status and prestige.

The mass media may *enforce social norms* as a result of their "exposure" of conditions which deviate from professed public morality. Publicity forces members of a group to acknowledge that these deviations have occurred and it requires individuals to take a stand. An individual is forced to choose between repudiating the norm and identifying himself or herself as outside the moral framework or supporting the norms, whatever his or her private beliefs. As the authors say, "Publicity closes the gap between 'private attitudes' and 'public morality.' " By preventing continued evasion of an issue publicity brings about pressure for a single rather than a dual morality. The mass media reaffirm social norms by publicly exposing deviations from them.

The authors observe that another consequence of the mass media is a *"narcotizing"* of the average reader or listener as a result of the flood of media stimuli. They call this the "narcotizing dysfunction" on the assumption that it is not in society's best interest to have a large portion of the population apathetic and inert. The authors suggest that the result of a flood of communications may be a superficial concern with problems and that this superficiality may cloak mass apathy. The interested and informed individual may know about the problems of the society without recognizing that he or she has failed to make decisions and do something about them. In this way, the authors say, mass media are among the most respectable and efficient of social narcotics, and increasing dosages may be transforming our energies from active participation to passive knowledge (1960, pp. 501–2).

Social Conformism

In much of western society the media are supported by the corporate business world which is a result of the social and economic system. The media, in turn, support that system. Lazarsfeld and Merton note that this support comes not only in the form of advertising but also in the content of the media which usually confirms and approves the present structure of society. In their words, ". . . this continuing reaffirmation underscores the duty to accept" (1960, p. 503).

The authors charge that this comes about not only through what is said, but, more importantly, from what is not said, for the media ". . . fail to raise essential questions about the structure of society." The authors say that the commercially sponsored media provide little basis for the critical appraisal of society and ". . . restrain the cogent development of a genuinely critical outlook" (p. 503). They note that there are occasional critical articles or programs but that they are so few that they are overwhelmed by the tide of conformist materials.

Because of the unthinking allegiance promoted by the commercial media, the authors say that the media cannot be expected to work for even minor changes in the social structure. Lazarsfeld and Merton note that social objectives are abandoned by commercial media when those objectives interfere with profits and this economic pressure results in conformity by omitting sensitive issues (1960, p. 504).

Conditions of Media Effectiveness

Lazarsfeld and Merton list three conditions which they say makes for media effectiveness: monopolization, canalization rather than change of basic values and supplementary face-to-face contact.

Monopolization occurs in the absence of mass media counterpropaganda. Besides authoritarian societies it also exists in any society for any issue, value, policy or public image for which there is nearly a complete absence of counterpropaganda. Sometimes this near complete absence of counterpropaganda is illustrated by the fact that when a "sacred" institution is questioned by the media the article or program becomes the center of a storm of controversy and is remembered years later as an outstanding exception to the norm. An example is the CBS documentary "The Selling of the Pentagon," which raised the question of what were termed "improper military information activities." Other memorable exceptions to the norm which resulted in storms of protest were the CBS documentaries "Harvest of Shame," dealing with migrant farm labor, and "Hunger in America," as well as the PBS documentaries "Who Invited US?" which questioned U.S. foreign policy and "Banks and the Poor." (Brown, 1971, pp. 328–332) Many other underlying assumptions, issues, policies and values are only peripherally dealt with, if at all. The television documentary "The Business of Religion" questioned some aspects of some religions, but the larger question of the overall value of religion in society is seldom, if ever, discussed in the major media. During the past decade the media have increasingly questioned business methods, without ever questioning the underlying assumptions—for example, the private ownership of natural resources. It is only in small and highly specialized publications that one finds any serious questioning of the family as the most effective basic unit for organizing post-industrial society, even with a national divorce rate currently reported at 40 percent. Whatever the intent of the framers of the first amendment, whatever the arguments of the enlightenment that "truth will win out in the marketplace of ideas," whatever the logic of Mill in his arguments for the liberty of thought and discussion, many basic assumptions which underlie society are never questioned or challenged in any meaningful way.

Lazarsfeld and Merton point out that advertising usually attempts to *"canalize"* existing patterns of behavior or attitudes. It often attempts to get the consumer to switch brands of a product he or she is already habituated to use, be it toothpaste or automobiles. Once a pattern of behavior or an attitude has been established it can be canalized in one direction or another. On the other hand, propaganda usually deals with more complex matters. Its objectives may be at odds with deep seated attitudes which must be reshaped, rather than the simple canalizing of existing value systems. The authors conclude that while the mass media have been effective in canalizing basic attitudes, there is little evidence of their bringing about attitude change by themselves.

Lazarsfeld and Merton cite a third condition: *supplementation* through face-to-face contacts. Here mass media which are neither monopolistic nor canalizing may, nevertheless, prove effective. The authors cite Father Coughlin who combined propagandistic radio talks with local organizations. Members listened to him and followed his radio talks with group discussions of the views he had expressed. This combination of radio talks, the distribution of newspapers and pamphlets, and the coordinated locally organized small discussion groups, all reinforcing one another, proved especially successful. (See Chapter 14, on the use of "media-forums.")

Such combinations of the mass media and reinforcing discussion groups are expensive and are usually found only in cases of planned change in the service of the status quo or in the case of the diffusion of innovation in developing countries. As Lazarsfeld and Merton point out, such media and discussion group collaboration has seldom been achieved by groups trying to bring about social change in modern industrial society. They say, "The forward looking groups at the edges of the power structure do not ordinarily have the large financial means of the contented groups at the center" (1960, p. 512).

The authors add, "Organized business does approach a virtual 'psychological monopoly' of the mass media. Radio commercials and newspaper advertisements are, of course, premised on a system which has been termed free enterprise."

The authors close by saying, "Face-to-face contacts with those who have been socialized in our culture serve primarily to reinforce the prevailing culture patterns." (Indeed, when those contacts do not do so, we often suffer the psychological discomfort of dissonance discussed in Chapter 11.) "Thus," the authors conclude, "the very conditions which make for the maximum effectiveness of the mass media of communication operate toward the maintenance of the going social and cultural structure rather than toward its change." (1960, p. 512).

Controlling the News Staff and Maintaining the Statue Quo

Why and how media maintain news and editorial policy is explored in two articles by Warren Breed, former newspaper reporter, Columbia PhD., and longtime faculty member at Tulane University. In "Social Control in the Newsroom" (1955, 1960), Breed explores the areas in which news and editorial policy is usually maintained and where it is bypassed. Breed observes that the newspaper publisher, as owner or a representative of ownership, has the right to set and enforce the newspaper's policy. However, conformity is not automatic.

By *policy* Breed means the orientation shown by a newspaper in its editorials, news columns and headlines regarding certain issues and events. "Slanting" almost never means prevarication, Breed points out, but rather it is the "omission, differential selection, and preferential placement, such as 'featuring' a pro-policy item, 'burying' an anti-policy story, etc." Breed contends that every newspaper, whether it admits it or not, has a policy. Politics, business and labor are the major areas of policy, much of which results from considerations of class. Breed points out that policy is usually *covert* because it is often against the ethical norms of journalism and media executives want to avoid being embarrassed by accusations that they have ordered the slanting of a news story.

Because of the covert nature of policy a new reporter can not be told what the policy is, but must learn to anticipate what is expected in order to win rewards and avoid punishments. Since policy is never made explicit a new reporter learns policy in a number of indirect ways. First, the staffer reads his or her own newspaper every day and learns to diagnose its character- istics. Usually his or her own output is patterned after that of newsroom colleagues. The newcomer's stories tend to reflect what is defined as standard procedure. The editing of a newcomers' copy is another guide as to what is or is not acceptable. Occasionally a staffer may, in an oblique way, be reprimanded. The implication is that punishment will follow if policy is not adhered to.

Through gossip among staffers and by other means the new reporter learns of the interests, affiliations and characteristics of the executives. News conferences, where the staffer outlines findings and executives discuss how to shape a story, offer insight through what the executives say and do not say. Again, policy is not stated explicitly. Other sources of information for staffers about executives are house organs, observation of the executives in meetings with various leaders and the opinions executives voice in unguarded moments.

Breed lists a number of reasons a staffer conforms to policy. The publish- er's power to fire or demote is one. However, editors have many opportunities to prevent a situation from reaching this point. Editors can ignore stories which allow for deviation from policy, or, if the story cannot be ignored it can be assigned to a "safe" reporter. Should a story reach an editor in an unacceptable form it can be edited and reasons other than policy can be given—such as the pressures of time and space.

New reporters may feel obligation and esteem for those who hired them, helped show them the "ropes" or did them other favors. Breed says that these "obligations and warm personal sentiments toward superiors play a strategic role in the pull to conformity." This factor seems to determine not only conformity to policy but morale and good news policy as well.

The desires that most young staffers have for status achievement are another reason for conforming to policy. Many reporters noted that a good path for advancement is to get big page one stories, and this means stories which do not oppose policy. Many staffers view newspapering as a stepping stone to more lucrative positions and a reputation as a "troublemaker" is a serious hurdle to such goals.

Among the other reasons for conformity to policy which Breed notes are: the absence of conflicting group allegiance; the pleasant nature of the activity (e.g., the in-groupness in the newsroom; the interesting nature of the work; non-financial perquisites); and the fact that news becomes a value and is a continuous challenge.

Through these many factors the new staffer identifies with veteran staffers and executives. Because of shared norms, his or her performance soon emulates theirs. The new staffer usually learns rapidly to put aside whatever personal beliefs or ethical ideals he or she may have brought to the job and conforms to policy norms.

Possibilities for Policy Deviation

However, there are situations which permit deviations from policy. Because policy is covert, its norms are not always entirely clear. If policy were spelled out explicitly, motivations, reasons, alternatives and other complicating material would have to be provided. Because policies are not spelled out a reporter often has an undefined zone which allows a certain amount of freedom.

Staffers who gather the news can use their superior knowledge of a story to subvert policy because executives may be ignorant of particular facts. Staffers are in a position to make decisions at many points. If a staffer cannot get "play" for a story because it violates policy then the story can be "planted" through a friendly staffer of a competitor. The reporter can then argue that the story has become too big to ignore.

Staffers covering "beats" (police, fire, city hall, courts, etc.) have greater leeway in deciding which stories to cover and which to ignore than those working on individual assignments from an editor. Beat reporters can sometimes ignore stories which would support policies they dislike or feel run counter to professional codes. Of course, this is only possible if potential competitors cooperate.

And, as one might expect, reporters who are considered "stars" can more often violate policy than others.

Breed contends that to the extent policy is maintained the existing system of power relationships is maintained. He says, "Policy usually protects property and class interests, and thus the strata and groups holding these interests are better able to retain them." (1960, p. 193). While much news is printed objectively so that the community can form opinions openly, important information is often denied the citizenry when policy news is buried or slanted.

Breed concludes that because the newsperson's source of rewards is from colleagues and superiors rather than from readers the staffer abandons societal and professional ideals in favor of the more pragmatic level of newsroom values. The staffer thereby gains both status rewards and group acceptance. Breed says, "Thus the cultural patterns of the newsroom produce results insufficient for wider democratic needs. Any important change toward a more 'free and responsible press' must stem from various possible pressures on

the publisher, who epitomizes the policy making and coordinating role."
(1960, p. 194).

A glaring example of newsroom "cultural patterns which produce results
insufficient for wider democratic needs" is the story told by the prize-winning
bureau chief of a national newspaper. As a young, beginning reporter in
the 1960s for another newspaper in a major southern city which has been
noted by one national publication for its "shackled press," the new staffer
began developing "initiative" stories in areas the paper had heretofore not
covered. Upon returning to her desk one day she found a crudely lettered
sign, "NIGGER EDITOR," and as she puts it, she "stormed out in a snit."

One of the often stated reasons for the urban riots by minorities in
the 1960s was the feeling that their grievances were not being communicated
to the general public. They recognized correctly, of course, that before one
can hope for change the problem must first be recognized. In the past decade
we have given currency to the shorthand term "consciousness raising."

Ten years after the publication of Breed's article, the Report of the
National Advisory Commission on Civil Disorders (The Kerner Report) said
this about media coverage of urban minority grievances:

> Our second and fundamental criticism is that the news media have failed
> to analyze and report adequately on racial problems in the United States and,
> as a related matter, to meet the Negro's legitimate expectations in journalism.
> By and large, news organizations have failed to communicate to both their black
> and white audiences a sense of the problems America faces and the sources of
> potential solutions. The media report and write from the standpoint of the white
> man's world. The ills of the ghetto, the difficulties of life there, the Negro's
> burning sense of grievance, are seldom conveyed. Slights and indignities are
> part of the Negro's daily life, and many of them come from what he now calls
> "the white press"—a press that repeatedly, if unconsciously, reflects the biases,
> the paternalism, the indifference of white America. This may be understandable,
> but it is not excusable in an institution that has the mission to inform and
> educate the whole of our society (1968, p. 366).

Mass Communication and Sociocultural Integration

In a second article, Warren Breed (1956, 1964) looks at the ways in
which the media function to maintain the status quo. He points out that in
a conflict of values the mass media sometimes sacrifice accurate reporting
of significant events for the virtues of respect for convention, public decency
and orderliness. Breed observes that newspapers generally speak well of the
home town and its leaders. Most of his examples are concerned with protecting
the dominant values and interests of American society.

Breed begins by observing that a major problem for any society is the
maintenance of order and social cohesion, including consensus over a value
system. He quotes E. C. Devereux, "Such head-on conflicts are prevented

also by various barriers to communication embedded in the social structure; taboo'd areas simply are not to be discussed, and hence the conflict need not be 'faced' " (1964, p. 186).

A rather dramatic example of "taboo'd areas" can be seen in the paucity of media discussion about the inequities of the draft during the Vietnam War. In most instances the sons of the middle class went to college while the sons of the poor went to Asia. In a rare and unusually candid article in the *National Observer* one writer, James Fallows, describes how in his senior year of college (1969) the draft lottery had been instituted and his number (45) indicated he would probably be called for military service. In a full-page article Fallows tells how he and his fellow students devised ways to escape service while the less sophisticated lads from across town were being drafted wholesale. It should be noted, however, that the article was published several years after American involvement in Vietnam ended. (Fallows, 1976).

Fallows concluded, ". . . our heritage from Vietnam is rich with potential for class hatred. World War II forced different classes of people to live together; Vietnam kept them rigidly apart, a process in which people like me were only too glad to cooperate . . . Among those who went to war, there is a residual resentment, the natural result of a cool look at who ended up paying what price. On the part of those who were spared, there is a residual guilt often so deeply buried that it surfaces only in unnaturally vehement denials that there is anything to feel guilty about."

The Rev. Theodore M. Hesburgh, president of the University of Notre Dame, in the foreword to a book dealing with this topic (Baskir and Strauss, 1978) wrote: "The great bulk of all those Americans deeply scarred by Vietnam were those already economically, socially, and educationally disadvantaged. They not only carried the burden of the fighting and dying, they now bear the lion's share of the penalties occasioned by the war and its aftermath. One often hears shocked people excoriating the President for pardoning deserters, but do these self-righteous critics ever advert to the fact that 15 million men of draft age completely avoided even one day of military service without penalty . . ."

An article titled "America's Foreign Legion," published in 1966 in *Ramparts,* (a magazine of relatively small circulation at that time) pointed out that while blacks were then being drafted at a rate of 11 percent, 22 percent of the total Vietnam casualities were black. Meanwhile, back home the rate of unemployment among blacks was twice as high as among whites.

The article went on to say:

During recent hearings before the House Armed Services Committee, Representative Alvin E. O'Konski told General Hershey, "The system is undemocratic and unAmerican. It nauseates me. How can I defend it to my people? They say that the poor are always with us, but if the draft goes on this way the poor won't be around much longer." O'Konski cited the shocking statistic that of 100 men drafted from his district in the previous six months, not one had come from a family with an annual income of more than $5000. Speaking was not a left wing populist but a relatively conservative Republican.

The article added:

. . . The President's son-in-law, Pat Nugent, managed a convenient six month reserve stint in the Air Force that put him in Washington. Actor George Hamilton, a sometimes rumored-to-be future son-in-law of the President, managed to avoid even that inconvenience. He is the sole supporter (a $200,000 home, a $30,000 Rolls Royce and a $100,000 income) of his four times married mother. That, according to Selective Service regulations, is a hardship case.

. . . A total of 146 senators and congressmen have one or more sons between the ages of 18 and 26—there are a total of 191 such sons in all. RAMPARTS was able to track down the whereabouts of all but 13 of them. Of the 178 thus accounted for, only 16 were serving in the Armed Services, and only one was in Vietnam.

The one man serving in Vietnam was a 22-year-old paratrooper with Special Forces who obviously wanted to be there. The other 15 were mostly commissioned officers (from the service academies or R.O.T.C.) or had enlisted in the Navy or the Air Force. None, apparently, had been drafted (Stern, 1966).

While other writers have said that the media maintain consensus through the dramatization of proper behavior, Breed sets out to demonstrate that they also do this by omission. He says, ". . . they (the media) omit or bury items which might jeopardize the sociocultural structure and man's faith in it." He cites considerable supporting evidence.

Politics and Economics

Breed found that items in the political and economic areas were most frequently omitted. Typically they involved ". . . an elite individual or group obtaining privilege through nondemocratic means." He notes that the most striking fact is that the word "class" is seldom mentioned in the media. Breed observes, ". . . class, being social inequality, is the very antithesis of the American creed" (p. 196). A glaring example of media omission came to public attention in 1968 when *The Reader's Digest,* owner of Funk and Wagnalls, stopped publication of a book critical of the advertising business *(The Permissible Lie)* written by a former advertising agency president. This happened after the book had been widely publicized, 5,000 copies had been printed, and the book had been attacked in pre-publication reviews in several advertising trade journals. The author, Samm Sinclair Baker, is quoted, "I was told that *The Reader's Digest* believes that advertising is good for business and that business is good for the country." Mr. Baker added, "The implication was that it was almost an unpatriotic book." (Raymont, 1968). The book was later published by another publisher.

Another topic seldom discussed in the mass media is the inequality in the distribution of income. When boosting the home town and the home state the media are usually quick to report improvements in average income, while remaining silent on its distribution. An example of this is a story detailing the increasing per capita average income in one state and in many of the state's cities (Associated Press, Nov. 19, 1978). Overlooked is the fact that according to federal income-tax returns from that state over a twenty-year period (1953–73) the share of income of the poorest 10 percent of the population declined from slightly less than two percent of the total income reported to less than one-half of one percent of the total income reported. In the same twenty year period the income of the richest 10 percent of the population increased from 26 percent of all income to 30 percent. In other words, in 1953 the richest 10 percent of the population had total incomes 13 times greater than the poorest 10 per cent. By 1973 the richest 10 percent had total incomes 70 times greater than the poorest 10 percent (*Texas Observer,* 1978).

The fact that the establishment media do not discuss the wide disparity in income is even more understandable when one considers that the state cited has neither a personal nor a corporate income tax. The income of the wealthiest 10 percent is probably even greater than that reported since that state is one of two which account for more than half of all the fraudulent tax returns each year.

Among other sacrosanct areas which Breed lists are religion, the family, patriotism, the community, health and doctors and justice. Already mentioned was an exception on the topic of religion, the television documentary, "The Business of Religion," one of the few critical attempts to explore some of the practices of established, "respectable" religions. Of religion Breed says, "It should be noted that religion is of double significance to social integration: It is not only a value in itself but it justifies and rationalizes other sentiments which bring order to a society."

Breed contends that the media portray the family as an institution without which society would perish. While it may be true that in recent years the media have devoted some time and space to alternate lifestyles, in general it seems difficult to dispute Breed's contention.

Breed observes that patriotism is another value which is protected by the media. He says, "When an individual is accused of disloyalty, favorable discussion of him by the media is sharply checked. He cannot be dramatized as an individual or a leader, only as a 'controversial' person under suspicion."

When Muhammad Ali (then known as Cassius Clay), the world heavyweight champion, reacted to the possibility of being drafted with, "I've got nothing against them Viet Congs," boxing commissioners, promoters and veterans groups found the remark "unpatriotic" and "disgusting." A title bout was called off, six other cities turned down the fight, and, finally, it was rescheduled for Toronto. Then sponsors of the radio broadcast and most of the theaters planning to show the fight on closed circuit TV cancelled their contracts. Ali was even denounced on the floor of the House of Representatives (March 15, 1966) by Rep. Frank Clark (D., Pa.). (*I. F. Stone's Weekly*, 1966.) Ali's heavyweight title was taken away from him and when he chose the Black Muslim name Muhammad Ali the media scoffed and refused to use it for many months.

Of the press and its policy regarding patriotism and national ethnocentrism, Breed says, "American soldiers overseas may violate norms involving persons and property for which they would be publicly punished in this country, but the press here minimizes overseas derelictions. In other countries, they are 'representatives' of our nationality and thus in a quasi-sacred position" (1964, p. 193).

For nearly two years the American mass media did not use the pictures of the Vietnam My Lai massacre in which American soldiers murdered 109 unarmed civilian prisoners. Only after a former GI, Ron Ridenhour, began a letter writing campaign to congressmen and an investigation was opened into the massacre were the pictures finally given national exposure, twenty months after the actual event (*Life*, Dec. 5, 1969). Seymour M. Hersh, the reporter who finally broke the story detailed the refusals he got at LIFE and LOOK as well as Ron Ridenhour's earlier refusal by LIFE before the story finally was made public (Hersh, 1972). The first publication of the My Lai photos was on Nov. 20, 1969, in the *Cleveland Plain Dealer.*

Writing of the media's coverage of their communities Breed says, "The progress, growth, and achievements of a city are praised, the failures buried." Breed notes the chamber of commerce attitude on the part of the media which another author, journalism professor Gene Burd, has termed the "Civic Superlative."

Burd wrote, "Moreover, as gatekeeper of the civic symbols and custodian of the civic relics, the press is the city's civic salesman and press agent who points with pride or cries with shame and alarm. It reminds the public of the central business district as *the* city with civic superlatives, the centerpiece, the showcase, the crown jewels, the face and facade, the newest, the biggest, the tallest, the longest, the largest, the cleanest, the safest, the greatest." (Burd, 1969, p. 307)

Later Burd wrote, "Such boosterism is most evident in news on sports and new urban developments, in news of national recognition of local natives . . ." (Burd, 1972, p. 3).

A notable example of this boosterism occurred when the Nobel Prizes were announced in October 1977. The prize in chemistry was awarded to Dr. Ilya Prigogine. The *Chronicle of Higher Education* (1977) identified him with the Free University of Brussels in Belgium. The *New York Times* described him likewise (1977) and in the sixth paragraph mentioned that the Russian born, European educated, naturalized Belgian citizen "spends part of each year at the University of Texas in Austin." The Austin *American-Statesman* described it as "The first Nobel Prize awarded a current UT professor . . ." Omitted was the fact that the only other one had been forced to leave the university (some claim fired) before he was awarded the Nobel (Dugger, 1974, pp. 26–32). In the next paragraph the *American-Statesman* described Prigogine as ". . . founding director of UT's Center for Statistical Mechanics and Thermodynamics and a professor at Belgium's Free University of Brussels . . ." (Daugherty, 1977).

The student daily, *The Texan,* under a banner, "UT Chemist Wins Nobel," (Hoppe, 1977) noted in the last paragraph of its story that Prigogine was in Belgium and was expected at the University of Texas in February— four months hence. Not until months later could a diligent reader discover, buried deep in a long story the following, "After a 50 percent research budget cut by the Legislature last spring, the UT-Austin administration reduced Prigogine's annual research funds to $28,000, and the Physics Department discussed abolishing his research center altogether" (Stuckey, 1978).

The civic boosterism in sports referred to by Burd can reach into even the smallest communities and down to the junior high school level as an ABC Evening News report by Bob Brown illustrates. In a November 23, 1978, report from Georgia, Brown reported that "football isn't everything in Thomaston, but it is an important source of prestige . . ."

In his report Brown cited cases of students at the junior high school who repeated years, although their grades were fine, in order to improve their prowess at football before their limited high school eligibility of eight semesters begins. The local coach said that parental permission must be received in advance and that two or three players were probably repeating the eighth grade at the time. Half of the repeaters take exactly the same courses as they had passed the year before. The coach said the situation was probably the same at other towns in Georgia.

In Thomaston football begins at age seven in the Youth League. In the fall of 1978, reported ABC News, there were five repeaters on the Robert E. Lee (high school) varsity and four on the junior varsity. It was estimated that the extra years in junior high school for these nine players alone cost about $10,000.

Brown closed his report with "as in many other communities football here is viewed as a measure of a town's image, reflected in its youth."

Whenever possible, our town, our school, our team, our paper is the biggest, the best or the first. To contrast this Breed quotes two authors who say, "There is silent recognition among members of the community that facts and ideas, which are disturbing to the accepted system of illusions are not to be verbalized . . ." (Vidich and Bensman, 1960, p. 308). (See Chapter 11 on consistency theories.)

A relatively rare example of a news item which included facts disturbing to the "accepted system of illusions" concerned a graduation ceremony. The son of a former governor and a presidential hopeful had just graduated from Air Force officer training school at the height of the Vietnam War. The father was quoted, "In the times we live in there are so many who have doubts about their country that it's critical that our young men recognize their responsibility to serve their nation. I'm particularly proud that my son has chosen to meet his responsibility."

The last paragraph of the page one news story, surprisingly uncut, read, "Lt. _____ will serve with headquarters, _____ Air National Guard in _____, where he will attend law school." (Associated Press, June 30, 1969).

Medicine

". . . physicians are almost never shown in a bad light by the press, and the treatment of doctors in other media such as daytime serials is often worshipful," says Breed. Rare indeed is coverage like the five-part in-depth series by the *New York Times* discussing the number of unfit physicians, incompetent surgery, bad prescriptions, and medical cover-ups (*New York Times,* January 26–30, 1976), or the six-part series by the *Milwaukee Journal* titled "The Ailing Blues" examining medical and surgical insurance in depth (*Milwaukee Journal,* May 30 to June 4, 1976).

The next chapter relates what followed as a result of the *Times* series on medical malpractice.

Even rarer are stories showing "doctors acting in selfish rather than professional fashion" (Breed, 1964, p. 195). One of these rare stories told of a white Alabama doctor who pulled the freshly sewn stitches from the arm of a 13-year-old black boy when the youth's father couldn't pay the $25 fee (Associated Press, April 16, 1976).

Law and Justice

Justice is another media policy area noted by Breed. On the subject of differential attention to crime a former Attorney General of the United States has said:

> The crimes to which we pay least attention are those committed by people of advantage who have an easier, less offensive, less visible way of doing wrong. White-collar crime is usually the act of respected and successful people. Illicit gains from white-collar crime far exceed those of all other crimes combined . . . One corporate price-fixing conspiracy criminally converted more money each year it continued than all of the hundreds of thousands of burglaries, larcenies or thefts in the entire nation during those same years . . . White-collar crime is the most corrosive of all crimes. The trusted prove untrustworthy; the advantaged dishonest. It shows the capability of people with better opportunities for creating a decent life for themselves to take property belonging to others. As no other crime, it questions our moral fiber. (Clark, 1970, p. 38).

Two researchers examined crime reporting during one month by the two daily newspapers in one of America's largest cities. They found that while nearly 36 per cent or 2814 of the 7901 crimes reported were larcenies, neither newspaper carried a story about any of them during that month (Antunes and Hurley, 1977).

Breed contends that the media function to protect "power" and "class." He observes that, "critics have for centuries noted the disproportionate power of elites and the winking by the media at their actions." Other values given protection by the media are capitalism, the home, religion, health, justice, the nation and the community.

Breed says that when television dramas do portray a businessman as a villian they focus on the individual, not on the institution. When newspapers report investigations detailing the structural faults of campaign financing, lobbying, concentrations of economic power, etc., Breed contends that they are usually not featured. He says that viewers become uncomfortable with exceptionally frank programs like Mike Wallace interviews and that this "exception proves the rule," the "media do not challenge basic institutions by exploring flaws in the working of institutions."

CONCLUSIONS

It becomes apparent, as only the naive might not expect, that the ideal functions of the mass media, are at considerable variance with actual practice. Wright, Lasswell, Lippmann, Lazarsfeld, Merton, and Breed are but a few of the many who have made such observations. The gap between the ideal and the reality remains one of the problems for a democratic society.

REFERENCES

Associated Press (June 30, 1969). Connally Pins AF Bars on Son. In *Austin* (Texas) *American-Statesman,* p. 1.

Associated Press (April 16, 1976). Patient can't pay, so doc pulls stitches. In *Austin* (Texas) *American-Statesman,* p. 1.

Associated Press (November 19, 1978). Texas gaining steadily in national income race. In *Austin* (Texas) *American-Statesman,* p. B 21.

Antunes, G. and P. Hurley (1977). The Representation of Criminal Event's in Houston's Two Daily Newspapers. *Journalism Quarterly* 54: 4: 756–60 (Winter)

Baskir, L. and W. Strauss (1978). *The Draft, the War, and the Vietnam Generation.* New York: Alfred A. Knopf.

Breed, W. (1955). Social Control in the Newsroom. *Social Forces,* May 1955. Also in W. Schramm (ed.), *Mass Communications* (2nd ed.) (1960). Urbana: University of Illinois Press.

Breed, W. (1958). Mass Communication and Sociocultural Integration. *Social Forces.* Reprinted in L. Dexter and D. White (eds.), *People, Society and Mass Communications* (1964). New York: The Free Press.

Brown, L. (1971). *Televi$ion: The Business Behind the Box*. New York: Harcourt Brace Jovanovich, Inc.

Burd, G. (1969). The mass media in urban society. In H. Schmandt and W. Bloomberg, Jr. (eds.) *The Quality of Urban Life*. Beverly Hills, Calif.: Sage.

Burd, G. (1972). The civic superlative: We're no. 1/The press as civic cheerleader. *Twin Cities Journalism Review 1* (April–May). Minneapolis, Minn.

The Chronicle of Higher Education (Oct. 17, 1977). Five Win Nobel Prizes, p. 2.

Clark, R. (1970). *Crime in America*. New York: Simon and Schuster.

Daugherty, J. (Oct. 12, 1977). UT honors Nobel Prize winner. In *Austin* (Texas) *American-Statesman*, p. 1.

Dugger, R. (1974). *Our Invaded Universities*. New York: W. W Norton & Co.

Fallows, J. (Feb. 21, 1976). Vietnam—the Class War. *The National Observer*. New York: Dow Jones & Co., p. 14.

Hersh, S. (1972). The Story Everyone Ignored. In M. Emery and T. Smythe (eds.), *Readings in Mass Communications*, (1st Ed.). Dubuque: Wm. C. Brown Co. Also see S. Hersh (1970). How I Broke the My Lai Story. *Saturday Review 53* (July) pp. 46–9; and *Columbia Journalism Review*, Winter, 1969–70.

Hoppe, C. (Oct. 12, 1977). UT Chemist Wins Nobel. In *The Daily Texan* (Austin, Texas), p. 1.

I. F. Stone's Weekly (March 28, 1966). No Free Speech for Cassius Clay, p. 2.

Lasswell, H. (1948, 1960). The Structure and Function of Communication in Society. In L. Bryson (ed.), *The Communication of Ideas* (1948). New York: Institute for Religious and Social Studies. Reprinted in W. Schramm (ed.), *Mass Communications* (1960). Urbana: University of Illinois Press.

Lazarsfeld, P. and R. Merton (1948). Mass Communication, Popular Taste and Organized Social Action. In L. Bryson (ed.), *The Communication of Ideas*. New York: Institute for Religious and Social Studies. Reprinted in W. Schramm (ed.), *Mass Communications* (1960). Urbana: University of Illinois Press.

Lippmann, W. (1922). *Public Opinion*. New York: The Macmillan Company. Chapter one reprinted in W. Schramm (ed.), *Mass Communications* (1960). Urbana: University of Illinois Press.

Mill, J. (1859). *On Liberty*. Reprinted 1956. Indianapolis: The Bobbs-Merrill Company, Inc.

National Advisory Commission on Civil Disorders (1968). *Report of the National Advisory Commission on Civil Disorders* (The Kerner Report). New York: Bantam Books.

New York Times (Oct. 12, 1977). 2 Americans Among 4 Nobel Science Winners. p. 1.

Raymont, H. (June 2, 1968). Reader's Digest Suppresses Book. *New York Times*, p. 88.

Siebert, F., T. Peterson and W. Schramm (1956). *Four Theories of the Press*. Urbana: University of Illinois Press.

Stern, S. (November 1966). America's Foreign Legion. *Ramparts*, pp. 6 and 8.

Stuckey, W. (Feb. 19, 1978). PR and the Nobel. *Austin* (Texas) *American-Statesman*, p. C1.

The Texas Observer (May 26, 1978). How Texans Fared, 1953–1973. Austin, Texas: p. 4.

Vidich, A. and J. Bensman (1960). *Small Town in Mass Society*. New York: Doubleday.

Wright, C. (1959). *Mass Communication*. New York: Random House.

Chapter 16

Newspaper Chains and Media Conglomerates

C LOSELY related to the charges that the media "omit or bury items which might jeopardize the sociocultural structure" and that "policy usually protects property and class interests," cited in the preceding chapter, is the accelerating pace at which media are being swallowed up by newspaper chains and media conglomerates.

Newspaper Chains

The newspaper industry is the third largest manufacturer in the United States in terms of employment, exceeded only by the auto and steel industries. Newspaper payrolls totaled 382,700 in 1976, up by 4,200 over 1975 (Jones and Anderson, 1977, p. 25).

By 1977 ten chains controlled one-third of the daily newspaper circulation in the U.S. and two-thirds of all U.S. dailies were part of group ownership arrangements. Knight-Ridder, with 32 dailies in mid-1977, led in total daily circulation with 3½ million, while Gannett held the largest number of dailies, 73, with a daily circulation of nearly 3 million. Forty nine independent dailies were bought by chains in 1975, and the following year saw the number of independent dailies bought by chains jump to 72 (Jones and Anderson, 1977, p. 25).

In one large state 70 per cent, or 79 of the 111 daily newspapers, and 67 per cent of the daily circulation was in the hands of chain owned newspapers. This was about average for the nation as a whole that year (Beutler, 1978a, p. 10).

Katharine Graham, publisher of the *Washington Post* and chairman of the Washington Post Company, was quoted in a rare series of articles in a newspaper about the newspaper industry as saying, "You have an irreversible trend going, and nothing can stop it short of government intervention and then, at that point, we all choke" (Jones and Anderson, 1977, p. 25).

The editor and publisher of the family-owned Louisville *Courier Journal,* Barry Bingham, Jr., says, "The idea of a family-owned newspaper in the future is not probable" (*Business Week,* Feb. 21, 1977, p. 58).

Many reasons have been advanced for the growth of media conglomerates. This phenomena is, of course, part of the larger economic trend in our society which favors concentration in general with the advantages of large scale operation. Another factor is the inheritance tax laws which make it difficult for a family owned newspaper to be passed on to heirs when large sums are needed to pay taxes. There is also the inability to challenge chain ownership under current anti-trust laws. Senator Edward Kennedy, as chairman of a subcommittee on anti-trust and monopoly, has expressed concern about this (Jones and Anderson, 1977, p. 25).

Another factor is the tremendous profitability or potential for profit of many of the media. Profit figures in the newspaper industry are hard to come by since only about 200 of the 1,762 dailies sell public stock and issue public business reports. The Times-Mirror Company, publisher of the *Los Angeles Times Mirror,* two other newspapers, four magazines, and owner of several book publishing houses, broadcasting and cable properties, newsprint mills and timberland, had an average annual growth in profits of 17 per cent for each of five years (1972–6), even with a drop of 19 per cent in profits in 1975 because of the recession and a long strike (*Business Week,* Feb. 21, 1977, p. 58).

An article on the buying up of independent newspapers by chains referred to papers "that either earn or have the potential to earn pretax profit margins of 25% to 30% or higher. The Speidel chain acquired by Gannett, had pretax margins of 34%." Speidel Newspapers, Inc., sold 13 newspapers in the West and Midwest to Gannett Co. for a reported $178.3 million (*Business Week,* Feb. 21, 1977, p. 57).

Otis Chandler of the Times-Mirror Company stresses local media competition as one of the biggest considerations in any prospective acquisition. The choicest property is one that has a market almost to itself. Chandler is quoted, "In these markets (large metropolitan areas) you worry about cost per thousand, or the other media buys that an advertiser could make. All that doesn't mean a thing in smaller media markets because the advertiser has no competitive buys." He adds that if a newspaper is noncompetitive, "it gives you a franchise to do what you want with profitability. You can engineer your profits. You can control expenses and generate revenue almost arbitrarily." Times-Mirror bought *Newsday* in 1970 and increased profits by 72 per cent in the first year, in part by doubling the price of the paper (*Business Week,* Feb. 21, 1977, pp. 58–9).

Harte-Hanks Communications, Inc., a San Antonio based nationwide communications company which went public from family ownership, owned at last count 26 daily newspapers, 48 non-daily newspapers, three VHF-TV stations, and the world's largest direct mail shopper organization, in Southern California. In five years (1970–75) its revenues increased 260 per cent and profits increased 320 per cent. Its president and chief executive officer, Robert Marbut, a 1963 Harvard MBA and a member of the advisory council of the largest school of communications in the United States, is quoted as saying, "Newspapers are very profitable . . . There are about 7,500 weeklies all over the country, and 1,762 dailies. Out of those dailies, only 39 cities have competing newspapers. We don't try to get a paper in those 39 cities" (Cook, 1977, pp. 35–6).

Former Secretary of the Treasury John Connally, speaking at the Houston Press Club, called the media conglomerates, "massive business empires built by entrepreneurs under the shelter of our free enterprise system" and said that they should be recognized for what they are (Phillips, 1977, pp. 23–4).

At the other end of the political spectrum, Senator Edward Kennedy wants the anti-trust laws to be ready and able to promote "a diverse and competitive press." Representative Morris Udall of Arizona and 25 of his colleagues introduced legislation for a study of concentration in newspapers as well as in other industries. Udall told an audience at the National Press Club in April 1977 that he feared "chain store news is upon us" as, he said, are chain store drugs and chain store gasoline. Udall sees disturbing social implications in this trend (Jones and Anderson, 1977, p. 25).

Concern about "chain store news," the maintenance of a "diverse and competitive press" and the effects of "massive business empires" on our media have been voiced for at least 50 years.

Of the more than 1,500 cities in the United States with dailies, more than 97 per cent are newspaper monopolies. Only 39 or 40 cities have newspaper competition. As a nationally known and highly regarded media critic has pointed out, residents of most American cities are apt to have available to them competing automobile dealerships even though we have only four manufacturers of automobiles in America. Not so with newspapers—most American cities have no competition in newspapers (Bagdikian, 1978, p. 31).

But, reply the defenders of newspaper chains and monopoly newspaper cities, the citizen has available other sources of news, including radio and television. However, the fact is that most of the news in all of the media comes from two wire services, the Associated Press and United Press International, who, in turn, rely very heavily on their local members and clients. The wire service clients most apt to gather news are the daily newspapers, which are, increasingly, in one-owner cities.

Broadcasting

Ownership in broadcasting is equally concentrated. By 1974 nearly three-fourths of all television stations in the 100 largest markets in the U.S. were group owned. These 100 markets accounted for 87 per cent of the nation's television households. In the top ten markets, 85 per cent of all the television stations were group owned. Group ownership of the nation's TV stations is now at an all-time high. Moreover, approximately one-third of the television chains in the nation are affiliated with newspaper publishing organizations. The three major networks, with five network owned-and-operated television stations each, top the list for net weekly audience. In January, 1975, each network reached approximately fifteen million homes a week with its five owned-and-operated stations alone (Howard, p. 404). Besides these network owned-and-operated stations the stations affiliated with each network carried network programming into tens of millions of more homes each week.

When examining one state's 54 commercial television stations one finds 74 per cent or 40 of them chain owned. The same percentage of the state's 225 cable television systems are also chain owned. In the top three media markets there is *not one* commercial television station which is not chain owned. Among the licensees listed for these three cities are chains and conglomerates with headquarters in Los Angeles, Beverly Hills, New York City, Oklahoma City, Virginia and Rhode Island. Of 23 commercial television stations in the top six media markets in that state only one station is not chain owned (Beutler, 1978b, pp. 4–5).

Media Conglomerates

One of the most rapidly expanding areas of media ownership is that of media conglomerates where a parent corporation may own newspapers, magazines, book publishing houses, news services, public opinion polling organizations, radio and television stations, cable TV, broadcasting networks and companies which produce records and tapes and the associated "clubs" which promote, sell and distribute those records and tapes.

Often the conglomerate derives only a fraction of its annual revenue from media activities while the bulk of its operations are in manufacturing and sales. These include such diverse activities as international telecommunications, the manufacture of electronic systems for defense and space, musical instruments, frozen foods, investment corporations, paper and wood products, timberlands, furniture manufacture, vehicle rental agencies, cement, sugar, citrus, livestock, cigars and candy. If these seem like a varied mixture indeed, that is, after all, the definition of conglomerate. A number of these conglomerates which are involved in the mass media rank well up among the Fortune 500 listings of the largest corporations in the United States.

Radio Corporation of America, one of the largest, not only owns NBC, but also television stations in Chicago, Los Angeles, Cleveland, New York City and Washington, D.C. It also owns one AM and one FM station in Chicago, New York, San Francisco and Washington, D.C. However, only 17.8 per cent of its total 1976 revenues were derived from broadcasting. Another 17.6 per cent came from publishing houses owned by RCA (Random

House, Alfred A. Knopf, Pantheon, Ballantine Books, Vintage, Modern Library). The biggest chunk of revenue in 1976 for RCA came, however, from its electronic products and services, a total of 38.4 per cent, much of it from defense and space contracts. The balance of RCA's 1976 revenues came from such diverse operations as Banquet frozen foods and Hertz vehicle renting (*Harper's,* July 1977, p. 28).

One writer points out that RCA is a major defense contractor supplying radar, electronic warfare and laser systems, guidance systems for missiles and bombs, intelligence processing hardware and other items. Through RCA Global Communications it controls telecommunications among 200 nations, and it was also a major supplier for the Alaska pipeline. RCA produced the guidance systems for the Apollo and Skylab spacecraft and the author wonders what RCA might have lost in multi-million dollar space contracts if its broadcasting network, NBC, had produced a powerful documentary against the vast expenditures on space exploration (Bagdikian, 1977, p. 20).

The Columbia Broadcasting System not only provides network news and entertainment, but also owns television stations in New York, Los Angeles, Philadelphia, Chicago and St. Louis, plus seven AM radio stations and seven FM radio stations (the legal limit). It owns Columbia, Epic and Portrait records and tapes and their affiliated clubs, manufactures Steinway pianos, Rogers drums, organs and other musical instruments, publishes books (Holt, Rinehart and Winston, etc.) and magazines (*Field and Stream, Road and Track, Mechanix Illustrated* and about twenty others).

Time, Inc., publishes not only *Time, Fortune, Sports Illustrated, Money* and *People* magazines, but also Time-Life Books, 17 weekly newspapers in suburban Chicago (Pioneer Press), the "other" daily in Washington, D.C., the *Star,* and Little-Brown books. It is heavily into films, broadcasting and cable television (Time-Life Films, Home Box Office, Manhattan Cable TV), investment corporations (Sabine and Lumberman's, including home mortgages), and forest products (pulp, paperboard, packaging, building materials, interior wall products, bedroom furniture, timberland, etc.).

Time, Inc.'s competitor in two areas, The Washington Post Company, publishes not only the *Washington Post* newspaper and *Newsweek* magazine, but also publishes newspapers in Trenton, N.J., owns 30 per cent of the *International Herald Tribune,* and owns television stations in Michigan, Florida and Connecticut, 49 per cent of a Canadian paper company and other varied properties.

The New York Times Company owns, besides *The New York Times,* six dailies and four weeklies in Florida, three dailies in North Carolina, a television station in Memphis, WQXR-AM and WQXR-FM in New York City, three book publishers (Quadrangle, Arno and Bambridge) and half-a-dozen magazines. In 1976 it sold eight professional magazines to Harcourt Brace and Jovanovich. Among the magazines the New York Times Company sold was *Modern Medicine,* one of seven specialized journals in the health field which it had bought from another media conglomerate, Cowles Communications, Inc. (former publishers of *Look* magazine, among other ventures). After the *New York Times* ran the series of articles (cited in the previous chapter) dealing with medical incompetence it faced a loss of 260 pages of advertising from medical related industries, not in the *New York Times,* but in its magazine *Modern Medicine.* One respected media critic, Ben Bagdikian, asks:

> One wonders whether Harcourt Brace Jovanovich will now think twice before publishing an otherwise acceptable manuscript if it contains material displeasing to the advertisers who are now a source of the concern's revenue. One wonders, moreover, if other newspaper conglomerates would have been as willing as the Times Company to get rid of such a property: it would strike many as simpler not to assign reporters to stories that might offend someone doing business with a subsidiary. (Bagdikian, 1977, p. 20).

The Times-Mirror Company publishes not only the *Los Angeles Times,* but also *Newsday* (Long Island) and the *Dallas* (Texas) *Times-Herald.* It owns television stations in Austin and Dallas, two newsprint mills, ten wood products mills, a third-of-a-million acres of timberland, and jointly owns the L.A. Times-Washington Post News Service. It is also involved in magazine and book publishing (*Outdoor Life, Popular Science, Golf, Ski, The Sporting News,* New American Library, Signet, and other magazines and book publishers).

Gulf and Western, near the top of the Fortune 500, deals in manufacturing, zinc, cement, apparel, paper, building products, auto replacement parts, sugar, citrus (Minute Maid), livestock, cigars, candy *and* owns Paramount Pictures and Simon and Schuster book publishers.

The Gannett newspaper chain (now rapidly becoming a media conglomerate) owns, in addition to its widespread newspapers (from New York to Hawaii and Guam) two radio stations in Ohio and one television station in New York state plus the public opinion polling organizations Louis Harris & Associates and Louis Harris International.

In May 1978 Gannett Company announced a pending deal to exchange stock valued at $370 million for Combined Communications Corporation of Phoenix, owners of the *Oakland* (Calif.) *Tribune* and the *Cincinnati Enquirer,* seven television stations, thirteen radio stations and an outdoor advertising company. The two newspapers would increase Gannett's holdings to 79 and would move Gannett's total newspaper circulation to nearly three-and-a-half million daily (1978 figures). Based on 1977 revenues it would rank second only to the Times-Mirror Company of Los Angeles (a billion dollar media conglomerate) (*Columbia Journalism Review,* July–August 1978, p. 10).

In late 1966 and early 1977 International Telephone and Telegraph attempted to buy the American Broadcasting Company. At that time ABC owned five VHF television stations, and six each AM and FM radio stations, all in the top ten markets, 399 theaters in 34 states, one of the three major television networks and one of the four major radio networks in the world. Through its network affiliates it could reach 93 per cent of the television households in the United States and 97 per cent of the homes with radio. Through its subsidiary "Worldvision Group" it had interests in or affiliations with stations in 25 other countries. Together with ABC films it was probably the largest distributor of films for theaters and television in the world. It also had major interests in record production and distribution and other subsidiaries published three agricultural newspapers (Johnson, 1968, p. 45).

ITT, on the other hand, was at that time the ninth largest industrial corporation in the world in size of work force. It derived about 60 per cent of its income from holdings in more than 40 foreign countries. Besides operating foreign countries' telephone companies and selling electronic equipment overseas, about half of its income at home came from U.S. space and defense contracts. It was also involved in life insurance, consumer financing, investment funds, small loan companies, car rentals (Avis), and book publishing (Johnson, 1968, p. 44).

Had ITT been allowed to acquire ABC, one of the largest purveyors of information in America would have been placed under one of the largest conglomerates in the world. In June 1967 the Federal Communications Commission approved the merger, with three commissioners, Bartley, Cox and Johnson, dissenting. They questioned, among other things, how the integrity of news judgment at ABC might be affected by ITT's economic interests. They asked, would ITT view ABC's programming as part of the overall corporate public relations, advertising or political activities? The commissioners did not have to wait long for an answer.

While the hearings on the issue were being debated before the FCC the *Wall Street Journal* carried on its editorial page an article titled, "Managing the News?" (Zimmerman, 1967) detailing the extraordinary lengths ITT was going to get favorable news coverage of hearings and the merger (Johnson, 1968, p. 46; Bagdikian, 1967, p. 10). As a result of the article the FCC heard testimony from three reporters (AP, UPI, and the *New York Times*), regarding the incidents related in the *Journal* article. The wireservice reporters told of phone calls to their homes by ITT public relations men requesting them to change their stories, to get information about the merger story being written by other reporters, and, if possible, to get confidential Justice Department information regarding its intentions in the case.

The *New York Times* reporter told how she had been visited at her office by ITT's senior vice president in charge of public relations. After he criticized her reporting in a manner which she described as "accusatory and certainly nasty," he inquired as to whether or not she had been following the stock prices of ITT and ABC. When she replied in the negative he asked if she didn't feel "a responsibility to the shareholders who might lose money as a result of what" she reported regarding the proposed merger. Her reply, "My responsibility is to find out the truth and print it."

The ITT senior vice president then told the *Times* reporter that an

FCC commissioner was working with a prominent senator on legislation to forbid newspapers from owning broadcasting stations. (The *New York Times* owns radio station WQXR in New York.) Later public statements made it clear that the senator and the commissioner had never met, let alone collaborated on legislation. The *Times* reporter testified that the ITT official told her that this false information was something she, ". . . ought to pass on to (her) . . . publisher before (she wrote) . . . anything further" about the proposed merger. She felt that the obvious implication of his remark was that since the Times owns WQXR its economic interests would play a part in how it would handle the ITT-ABC merger story (Johnson, 1968, p. 46).

FCC Commissioner Nicholas Johnson wrote of this behavior,

> To me, this conduct, in which at least three ITT officials, including a senior vice president, were involved, was a deeply unsettling experience. It demonstrated an abrasive self-righteousness in dealing with the press, insensitivity to its independence and integrity, a willingness to spread false stories in furtherance of self-interest, contempt for government officials as well as the press, and an assumption that even as pretigious a news medium as the *New York Times* would, as a matter of course, want to present the news so as to serve best its own economic interests (as well as the economic interests of other large business corporations).
>
> But for the brazen activities of ITT in this very proceeding, it would never have occurred to the three of us who dissented to suggest that the most probable threat to the integrity of ABC news could come from *overt* actions or written policy statements. After the hearing it was obvious that that was clearly possible. But even then we believed that the most substantial threat came from a far more subtle, almost unconscious, process: that the questionable story idea, or news coverage, would never even be proposed, whether for reasons of fear, insecurity, cynicism, realism, or unconscious avoidance." (Johnson, 1968, p. 46).

In the face of a Justice Department appeal of the FCC approval of the ITT-ABC merger, the ITT aborted the merger on New Year's Day of 1968.

In the spring of 1967 the Justice Department got a decree against the Lindsay-Schaub chain which had been accused of violating anti-trust laws. The chain's Champaign-Urbana, Illinois paper cut ad rates and intentionally took a $3-million loss between 1956 and 1963 in an attempt to drive a competitor out of business. The Justice Department charged the chain offset the loss by profits from other papers. The chain's A.M.-P.M. daily combination in Decatur, Illinois alone, with a combined circulation of less than 65,000, made more than $5-million during the same period (Bagdikian, 1967, p. 5).

In January 1979 the American Express Company attempted to take over one of the nation's largest publishers, McGraw-Hill, Inc. In addition to book publishing the company also publishes 60 magazines including *Business Week* and owns Standard and Poor's investment advisory service. The offer of $830-million (later increased to $976-million) or $34 per share (later $40) in cash or securities to stockholders make it one of the biggest takeover attempts on record. The day after the announcement (January 10,

1979) McGraw-Hill stock jumped 4⅞ on the New York Stock Exchange. The reaction of Harold W. McGraw, Jr., chairman of McGraw-Hill to the attempted takeover was "negative" (*New York Times,* January 10, 1979).

In February the Federal Trade Commission expressed four "serious concerns" about the takeover effort, now "bitterly opposed" by McGraw-Hill directors. The areas of concern were:

1) possible unfair advantage to American Express from advance notice of business information to be published in McGraw-Hill publications and possible influence by American Express on the selection of material to be published by McGraw-Hill;
2) potential conflict of interest if McGraw-Hill, a leading bond rating firm is taken over by American Express, a leading underwriter of bonds;
3) the possibility of a reduction in competition between the two companies in services related to bond sales;
4) possible unfair business advantage to American Express through reduced advertising rates in McGraw-Hill publications.

In mid-February 1979 several stockholder's lawsuits were filed against the McGraw-Hill directors. The company's stock which sold for $26 per share before the announced takeover was back down to $27.125 on February 14. American Express had first offered $34 per share and then $40 per share, driving the market price per share up considerably.

At this writing the takeover attempt appears dead.

Media Cross-Ownership

From the standpoint of the individual citizen probably one of the greatest threats to diversity of news and opinion about local issues is media cross ownership or joint ownership (where a newspaper and a television station are under a single ownership).

In 1975 the Federal Communication Commission proposed a ban on single-community broadcast-newspaper links in the future. It did, however, "grandfather" or make immune from divestiture all existing combinations except those amounting to outright monopolies. The exemption for existing cross-ownerships was challenged in D.C. Circuit Court by the Justice Department. Although the court ruled against exempting existing cross-ownerships, the U.S. Supreme Court ruled in a unanimous (8–0) decision in 1978 that the FCC had reasonably exercised the power delegated to it by Congress.

The Newhouse Broadcasting Corporation announced in December 1978 the sale of five television stations to the Times-Mirror Company for $82 million. The reason given for the sale was the growing opposition by federal regulatory agencies to cross ownership of newspapers and television stations in the same communities. The Newhouse group publishes newspapers in each of the cities in which the five television stations they sold are located.

Newhouse retains its radio, cable television and microwave facilities as well as its newspaper properties.

In a large scale study of joint ownership of a newspaper and a television station in the same city, one researcher concluded that it often means less diversity in coverage (Gormley, 1977). The author notes that more than 60 million Americans live in cities where at least one newspaper and television station have the same owner. In 1975 there were 66 newspaper-television cross ownerships.

The investigator sent questionnaires to 349 news directors and managing editors of both cross-ownership and separately owned media. As a result of the 214 responses he then visited ten cross-ownership cities where he interviewed 44 news executives and reporters. Then he analyzed 9,335 news stories for a comparison of overlap of coverage between cross-owned and separately owned pairs of newspaper and television stations.

The researcher says

> What I found was that jointly owned newspaper and television news staffs were engaged in cooperative practices that might not be described as "abuses" but which nevertheless belied assurances by owners of newspaper-television combinations that their news staffs functioned separately and independently (Gormley, 1977, p. 39).

He adds that cross-ownership increases the likelihood that:

1) a newspaper and a television station will share carbons; 2) a television station will hire a reporter or editor who has worked for the newspaper that owns the television station; 3) a newspaper and a television station will be located within the same complex of buildings ". . . sharing the same roof, the same parking lot, or the same cafeteria reminds newspaper and television reporters that they are members of the same corporate family—which encourages cooperation" (Gormley, 1977, pp. 42–3).

Besides undermining diversity in the flow of news, the author points out that while a fourth of the stations not owned by a newspaper never editorialize, more than half of those which are newspaper owned never editorialize. A newspaper-owned television station which editorializes in accord with a newspaper's view faces charges of collusion, yet if it editorializes against those views it tends to offset the view of a corporate partner. If it chooses not to editorialize it avoids the dilemma, which is what most have chosen to do. By not editorializing television stations increase dependence on local newspapers for views on local issues. The investigator found that the "homogenizing effects of newspaper-television cross-ownership are strongest in cities with populations under 125,000" (Gormley, 1977, p. 43). It is precisely these cities which can least afford reduced diversity since they usually have only one or two television stations.

If one accepts the position of Judge Learned Hand who wrote in *U.S. v. Associated Press* that, "Right conclusions are more likely to be gathered out of a multitude of tongues," then when cross-ownership reduces diversity in news and opinions it also threatens truth and understanding.

Ben Bagdikian notes that when contamination of the news does occur it can be on a massive scale. He cites Atlantic Richfield's purchase of *The London Observer* in late 1976 and notes that Mobil Oil says it is also in the market to buy a daily newspaper. Bagdikian observes that we might judge Mobil's dedication to independent journalism from the fact that it withdrew support from the Bagehot Fellowships in economic journalism at Columbia University because the new director of the fellowships once wrote a book about the oil industry that Mobile dislikes (Bagdikian, 1978, p. 32).

Today there are so few desirable newspapers and broadcasting stations left that chains are buying other chains. Already mentioned was the sale of 13 newspapers by the Speidel chain to Gannett for $178 million. In 1976 the Newhouse chain bought the Booth Newspapers (Michigan) for $305 million, a purchase called "the biggest single newspaper deal in history." As this is written, Gannett is negotiating the deal to add to its empire Combined Communications Corporation of Phoenix with two daily newspapers, seven television stations and thirteen radio stations. The pace of consolidation in the media accelerates with the prices spiraling ever higher and the trading becoming ever more hectic (Bagdikian, 1977; *Columbia Journalism Review,* July/August 1978, p. 10).

In June 1978 the National News Council, an independent agency which evaluates and comments on the national news media, began to examine what forms of ownership of the news media best serve to insure a free flow of information. Among topics to be explored are the advantages and disadvantages of chain ownership or other forms of economic concentration especially as regards freedom of the press, autonomy of news and editorial decisions, adequacy of budget, and quality of coverage (*Columbia Journalism Review,* September/October 1978, p. 87).

Ben Bagdikian has observed (1977, p. 22; 1978, p. 34) that what is really needed is more profound change—for the professional staffs of newspapers and broadcasting stations to choose their own top editors, to have representatives on the board of directors and to have a voice in determining the annual news budget. He points out that this is done on a number of quality European papers including *Le Monde,* often cited as one of the ten best in the world. Bagdikian gets to the heart of the matter when he says:

> Broadcast and newspaper news is too important an ingredient in the collective American brain to be constantly exposed to journalistically irrelevant corporate policy . . . Staff autonomy in the newsroom has not been the ordinary way of running business, even the news business. But there is no reason to expect that a person skilled at building a corporate empire is a good judge of what the generality of citizens in a community need and want to know. Today, news is increasingly a monopoly medium in its locality, its entrepreneurs are increasingly absent ones who know little about and have no commitment to the social and

political knowledge of a community's citizens. More and more, the news in America is a by-product of some other business, controlled by a small group of distant corporate chieftains. If the integrity of news and the full information of communities are to be protected, more can be expected from autonomous news staffs than from empire builders mainly concerned with other businesses in other places (Bagdikian, 1977, p. 22).

Ownership to the Employees

One major daily newspaper, *The Milwaukee Journal,* found a way in 1937 to prevent the "irreversible trend" of chain ownership (Conrad, Wilson and Wilson, 1964, pp. 175–81). Today nearly all of the stock in the *Journal* is in employee hands. The Employees' Stock Trust Agreement of 1937 insures that it will probably remain so (Severin, 1979). The agreement was set up to prevent ownership of the actual stock from passing into the hands of persons without direct involvement with the company.

A former editor and president of the company, John Donald Ferguson, said, "The allotment of stock has been such that no single group, and no possible combinations of two or three groups, including the executive group, could control the company."

In 1947, on the 10th anniversary of the employee ownership plan scrolls were presented to former owners by the employees which stated, ". . . Employee ownership knits our lives together. We don't work FOR The Journal. We ARE The Journal . . . Above all we are grateful for the security which sharing ownership has brought into our lives . . . We stand on guard to preserve and perpetuate this institution in our time, and beyond . . ."

The Financial Effect

By the end of 1976, a total of 1,865 employees of the Journal Company owned more than $88-million worth of stock. Over the ten-year period of 1966–76 the price per unit increased nearly 154 per cent with an average annual return of 23.7 per cent on a unit, including dividends paid per unit and increases in value per unit. By December 31, 1976, more than $51 million in dividends had been paid out to unitholders.

Irwin Maier, Chairman of the Board of Directors of the Journal Company from 1968 to 1977 says, "What this stock plan has done has been not only to keep secure a newspaper's future, but it has helped finance college educations for children, helped buy homes and secure loans for home remodeling, supported parents in nursing homes and paid for parents' medical expenses."

Maier adds, "Employees can use their Certificates of Beneficial Interest in the Unitholder Plan as collateral for loans at Milwaukee banks and get favorable interest rates."

More Than Profits

The annual balance sheet shows how the vision of Harry J. Grant has paid off financially. But, many hold that there is another balance sheet to be considered in the only industry named in and protected by the Constitution—the fulfillment of a social responsibility to a community.

Nearly any national poll of the ten best daily newspapers in the United States includes *The Milwaukee Journal.* Often it is ranked among the first five.

In the Spring of 1977 the paper won its fifth Pulitzer Prize, in local reporting, for a series on problems of the aged by Margo Huston. Its 1968 Pulitzer, for distinguished public service, was for a color Sunday supplement dealing with water pollution. Shortly thereafter Wisconsin passed a model law to regulate the pollution of public waters. Other Pulitzers were awarded the paper in 1953, 1935 and 1919.

There is no question that the employee-owned *Milwaukee Journal* is one of the best newspapers in the nation.

Irwin Maier says, "The employees take a pride in ownership, they want it to succeed." Of his own role in the company, which spans more than half of a century, including the positions of publisher, executive vice-president, president and chairman of the board, Maier says, "You feel that anything you do affects them so you give it extra thought. You are working as an owner, but you are also working for all other owners who are your friends and associates. You don't go to New York to report to security analysts. The people you report to are right here—they are us. I wouldn't want it any other way—."

Editorial page editor of the *Journal,* Sig Gissler, says, "We have preserved many of the features of a family-owned newspaper but have avoided the eccentricities of family ownership. Whoever is chairman of the board here cannot say, 'this is my newspaper' and do whatever he wants. It is amazing that we can still preserve a family feeling with 2,000 employees and our many subdivisions."

Gissler adds, "I think primarily the difference between the *Journal* and other newspapers is the depth and diligence of its local, regional and state coverage. We plow an awful lot of our resources into coverage."

The Employees' Stock Trust Agreement is now in its fifth decade with no indication that the Journal will ever become part of a chain or conglomerate. All indications are, however, that it will continue its high level of journalism.

CONCLUSIONS

A number of arguments have been put forth against the increasing concentration of ownership in the mass media. Among them are:

1) Conflict of interest may restrict reporting when a news medium is owned by corporations with extensive non-media activities. News values may become distorted.
2) A concentration of political and economic power may result which may rival or exceed that of any other segment of society, including the government.
3) There may be violations of those sections of the anti-trust laws which in no way conflict with the First Amendment guarantees of a free press (see Bagdikian, 1967, p. 6).
4) A reduction in the diversity of news and opinions which is available undermines the intent of the First Amendment and is contrary to the spirit of the Libertarian and Social Responsibility theories of the press.

Many possible remedies have been suggested by media scholars. Some of the more prominent ones are:

1) Divestiture of cross-owned media in single communities.
2) Divestiture of network owned-and-operated stations.
3) Reduction in the amount of programming which is network originated.
4) Limits upon how many newspapers or how much circulation one corporation may control (see Bagdikian, 1978, p. 33).
5) More autonomy for news staffs, including, if necessary, employee ownership.

REFERENCES

Bagdikian, B. (1967). News as a byproduct. *Columbia Journalism Review,* Spring, pp. 5–10.

Bagdikian, B. (1977). Newspaper mergers—the final phase. *Columbia Journalism Review,* March/April, pp. 17–22.

Bagdikian, B. (1978). The Media Monopolies. *The Progressive,* June, p. 31–7.

Beutler, M. (1978a). Chain gang journalism. *Texas Observer,* May 12, pp. 7–10.

Beutler, M. (1978b). Texas broadcasting: who shall govern? *Texas Observer,* Oct. 20, pp. 4–8.

Business Week (Feb. 21, 1977). The Big Money Hunts for Independent Newspapers, pp. 56–60; 62.

Columbia Journalism Review (July/August 1978). Deals, Gannett's Biggest Gulp, p. 10.

Columbia Journalism Review (Sept./Oct. 1978). Council to study ownership impact on press, p. 87.

Conrad, W., K. Wilson and D. Wilson (1964). *The Milwaukee Journal: The First Eighty Years.* Madison: University of Wisconson Press. Especially chapter 28, "The Employees Become Owners," pp. 175–81.

Cook, A. (1977). Extra! Extra! Read All About It! *Texas Parade,* October, pp. 35–6.

Gormley, W. (1977). How cross-ownership affects news-gathering. *Columbia Journalism Review,* May/June, pp. 38–9; 42–3; 46.

Harper's (1977). The Media Goliath: A Sample of Conglomerates in the Communications Industry. July, pp. 28–9.

Howard, H. (1976) The Contemporary Status of Television Group Ownership. *Journalism Quarterly* 53:399–405.

Johnson, N. (1968). The Media Barons and the Public Interest. *The Atlantic,* June, pp. 43–51.

Jones, W. and L. Anderson (1977). The Newspaper Business. Washington Post News Service. In the Madison, Wisconsin, *Capital Times,* August 15, p. 25.

Phillips, K. (1977). Busting the Media Trusts. *Harper's,* July, pp. 23–7; 30–4.

Severin, W. (1979). The Milwaukee Journal: Employee Owned Prizewinner. *Journalism Quarterly* (in press).

Zimmerman, F.(1967). Managing the News? *Wall Street Journal,* April 17. Extensive excerpts in *Columbia Journalism Review,* Spring 1967, p. 10.

Chapter 17

The Effects of
Mass Communication

THE search goes on for a single comprehensive theory that will explain the effects of mass communication. Theories about the effects of mass communication appear to go in cycles. For a time, one theory will be dominant, but eventually it comes to be replaced by another.

During the 50 years in which mass communication has been the subject of serious study, we have seen the Bullet Theory, the Limited Effects Model, and the present focus of attention, which we will call the Moderate Effects Model. In addition, there are some indications that the future might see a return to a new version of the Bullet Theory we might call the Powerful Effects Model. These models differ primarily in the size of the effect that they are willing to attribute to mass communication in general, but also in some other ways. They can be illustrated in a diagram that shows the size of this effect and the period in which the model has been popular (Figure 1).

The cyclical nature of the theorizing is apparent in the diagram. The theorizing could even come full circle if the Powerful Effects Model were to grant as much influence to mass communication as the Bullet Theory did. It appears, however, that the Powerful Effects Model will be much more subject to qualifications than the Bullet Theory. In that sense, our knowledge about mass communication will not be moving in a circle, as this diagram might suggest, but will be progressing forward. The word "theory" is probably too grand for these ideas. They are instead views of the magnitude of the effects of mass communication. They are convenient and useful because they allow us to sum up in a single phrase what we seem to know about the

Figure 1 Various Models of the Effects of Mass Communication Developed Over a Fifty-Year Period

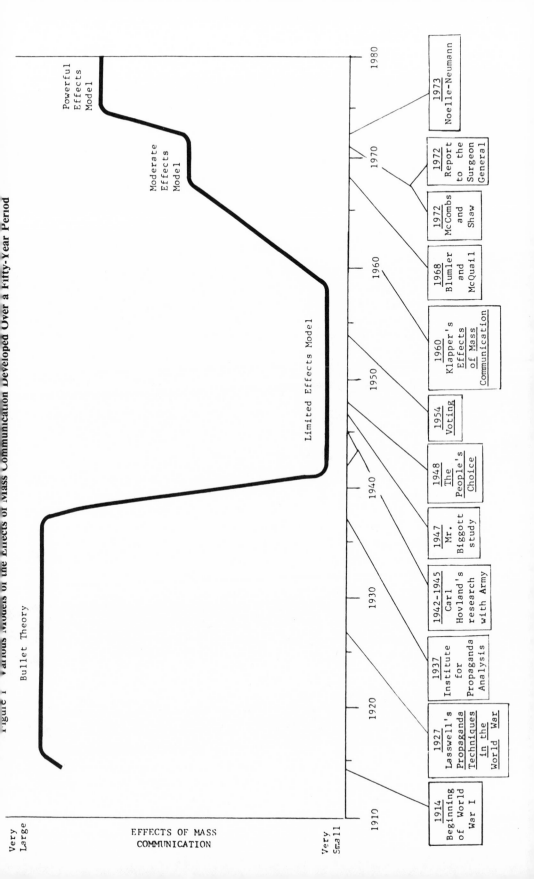

effects of mass communication. But they are far from being systematic scientific theories, and in fact each of them contains within it a number of theoretical approaches or sets of research findings.

The Bullet Theory

The Bullet Theory, also known as the hypodermic needle theory or the Mechanistic S-R Theory (DeFleur, 1970), was a view that attributed great power to mass communication. It was a view that was influenced by the apparent power of propaganda in World War I, as we have described in Chapter 8. This view was popular in the years before World War II, when many people feared that a Hitler-type demagogue could rise to power in the United States through the use of mass communication. The Institute for Propaganda Analysis was created in response to this fear, and it began a massive campaign of educating the American people on the techniques of propaganda.

Although the Bullet Theory has largely been discarded by mass communication researchers, many members of the public may believe in it still today. For instance, John Lilly, an expert on interspecies communication but apparently not on mass communication, wrote recently, "We have all been educated on the fantastic power of the media in changing public opinion" (Lilly and Lilly, 1976, p. 208).

The Limited Effects Model

The Limited Effects Model began to emerge in the 1940s. Some of the key research leading to this view of mass communication as having small effects included Hovland's Army studies showing that orientation films were effective in transmitting information but not in changing attitudes, Cooper and Jahoda's research on the "Mr. Biggott" cartoons indicating that selective perception could reduce the effectiveness of a message, and the election studies of Lazarsfeld and his associates that showed few people were influenced by mass communication in election campaigns.

The Limited Effects Model was stated well in Joseph Klapper's book *The Effects of Mass Communication.* Klapper presented five generalizations about the effects of mass communication, with the first two being the following:

1. Mass communication *ordinarily* does not serve as a necessary and sufficient cause of audience effects, but rather functions among and through a nexus of mediating factors and influences.
2. These mediating factors are such that they typically render mass communication a contributory agent, but not the sole cause, in a process of reinforcing the existing conditions. . . . (Klapper, 1960, p. 8).

The mediating factors that Klapper was referring to include the selective processes (selective perception, selective exposure and selective retention), group processes and group norms, and opinion leadership.

This position, that the effects of mass communication are limited, is sometimes referred to as "the law of minimal consequences." This phrase does not appear in Klapper's book, but was coined by his wife, Hope Lunin Klapper, a faculty member at New York University (Lang and Lang, 1968, p. 273).

The Moderate Effects Model

What we are calling the Moderate Effects Model characterizes the research on the effects of mass communication being done in the 1970s. It includes a number of approaches: the information seeking paradigm, the uses and gratifications approach, the agenda setting function and the cultural norms theory. These approaches share a number of assumptions:

1. That the Limited Effects Model overstated the smallness of the effects of mass communication, and that in certain situations mass communication might have important effects.
2. That past research has to a large extent looked for effects of mass communication on attitudes and opinions, whereas looking at other dependent variables might have found greater effects.
3. That past research has been one-sided in conceptualization in that it has asked "What is mass communication doing to the audience member?" to the exclusion of another important question, "What does the audience member do with mass communication?"
4. That past research has studied short-term effects of mass communication almost to the exclusion of long-term effects.

The Information Seeking Paradigm

The information seeking paradigm focuses on the individual's information seeking behavior and attempts to identify the factors that determine that behavior. The paradigm represents a shift from a focus on the mass communicator or the message, which was prevalent in much earlier research, to a focus on the receiver.

One of the first articles to use the phrase "information seeking" was a 1959 study by Bruce Westley and Lionel C. Barrow, Jr., who developed two measures of news seeking behavior and showed that they were both related to retention from a news broadcast. Westley and Barrow did not, however, make information seeking the dependent variable and try to find the variables affecting it, as most of the later investigators of information seeking did. It is understandable that Westley might be involved in some of the first research focusing on "information seeking," since the Westley and MacLean model differs from earlier models in stressing the need of the receiver for information.

Research on information seeking was also greatly influenced by the work on selective exposure. Many studies had been done attempting to test the prediction from selective exposure that people should select information that was supportive of their present attitudes. Some of the research supported this prediction and some did not (see Sears and Freedman, 1971). Researchers began to realize there were other factors that could influence the selection of a message, and that sometimes these factors were more important determinants than the desire for supportive information. Some of these other factors include information utility or usefulness, intrinsic interest in a particular topic, entertainment value, need for variety, and personality characteristics such as high or low dogmatism.

The findings of the information seeking approach are not easily summarized in a sentence or two. The research has been heading in the direction of developing rather complex models that attempt to summarize the relationships between information seeking and the numerous variables that influence it (Atkin, 1973; Donohew and Tipton, 1973).

To some extent, the information seeking paradigm appears to have been subsumed under the uses and gratifications approach, to which it is similar.

The Uses and Gratifications Approach

The uses and gratifications approach attempts to determine the functions that mass communication is serving for audience members, and it does this largely by asking them. Like the information seeking paradigm, it represents a shift of focus from the purposes of the communicator to the purposes of the receiver. It differs from the information seeking paradigm in being a somewhat broader approach, although recently the two have practically merged. For instance, quite a bit of the data cited by Atkin (1973) in his presentation of his information seeking model comes from Blumler and McQuail's *Television and Politics,* one of the major studies using the uses and gratifications approach.

The uses and gratifications approach was first described in an article by Elihu Katz (1959) in which he was reacting to a claim by Bernard Berelson (1959) that the field of communication research appeared to be dead. Katz argued that the field that was dying was the study of mass communication as persuasion. He pointed out that most communication research up to that time had been aimed at investigating the effects of persuasive campaigns on audiences. Katz said this research was aimed at answering the question, "What do the media do to people?" Most of this research had shown that mass communication had little effect in persuading people, and so there had been a turning away of researchers to variables that did have more of an effect, such as group influences.

Katz suggested that the field might save itself by turning to the question, "What do people do with the media?" He cited a few studies already done of this type. One of them was, curiously enough, Berelson's "What Missing the Newspaper Means," a 1949 study conducted by interviewing people during a newspaper strike about what they missed in their papers (Berelson, 1965).

Another example was Riley and Riley's study (1951) showing that children well integrated into groups of peers "use" adventure stories in the media for group games while children not well integrated use the same communications for fantasizing and daydreaming. The latter example shows the importance of the uses and gratifications approach: different people can use the same mass communication message for very different purposes.

The uses and gratifications approach, with its emphasis on the uses of mass communication, has some similarities to Raymond Bauer's idea of an active or obstinate audience, originally proposed in 1964 (Bauer, 1971).

Blumler and McQuail (1969) used the uses and gratifications approach as the overall research strategy in a study of the 1964 General Election in Britain. The central aim of their study was "to find out why people watch or avoid party broadcasts; what uses they wish to make of them; and what their preferences are between alternative ways of presenting politicians on television" (pp. 10–11). Part of their aim was to answer the challenging question posed by earlier election studies which indicated mass media election campaigns had little effect on voters: if voters are not influenced by mass media election programming, why do they follow it at all? Also, the researchers expected that classifying viewers according to their motives for viewing might disclose some previously undetected relationships between attitude change and campaign exposure, and thus might tell us something about effects after all. The uses and gratifications approach of Blumler and McQuail is reflected in some of their chapter titles: "Why do People Watch Political Programmes?" and "What Kind of Political Television Do Viewers Want?"

Blumler and McQuail began the task of determining people's motives for watching political broadcasts by interviewing a small sample with open-ended questions. On the basis of the responses to these questions, they drew up a list of eight reasons for watching political broadcasts. This list was used in subsequent interviewing with a large sample survey. On the basis of this interviewing, the researchers determined the frequency with which each reason was cited (Table 1).

The three most frequently mentioned reasons reflect a desire for what Blumler and McQuail call surveillance of the political environment. These reasons, each cited by more than half the respondents, indicated that people used the political broadcasts as a source of information about political affairs. Other data from the survey indicated that one of the specific purposes of this surveillance was to find out about campaign promises and pledges. Only about a third of the respondents chose "To remind me of my party's strong points," a reason that would indicate the political broadcasts were being used for reinforcement of existing attitudes. This casts some doubt on the indication from some earlier research that people turn to the mass media primarily for reinforcement.

Blumler and McQuail also found some support for their notion that classifying viewers according to motives for viewing might disclose some relationships between attitude change and campaign exposure. The most use-

Table 1

**Reasons for Watching Party Broadcasts in the
British General Election of 1964,
As Endorsed by TV Owners***

	Percent
To see what some party will do if it gets into power	55
To keep up with the main issues of the day	52
To judge what political leaders are like	51
To remind me of my party's strong points	36
To judge who is likely to win the election	31
To help make up my mind how to vote	26
To enjoy the excitement of the election race	24
To use as ammunition in arguments with others	10

* Respondents could endorse more than one reason.

Reprinted by permission of Faber and Faber Ltd. and The University of Chicago Press from *Television in Politics: Its Uses and Influence,* by Jay G. Blumler and D. McQuail. Chicago: The University of Chicago Press, 1969. Copyright 1969 by Jay G. Blumler and Denis McQuail.

ful variable they found for this purpose was an index of the strength of a viewer's motivation for following an election campaign on television. They divided viewers into two groups: those "strongly motivated" to follow the campaign and those with "medium and weak" motivation. For those with medium and weak motivation, there was a strong and regular relationship between exposure to Liberal Party broadcasts and shift in favor of the Liberal Party. This relationship was not found for those who were strongly motivated to follow the campaign. This finding indicates that a uses and gratifications approach can actually increase our knowledge about *effects* of mass communication. Effects may be dependent upon or related to audience members' needs and motives.

The finding also indicates the complexity that our knowledge about the effects of mass communication might take on in the future. There is an effect of exposure to the campaign on change in voting attention, but it occurred only for those with low motivation to follow the campaign and when they were exposed to Liberal Party programming.

Blumler and McQuail went on to make some policy recommendations for television election coverage in Britain. One was that the policy of putting political party broadcasts on all British television channels simultaneously be discontinued. The other was that there should be more programming in which candidates are challenged, either by television correspondents or by other candidates in a debate format. Both of these recommendations grew rather directly out of expressed desires of the television viewing public, and show the value of the uses and gratifications approach for formulating policy.

The uses and gratifications approach has come under some criticism, particularly for being non-theoretical, for being vague in defining key concepts and for being basically nothing more than a data-collecting strategy (see Elliott, 1974, and Swanson, 1977). In light of the research since Freud indicating the complexity and obscurity of human motivation, there is also something a little simplistic or naive about using self reports to determine motives.

As a healthy antidote to the emphasis on passive audiences and persuasion in much earlier research, however, the uses and gratifications approach is valuable.

The Agenda Setting Function

The agenda setting function of the mass media is the capability of the mass media to select and emphasize certain issues and thereby cause those issues to be perceived as important by the public. Maxwell E. McCombs and Donald L. Shaw, the researchers most responsible for the current research on agenda setting, state it this way:

> This notion of the agenda-setting function of the mass media is a relational concept specifying a strong positive relationship between the emphases of mass communication and the salience of these topics to the individuals in the audience. This concept is stated in causal terms: increased salience of a topic or issue in the mass media influences (causes) the salience of that topic or issue among the public (McCombs and Shaw, 1977, p. 12).

Agenda setting was not a new idea when McCombs and Shaw first presented it in 1972. The idea, and in some cases, the very phrase, have appeared in the literature of political science for some time. Some authors trace it back to Walter Lippmann's *Public Opinion,* published in 1922, in which he discussed the role of mass communication in shaping the "pictures in our heads." Lippmann's notion was a much vaguer one than the rather specific agenda setting hypothesis, however, and the connection with his work seems rather indirect.

A rather direct statement of the agenda setting function appears in a 1958 article by Norton Long:

> In a sense, the newspaper is the prime mover in setting the territorial agenda. It has a great part in determining what most people will be talking about, what most people will think the facts are, and what most people will regard as the way problems are to be dealt with (Long, 1958, p. 260).

Agenda setting researchers frequently cite the influence of Bernard C. Cohen's *The Press and Foreign Policy,* and hardly an article appears on agenda setting that does not quote or paraphrase his catchy statement of the power of the press: "It may not be successful much of the time in telling people what to think, but it is stunningly successful in telling its readers what to think *about*"(Cohen, 1963, p. 13). This is the agenda setting idea in a nutshell, even though Cohen did not use the phrase "agenda setting."

Other political scientists discussing "agenda changing" or "agenda building" include Walker (1966) and Cobb and Elder (1971, 1972).

McCombs and Shaw (1972) also credit Lang and Lang (1966) with one of the early statements of the agenda setting power of the mass media, although Lang and Lang did not use the phrase "agenda setting" either.

The first empirical test of the agenda setting hypothesis was conducted by McCombs and Shaw (1972). They studied the 1968 presidential election in Chapel Hill, N.C., and compared actual campaign content of the mass media with what people said were the most important issues.

To determine the public's agenda, interviews were conducted with 100 randomly selected voters who had not yet decided how to vote. These "undecideds" were studied because they should have been most susceptible to campaign influence. Respondents were asked to outline the key issues as they saw them, regardless of what the candidates might be saying at the moment. These responses were used to prepare a list of issues ranked according to importance by the public.

To determine the mass media's agenda, a content analysis was conducted of the five newspapers, two news magazines, and two television network evening newscasts widely used in the Chapel Hill area. This was done from Sept. 12 to Oct. 6, and news and editorial content items were placed in 15 categories representing the key issues and other kinds of campaign news. Items were classified as *major* or *minor,* depending on amount of time or space used. This content analysis was used to prepare a list of issues ranked according to importance by their frequency of appearance in the news media.

The crucial test of the agenda setting hypothesis was to see if the mass media's rankings of issues correlated with the public's rankings of issues. This correlation was .967 for major items and .979 for minor items.

These correlations are striking, but the McCombs and Shaw study has the weakness that it does not establish causal direction. They interpret the correlations as indicating that the media agenda has influenced the public's agenda. But an equally plausible interpretation is that the public's agenda has influenced the media's agenda. In fact, this interpretation follows logically from such ideas as the active audience or the suggestion of the Westley-MacLean model that media survive to the extent that they give the audience what it wants.

In order to show causal direction, it is necessary to establish time order. Which comes first, the public's agenda or the media's agenda? This can only be answered by a study that examines the media's content and the public's views at two or more points in time. McCombs and Shaw conducted this kind of study four years later in Charlotte, N.C. (McCombs, 1977). Data were collected in June and October and then were evaluated with a technique called cross-lagged correlation. Unfortunately for the agenda setting hypothesis, the results were ambiguous at best. The data for newspapers supported the agenda setting hypothesis. But the data for television news gave more support to the opposite notion, that the public's agenda was influencing the media's agenda. McCombs and Shaw argue that the two media are playing different roles in the agenda setting process, with television coming into play later in the campaign, but their data do not really show that television influences the public agenda. Communication researcher Bruce Westley (1978) has pointed out another problem. Although the newspaper results appear at first to support agenda setting, a closer look at the cross-lagged correlation diagram shows the public's agenda in June correlating with a coefficient of .94 with the public's agenda in October. Westley asks how the media can be having much of an effect on the public's agenda if the public's agenda is not changing any more than that over a four-month period?

At this point, the research on agenda setting must be labeled inconclusive. Despite the lack of clear evidence, agenda setting is now being presented in some books as if it is established fact. Oskamp (1977) states that "probably the most important effect of the mass media is their agenda-setting function" (p. 161). Patterson and McClure (1976) wrote, "The media's agenda-setting role affects the public's view of presidential elections" (p. 75).

One reason for the popularity of the agenda setting hypothesis is its basic attractiveness. To mass communication researchers faced with growing evidence that the effects of mass communication were practically nonexistent, the agenda setting hypothesis was a welcome idea. To journalism researchers, it had the additional advantage that it gave them another theory to research and teach besides persuasion theory. Agenda setting is a theory that is much more compatible with reporting. Journalism researchers might also be attracted to agenda setting research because they to some extent can claim it as "their" theory, while most of the theorizing about persuasion had to be "borrowed" from psychologists. In fact, however, even the agenda setting function is "borrowed;" it was being written about by political scientists (Long, 1958; Walker, 1966; Cobb and Elder, 1971) before communication researchers.

The Cultural Norms Theory

The cultural norms theory states that mass communication has an indirect effect on behavior through its ability to shape norms.

Melvin DeFleur, the developer of the theory, stated it this way:

> Essentially, the cultural norms theory postulates that the mass media, through selective presentations and the emphasis of certain themes, create impressions among their audiences that common cultural norms concerning the emphasized topics are structured or defined in some specific way. Since individual behavior is usually guided by cultural norms (or an actor's impressions of what the norms are) with respect to a given topic or situation, the media would then serve *indirectly* to influence conduct (DeFleur, 1970, p. 129).

This theory, like the agenda setting function, can be traced back to Walter Lippmann's notion that mass communication shapes the "pictures in our heads."

Some of the strongest evidence supporting DeFleur's cultural norms theory comes from George Gerbner's research on television viewing. Gerbner has found that, on a number of different topics, heavy television viewers tend to answer questions differently from light television viewers (Gerbner and Gross, 1976; Gerbner, et al., 1977). The answers that the heavy television viewers tend to choose are ones that are presented and reinforced by television itself. For instance, heavy television viewers were more likely to overestimate the percentage of the world population that is American. Of course, the leading characters in most television programs are Americans. Television is also heavy in programs featuring violence and police: Gerbner found that heavy television viewers were more likely than light viewers to overestimate the percentage of the population actually employed in law enforcement work. Perhaps most disturbing, the heavy television viewer seems to be getting the lesson from all that television violence that the world is a mean and dangerous place. Heavy television watchers tended to overestimate their own chance of being involved in some type of violence in the next week and were more likely to answer "Can't be too careful" when asked "Can most people be trusted?"

These results alone, while supporting the cultural norms theory, are open to challenge. There is a plausible rival hypothesis to the notion that television is influencing people to these views. It could be that people lower in education tend to be the heavy television watchers, and perhaps they just don't know the answers to these questions because of their lower education. Gerbner has considered this rival hypothesis and has rather effectively ruled it out. His research shows that if you look at people with the same level of education, you still find these differences between heavy and light television viewers. Furthermore, the same thing is true for a number of other variables that might explain the relationship: sex, age, income, newspaper reading and church attendance.

DeFleur's cultural norms theory seems to offer a great deal of promise, even though it appears that DeFleur himself might have become disillusioned with it. The theory has been left out of the third edition of his book (DeFleur and Ball-Rokeach, 1975). However, certain topics involving mass communication that many people are currently interested in seem to be handled nicely by the cultural norms theory. These include the role of television in influencing our norms about violence as a way of relating to others, the role of the mass media in shaping our sexual stereotypes and our images of minority group members, and the role of the mass media in shaping our values, particularly in the directions of materialism and consumerism.

The Powerful Effects Model

The powerful effects model is just beginning to emerge, so it is not clear yet exactly what form it will take. But a number of studies seem to agree that mass communication can have powerful effects after all if it is used in programs or campaigns that are carefully prepared according to communication theory principles. Some of the important principles seem to be that it takes repeated messages over a period of time rather than a single message to have a significant effect (although there are exceptions), that it is important to identify and focus on a target audience, that the objectives of the campaign should be identified very specifically and the messages produced should be related to those objectives, and that ideas from communication theory can be used in development of themes, messages and media.

Mass media campaigns that have had important effects on attitudes and behavior have been reported by Mendelsohn (1973) and Maccoby and Farquhar (1975).

Mendelsohn describes his own participation in three projects. The first, the CBS "National Drivers Test," resulted in 35,000 viewers enrolling in driver training courses. A second project, a short film on drinking and driving that was entertaining enough to be shown as a short in commercial theaters, led to three out of 10 viewers saying they would consider changing some of their previously held ideas regarding safe driving. A third project, an informational soap opera series aimed at Mexican-Americans in Los Angeles, led to 6 per cent (or 13,400 persons) of the viewers reporting they had joined a community organization, one of the prime objectives of the series.

Maccoby and Farquhar undertook an ambitious program attempting to use mass communication to reduce heart disease. The study was conducted in three towns, with one (Gilroy) receiving an eight-month mass media campaign, one (Watsonville) receiving the same mass media campaign plus intensive group instruction for a sample of high risk adults and the third (Tracy) serving as a control and receiving neither type of communication. Pretests in all three towns before the campaign included measures of information, attitudes and reported behaviors as well as a physical examination. Both the mass media campaign and the intensive instruction were aimed at producing in people behavior changes that would reduce the risk of coronary disease. These behaviors included reducing or stopping smoking, improving diets (particularly by eliminating foods high in cholesterol) and increasing amounts of exercise. Results showed that both types of communication campaigns were effective in reducing the amounts of eggs consumed and the number of cigarettes smoked and in lowering the cholesterol level as well as an overall measure of heart disease risk, the Cornfield risk score. The greatest effects were in Watsonville, the town with the mass media campaign and the intensive instruction for a selected group, but there were also significant effects in Gilroy, the town with mass media only.

Another version of the powerful effects model has been described by Elisabeth Noelle-Neumann (1973), a West German communication researcher, in her article "Return to the Concept of Powerful Mass Media." Noelle-Neumann argues that the mass media do have powerful effects on public opinion, but that these effects have been underestimated or undetected in the past because of limitations of the research. Noelle-Neumann argues that we need more longterm studies of the effects of mass communication conducted outside laboratory settings. She has conducted some of these studies herself, using public opinion poll data and content analysis of the mass media. Noelle-Neumann suggests that three characteristics of mass communication—its cumulation, ubiquity and consonance—combine to produce powerful effects on public opinion. By consonance, she refers to the unified picture of an event or issue that can develop and which is often shared by different newspaper, television stations, etc. The effect of this consonance is to overcome selective exposure, since people cannot select any other message, and to present the impression that most people look at the issue in the way that the mass media are presenting it. For example, in West Germany in 1971, most people thought the majority of the public was against the death penalty, even though the poll data showed a fifty-fifty split on the issue. Noelle-Neumann suggests that the consonant attitude of the mass media, which were generally opposed to capital punishment, was the reason. Another factor that might come into play in such a situation is what Noelle-Neumann calls the "hypothesis of silence." A member of society who disagrees with a majority opinion (or what appears to be a majority opinion) often chooses to remain silent on that issue. This adds even further to the strengthening of the view that appeared to be a majority opinion. Noelle-Neumann's "hypothesis of silence" is somewhat similar to John Stuart Mill's idea of "reticence on the part of heretics" (Mill, 1956, p. 41).

Noelle-Neumann relates her concept of consonance back to Lippmann's idea that the mass media produce a certain "picture of reality." She also describes a number of factors which operate to produce consonance, including widely shared news values, common dependence on certain sources, studying rival media too closely, and striving for approval from colleagues and superiors. This list is similar to the factors Warren Breed identified as operating in the newsroom (see Ch. 15).

Noelle-Neumann calls for more field studies investigating the combination of consonance, cumulation and ubiquity, since the three factors can hardly be simulated realistically in a laboratory experiment.

Effects in Particular Areas

This chapter so far has looked at some very general paradigms for viewing the effects of mass communication. But it is also possible to consider the effects of mass communication in more restricted areas of concern. It is merely a matter of narrowing our interest to a particular kind of content or a more limited type of behavior that might be affected. Then, within that area, many of the theories or paradigms that we have discussed in the beginning of the chapter might apply, although some will be more appropriate than others.

Two of these areas in which there has been a lot of interest and research are the effects of mass communication on political behavior and the effects of television violence on aggressive behavior.

Effects on Political Behavior

Careful study of the effects of mass communication on political behavior began with the classic election studies of the 1940s—*The People's Choice and Voting.* These studies suggested that mass communication had only limited effects on people's voting decisions. They showed that 80 per cent of the voters made their voting decisions before the campaign began, and that for the remaining persons personal influence was often more important than mass media influence.

These classic studies have made some important contributions, such as the two-step flow hypothesis, but communication researchers have also come to see that they had some shortcomings. These include: 1). They focused on elections and ignored possible effects between elections. 2). They focused on opinion change as the effect to the exclusion of other possibly important effects. 3). They left out television, which had not come into wide use yet.

Lang and Lang (1968) have criticized the classic studies for focusing on election campaigns and then concluding that the effect of the mass media on voting behavior is minimal. They suggest that the preconceptions and impressions that enter into a vote decision are gradually built up in the periods between elections, and that the mass media play a large part in shaping those impressions. The mass media do this, Lang and Lang suggest, by forcing attention to some issues and not others—the process that McCombs and Shaw called "agenda setting."

Blumler and McQuail (1969) have criticized the classic studies for focusing on opinion change as the effect of mass communication on political behavior. They attempted in their British study to apply a more user-oriented approach aimed at determining why people bother to attend to political campaigns if they have already decided for whom to vote. This approach turned up some interesting functions of mass communication in a campaign—particularly the widespread use for surveillance of the political environment. They also found that the uses and gratifications approach helped them to identify some particular groups for whom the mass media campaigns did have direct effects on voting decisions—particularly those unmotivated to follow the campaign who happened to be exposed to material from one party, the Liberal party. This suggested that effects of mass communication on voting decisions can be identified if we are willing to accept rather complicated findings involving particular types of messages and people with particular types of motivations.

The role of television in election campaigns has been studied recently, particularly by two political scientists at Syracuse University, Thomas E. Patterson and Robert D. McClure (1976). Their book is based on a panel survey of viewers and a content analysis of television during the 1972 presidential campaign. It has the subtitle "The Myth of Television Power in National Politics," and it presents the surprising conclusion that "television's only effect on the American voter is to cheapen his conception of the campaign process and to stuff his head full of nonsense and trivia" (p. 144). They found that network evening news coverage of a presidential campaign is so devoted to exciting visuals that it hardly deals with issues. They found that political "image" commercials, designed to sell candidates like soap, have little or no effect because viewers see through them and practice selective perception. Surprisingly, they found that political commercials did pass on to viewers a significant amount of information about campaign issues—more, in fact, than the network evening news did. Patterson and McClure argue that television does not have as great an agenda setting effect as newspapers because of the selection for television of stories that are brief, visual and entertaining.

Patterson and McClure's surprising findings of the slight effect of television in campaigns and Blumler and McQuail's finding that significant effects of campaigns can be identified if we are willing to consider a number of variables simultaneously suggest that quite a bit of research is still needed on the topic of the effects of mass communication on political behavior. A recent review of the literature in the area (Kraus and Davis, 1976) reached this conclusion: "What we know is not what we thought we knew and what we thought we knew is more persistent in the literature than what we know" (p. 283).

Effects of Television Violence

Violence and the mass media have been intertwined almost from the beginning of mass communication. "The Great Train Robbery," one of the first entertainment films, was a violent western. Concern about the effects of violent content is not a new phenomenon, either. For a while it centered on comic books, but in more recent years it has focused on television.

It is easy to see why. Content analysis has revealed a staggering amount of violence on television. One set of figures indicates that by the age of 12, the average child will have watched 101,000 violent episodes on television, including 13,400 deaths (Steinfeld, 1973).

This concern about the effects of violence on television has been gradually transmitted to Congress, which has looked into the matter several times over the years. Hearings on the question were held by the Kefauver Subcommittee in 1954 and the Dodd Subcommittee in 1961 and 1964. About the same time, social science researchers were becoming interested and were conducting some of the first experiments investigating the question.

The National Commission on the Causes and Prevention of Violence, appointed in 1968 after the assassination of Robert Kennedy, paid particular attention to television violence. It looked at all the research that had been conducted up to that time and concluded, "We believe that the television networks, network affiliates, independent stations, and other members of the broadcasting industry should recognize the strong probability that a high incidence of violence in entertainment programs is contributing to undesirable attitudes and even to violence in American society" (National Commission on the Causes and Prevention of Violence, 1969, p. 201).

Senator John O. Pastore apparently was not satisfied with that finding, for in 1969 he asked the Secretary of Health, Education and Welfare to direct the Surgeon General to appoint a committee to come up with "definitive information" on whether there is a causal connection between televised crime and violence and antisocial behavior by individuals, particularly children. This request led to the appointment of the Surgeon General's Scientific Advisory Committee on Television and Social Behavior and a $1.5 million program of research.

Unfortunately, the appointment of this committee was handled in an unusual manner, leading to quite a bit of criticism and a somewhat confusing final report. William H. Stewart, the Surgeon General at the time, submitted his list of possible committee members to the broadcasting industry for its approval. CBS declined to challenge any names, but NBC, ABC and the National Association of Broadcasters did not hesitate to strike names, with the result that seven of the best known researchers on television violence were excluded from the committee. Furthermore, the final committee of 12 included four or five people with strong network connections, including Joseph Klapper, who was director of social research for CBS. Stewart apparently allowed this prior screening by the broadcast industry to head off any possible criticism of the committee make-up after the report was released. But some critics have said a fairer way to do it might have been to permit the academic community to go over the list and strike names if this privilege was going to be given to the television industry. At any rate, this background on the composition of the Surgeon General's committee is important information for anyone attempting to interpret its final report.

A number of different hypotheses have been suggested concerning the possibile effects of television violence on human behavior. One is the catharsis hypothesis, which suggests that viewing television violence causes a reduction of aggressive drive through a vicarious expression of aggression. Then there are several different stimulation hypotheses which predict that watching television violence will lead to an increase in actual aggressive behavior. One of these is an imitation hypothesis, which suggests that people learn aggressive behaviors from television and then go out and reproduce them. A slightly different hypothesis is the disinhibition hypothesis, which suggests that television lowers people's inhibitions about behaving aggressively toward other people. If this latter hypothesis is correct, television violence might be teaching a general norm that violence is an acceptable way to relate to other people. This hypothesis has some resemblance to the cultural norms theory.

The Surgeon General's advisory committee reviewed prior research but also commissioned quite a bit of new research. In all of this research—perhaps hundreds of studies—there are only a handful giving any support to the catharsis hypothesis. Many more studies support the two stimulation hypotheses—imitation and disinhibition. One of the most striking of these studies is the Walters and Llewellyn Thomas (1963) experiment, which indicated that subjects who saw a film of a knife fight scene were more likely to increase the levels of shock they would give another person than subjects who saw a film of adolescents involved in crafts. This supports the disinhibition hypothesis, since the type of aggression engaged in was not the same as that portrayed in the film. A study conducted especially for the Surgeon General's committee which dealt with young children and a violent sequence from the television program *The Untouchables* (Liebert and Baron, 1972) produced a very similar result.

It is possible to criticize these experiments for dealing only with short-term effects of televised violence and for being somewhat artificial in that they take place in laboratory settings. It could be, for instance, that people are more willing to behave aggressively in the laboratory because they do not have to worry about reprisals, which they would almost always have to in real life. The research done for the Surgeon General's committee also includes a panel study done over a ten-year period (Lefkowitz, Eron, Walder and Huesmann, 1972), however, and this deals with long-term effects and a real world setting. Lefkowitz and his colleagues had started a study of aggression in young people in 1959–60. When the Surgeon General's study came along in 1969, they were able to take advantage of their earlier research to do a follow-up study. Their cross-lagged correlation data for boys showed in real-life the same relationship that most of the experiments had shown in the laboratory: that watching television violence leads to an increase in aggressive behavior. In fact, the best predictor in their study of aggressive behavior at age 19 was violent television watching while in the third grade. The home environment is often thought to have an effect on whether a person becomes violent. The Lefkowitz, et al. study investigated several aspects of the home environment that might have been related to later aggression: the amount of disharmony between the parents, the tendency of the parents to punish the children and the regularity of church attendance of the parents. None of these measures taken while boys were in the third grade predicted aggressive behavior at age 19 as well as did television violence viewing in the third grade.

These two types of studies—the experiments in the laboratories and the correlation studies from surveys outside the laboratories—agreed in their general finding, that viewing television violence leads to an increase in aggressive behavior. And that was the conclusion of the report of the Surgeon General's advisory committee in 1972, although the committee stated it in a rather qualified manner:

> Thus, the two sets of findings converge in three respects: a preliminary and tentative indication of a causal relation between viewing violence on television and aggressive behavior; an indication that any such causal relation operates only on some children (who are predisposed to be aggressive); and an indication that it operates only in some environmental contexts (Surgeon General's Scientific Advisory Committee on Television and Social Behavior, 1972, p. 11).

Some critics have said this is a watered-down conclusion, heavily influenced by the network members of the committee, and that the research done for the committee really justifies a stronger conclusion. Some researchers have objected particularly to the statement that the causal relationship only applies to those children already predisposed to be aggressive. In the overview to one of the five volumes summarizing the research done for the committee, researcher Robert Liebert concludes that television violence may be contributing to the aggressive behavior "of many normal children" (Liebert, 1972, p. 30).

Another way to look at the committee's conclusion is this: even with a somewhat one-sided committee, they still concluded that there was a causal relationship between watching television violence and behaving aggressively. Viewed this way, one might conclude that the evidence must be pretty strong.

Jesse L. Steinfeld, the Surgeon General who replaced Stewart, stated the relationship more strongly in a hearing before a Congressional committee: "It is clear to me that the causal relationship between televised violence and antisocial behavior is sufficient to warrant appropriate and immediate remedial action" (Cater and Strickland, 1975, p. 86).

At any rate, the evidence appears to be strong enough for a number of groups, including the PTA, the American Medical Association, and the National Citizens Committee for Broadcasting, to demand a reduction in the amounts of violence in television. Gerbner's most recent content analysis results indicated these demands were having an effect; the amount of violence on TV had dropped significantly in the Fall 1977 TV season (Gerbner, et al., 1978).

The findings of the Surgeon General's Advisory Committee have had another effect—the adoption by the networks of a "family viewing hour" that is supposed to contain less violence and sex. This has led to additional complications, including law suits by television writers and producers who say their creativity is being restricted, and a court finding that the family hour was unconstitutional because it resulted from FCC pressure on the networks.

Some of the research on television violence is now aimed at determining which kinds of children are more susceptible to influence by violent programming. This is a development that is nicely compatible with the uses and gratifications approach to the effects of mass communication.

Another new direction for television research is attempting to explore the positive lessons that television could teach—the opposite side of the coin (see Liebert and Poulos, 1972).

CONCLUSIONS

Theories of the effects of mass communication have varied widely over the last fifty years, ranging from the Bullet Theory to the Limited Effects Model, as well as a number of positions in between these extremes. Theories that suggest moderate effects of mass communication are the popular ones now. These include the information seeking paradigm, the uses and gratifications approach, the agenda setting function, and the cultural norms theory. Interestingly, there are also some hints of a return to the idea that the mass media can have powerful effects, at least in certain areas. Evidence supporting this view comes from Noelle-Neumann's research on the formation of public opinion, work on public service campaigns of various types by Mendelsohn and work on health communication by Maccoby and Farquhar.

REFERENCES

Atkin, C. (1973). Instrumental Utilities and Information Seeking. In Peter Clarke (ed.), *New Models for Communication Research,* pp. 205–242. Beverly Hills: Sage.

Bauer, R. A. (1971). The Obstinate Audience: The Influence Process from the Point of View of Social Communication. In W. Schramm and D. Roberts (eds.), *The Process and Effects of Mass Communication,* rev. ed., pp. 326–346. Urbana: University of Illinois Press.

Berelson, B. (1959). The State of Communication Research. *Public Opinion Quarterly* 23:1–6.

Berelson, B. (1965). What "Missing the Newspaper" Means. In Wilbur Schramm (ed.), *The Process and Effects of Mass Communication,* pp. 36–47. Urbana: University of Illinois.

Blumler, J. G., and D. McQuail. (1969). *Television in Politics: Its Uses and Influence.* Chicago: The University of Chicago Press.

Cater, D., and S. Strickland. (1975). *TV Violence and the Child: The Evolution and Fate of the Surgeon General's Report.* New York: Russell Sage Foundation.

Cobb, R. W., and C. D. Elder. (1971). The Politics of Agenda-Building: An Alternative Perspective for Modern Democratic Theory. *Journal of Politics* 33, no. 4:892–915.

Cobb, R. W., and C. D. Elder. (1972). *Participation in American Politics: The Dynamics of Agenda-Building.* Boston: Allyn and Bacon.

Cohen, B. C. (1963). *The Press and Foreign Policy.* Princeton: Princeton University Press.

DeFleur, M. L. (1970). *Theories of Mass Communication,* 2nd ed. New York: David McKay.

DeFleur, M., and S. Ball-Rokeach. (1975). *Theories of Mass Communication,* 3rd ed. New York: David McKay.

Donohew, L., and L. Tipton. (1973). A Conceptual Model of Information Seeking, Avoiding, and Processing. In Peter Clarke (ed.), *New Models for Communication Research,* pp. 243–268. Beverly Hills: Sage.

Elliott, P. (1974). Uses and Gratifications Research: A Critique and a Sociological Alternative. In J. G. Blumler and E. Katz (eds.), *The Uses of Mass Communications: Current Perspectives on Gratifications Research,* pp. 249–268. Beverly Hills: Sage.

Gerbner, G., and L. Gross. (April, 1976). The Scary World of TV's Heavy Viewer. *Psychology Today* 9, no. 11:41–45, 89.

Gerbner, G., L. Gross, M. F. Eleey, M. Jackson-Beeck, S. Jeffries-Fox and N. Signorielli. (1977). TV Violence Profile No. 8: The Highlights. *Journal of Communication* 27, no. 2:171–180.

Gerbner, G., L. Gross, M. Jackson-Beeck, S. Jeffries-Fox and N. Signorielle. (1978). Cultural Indicators: Violence Profile No. 9. *Journal of Communication* 28, no. 3:176–207.

Katz, E. (1959). Mass Communication Research and the Study of Popular Culture: An Editorial Note on a Possible Future for this Journal. *Studies in Public Communication* 2:1–6.

Klapper, J. T. (1960). *The Effects of Mass Communication.* New York: The Free Press.

Kraus, S., and D. Davis. (1976). *The Effects of Mass Communication on Political Behavior.* University Park: Pennsylvania State University Press.

Lang, K., and G. E. Lang. (1966). The Mass Media and Voting. In B. Berelson and M. Janowitz (eds.), *Reader in Public Opinion and Communication,* pp. 455–472. New York: The Free Press.

Lang, K., and G. E. Lang. (1968). *Politics and Television.* Chicago: Quadrangle Books.

Lefkowitz, M. M., L. D. Eron, L. O. Walder and L. R. Huesmann. (1972). Television Violence and Child Aggression: A Followup Study. In G. A. Comstock and E. A. Rubinstein (eds.), *Television and Social Behavior,* vol. 3, pp. 35–135. Washington, D.C.: U.S. Government Printing Office.

Liebert, R. M. (1972). Television and Social Learning: Some Relationships Between Viewing Violence and Behaving Aggressively (Overview). In J. P. Murray, E. A. Rubinstein and G. A. Comstock (eds.), *Television and Social Behavior,* vol. 2, pp. 1–42. Washington, D.C.: U.S. Government Printing Office.

Liebert, R. M., and R. A. Baron. (1972). Short-term Effects of Televised Aggression on Children's Aggressive Behavior. In J. P. Murray, E. A. Rubinstein and G. A. Comstock (eds.), *Television and Social Behavior,* vol. 2, pp. 181–201. Washington, D.C.: U.S. Government Printing Office.

Liebert, R. M., and R. W. Poulos. (November, 1972). TV for Kiddies. Truth, Goodness, Beauty—and a Little Bit of Brainwash. *Psychology Today* 6, no. 6:122–128.

Lilly, J., and A. Lilly. (1976). *The Dyadic Cyclone: The Autobiography of a Couple.* New York: Simon and Schuster.

Lippmann, W. (1965). *Public Opinion.* New York: The Free Press.

Long, N. E. (1958). The Local Community as an Ecology of Games. *American Journal of Sociology* 64:251–261.

Maccoby, N., and J. W. Farquhar. (1975). Communication for Health: Unselling Heart Disease. *Journal of Communication* 25, no. 3:114–126.

McCombs, M. E. (1977). Newspapers Versus Television: Mass Communication Effects Across Time. In D. L. Shaw and M. E. McCombs (eds.), *The Emergence of American Political Issues: The Agenda-Setting Function of the Press,* pp. 89–105. St. Paul, Minn.: West.

McCombs, M. E., and D. L. Shaw. (1972). The Agenda-Setting Function of Mass Media. *Public Opinion Quarterly* 36:176–187.

McCombs, M. E., and D. L. Shaw. (1977). The Agenda-Setting Function of the Press. In D. L. Shaw and M. E. McCombs (eds.), *The Emergence of American*

Political Issues: The Agenda-Setting Function of the Press, pp. 1–18. St. Paul, Minn.: West.

Mendelsohn, H. (1973). Some Reasons Why Information Campaigns Can Succeed. *Public Opinion Quarterly* 37:50–61.

Mill, J. S. (1956). *On Liberty.* Indianapolis: Bobbs-Merrill.

National Commission on the Causes and Prevention of Violence. (1969). *To Establish Justice, To Insure Domestic Tranquility: Final Report of the National Commission on the Causes and Prevention of Violence.* Washington, D.C.: U.S. Government Printing Office.

Noelle-Neumann, Elisabeth. (March, 1973). Return to the Concept of Powerful Mass Media. In H. Eguchi and K. Sata (eds.), *Studies of Broadcasting: An International Annual of Broadcasting Science,* pp. 67–112. Tokyo: The Nippon Hoso Kyokai.

Oskamp, S. (1977). *Attitudes and Opinions.* Englewood Cliffs, N.J.: Prentice-Hall.

Patterson, T. E., and R. D. McClure. (1976). *The Unseeing Eye: The Myth of Television Power in National Politics.* New York: G. P. Putnam's Sons.

Riley, M. W., and J. W. Riley, Jr. (1951). A Sociological Approach to Communications Research. *Public Opinion Quarterly* 15:445–460.

Sears, D. O., and J. L. Freedman. (1971). Selective Exposure to Information: A Critical Review. In W. Schramm and D. F. Roberts (eds.), *The Process and Effects of Mass Communication,* rev. ed., pp. 209–234. Urbana: University of Illinois Press.

Steinfeld, J. L. (April, 1973). TV Violence *Is* Harmful. *Reader's Digest,* pp. 37–38, 40, 43, 45.

Surgeon General's Scientific Advisory Committee on Television and Social Behavior. (1972). *Television and Growing Up: The Impact of Televised Violence.* Washington, D.C.: U.S. Government Printing Office.

Swanson, D. L. (1977). The Uses and Misuses of Uses and Gratifications. *Human Communication Research* 3:214–221.

Walker, J. L. (1966). A Critique of the Elitist Theory of Democracy. *American Political Science Review* 60:285–295.

Walters, R. H., and E. Llewellyn Thomas. (1963). Enhancement of Punitiveness by Visual and Audiovisual Displays. *Canadian Journal of Psychology* 17:244–255.

Westley, B. H. (1978). Review of *The Emergence of American Political Issues: The Agenda-Setting Function of the Press. Journalism Quarterly* 55:172–173.

Westley, B. H., and L. C. Barrow, Jr. (1959). An Investigation of News-Seeking Behavior. *Journalism Quarterly* 36:431–438.

Chapter 18

The Overall Picture

E ARLY in this book the authors discussed the need for research and theory in communication and their application to the fields of journalism, advertising, radio-television-film and public relations. After defining communication and mass media and discussing the scientific method a number of models of the communication process were presented and discussed. We now attempt to bring most of the material discussed in earlier chapters together by relating it to an overall model—the Westley-MacLean model.

The Westley-MacLean model (Chapter 3) expanded the Newcomb model of interpersonal "Symmetry" (Chapters 3 and 11) to include a communicator role (C) and to accommodate a number of "objects of orientation" (Xs).

When they presented their model in 1957 Westley and MacLean said:

> Communications research and theory have blossomed from a variety of disciplinary sources in recent years. People probing the communications area have here focused on theoretical issues and there on "practical" concerns. Thus, one finds today a jungle of unrelated concepts and systems of concepts on the one hand and a mass of undigested, often sterile empirical data on the other. (Westley and MacLean, 1957, p. 31).

The authors go on to say,

> In this paper, we are trying to develop a single communications model which may help to order existing findings. It also may provide a system of concepts which will evoke new and interrelated research directions, compose old theoretical and disciplinary differences, and in general bring some order out of a chaotic situation . . . Can a simple, parsimonious model be built capable

267

Figure 1

Westley-MacLean Model

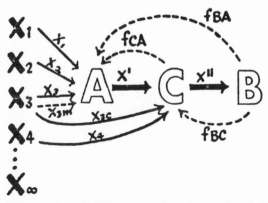

The messages C transmits to B (X") represent his selections from both messages to him from As (X') and C's selections and abstractions from Xs in his own sensory field (X$_{3c}$, X$_4$), which may or may not be Xs in A's field. Feedback not only moves from B to A (f$_{BA}$) and from B to C (f$_{BC}$) but also from C to A (f$_{CA}$). Clearly, in the mass communication situation, a large number of Cs receive from a very large number of As and transmit to a vastly larger number of Bs, who simultaneously receive from other Cs.

From Westley, B. and MacLean, M. (1957). A conceptual model for communication research. *Journalism Quarterly* 34:31–8. Reprinted with permission.

of drawing together many of the existing approaches to mass communications without serious loss in utility?

The Model and Communications Research

In the Westley-Maclean model the As (advocacy roles) or communicators select and transmit messages purposively. Information theory (chapter 4) deals with sources which select messages out of all those possible and produce suitable signals for transmission over whatever channel is used. The chapter also discussed the role of gatekeepers and coupling. The following chapter (semantics) dealt with the effects of language on perception and abstraction and the misuses of language, including overgeneralization, two-valued thinking and unconscious projection. Consistency theories have equal meaning for both communicators and receivers. To a greater or lesser extent, depending upon the issue, we all practice selective exposure and perception. Attitude change research indicates that single messages are unlikely to change strongly held attitudes while research about the communication of innovation indicates that such attitudes are probably best changed with a combination of interpersonal and media messages used as "media forums." The studies dealing with the credibility of the source or communicator are, of course, of direct application here.

The Cs (channel roles) provide the Bs (behavioral system roles) with a more extended environment by selecting and transmitting the information Bs require, especially information which is beyond the immediate reach of B. Cs make abstractions from objects (Xs) which are appropriate to Bs need satisfactions or problem solutions. We have already mentioned information theory, semantics and selective exposure as they relate to abstraction in connection with A roles. In a like manner they apply to C roles.

In the Westley-MacLean model Cs select and transmit non-purposively the information Bs require. By non-purposively the authors mean without intent to influence. However, as gatekeepers, Cs often engage in transmitting messages designed to engender attitude change as in the case of advertising and public relations campaigns and in more general ways (c.f., Lasswell and Breed). Cs also serve different roles in various types of societies and may have several functions as well as dysfunctions. Lasswell has pointed to distortions of media content as a method of achieving or maintaining social control. Breed discusses news policy and slanting, areas omitted or seldom dealt with by communicators, and the distortions brought about by civic boosterism. Media chains, conglomerates and cross-ownership in single communities can all result in distortions and omissions of news and a reduction in the diversity of news as a threat to truth and understanding. Some researchers suggest that the communicator is often in a position to exercise great influence as to what readers and viewers will think about (the agenda setting function) even if not what conclusions they will reach about an issue.

The Bs in the Westley-MacLean model are the behavioral system roles or the "receivers." They can be an individual (a personality system), a primary group or a social system. A B needs "transmissible messages as a means of orienting itself in its environment and as a means of securing problem solutions and need satisfactions." Bs can select from a number of Cs which is why C remains an agent of B only so long as C fulfills Bs needs. Bs are the destination in information theory terms and must decode the messages. Bs bring their backgrounds to the messages to provide connotative meanings. They exercise selective perception as a result of their past experiences, cultural expectations, needs, moods and attitudes. They also utilize selective exposure and selective retention when dealing with messages. As chapter 9 concludes, "meaning is invented, assigned, given, rather than received."

Consistency theories predict that when messages which cause psychological discomfort are directed at Bs (receivers) they will use selective exposure, perception and retention or fall back on rationalization, incredulity or attacks on source credibility to avoid or reduce the psychological discomfort. Communicators who wish to change attitudes held by receivers must first understand the functions of those attitudes for receivers if any measure of success is to be achieved. Inoculation theory provides the other side of the coin, making attitudes resistant to persuasion.

If receivers are to be reached through opinion leaders then the two-step flow and the communication of innovation research indicate that media appropriate to the particular sphere of influence must be carefully selected.

The media serve several functions for receivers, but as we have seen, they can also have a number of dysfunctions. Walter Lippmann, more than a half-century ago, discussed the gap between reality and the pictures of reality we carry around in our heads. For the receiver the media supply information, gratify needs and have other uses. These are areas which need further research along with the effects of the media on political behavior and the effects of viewing violence on television.

In the model "messages" about Xs (objects or events "out there" which have characteristics capable of being transmitted in some abstracted form) are transmitted through channels from As and/or Cs to Bs. These messages can inform, persuade, and educate. Information theory introduces the concepts of channel capacity, the notion that in one sense information is not meaning, the important use of redundancy to offset noise, and the use of entropy as a measure of the difficulty of a message. General semantics sheds light on the problems we encounter in using language to communicate abstractions about reality and readability measures provide a way of judging the difficulty of textual materials. As was noted, more research is needed on the effects of organization of material, the directness of approach and the conceptual difficulty of textual materials as well as on the "listenability" of spoken messages.

Message symbols contain connotative as well as denotative meanings. The semantic differential provides a way for measuring the meanings or "images" receivers assign to products, political candidates, organizations and ideas. Messages often contain the techniques identified in studies of propaganda, an area which provided the roots for attitude change research and the general studies of the effects of mass communication. An understanding of these techniques for designing messages is of considerable value to the receiver as well as the communicator. Persuasive messages can be designed from a number of theoretical viewpoints: stimulus-response; motivational; cognitive; social; and personality. Message content is under increasing scrutiny, especially for sex and violence during prime-time television.

Mass Media Research

Communication research is the application of social science research methods to the problems communicators deal with. It is an attempt to replace as much guesswork as possible with verified theories. Theories and research methods in the social sciences are not as accurate and refined as those used in the physical sciences. Understanding and predicting human behavior is extremely difficult; nevertheless the imperfect statements which can be made about human behavior as a result of research are better than the guesswork upon which much of communication has been based.

Research provides the information to help plan communication and evaluate its results. Some of the uses of research in mass communication are:

1) *Audience studies* are usually survey type research designed to measure the amount of interest in various mass media content and the reasons for it. With print media audience studies are usually in the form of "one-time" surveys while television ratings most often use an adaptation of the "panel" method where samples of the audience are repeatedly measured over a period of years. Studies of media use and media credibility, reader interest surveys and broadcast "ratings" are examples of this type of research.

2) *Message content and design* immediately brings to mind the content analysis of messages, but content analysis can often be used in conjunction with other research methods to great advantage. Experimental designs in a "laboratory" setting are often used to determine the most effective version of a message to achieve a desired objective with a specific population. Research on the advantages of presenting one side of an issue or two sides of an issue, the use of fear appeals, the optimum levels of redundancy, the uses of language and the various methods of counter persuasion are examples of message content and design studies. So are "field" studies done by advertising agencies and public relations firms to determine the most effective form or versions for their commercials and advertisements.

3) *Effect studies* involve the planning and evaluation of the effects of media campaigns as well as the choice of media used. Studies involving the diffusion of innovations, the functions and dysfunctions of the media, the agenda setting function of the media and the effects of viewing television violence are obvious examples. In the commercial world, advertisers are interested in the most effective means of increasing sales, public relations practitioners seek the best ways to improve a corporate image, campaign managers need the means to get a candidate elected, and statesmen want the best ways to win acceptance for a policy or a program. Effect studies can utilize many research methods: experimental designs, survey research, content analysis, case studies, as well as combinations of them.

4) *Communicator analysis* has traditionally been linked with "gatekeeper" studies (case studies). Studies dealing with the effects of language on perception and abstraction can also be classified as communicator analysis. The effects of source credibility on the acceptance of a message are also directly related to communicator studies. Research into the effects of media chains, conglomerates and cross-ownership on the content of the media are all examples of communicator analysis.

As can be seen, any listing of research in mass communication contains a great deal of overlap. One cannot separate media effects from message content, nor communicator analysis from message content. Communicators, messages, audiences and effects are all interrelated—that interrelation is necessary for communication. Research methods are tools to aid communicators in understanding the communication process and predicting the effects of their efforts.

RELATED FIELDS

By now the reader is aware that communications theory and research stands at the crossroads of many other fields. The student seeking related courses and the practitioner seeking related reading might wish to consider some of the following, which is by no means an exhaustive list.

Psychology—social psychology; perception; psychology of language; sensory psychology; information processing; and human learning.

Sociology—public opinion; collective behavior; formal organizations; social change; communication.

Government—public opinion; theory construction; empirical theory and modeling; research design.

Philosophy—philosophy of science; science and the modern world; communication and culture.

Linguistics—study of language; language and society.

Computer Sciences—computer applications courses.

Also, research methods (survey research, experimental design, content analysis, case studies, etc.) and statistics in a number of fields, especially psychology, educational psychology, sociology and government.

Index

Abelson, R. P., 155, 156, 163

Abstraction, 55–57, 268; dead-level, 57–58; high-level, 57, 58; low-level, 57, 58

Abstraction ladder, 56

Access magazine, 53

Accuracy factor in newspaper attitudes, analysis of, 97, 98

Action for Children's Television, 3

Activity dimension of semantic space, 96, 97, 100

Adjustive function in attitude, 183, 185

Advertising, 165, 217, 218, 219, 224, 271; cognitive design used in, 194–95; motivational approach in, 194; personality design used in, 196; propaganda devices used in, 114, 118, 120, 121, 122, 123, 124, 151; Semantic Differential Technique in, 102–03; social design used in, 195; stimulus-response design used in, 193; subliminal, 138

Agenda-setting function of mass media, 253–55, 259

Agnew, Spiro, 2, 64, 103, 105

Air Force, United States: *see* United States Air Force

Ajzen, I., 190, 191

Alcoholics Anonymous, 150, 151

Ali, Muhammad, 225–26

"All in the Family" (TV program), 135–36, 137, 140

Allen, B. P., 192

Allen, Woody, 79

Allman, Gregg, 120

Allport, Gordon, 137, 166

Ambiguity in communication, 140

American Association for Adult Education, 72

American Broadcasting Company (ABC), 227, 236, 237, 238, 261

American Civil Liberties Union, 111

American Express Company, 238, 239

American Jewish Committee, 135

American magazine, 68

American Medical Association, 3, 263

Ames, Adelbert, Jr., 129

Anderson, L., 231, 232, 233

Antunes, G., 229

Apple, R. W., 134

Arafat, Fathi, 122

Arafat, Yasir, 122

Arbitron, 5

Aristotle, 4

Art of Plain Talk, The (Flesch), 73
Art of Readable Writing, The (Flesch), 74
Art of War, The (Sun Tsu), 115
Asch, Solomon, 124, 143, 145–46, 147, 149, 195
Associated Press (AP), 76, 79, 122, 225, 228, 233, 237
Atkin, C., 250
Atkinson, J. W., 132
Atlantic Richfield Company, 241
Attitude: and behavior, 188–92, 197–98; concept of, 166–67
Attitude change, 2, 4, 159, 160, 161, 165, 166, 268, 269; consistency-theory approach to, 156–63 *passim*, 182, 194, 197; and fear appeals, 175–77, 179, 189; following forced compliance, 162–63; functional approach to research on, 182–86, 192, 197; and Inoculation Theory, 179, 180, 182, 186–88, 197, 269; learning-theory approach to, 167–79 *passim*, 182, 197; and Lerbinger's designs, 192–97, 198; military research on (Hovland), 166, 167–72, 179, 182, 248; and resistance to counterpropaganda, 178–79; and source credibility, 172–75; and Yale Communication Research Program, 172–79; *see also* Persuasion
Attitude Organization and Change (Rosenberg et al.), 172, 179
Audience studies, 271
Autokinetic light effect, 144
Avoiders and copers, 177

Bacharach, Burt, 120
Bagby, J. W., 130
Bagdikian, Ben, 233, 235, 236, 237, 238, 241, 244
Baker, Samm Sinclair, 224
Balance Theory, Heider's, 155–56, 157, 158
Ballachey, E. L., 166
Ball-Rokeach, S., 125, 151, 256
Band-wagon device in propaganda, 123, 124, 151, 195
Barnlund, Dean C., 140
Baron, R. A., 262

Barrow, Lionel C., Jr., 249
Baskir, L., 223
"Battle of Britain" (film), attitude change research on, 168–69
Bauer, Raymond, 251
Bavelas, Alex, 147
Becker, Hal, 139, 140
Bell, Daniel, 119
Bellow, Saul, 79
Bensman, J., 227
Berelson, Bernard, 17, 18, 129, 139, 148, 149, 250
Berlo, David, 6, 125
Beutler, M., 231
Bias factor in newspaper attitudes, analysis of, 97, 98
Bill, J. A., 14, 28
Bingham, Barry, Jr., 232
Blumler, J. G., 250, 251, 252, 259, 260
Bock, H. de, 137
Boorstin, Daniel, 213
Boosterism, civic, 226, 227
Booth Newspapers, 241
Bormuth, J. R., 85
Bramsted, E. K., 125
Brauer, S., 23
Breed, Warren, 219, 220, 221, 222, 224, 225, 226, 227, 228, 229, 258, 269
Brehm, J. W., 162, 163
Breslin, Jimmy, 79
Brigham, J. C., 136
Brinkley, David, 61
Broadcasting, concentrated ownership in, 233–34; *see also* Radio; Television
Bronowski, J., 12
Brown, Bob, 227
Brown, L., 218
Brown, Roger, 114, 123, 124
Brucker, Herbert, 61
Bryan, Sam Dunn, 75, 76
Bryan, William Jennings, 166
Bryson, Lyman, 72
Buber, Martin, 7
Buckley, William, 58
Budd, R., 17
Bullen, Dana, 23
"Bullet Theory" of media effects, 125–26, 148, 161, 246, 247, 248

Bulletin of National Resources Planning Board, 173

Burd, Gene, 226

Bureau of Applied Social Research (Columbia University), 148, 201

Business Week, 232, 238

Byrne, D., 139

Campbell, D. T., 25

Canalization, as condition of media effectiveness, 218

Canby, Vincent, 122

Cantril, Hadley, 115, 116, 129, 133

Capra, Frank, 168

Card stacking, as propaganda device, 121–23, 169

Carter, Jimmy, 80, 117, 118, 120, 121, 134, 152

Carter, R., 101

Cartoons, anti-prejudice, 135, 152, 168, 196, 197, 248

Cartwright, Dorwin, 147

Case studies in communication research, 22–23

Castro, Fidel, 118

Categorical thinking, 58–59

Cater, D., 263

Catholic Church, 115

Causality, and experimental design, 19

Century magazine, 68

Chaffee, S., 101

Chall, J. S., 80

Chandler, Otis, 232

Change agents in diffusion-of-innovation paradigm, 209–10

Charnley, Mitchell, 1*n.*

Chen, W., 166

Cherry, C., 7

Chicago American, 68

Chicago Evening Post, 68

Chicago Tribune, 159

Chronicle of Higher Education, 226

Cincinnati Enquirer, 236

Clark, Frank, 226

Clark, R., 228

Cleaver, Eldridge, 54

Cleveland Plain Dealer, 226

Cloze Procedure, 49, 83–85

Cobb, R. W., 254, 255

Coder reliability, 3

Cognitive consistency, and mass communication, 154–63, 194, 268, 269

Cognitive design in persuasion, 194–95

Cognitive dissonance, 2, 136, 161–62, 163, 189

Cohen, Arthur R., 163, 189

Cohen, Bernard C., 253

Cohen, M. R., 14

Colby, William, 59

Cole, R., 17

Collings, V. B., 144

Color-music synesthesia, 90

Columbia Broadcasting System (CBS), 134, 159, 218, 235, 261

Columbia Bureau of Applied Social Research, 148, 201

Columbia Journalism Review, 236, 241

Combined Communications Corporation, 241

Commercials: *see* Advertising

Commission on Federal Paperwork, 80

Communication: ambiguity in, 140; definitions of, 5–8; feedback in, 31; and groups, 143–52 *passim;* interpersonal, and mass media, 200–11; mass, *see* Mass communication; Mathematical Theory of, 31–32, 43, 46, 48, 50 (*see also* Information Theory); and perception, selective, *see* Selective perception; statistical foundation of, 31; two-step flow of, 201, 205–06, 207, 269

Communication and Persuasion (Hovland, Janis and Kelley), 172, 176, 178

Communication model(s), 29, 30–41; evaluation of, 29–30; functions of, 29; Gerbner, 39–40; Lasswell, 30, 37, 39, 40; Newcomb A-B-X, 23, 35–36, 37, 157, 267; originality of, 30; Osgood, 32–35; parsimony of, 30; realism of, 30; Schramm, 34, 35; Shannon-Weaver, 31–32, 35, 37, 40; symmetry in (Newcomb), 23, 35–36, 37, 157, 267; Westley-MacLean, 37–39, 249, 254, 267–69; *see also* Models in science

Communication networks, 49

Communication of Innovations (Rogers and Shoemaker), 207

Communication research, 20, 21, 25; case studies in, 22–23; interviews in, personal, 16; split-run technique in, 21

Communication Research Center (Michigan State University), 99

Communication system: definition of, 48; corresponding, 48, 49; as functional system, 48; non-corresponding, 48, 49; *see also* Information Theory

Communicator analysis, 271

Computer sciences, and communications theory, 272

Cone, A. L., 78

Conglomerates, media, 231, 232, 233, 234–39

Congruity Theory, Osgood and Tannenbaum's, 157–59, 161

Connally, John, 233

Connotative meaning, 89, 270; measurement of, 89–111 *passim*

Conrad, W., 242

Consistency, cognitive, and mass communication, 154–63, 194, 268, 269

Content analysis, 3, 17–19, 260, 263, 271, 272

Cook, A., 233

Cooper, Eunice, 135, 143, 152, 168, 196, 197, 248

Copernicus, Nicolaus, 11, 12

Copers and avoiders, 177

Costello, Jan, 80, 83

Coughlin, Charles E., 116, 119, 151, 219

Counterpropaganda, resistance to, 178–79

Cousins, Norman, 138

Cowles Communications, Inc., 235–36

Crist, Judith, 122

Cronkite, Walter, 159

Crutchfield, R. S., 166

Culhane, J. W., 85

Cultural-norms theory, and mass communication, 255–56

Cybernetics (Wiener), 30, 45

Dale, Edgar, 80, 116

Daley, Lar, 119

Daley, Richard, 159

Dallas Times-Herald, 236

Dance, F. E. X., 5

Daniel, Clifton, 61

Danielson, Wayne, 21, 75, 76, 78, 79

Darley, J. M., 177, 192

Darley, S. A., 177, 192

Daugherty, J., 227

Davis, D., 260

Dead-level abstracting, as misuse of language, 57–58

Decision making, 162, 203, 209, 210

Decoding, 39, 45, 129

Deductive logic, 14

DeFleur, Melvin, 125, 151, 205, 248, 255, 256

Dembroski, T. M., 192

Deneuve, Catherine, 120

Denial, and incongruity, 159–60

Denotative meaning, 89, 270

Dependent variable in experimental design, 19

Designs for Persuasive Communication (Lerbinger), 192

Deutsch, K., 29, 30

Deutschmann, Paul, 99, 103

Devereux, E. C., 222

Dewey, Thomas E., 148

Dichter, Ernest, 194

Dickinson, Angie, 120

Diffusion studies, 21, 200, 207

Dissonance theory, 2, 136, 161–62, 163, 189

Dollard, Charles, 167

Donohew, L., 250

Doob, Leonard, 116

Dugger, R., 227

Dulles, F. R., 113

Effect studies, 246–64, 271

Effects of Mass Communication, The (Klapper), 248

Efron, Edith, 3

Ego-defensive attitude, 183, 184, 185, 186, 196, 197

Ehrlich, D., 162

Einstein, Albert, 11, 30, 54

Eisenhower, Dwight D., 21, 22, 63, 64

Eisinger, R. A., 3

Either-or thinking, 59–60

Elder, C. D., 254, 255
Elliott, P., 253
Ellsberg, Daniel, 117
Ellul, Jacques, 125–26
"Embeds" (Key), 139
Empiricism, 11, 14
Encoding, 39, 51; implications for, 65; *see also* General Semantics
Engels, Edward, 129
Engle, Clair, 122
English, A. C., 166
English, H. B., 166
Entertainment factor in ratings for media, 99
Entropy concept in Information Theory, 46, 47, 49, 50, 270
Eron, L. D., 262
ETC.: A Review of General Semantics, 53
Ethical factor in ratings for media, 99, 100
Evaluation: multi-valued, 60; two-valued, 59–60
Evaluative dimension of semantic space, 96, 100
Evans, R., 192
Excluded middle, thinking with, 59–60
Experimental design, 19–22, 272; variables in, 19
Experiments on Mass Communication (Hovland, Lumsdaine and Sheffield), 167

Fact magazine, 122
Factor Analysis, 93–94, 97, 99, 100
Factor loadings: of newspaper scales, 93; of television scales, 94
Fallows, James, 223
Family, media portrayal of, 225
Farquhar, J. W., 5, 152, 192, 257, 264
Farr, J. N., 86
Farrell, Barry, 121
Fear appeals, 175–77, 179, 189
Fearing, Franklin, 140
Federal Communications Commission, 4, 237, 238, 239, 263
Federal Trade Commission, 118, 239
Feedback, concept of, 45–46

Feinberg, M., 3
Ferguson, John Donald, 242
Feshbach, 176, 177, 179, 189, 196
Festinger, Leon, 2, 136, 147, 161, 179, 182, 189, 191, 197
Filene, Edward A., 115
Fine Art of Propaganda, The, 116
Finnegan's Wake (Joyce), 84, 85
First Amendment, 244
Fishbein, Martin, 190, 191
Flesch, Rudolf, 68, 72, 73, 74, 75, 76, 78, 79, 80, 83, 84, 86
Fog Index (Gunning), 74–75
Food habits studies (Lewin), 147–48
Forced compliance, attitude change following, 162–63
Ford, Jerry, 118, 134
Formula(s) for readability measurement, 67–86 *passim;* applications of, 78–83; Dale-Chall, 80, 86; Farr-Jenkins-Paterson, 86; and government regulations, 80–83; Human Interest (Flesch), 73, 74, 75, 76, 78, 80, 82, 83; and insurance policies, 83; and mass communication, 78–79; and "New Literates," 80; Reading Ease (Flesch), 74–86 *passim;* textbooks evaluated by, 78; use of, 76–77
Fortune magazine, 173, 174, 235
Four Theories of the Press (Siebert et al.), 212
Foyt, A. J., 120
Freedman, J. L., 137, 163, 250
Frost, David, 117
Fry, Edward, 75
Fulbright, William J., 121
Functional approach to attitude change research, 182–86, 192, 197

Galileo, 11, 12, 115
Gamble, L. G., 85
Gannett Company, 236
Gannett newspapers, 231, 232, 236, 241
Garvin, G., 139
Gatekeeper point, definition of, 48
Gatekeeper studies, 22, 30, 147, 210, 268, 269, 271
Gaudet, H., 148

General Semantics, 51–65, 270; *see also* Encoding; Language

Generalization, definition of, 14; in science, 12, 13, 14, 24

Geography and Plays (Stein), 84, 85

Gerbner, George, 5, 39, 40, 256, 263

Germany, Nazi propaganda in, 116, 124–25

Gestalt Psychology (Koffka), 73

Gibbons, Euell, 121

Giesbrecht, L. W., 136

Gillen, B., 78

Gillig, P. M., 174, 175

Ginzburg, Ralph, 122

Gissler, Sig, 243

Glittering generality, as propaganda device, 118–19

Gode, Alexander, 6

Goebbels, Joseph, 116, 125

Goldstein, M. I., 177

Goldwater, Barry, 122

Goodman, Steve, 119

Gormley, W., 240

Government, studies of, and communications theory, 272

Graham, Billy, 120

Graham, Katharine, 231

Grant, Harry J., 243

Grant, M. N., 123

Gray, W. S., 70, 71, 72, 73, 78, 79

Greenberg, Bradley, 99, 105

Greenwald, A. G., 174, 175

Greer, Germain, 58

Grey, D. L., 23

Gross, L., 136, 256

Gross, S. J., 190

Group Dynamics, 143, 147, 151

Group norms, 144–45

Group pressure, 145–47

Groups, 2, 143; casual, 144; and communication, 143–52 *passim;* as instruments of change, 150–51; and mass communication, 151; and political attitudes, 148–50; primary, 143, 149; reference, 143–44

Gulf and Western, 236

Gunning, Robert, 74, 75, 78, 79

Gunning Fog Index, 74–75

Guthrie, Arlo, 119

Hall, E., 195

Hand, Learned, 240

Hardgrave, R. L., Jr., 14, 28

Harper's magazine, 235

Harte-Hanks Communications, Inc., 232–33

Hastorf, Albert, 129, 133

Hayakawa, S. I., 52, 53, 56, 57, 61, 63, 64

Hearst, Patricia, 59, 64

Heider, F., 179, 182; Balance Theory of, 155–56, 157, 158

Hemingway, Ernest, 9

Hersh, Seymour M., 226

Hesburgh, Theodore M., 223

Heterophily, 207

Heuristic function of communication model, 29, 30

Hidden Persuaders, The (Packard), 194

Hitler, Adolf, 116, 200

Hofmann, R. J., 78

Homophily, 207

Hope, Bob, 120

Hoppe, C., 227

Horowitz, Irving Louis, 111

Hovland, Carl, 2, 6, 20, 21, 123, 124, 166, 167, 168, 169, 171, 172, 173, 174, 175, 176, 178, 179, 180, 182, 248

How to Talk Back to Your Television Set (Johnson), 53

Howard, H., 234

Huesmann, L. R., 262

Hull, Clark, 167

Human Interest formula for readability (Flesch), 73, 74, 75, 76, 78, 80, 82, 83

Humphrey, Hubert H., 106

Hurley, P., 229

Huston, Margo, 243

Huxley, Thomas H., 11

Hypothesis: definition of, 14; operationally defining, 24; and scientific method, 11, 12, 13, 14

Identification, undue, as misuse of language, 58–59

Illiteracy, world, 80

Incredulity, and incongruity, 159–60

Independent variable in experimental design, 19
Index numbers to prevent undue identification, 59
Inductive logic, 14
Inference: definition of, 61–62; labeled, 62
Information seeking paradigm, 249–50
Information Theory, 2, 32, 43–50, 268, 270; applications of, 48–49; channel capacity in, 45; concepts of, basic, 44; and coupling of corresponding communication systems, 49; destination concept in, 44, 45, 47; and encoding and decoding of message, 45; entropy concept in, 46, 47, 49, 50, 270; and feedback, 45–46; information in, as special term, 46, 47; and information source, 44; and noise, definition of, 47; and readability, application to, 49; receiver concept in, 44, 45; redundancy concept in, 46–47, 49, 50, 270; as theory of signal transmission, 44–45; *see also* Communication, Mathematical Theory of; Communication system
Informative-vitality factor in ratings for media, 99, 100
Innovation, diffusion of, 207–10
Inoculation Theory (McGuire), 179, 180, 182, 186–88, 197, 269
Insko, C. A., 166, 188
Institute for Communication Research (University of Illinois), 90, 96
Institute for Propaganda Analysis, 116, 123, 124, 125, 126, 165, 169, 248
Insurance policies, readability of, 83, 85
Internal Revenue Service, 80
International Telephone and Telegraph Company (ITT), 236, 237, 238
Interpersonal communication, and mass media, 200–11
Interviews, personal, in communication research, 16
Ittelson, William H., 129
Ivins, M., 105

Jahoda, Marie, 135, 143, 152, 168, 196, 197, 248
James, William, 73, 78

Janis, Irving, 6, 20, 123, 167, 172, 176, 177, 178, 179, 186, 189, 196
Jenkins, J. J., 86
Jenner, Bruce, 118, 120
Johnson, Nicholas, 53, 237, 238
Johnson, Wendell, 52–53, 54, 57, 60
Jones, E. E., 137
Jones, W., 231, 232, 233
Jong, Erica, 60
Journalism: objectivity in, 61, 63; slanting in, 61, 63, 64
Joyce, James, 84, 85
Judgment, definition of, 62–63
Justice and law, media portrayal of, 225, 228–29
Justice Department, U.S., 238, 239

Karwoski, Theodore, 90
Katz, Daniel, 182, 183, 184, 186, 192, 196, 197
Katz, Elihu, 201, 202, 205, 250
Katz, Harold, 6, 20, 172
Kennedy, Edward M., 233
Kennedy, John F., 63, 64, 134
Kennedy, Robert F., 117, 260
Kerner Report, 222
Key, Wilson Bryan, 139
Kiel, Donald, 99
Kiesler, C. A., 155, 156, 162
Kilpatrick, Franklin P., 129
Kincaid, J. P., 85
Kitson, H. D., 68
Klapper, Hope Lunin, 249
Klapper, Joseph, 126, 248, 249, 261
Klare, G. R., 67, 68, 74, 86
Klass, B., 139
Knight-Ridder newspapers, 231
Knowledge function in attitude, 183–84, 185
Koffka, Kurt, 73, 78
Kohler, R., 137
Korean War, 186
Korzybski, Alfred, 2, 51–52, 53, 56
Kotok, A. B., 3
Kraus, S., 134, 260
Krech, D., 166
Kris, E., 125
Krisher, H. P., 177, 192

Krumm, Philip O., 117
Ku Klux Klan, 117, 119

Labeled inference, 62
Lang, G. E., 249, 254, 259
Lang, K., 249, 254, 259
Language, 52, 53, 89, 268; abstractness of, 55–57; changes in, 89; characteristics of, 53–57; limited nature of, 54–55; and mental health, 52, 53; misuses of, 57–61, 268; static nature of, 54: see also General Semantics
Language in Thought and Action (Hayakawa), 53
LaPiere, Richard, 189
Larsen, O., 205
Larson, C., 113, 115
Lasater, T. M., 192
Lasswell, Harold, 2, 30, 37, 39, 40, 113, 114, 115, 212, 214, 215, 229, 269
Laubach, F. C., 80
Laubach, R. S., 80
Law and justice, media portrayal of, 225, 228–29
Laws of science, 13; definition of, 14
Lazarsfeld, Paul, 126, 143, 148, 149, 152, 201, 205, 213, 216, 217, 218, 219, 229, 248
Lazarus, R. S., 139
Lear, Norman, 135, 136
Leary, B. E., 70, 71, 72, 73, 78, 79
Lee, Alfred McClung, 116, 118, 119, 120, 121, 123
Lee, Elizabeth Briant, 116, 118, 119, 120, 121, 123
Lefkowitz, M. M., 262
Lemon, J., 19
Lerbinger, Otto, 182, 192, 193, 194, 195, 197, 198, 210
Leuba, C., 132
Levine, J. M., 137
Lewin, Kurt, 2, 143, 147, 148, 195
Lewis, Jerry, 173
Lewis, John L., 117
Liddy, G. Gordon, 147
Liebert, Robert, 262, 263
Life magazine, 226
Lilly, A., 248

Lilly, John, 248
Lin, N., 206
Lindsay-Schaub newspaper chain, 238
Linguistics, and communications theory, 272
Lippitt, Ron, 147
Lippmann, Walter, 2, 215, 216, 229
Lively, B. A., 68, 69, 70, 78, 79
Logic: deductive, 14; inductive, 14
London Observer, 241
Long, Norton, 253, 255
Look magazine, 226, 236
Lorge, Irving, 72
Los Angeles Times, 236
Louisville Courier-Journal, 232
Lowry, Dennis, 64
Lucas, C., 132
Lumsdaine, Arthur A., 123, 167, 174, 175, 178, 179, 186
Lyle, Jack, 96, 97, 98, 103
Lysenko, Trofim, 13

Maccoby, Nathan, 4, 5, 152, 167, 179, 192, 257, 264
MacLean, M. S., 1, 37, 129, 249, 254, 267
Maddox, John, 106
Maddox, Lester, 117
Magazine research, Semantic Differential Technique in, 100
Maier, Irwin, 242, 243
Mail questionnaires, 15
Mann, Leon, 63
Marbut, Robert, 233
Marks of a Readable Style (Flesch), 73
Marrow, A. J., 2, 147
Maslow, Abraham, 193
Mass communication, 1–9, 53, 67, 152; and "Bullet Theory," 125–26, 148, 161, 246, 247, 248; and cognitive consistency, 154–63, 194, 268, 269; and cultural-norms theory, 255–56; definition of, 8; effects of, 246–64, 271; fear appeals in, 175–77, 179, 189; feedback in, 5, 31; and groups, 151; and Limited Effects Model, 246, 247, 248–49; and Moderate Effects Model, 246, 247, 249; motivational design in, 193–94; and

perception, 128, 133–36, 137, 140; personality design in, 196–97; and persuasion, *see* Persuasion; and Powerful Effects Model, 246, 247, 256–58; and readability formulas, 78–79; research on, 270–72; selective exposure in, 136, 137, 159, 268; and sociocultural integration, 222–24; and source credibility, 172–75; stimulus-response design in, 192–93; uses-and-gratifications approach in, 250–53; *see also* Communication model(s); Mass media

Mass Communication Research Center (University of Wisconsin), 98

Mass media, 200, 214; agenda-setting function of, 253–55, 259; cross-ownership of, 239–42; dysfunctions of, 213, 214, 216, 270; effectiveness of, conditions of, 218–19; and entertainment, 214; functions of, 212–13, 216, 270; and interpersonal communication, 200–11; in modern society, 212–29, 270; narcotizing dysfunction of, 216, 217; research on, 270–72; and social conformism, 217; social norms enforced by, 216–17; status conferred by, 216; as transmitters of culture, 213; *see also* Communication model(s); Mass communication

Mathematical Theory of Communication, The (Shannon and Weaver), 31, 44

McBurney, D. H., 144

McCleary, R. A., 139

McClelland, D. C., 132

McCleneghan, J., 108

McClintock, Charles, 183, 184, 186

McClure, Robert D., 128, 255, 259, 260

McCombs, Maxwell E., 253, 254, 255, 259

McGinniss, Joe, 105, 106

McGovern, George, 120, 128

McGraw, Harold W., Jr., 239

McGraw-Hill Book Company, 78, 238, 239

McGuire, William, 179, 180, 182, 186, 187, 188, 197

McPhee, W. N., 148, 149

McQuail, D., 250, 251, 252, 259, 260

Mead, Margaret, 147

Meaning: connotative, *see* Connotative meaning; denotative, 89, 270

Measuring function of communication model, 29, 30

Media, mass: *see* Mass media

Media conglomerates, 231, 232, 233, 234–39

Media forums, 210, 211, 219, 268

Media Sexploitation (Key), 139

Medicine, media portrayal of, 225, 228

Mendelsohn, H., 257, 264

Menzel, H., 201

Merrill, John, 63

Merton, Robert K., 12, 126, 213, 216, 217, 218, 219, 229

Merwin, John, 103, 105, 110

Message content and design, 271

Michigan State University, 97, 99

Military research on attitude change (Hovland), 166, 167–72, 179, 182, 248

Mill, John Stuart, 212, 218, 258

Miller, George, 5, 54, 93

Mills, J., 163

Milwaukee Journal, 98, 99, 228, 243; employee ownership of, 242, 243

Mindak, William, 102, 103

Mobil Oil Corporation, 241

Mock, J. R., 113, 115

Models in science, 15, 28–30; definition of, 14, 28; *see also* Communication model(s)

Modern Medicine magazine, 235, 236

Monde, Le, 241

"Monocular distorted room," 129–30

Monopolization, as condition of media effectiveness, 218

Motivational design in mass communication, 193–94

Moyers, Bill, 61

Multi-valued evaluation, 60

Multivariate statistics, 90

Murphy, G., 137, 166

Murphy, L. B., 166

My Lai massacre, 226

NAACP, 136

Nagel, E., 14

Namath, Joe, 120

Name calling, as propaganda device, 116–18

National Association of Broadcasters, 138, 261

National Broadcasting Company (NBC), 234, 235, 261

National Citizens Committee for Broadcasting, 263

National Commission on the Causes and Prevention of Violence, 260

National News Council, 61, 241

National Observer, 155, 223

National Press Club, 233

National PTA, 3, 263

Nazis, 116; effectiveness of propaganda by, 124–25

Networks, communication, 49

New England Journal of Biology and Medicine, 173

"New Literates," 80

New York *Daily News*, 122

New York Magazine, 122

New York Times, 64, 79, 96, 122, 134, 155, 226, 228, 235, 236, 237, 238, 239

New York Times Company, 235–36

Newcomb, Theodore M., 23, 35, 36, 37, 39, 157, 166, 182, 267

Newhouse Broadcasting Corporation, 239, 240, 241

Newman, L. S., 191

Newman, Paul, 120

News Twisters, The (Efron), 3

Newsday, 232, 236

Newspaper chains, 231–32, 233, 241

Newspaper research, Semantic Differential Technique in, 93, 96–99, 100, 104, 105

Newsweek, 235

Newton, Isaac, 12

Nielsen, A. C., 5

Niman, C. M., 190

Nimmo, D., 122

Nixon, Richard M., 2, 3, 60, 61, 105, 106, 117, 119, 120, 121, 134, 146, 195

Nobel Prize, 226, 227

Noelle-Neumann, Elisabeth, 257–58, 264

Noise in information theory terms, definition of, 47

Oakland Tribune, 236

Objectivity, 61, 63; studies of, 63–64

O'Connor, Carroll, 136

O'Connor, D. Vincent, 134

On Liberty (Mill), 212

One-sided and two-sided messages, 169–72, 178, 179, 186

Opinion leaders, 201, 202, 203–05, 206, 207, 269

Opinion measurement, and Semantic Differential Technique, 101–02, 108–09

Oppenheimer, Robert J., 173

Order of Presentation in Persuasion, The (Hovland et al.), 172

Organizing function of communication model, 29, 30

Osgood, Charles, 2, 32, 35, 90, 91, 95, 96, 97, 99, 100, 101, 109, 110, 158, 167, 179, 182, 195

Oskamp, S., 255

Overgeneralization, 58–59

Oxford University Press, 78

Packard, Vance, 194

Palo Alto Times, 96, 97

Papageorgis, Demetrios, 186, 187, 188

Parent-Teacher Association (PTA), 3, 263

Pastors, John O., 261

Paterson, D. G., 86

Patriotism, media portrayal of, 225

Patterson, Thomas E., 128, 255, 259, 260

Pelz, Edith Bennett, 148

Penrose, J., 17

People in Quandaries (Johnson), 53

People's Choice and Voting, The, 259

Perception: and attitude, 133; and cultural expectations, 130–31; definition of, 129; influenced by assumptions, 129–30; and mass communication, 128, 133–36, 137, 140; and mood, 132–33; and motivation, 132; selective, 128–29, 136, 137, 139, 140, 268; subliminal, 138–40; transactional view of, 129

Permissible Lie, The (Baker), 224

Personality and Persuasibility (Janis et al.), 172

Personality design in mass communication, 196–97
Persuasion, 4, 165; and propaganda, 114; *see also* Attitude change
Peterson, T., 212
Phillips, K., 233
Philosophical Review, 43
Philosophy, and communications theory, 272
Plain-folks device in propaganda, 121
Politics: and economics, 224–28; and group attitudes, 148–50; group pressures in, 146–47; propaganda in, 114, 119, 120, 121; and Semantic Differential Technique, 103–06; *see also* Voting behavior
Postman, L., 137
Potency dimension of semantic space, 96, 97
Poulos, R. W., 263
Pravda, 173
Predictive function of communication model, 29
Press and Foreign Policy, The (Cohen), 253
Pressey, S. L., 68, 69, 70, 78, 79
Prigogine, Ilya, 226, 227
Projection, unconscious, as misuse of language, 60–61
Propaganda, 113–26, 216; and advertising, 114, 118, 120, 121, 122, 123, 124, 151; and "Bullet Theory," 125–26; definitions of, 114; devices used in, 116–23, 126; and effectiveness of devices, 123–25; history of, 115; objectives of, 114; and persuasion, 114; in politics, 114, 119, 120, 121; in public relations, 114, 216; wartime, 113, 114, 115, 122, 125, 200, 248
Propaganda Technique in the World War (Lasswell), 114
Pseudo-environment, 215
Pseudo-event, 213
Psychology, and communications theory, 272
Ptolemy, 11
Public Opinion (Lippmann), 2, 215, 216, 253

Public relations, and propaganda, 114, 216
Pulitzer Prize, 243
Pyrczak, F., 80

Questionnaires, mail, 15
Quinn, J. B., 80

Radio, 200, 213, 216, 233, 234; and Semantic Differential Technique, 100; *see also* Broadcasting
Radio Corporation of America, 234–35
Ramparts magazine, 223
Rankin, E. F., 85
Rapoport, A., 52, 53
Rather, Dan, 159
Rationalization, 154
Raven, Bertram H., 146, 147
Raymont, H., 224
Read, J. M., 115
Readability, Information Theory applied to, 49
Readability Laboratory of Teachers College (Columbia University), 72
Readability measurement, 67–86; and Cloze Procedure, 49, 83–85; formula(s) for, *see* Formula(s) for readability measurement; future research on, 86; and government regulations, 80–83; history of, 68–76; and insurance policies, 83, 85; and mass communication, 78–79; and "New Literates," 80; textbooks evaluated by, 78
Reader's Digest, 79, 224
Reading Center (Rutgers University), 75
Reading Ease formula (Flesch), 74–86 *passim*
Redundancy concept: and Cloze Procedure, 84; in information theory, 46–47, 49, 50, 270
Reed, Rex, 122
Reliability of scientific findings: external, 25; internal, 25
Religion, media portrayal of, 225, 229
Report, definition of, 61
Rickles, Don, 120
Ridenhour, Ron, 226

Riley, J. W., Jr., 251
Riley, M. W., 251
Rise and Fall of Project Camelot, The (Horowitz), 111
"Risky-shift" group pressure, 146–47
Robards, Jason, 120
Rockefeller, Nelson, 121
Rogers, Everett, 206, 207, 209, 210
Rogers, Lorene, 63
Rokeach, Milton, 136
Roosevelt, Franklin D., 119, 148, 200
Rosenberg, M. J., 166, 172, 179
Rozelle, R. R., 192
Ruggels, L., 101
Rumor transmission, studies of, 137
Ryan, M., 15, 16

Salisbury, H., 13
Salter, P., 18
Sarnoff, Irving, 183, 184, 186
Satire, 135
Saturday Review, 138
Schiller, Herbert, 111
Schiller, P. H., 138
Schramm, Wilbur, 6, 7, 8, 34, 35, 48, 49, 125, 212
Schulte, R., 130
Science: closure in, 13; cumulative nature of, 12, 90; generalization in, *see* Generalization; laws of, *see* Laws of science; models in, *see* Models in science; non-ethical nature of, 111; parsimony in, 13; predictability in, 13, 154; reliability in, *see* Reliability of scientific findings; and religion, struggle between, 115; validity in, *see* Validity of scientific findings; *see also* Scientific method
Science and Sanity (Korzybski), 2, 52
Scientific method, 2, 11–25; definition of, 11–14; experimental design in, *see* Experimental design; and hypothesis, *see* Hypothesis; and replicability, 13, 14; and theory, *see* Theory; *see also* Science
Scripps-Howard Research, 99
Sears, D. O., 137, 163, 250
Seib, Charles, 79
Selective exposure, 136, 137, 159, 268

Selective perception, 128–29, 136, 137, 139, 140, 268
Selective retention, 137, 161
Selling of the President, The (McGinniss), 105
Semantic Differential Technique, 90, 94, 96, 97, 98, 101, 158, 270; in advertising and marketing, 102–03; and generality of findings, 95–96; and media images, 99–101; misuse of, 109–10; in newspaper research, 93, 96–99, 100, 104, 105; and opinion measurement, 101–02, 108–09; and politics, 103–06; in radio research, 100; in television research, 94, 100, 104, 105; and United States Air Force, *see* United States Air Force; use of, for comparisons, 95
Semantic space, 91–93, 94, 95, 96; dimensions of, 96, 100, 101
Semantics, General: *see* General Semantics
Severin, W., 16, 17, 105, 242
Shannon, Claude, 2, 31, 32, 35, 37, 40, 43, 44, 48, 50
Shaw, Donald L., 17, 23, 263, 254, 255, 259
Sheffield, Fred D., 123, 167, 174, 175, 178, 179
Sherif, Muzafer, 124, 143, 144–45, 147, 172, 195
Sherman, L. A., 68
Shoemaker, F., 206, 207, 209, 210
Shoup, D. M., 155
Siebert, F. S., 23, 212
Sies, Luther F., 53
Skedgell, R. A., 150
Slanting, journalistic, 61, 63, 64
"Sleeper" effect, 169, 174
Smith, Kate, 173
Snider, J., 90
"Social Control in the Newsroom" (Breed), 219
Social design in persuasion, 195–96
Social Judgment (Sherif and Hovland), 172
Social Justice magazine, 116
Sociology, and communications theory, 272
Source credibility, 172–75

Speidel Newspapers, Inc., 232, 241
Speier, H., 125
Spinoza, Baruch, 143
Split-run technique in communication research, 21
Stanford Test for newspaper attitudes, 98
Stanford University, 96, 97
Stanley, J. C., 25
Statements, kinds of, 61–63
Statistics, 23–24, 31, 272; multivariate, 90
Stein, Gertrude, 84, 85
Steiner, G. A., 129, 139
Steinfeld, Jesse L., 260, 263
Stereotyping, 58
Stevens, S. S., 7, 73, 78
Stevenson, R., 3
Stewart, William H., 261, 263
Stimulus-response design in mass communication, 192–93
Stoen, D., 58
Stone, G., 73, 78
Stouffer, Samuel, 167
Strategy of Desire, The (Dichter), 194
Strauss, W., 223
Strickland, S., 263
Structural differential, 56
Stuckey, W., 227
Subliminal perception, 138–40
Subliminal Projection Company, 138
Subliminal Seduction (Key), 139
Sun Tsu, 115
Supplementation, as condition of media effectiveness, 219
Supreme Court, U.S., 239
Surgeon General's Scientific Advisory Committee on Television and Social Behavior, 261, 262, 263
Surveys, 15–17, 24, 272
Swanson, C., 79
Swanson, D. L., 253
Swift, Jonathan, 135
Symbionese Liberation Army, 59, 64, 65
Symmetry theory (Newcomb), 23, 35–36, 37, 157, 267
Synesthesia, color-music, 90

Tankard, E. F., 78
Tankard, J. W., 15, 16, 78

Tannenbaum, Percy, 98, 99, 103, 159, 179, 182
Taylor, Wilson L., 49, 83, 84, 85
Teacher's Word Book, The (Thorndike), 69
Television, 3, 53, 61, 64, 92, 94, 100, 152, 193, 197, 229, 233, 234, 256; cable, 234; in election campaigns, 259–60; and Semantic Differential Technique, 94, 100, 104, 105; violence on, 3, 179, 256, 258, 260–63, 270; *see also* Broadcasting
Television and Politics (Blumler and McQuail), 250
Testimonial, as propaganda device, 120–21, 123, 124, 173
Textbook evaluation by readability formulas, 78
Theory: definition of, 14; and scientific method, 12, 13
Thomas, Llewellyn, 361
Thomas, W. I., 166
Thompson, Hunter, 61
Thorndike, E. L., 69
Time, Inc., 235
Time magazine, 63, 64, 79, 96, 134, 235
Times-Mirror Company, 232, 236, 239
Tipton, L., 250
Toch, Hans, 129, 130
Toward World Literacy (Laubach and Laubach), 80
Transfer, as propaganda device, 119–20
Treffert, D. A., 60
Trendex, 5
Troldahl, V., 206
Trudeau, Garry, 135
Truman, Harry S., 63, 64, 148
Turner, W., 65
Two-step flow of communication, 201, 205–06, 207, 269
Two-valued evaluation, as misuse of language, 59–60

Udall, Morris, 233
Unconscious projection, as misuse of language, 60–61
Undue identification, as misuse of language, 58–59
UNESCO, 80

United Press International (UPI), 62, 233, 237

United States Air Force: image of, and Semantic Differential Technique, 106–08, 110; and identification of high school opinion leaders, 108–09

"Untouchables, The" (TV program), 262

Uses-and-gratifications approach in mass communication, 250–53

Ustinov, Peter, 121

Validity of scientific findings: external, 24–25; internal, 25

Value-expressive attitude, 183, 185

Van Dam, R., 206

Variables in experimental design, 19

Vicary, James M., 138

Vidich, A., 227

Vidmar, Neil, 136

Vietnam, 106, 155, 161, 215, 223, 224, 226, 227

Vogel, M., 70

Voting behavior, 201, 202, 251, 252, 259; see also Politics

Vyhonsky, P. J., 78

Walder, L. O., 262

Waldron, M., 111

Walker, J. L., 254, 255

Wall Street Journal, 237

Wallace, Mike, 229

Walters, R. H., 261

"War of the Worlds" broadcast, 200, 213

Washburne, C., 70

Washington Post, 79, 231, 235

Washington Post Company, 232, 234

Washington Star, 23, 79, 235

Wayne, John, 120

Weaver, D., 17

Weaver, Warren, 7, 31, 32, 43, 44, 46

Weigel, R. H., 191

Weiss, W., 20, 124, 173, 174, 175

Welles, Orson, 213

Wells, H. G., 200

Westley, Bruce, 12, 13, 16, 17, 37, 105, 249, 254, 255, 267

Westley-MacLean communication model, 37–39, 249, 254, 267–69

What Makes a Book Readable (Gray and Leary), 70

White, D., 22

White, William Alanson, 52

Whiteside, T., 61

Whitman, A., 12

Whor, Benjamin Lee, 96

"Why We Fight" film series, 168, 196

Wicker, A. W., 190

Wiener, M., 138

Wiener, Norbert, 30, 31, 45

Wiley and Sons, John, 78

Wilhoit, G. C., 137

Wilkins, Mac, 117

Williams, F., 93

Williams, J., 106

Willkie, Wendell, 148

Wilson, D., 242

Wilson, K., 242

Wilson, M. L., 147

Wisconsin, University of, 98

Words That Won the War (Mock and Larson), 113

World War I, 113, 115, 122, 125, 200, 248

World War II, 18, 113, 115, 125, 147, 167, 168, 173, 179, 182, 223, 248

Wright, Charles, 212, 229

Yale Communication Research Program, 172–79

Zajonc, R. B., 156

Zimmerman, F., 237

Znaniecki, F., 166